THE
REPUBLIC
OF
LETTERS

Nostalgia unfures the book —
perhaps b/c of sources? Memoirs,
histories → often written after the Rev.
Deal w/ the distortions more?
Nostalgic for some golden age of women
Nostalgic for somewhat heavy-handed.
Treatment of salonnières — salonnières = unique?
Dirge for the loss of — "Masculine" chapter to
public opinion — not enough explanation
value-laden — I want more on the way
for How transition occurred — does not
Narrative of women's exclusion/central story
seem like the most interesting/
to tell — and seems to sour the whole
account.

Abbé Delille reciting his poem "La Conversation" in the salon of Madame Geoffrin, from Jacques Delille, *La Conversation* (Paris, 1812). Courtesy of Harvard University Library.

THE
REPUBLIC
OF
LETTERS

A Cultural History of the French Enlightenment

Dena Goodman

CORNELL UNIVERSITY PRESS

Ithaca and London

First published 1994 by Cornell University Press.

Library of Congress Cataloging-in-Publication Data

Goodman, Dena, 1952–
    The republic of letters : a cultural history of the French
enlightenment / Dena Goodman.
        p.   cm.
    Includes bibliographical references and index.
    ISBN 0-8014-2968-4
    1. French prose literature—18th century—History and criticism.
2. France—Intellectual life—18th century.   3. France—
Civilization—18th century.   4. Enlightenment—France.   I. Title.
PQ618.G66   1994
944'.034—dc20   93-40493

Printed in the United States of America

À mes compatriotes, les gens de lettres

Contents

Acknowledgments

This book is a history of the Republic of Letters in the eighteenth century. It is also a reflection and a product of the Republic of Letters in the late twentieth century. It is a product of a community of my imagination, will, and desire, but if the community exists only by force of imagination, the institutions and individuals who compose it do not. They are very real, and without them this book would not have been possible. As the book takes the form of a narrative, so too do these acknowledgments.

The story begins with what, in retrospect, must have been the matrix and the inspiration for this project: Lynn Hunt's Berkeley French History Group. There I learned about the intimate and symbiotic relationship between discourse and dining, but I also discovered the possibility of a discourse that was both critical and collaborative. And over the years, as I have joined and formed other reading and discussion groups, I have come to understand and appreciate Lynn Hunt's brilliance and her hard work in shaping that discourse with generosity and wit.

From California I went to Madison, where the Institute for Research in the Humanities at the University of Wisconsin and its director, Robert Kingdon, welcomed me and supported this research for the year 1985–1986. John Tedeschi was extremely helpful in his capacity as head of special collections in the university library and also as an enthusiastic early modernist. During that year I profited from discussions with Diane Rubenstein and especially Suzanne Desan. These have continued over the years, developing into friendships that cannot be distinguished from the best kind of collaboration in the Republic of Letters.

Keith Baker's Workshop on Political Culture at the University of Chicago was the first venue in which I presented this research. There it received the kind of critical reading for which any citizen of the Republic of Letters should be grateful. I am especially indebted to Daniel Gordon, with whom I have continued to discuss and debate the issues raised by this work and by his on sociability.

In 1988–1989 the Mellon Foundation supported this research at Harvard University. Harvard's Center for European Studies welcomed me as an associate, and the Center for Literary and Cultural Studies gave me a much-coveted office. A version of Chapter 1 was first read by one of the study groups at CES, through which I exchanged manuscripts and ideas about the Republic of Letters with Ann Goldgar and Larry Wolff. I also benefited from the Eighteenth-Century Seminar at CLCS. At the Feminist Seminar I met other women who shared an interest in early modern France, and with them and the support of CLCS we formed the reading group Forgotten Women of Early Modern France. From that group, Nadine Bérenguier, Elizabeth Goldsmith, and Erica Harth have continued to help me to understand the women of the Enlightenment Republic of Letters. The group itself is a model of social and intellectual interaction of the highest sort.

Chapter 3 got a first hearing as part of the Women's History Week celebration (1989) organized by women graduate students of Harvard's history department. Caroline Ford, who joined the department that year, was both a good friend and a tireless partner in discussions of French history. Olwen Hufton, Patrice Higonnet, Margaret Higonnet, and Simon Schama were always encouraging. Johanna Drucker and Nancy Paxton were a tribute to the implied fellowship of the Mellon program.

When I came to Louisiana State University in 1989, I found a Works-in-Progress Seminar that was a small corner of the Republic of Letters. Through it I discovered common interests with David Lindenfeld, whose insights into and criticism of parts of this book have been very helpful.

I took up residency again in the Republic of Letters in 1991–1992, as a fellow of the Davis Humanities Institute at the University of California. The institute and its directors, Michael Hoffman and Clarence Walker, fully supported this research. As associate director of the institute, Kay Flavell stamped it with her own virtues of intellectual curiosity, energy, and generosity. Many of the traditional services of the Republic of Letters were furnished cheerfully and competently by Jeanette Trieber. Formal and informal discussions with other fellows and members of the Davis faculty were often useful, but most of all I am grateful to Christine Di Stefano, whose fellowship and friendship cannot be distinguished from her intellectual contribution to this work.

Two other interrelated institutions of the Republic of Letters were crucial to the development of this project: scholarly associations and journals. Most of the work that ended up in this book was presented at the annual meetings of societies whose members have helped me to shape my ideas: the Society for French Historical Studies, the Western Society for French History, the American and International Societies for Eighteenth-Century Studies (and their western and northeastern affiliates), the American Historical Association, and the International Society for the History of Rhetoric. Parts of Chapters 2 and 4 were drawn from "Enlightenment Salons: The Convergence of Female and Philosophic Ambitions," *Eighteenth-Century Studies* 22 (Spring 1989): 329–50; Chapter 3 is a much-expanded version of "Governing the Republic of Letters: The Politics of Culture in the French Enlightenment," *History of European Ideas* 13 (1991): 183–99. I am grateful to both journals for permission to include this work here.

I have also benefited greatly from the hospitality of those who have invited me to present my work for critical discussion at their universities: Bonnie Smith, then at the University of Rochester; Peta Howard at Tunxis Community College; Linda Colley at Yale University; Jerry Micelle at McNeese State University; David Lieberman at the University of California at Berkeley; Lawrence Bryant at California State University at Chico; Keith Baker, both at the University of Chicago and at Stanford University; Dario Castiglione and Colin Jones at Exeter University. In a category by itself is the William Andrews Clark Library of the University of California at Los Angeles, where successive directors of its Center for Seventeenth- and Eighteenth-Century Studies, John Brewer and Peter Reill, Clark Professor Susan Staves, and workshop organizers Mary Sheriff and Jay Tribby gave me the opportunity to participate in a discursive setting that has surely not been duplicated since the eighteenth century.

Lest I be accused of neglecting the material base, let me acknowledge the financial support of my own universities: summer research grants from the University of Alabama at Birmingham and Louisiana State University, and a Manship Faculty Summer Fellowship, also from LSU. On another level, this book could not have reached material form without John Ackerman of Cornell University Press, who has revived and redefined printshop sociability for the twentieth-century Republic of Letters.

This project has also brought me as a *femme de lettres* into the sphere of *les grands*. I am grateful to Madame la comtesse Edouard de Bruce and her son, le comte Charles Edouard de Bruce, who generously opened the Geoffrin papers to me and welcomed me into their home to study them. I thank them for permission to quote from the papers.

There are individuals whose support and friendship and critical

reading and discussion of this work transcend the institutional boundaries of the Republic of Letters, and I am especially indebted to them:
Carolyn Lougee, with whom I have spent many fruitful hours discussing salons; Mary Sheriff, Karen Offen, Pierre Saint-Amand, and Paula
Radisich, who generously shared their work with me and with whom I
have discussed various aspects of mine; Sarah Maza, Gary Kates, and
Nina Gelbart, who read the whole manuscript and from whose insights
it has benefited enormously; Jeremy Popkin, Jack Censer, and Elizabeth Eisenstein, who read and commented on substantial portions of
the manuscript; Lawrence Klein and Suzanne Desan, who may as well
have read it through, since what they have not read in bits and pieces
they have heard in conversations in which scholarship and friendship
are inextricably entwined; and Keith Baker, whose understanding of
the French Enlightenment I have come to know and appreciate ever
more deeply through the writing of this book, who posed the first
questions that it seeks to answer, and whose friendship, too, is inscribed
within it.

DENA GOODMAN

Baton Rouge, Louisiana

A Note to the Reader

Unless otherwise noted, all translations from the French are my own. Letters are always identified by date and, when there is a choice, they have been cited from the *sender*'s published correspondence. For the reader's convenience, citations from Voltaire's correspondence also include the letter numbers.

Also to assist the reader, I have provided short biographical sketches of the main persons who figure in the story that follows, both philosophes and salonnières. They will be found after the Conclusion.

D. G.

Enlightenment in the individual is easily established. . . . But to enlighten an age is a very protracted task, for there are many external obstacles which in part hinder and in part prevent that kind of education.

—IMMANUEL KANT

A Cultural History of
the French Enlightenment

This book is a cultural history of the Enlightenment as a moment
in the history of the Republic of Letters. Like France, the Republic of Letters is a polity with a much-contested history.
François Furet, Lynn Hunt, and Keith Baker argue for collapsing the
distinction between discourse and political reality if we are to understand such political constructions as the French monarchy, the Old
Regime, and the Revolution.[1] In these terms, the Republic of Letters
has the same status as the monarchy: in the eighteenth century, it too
had a political culture constructed out of discursive practices and institutions that shaped the actions, verbal and otherwise, of the people to
whose lives it gave structure, meaning, and purpose. Jürgen Habermas
and Reinhart Koselleck have argued that in the eighteenth century the
Republic of Letters constituted the public sphere that became the
ground for political discourse that contested the closed culture of
the monarchy.[2] As the history of the monarchy and of the political
cultures of the Old Regime and Revolution are revised, the Republic of
Letters emerges as a polity parallel to the monarchy but entwined with

[handwritten marginal note: What exactly is the Republic of Letters?]

---

1. François Furet, *Interpreting the French Revolution*, trans. Elborg Forster (Cambridge, 1981); Lynn Hunt, *Politics, Culture, and Class in the French Revolution* (Berkeley,
1984); Keith Michael Baker, *Inventing the French Revolution: Essays on French Political
Culture in the Eighteenth Century* (Cambridge, 1990).

2. Jürgen Habermas, *The Structural Transformation of the Public Sphere: An Inquiry into
a Category of Bourgeois Society*, trans. Thomas Burger with Frederick Lawrence (Cambridge, Mass., 1989), pp. 51–56; Reinhart Koselleck, *Critique and Crisis: Enlightenment and
the Pathogenesis of Modern Society* (Cambridge, Mass., 1988), pp. 110–16.

it: the double helix of early modern France. As such, the republic, its citizens, its practices and institutions, its structures of power, its conflicts—its history, in short—need to be taken seriously.

The Republic of Letters rose with the modern political state out of the religious wars of the sixteenth century, out of the articulation of public and private spheres, citizen and state, agent and critic. During the early modern period, its citizenry came to value reciprocal exchange based on a model of friendship that contrasted markedly with the absolutist state, corporative society, and the family. In the forms in which it still exists, the republic continues to be at odds with the dominant culture and to question its hegemony. Since the eighteenth century, those who participate in it have tried to work out a way of maintaining citizenship in the political and geographical states that define their nationality without compromising their primary allegiance to the values of the republic. The critical position of the citizen of the Republic of Letters, first articulated by Pierre Bayle at the end of the seventeenth century and then translated into the social and discursive practices of conversation and epistolarity by the philosophes and salonnières of the Enlightenment, is a product of the tension this dual citizenship generates. The transformative impulse, the desire to change the world to conform to the Republic of Letters, its values and practices, is the constructive result of this critical position. It is the project of Enlightenment.

A cultural history of the French Enlightenment is not simply an intellectual history with a new name or even a broadening of intellectual history's field of inquiry from a small canon of elite texts to a wider range of cultural materials. Unlike intellectual history, cultural history does not assume that ideas, or even those who articulate them, are the primary subject matter of historical inquiry. Rather, cultural history focuses on social and discursive practices and institutions: both the ground on which particular discursive actions take place and those actions themselves. Ideas are not of a different order from the practices and institutions that constitute them, and those practices and institutions are not without meaning. The job of the cultural historian is to understand the ways in which human beings have shaped and been shaped by the social and discursive practices and institutions that constitute their lives and actions.[3]

A cultural history of the French Enlightenment must also be a feminist history, because it challenges the conceptualization of intellectual

3. See Roger Chartier, *The Cultural Origins of the French Revolution* (Durham, 1991), pp. 17–18. See also Michel Foucault, "What Is Enlightenment?" trans. Catherine Porter, in *The Foucault Reader*, ed. Paul Rabinow (New York, 1984), pp. 32–50. On discursive practices, see Foucault, "What Is an Author?" in the same collection (101–20).

activity as the product of masculine reason and male genius.[4] The central discursive practices of the Enlightenment Republic of Letters were polite conversation and letter writing, and its defining social institution was the Parisian salon. Cultural history shifts attention away from ideas and texts as the products of masculine reason and male genius and toward these practices and institutions in which women figured centrally. If we recognize that the French Enlightenment cannot be abstracted from these practices that constituted it, then we can no longer conceive of it as part of a mythical history of masculine reason said to begin with the Greeks and to move triumphantly through Aquinas, Descartes, Locke, Voltaire, and Rousseau, to culminate in Kant, Hegel, and modern science.[5] Rather, we can see it as part of a very different history in which men and women have both played roles. It is one of the aims of this book to elucidate those roles as they changed over time, from the origins of the Republic of Letters in the seventeenth century through the first years of the French Revolution, in order to locate the particular gender configuration of the Enlightenment Republic of Letters.

The practices of intellectual sociability and discourse which defined the Enlightenment Republic of Letters were grounded in cultural and epistemological assumptions shared by those who considered themselves to be citizens of that republic. These assumptions gendered the cultural and discursive practices that defined it and structured the participation of women in the French Enlightenment. In Chapter 1 I discuss the values that shaped the Republic of Letters from its beginnings in the seventeenth century and the critical and collaborative epistemology drawn from Bayle and Francis Bacon on which the encyclopedists grounded an Enlightenment Republic of Letters centered in Paris. Here I would like to say something about certain cultural assumptions shared by the French philosophes which shaped the practices of discourse and sociability they brought to the Republic of Letters in the eighteenth century.

By the eighteenth century, French men of letters had come to identify French culture with sociability and sociability with the polite society of men and women referred to as *le monde* or *la bonne compagnie*. They viewed their own culture as the best in the world because the most sociable and the most polite; it had reached the highest point civiliza-

---

4. This tradition is critiqued by feminist philosophers such as Genevieve Lloyd, *The Man of Reason: "Male" and "Female" in Western Philosophy* (Minneapolis, 1984); Jean Grimshaw, *Philosophy and Feminist Thinking* (Minneapolis, 1986); Susan J. Hekman, *Gender and Knowledge: Elements of a Postmodern Feminism* (Boston, 1990).

5. Lloyd, *Man of Reason*.

tion had yet attained. Women were central to their understanding of sociability and civilization.

The idea of sociability, as Daniel Gordon has shown, was located in two independent discourses, one of natural law and the other of conviviality derived from *le monde* and *la bonne compagnie*. Within natural law discourse, French thinkers maintained the inherent sociability of human beings, in contrast to a Hobbesian unsociable man. Some made natural sociability the basis for a moral philosophy of benevolence. Others held that whereas human beings are born sociable, their passions undermine their ability to live peaceably with their fellows, and thus monarchy is necessary to establish the peace and order that humans by nature desire. The discourse of conviviality, in contrast to both these theories, represented human sociability as an achievement of civilization, the product of history.[6]

By the middle of the eighteenth century French men of letters had merged the discourses of sociability to forge the commonplace that France was the most civilized because it was the most sociable and most polite of nations. By implication, moreover, it was also the most moral. French men of letters saw themselves as the leaders of a project of Enlightenment that was both cultural and moral, if not political. By representing French culture as the leading edge of civilization, they identified the cause of humanity with their own national causes and saw themselves as at the same time French patriots and upstanding citizens of a cosmopolitan Republic of Letters.

Voltaire, both a zealous champion of French culture and the leading citizen of the Enlightenment Republic of Letters, contributed more than anyone else to this self-representation of national identity. "Since the reign of Anne of Austria, they have been the most sociable and polite people on earth," he wrote of the French in 1736, "and this politeness is not something arbitrary, like that which is called civility; it is a law of nature which they have fortunately cultivated more than other peoples."[7] In the eighteenth century, as Roger Chartier has shown, civility was devalued as mere formality associated with courtly notions of superiority and inferiority, as mere appearance disengaged from any moral basis.[8] Sociability was retained as a value and a valued practice within moral and political discourse because it was dissociated from this bankrupt concept of civility and aligned with politeness in-

---

6. Daniel Gordon, "The Idea of Sociability in Pre-Revolutionary France" (Ph.D. diss., University of Chicago, 1990), pp. 35–54.

7. Quoted ibid., p. 61.

8. Roger Chartier, "From Texts to Manners, a Concept and Its Books: *Civilité* between Aristocratic Distinction and Popular Appropriation," in *The Cultural Uses of Print in Early Modern France*, trans. Lydia G. Cochrane (Princeton, 1987), pp. 91–96.

stead. Polite sociability, rather than mere civility, became the hallmark of civilization.

Gordon writes that by midcentury a "politics of sociability" was attempting to replace traditional conceptions of political power with manners. The new political order was based on the reciprocal exchange of conversation among equals rather than the hierarchy of the society of orders and the absolutist state. The discipline of politeness would replace the coercion of military force. According to the conception of history from which this politics derived, contemporary France was a specifically "civilized" world that had emerged from the "barbarism" of the Middle Ages. The temporal vision was complemented by a spatial one, an anthropology in which civilized France was contrasted with "primitive" peoples across the seas.[9] In his *discours de réception* at the French Academy in 1774, Jean-Baptiste-Antoine Suard could speak of his age as both enlightened and sociable, a modern age in which the printing press, polite conversation, and public opinion were the defining discursive institutions.[10]

This new politics of sociability, with its egalitarian basis and potential for critical practice, did not overtly challenge the politics of the monarchy and the society of orders. Nevertheless, a discourse of natural sociability which substituted reciprocity and equality for hierarchy and the rules of polite conversation for absolute power and military force could hardly be compatible with an absolutist discourse that legitimated the monarchy as a policing power necessary to the realization of natural sociability. Or could it?

Enlightenment sociability upheld both reciprocal exchange and the principle of governance by substituting a female salonnière for a male king as the governor of its discourse.[11] The salonnière's position also made sense of the seeming contradiction between the natural law contention that human beings are endowed with sociability and the tenet of the discourse of conviviality that they achieve it. Her role as civilizer was the historical key to the realization of sociability and civilization. In the civilized world of the Republic of Letters, she was both the basis of

9. On the anthropological axis, see Michèle Duchet, *Anthropologie et histoire au siècle des Lumières: Buffon, Voltaire, Rousseau, Helvétius, Diderot* (Paris, 1971); and Peter France, *Politeness and Its Discontents: Problems in French Classical Culture* (Cambridge, 1992). By the 1770s, philosophes such as Diderot and Raynal were calling into question any simple opposition between the civilized and the primitive. Although such a critique had been mounted as early as the sixteenth century by Montaigne in his *Essais*, it was again new and atypical after more than a century of French cultural boosterism.

10. Gordon, "Idea of Sociability," pp. 72–73.

11. The adoption of the Salic Law in the fourteenth century had excluded women from the succession to the throne, thus forever after gendering the French monarchy male.

social order and the governor of its discourse. Her legitimacy had a completely different foundation from that of the monarchy. It was based on her acceptance of the rules of polite conversation which structured reciprocal exchange; on her difference as a woman from the men she governed and her position, therefore, outside their discourse; and on the Neoplatonic assumption of gender complementarity which saw the ideal whole as a product of the complementary actions of male and female, masculine and feminine qualities. That legitimacy, however, was both tenuous and temporary, for it was undermined by a masculinist assumption of the illegitimacy of female power and authority, especially over men.[12]

chronologi?

Women played a central role both in the representation of history upon which the convivial idea of sociability was based and in the practice and representation of polite conversation in the Parisian salons in which French men of letters experienced sociability. The French Enlightenment was grounded in a female-centered mixed-gender sociability that gendered French culture, the Enlightenment, and civilization itself as feminine.

"Of all the nations France is the one which has most experienced society," wrote Voltaire in the introduction to his tragedy *Zaire* in 1736. "The continual commerce between the two sexes, so lively and so polite, has introduced a politeness quite unknown elsewhere. Society depends on women."[13] The status of women was also seen as the measure of France's level of civilization relative to other cultures.[14] Most significant, women figured as the civilizing force in both history and contemporary society.[15]

In Voltaire's history of the age of Louis XIV, women were central to the transformation of France from a barbaric to a civilized nation. This was a seventeenth-century argument based on the self-representation of an aristocratic culture that based its claim of superiority on its transcendence of brute force for gentler virtues. "Woman's very weakness predisposed her to virtue and suited her to ends higher than the physi-

12. On women and power, see Barbara Garlick, Suzanne Dixon, and Pauline Allen, eds., *Stereotypes of Women in Power: Historical Perspectives and Revisionist Views* (New York, 1992).

13. Quoted in Gordon, "Idea of Sociability," p. 65.

14. Sylvana Tomaselli, "The Enlightenment Debate on Women," *History Workshop Journal* 20 (1985): 115.

15. Ibid., 101–24. Norbert Elias inscribes this version of history in *The Civilizing Process*. He locates the "civilizing" influence of women in the shift from a feudal warrior society to the court society and also argues that the absolutist courts of the seventeenth and eighteenth centuries allowed for more equality between men and women than existed at any other time in European history. Elias, *Power and Civility*, vol. 2 of *The Civilizing Process*, trans. Edmund Jephcott (New York, 1982), pp. 77–82.

cal," writes Carolyn Lougee of this line of reasoning. "She was seen as the creator and peaceful sustainer, man as the brute destroyer. Man's duty was to adopt the feminine value system, and the best man was the one who did so most effectively." Women's role in history was to pacify men. One writer, for example, urged France to model itself not on male-dominated and war-torn Germany but on peaceful Italy, where "the sovereigns indulge more fully the temperament and inclination of the ladies." "Under the goodness of the governance of ladies," he wrote, France would return to a golden age of universal brother-hood.[16] After the terrors of the Wars of Religion and the scare of the Fronde, a new, peaceful order would be founded on the antimartial virtues ascribed to women.

In the eighteenth century, Montesquieu was to make a similar argument. Women, he wrote, make good rulers because "their very weakness gives them more gentleness and moderation; which can make for good government, rather than tough and ferocious virtues."[17] Similarly, Buffon noted that "women are not nearly as strong as men are, and the greatest use, or the greatest abuse, which man has made of his strength is to have enslaved and often treated in a tyrannical manner this half of the human race, which was made in order to share with him the pleasure and pains of life." Gender equality was the sign of civilization. "It is only among the nations civilized to the point of politeness that women have obtained that equality of condition, which however is so natural and so necessary to the gentleness of society," he wrote elsewhere. Women were the civilizing force that had brought about this transformation from brutal oppression to gentle equality.[18]

The men who made these arguments submitted themselves to female governance in the salons of Paris, where the sociability by which they defined civilization was not simply an idea but a social practice. Salon sociability reflected both the conversational ideal of reciprocal exchange based on a belief in natural sociability and the perceived need to bring about order and harmony among men through strong discipline and a means to enforce it. It called for a civilizing force to enable conversing men to attain the sociability that they naturally sought. That civilizing force was identified as feminine. Was history constructed to ground the social practice of salon conversation? Or was salon gover-

good summary

16. Carolyn C. Lougee, *"Le Paradis des Femmes": Women, Salons, and Social Stratification in Seventeenth-Century France* (Princeton, 1976), pp. 32–33. The quotation is from Saint-Gabriel, *Mérite des dames* (1660).

17. Charles-Louis de Secondat, baron de Montesquieu, *De l'esprit des lois*, bk. 7, chap. 16, in *Oeuvres complètes*, ed. Daniel Oster (Paris, 1964), p. 570.

18. Quoted in Joel Schwartz, *The Sexual Politics of Jean-Jacques Rousseau* (Chicago, 1984), p. 21.

nance legitimated by an appeal to history? In either case, social practice
and the construction of history supported each other in giving women
a particular and central role in the formation of modern, civilized
society, defined as peaceful, gentle, sociable and—eventually—enlightened.

Positing the fundamental sociability of human beings as the basis of
both society and knowledge, Enlightenment epistemology embedded
the pursuit of knowledge in the social world, conceived of it as continuous with the everyday life of men of letters. Because the pursuit of
knowledge and intellectual activity of all sorts were not dissociated
from the world, because they were not abstracted from it but purposely
resituated in it, the seventeenth-century term "Republic of Letters"
gained new meaning. The Republic of Letters took on a *life* of its own
and the possibility, therefore, of a history.

As a worldly activity, philosophy now had two major implications:
first, it was not confined within the individual, disembodied (Cartesian)
mind; and, second, its tasks could be completed only in a social setting,
as a social practice. And since sociability was understood to be mixed-
gender and woman-centered, the collaboration of women in completing the tasks of philosophy was also implied. The necessity for this
collaboration, moreover, was reinforced by Neoplatonic theories of
complementarity.[19]

Gender complementarity began from the assumption (often but not
always based on biological definitions of nature) that men and women
(being male and female) are fundamentally different and these differences, however defined, are complementary.[20] *Completion*, the realization of any ideal, the achievement of any goal or project, could result
only from the complementary actions of men and women or of masculine and feminine qualities. Complementarity did not imply equality.
Indeed, the case for equality was sometimes made from an assumption
of undifferentiation.[21] Like the idea of natural sociability, however,

19. For a definition of complementarity, see Londa Schiebinger, *The Mind Has No
Sex?: Women in the Origins of Modern Science* (Cambridge, Mass., 1989), pp. 216–17. On
Neoplatonism, see Lougee, "*Paradis des Femmes,*" pp. 34–40.

20. On the grounding of gender differences in biological understandings of sex, see
Thomas Laqueur, *Maxing Sex: Body and Gender from the Greeks to Freud* (Cambridge, Mass.,
1990).

21. François Poulain de la Barre, for example, who wrote *L'Egalité des deux sexes*
(1673), was a Cartesian. On the feminist implications of Cartesian thought, see Erica
Harth, *Cartesian Women: Versions and Subversions of Rational Discourse in the Old Regime*
(Ithaca, 1992). For recent critiques of complementarity as inegalitarian, see Cécile Dauphin et al., "Women's Culture and Women's Power: An Attempt at Historiography,"
trans. Camille Garnier, *Journal of Women's History* 1 (Spring 1989): 63–88; and Evelyn Fox
Keller, "The Gender/Science System, or Is Sex to Gender as Nature Is to Science?"
Hypatia 2 (Fall 1987): 37–49. Most interesting is Joan W. Scott's argument that the binary

complementarity did imply that autonomous, rational beings (gendered male) were not sufficient to the attainment of the ends they sought by nature, whether philosophical, social, or political. "Feminine" virtues must compensate for "masculine" vices to create an ideal whole. In the realm of intellectual sociability, this gender complementarity was institutionalized in the salon. The French Enlightenment was built on the complementarity of "feminine" sensibility and "masculine" reason, on the compensation of female selflessness for male ego.

The Republic of Letters as it was conceived and constituted in France in the second half of the eighteenth century was composed of men and women who played particular complementary (but not equal) roles. The role of women in the Enlightenment and the attitude of male philosophes toward women (as well as the subsequent historiography of the Enlightenment) were founded on a tension between the *recognition* of a need for women in Enlightenment cultural practice and discomfort with that recognition. Historically, this tension was "resolved" by the decentering and displacement of women by men in new institutions of intellectual sociability in the 1780s; intellectually, it was "resolved" by the abstraction of philosophy (both epistemology and ethics) from the concrete social world, most notably by Kant, which reconceived reasoning and conversing males as sufficient to the attainment of philosophical ends (and relegated women to the sphere of antireason); historiographically, the tension has been continually redisplaced rather than resolved as historians, unable to efface women from history, have yet failed to develop an understanding of the Enlightenment which satisfactorily accounts for them. In the eighteenth century, the Republic of Letters was composed of French men and women, philosophes and salonnières, who worked together to attain the ends of philosophy, broadly conceived as the project of Enlightenment.

To say that men and women needed one another or that ends could be attained only by the complementary actions of men and women neither obviates the question of hierarchy nor addresses the question of power. Indeed, it begs these very questions, and that is why the *querelle des femmes,* or "woman question," raged throughout the seventeenth and eighteenth centuries.[22] Karen Offen contends that from the sixteenth century French culture was characterized by a fear of the power of women, defined as "influence." No matter how men revised the laws regarding issues as seeemingly diverse as marriage and mon-

---

opposition between equality and difference which structures so much debate within feminism needs to be deconstructed. See "Deconstructing Equality-versus-Difference, or The Uses of Post-structuralist Theory for Feminism," *Feminist Studies* 14 (Spring 1988): 33–50.

22. Lougee, "*Paradis des Femmes,*" p. 3.

archical succession, the specter of extralegal female "influence" continued to haunt and threaten them.[23]

Complementarity did not resolve the ultimate questions about the relations between the sexes, questions of power and hierarchy, of equality and subordination, which were deeply embedded in Western culture. It simply allowed them to be reinscribed, with "female virtues," however they might be defined, subordinated to "male" ones. In 1772 Louise d'Epinay made this a central point of her critique of Antoine-Léonard Thomas's "Essai sur les femmes," a classic of complementary thinking by a habitué of Enlightenment salons. "It is quite constant that men and women are of the same nature and the same constitution," wrote Epinay. "Men and women, being of the same nature, are susceptible to the same faults, the same virtues and the same vices. The virtues that people wish to give to women in general are almost all virtues against nature, which produce only small artificial virtues and some very real vices."[24]

Voltaire had identified the regency of Anne of Austria in the 1640s as the beginning of France's reign as the most civilized and sociable country on earth. Thomas called it "a singular epoch" of anarchy and faction "led by women." "They all had in this epoch that type of anxious agitation that makes for partisan spirit, a spirit less distant from their character than one might think," he said. In his own time "sociability [had been] pushed to excess" in France, with serious results. Overextension of the "spirit of society" had loosened the bonds of the family, and domestic life was unknown. "All the feelings of Nature that are born in retreat, and which grow in silence, must be weakened. Women must thus be less wives and mothers." Worse yet, the esteem in which women had been held was now falling through too much familiarity:

> In societies, in this eternal mixing of the sexes, one learns to praise less, because one learns to be more severe.... Such is the case with regard to women themselves, the influence of this general spirit of society that is their work, and which they do not cease to vaunt. They are like the sovereigns of Asia who are never more honored than when they are less seen: in communicating too much to their subjects, they encourage them to revolt.[25]

23. Karen Offen, "The Woman Question in Modern France" (unpublished ms.). I am grateful to Dr. Offen for sharing this manuscript with me.

24. Louise d'Epinay to Ferdinando Galiani, 14 March 1772, in Elisabeth Badinter, ed., *Qu'est-ce qu'une femme?* (Paris, 1989), p. 193.

25. Antoine-Léonard Thomas, "Essai sur le caractère, les moeurs, et l'esprit des femmes dans les différents siècles," in Badinter, *Qu'est-ce qu'une femme?* pp. 134, 152,

Thomas concluded his essay with a portrait of the ideal woman, who "at the risk of displeasing would know how, in her home and outside it, to protect her esteem for virtue, her contempt for vice, her sensitivity to friendship, and, despite the desire to have an extended society, in the very midst of that society, would have the courage to publish a way of thinking so extraordinary, and the greater courage to sustain it."[26]

Thomas was in fact drawing a portrait of Suzanne Necker, whose salon he frequented. Although Thomas praised Necker as a woman who could transcend her age by being both sociable and a real woman—a wife and mother—Diderot criticized him for ingratitude. "Thomas," he wrote, "says not one word about the advantages of the commerce of women for a man of letters."[27]

Thomas, however, was right: a revolt was brewing. As the philosophes grew stronger and the Republic of Letters grew broader through their successful efforts to create a critical reading public, they and those who read their work did not always see the need for an external form of governance. Sociability and enlightenment could perhaps be achieved without women to maintain order by disciplining unruly discourse. If men of letters were able to "forget" social distinctions and hierarchy in the controlled society of the salon, they could also "forget" why government had been necessary in the first place: to make possible the polite sociability on which Enlightenment discourse and civilization itself were predicated. The revolt against the monarchy in 1789 was prefigured by the revolt against salon governance in the 1780s, when young male citizens of the Republic of Letters formed their own societies based on a fantasy of masculine self-governance which displaced women from their central governing role and resituated them as the objects of male desire and male learning. After 150 years of female governance, the "natural order" was restored in the Republic of Letters.

157–58, 160. Epinay pointed specifically to the phrase "anxious agitation" as being particularly "unscientific" in her critique of Thomas's essay. (Epinay to Galiani, 14 March 1772, in Badinter, *Qu'est-ce qu'une femme?* p. 192.)

26. Thomas, "Essai sur les femmes," p. 160.

27. Denis Diderot, "Sur les femmes," in Badinter, *Qu'est-ce qu'une femme?* p. 184. Diderot identified Thomas's subject as Suzanne Necker in Friedrich-Melchior Grimm et al., *Correspondance littéraire, philosophique, et critique*, ed. Maurice Tourneux, 16 vols. (Paris, 1877–82), 1 April 1772; see also *Mémoires secrets pour servir à l'histoire de la République des Lettres en France, depuis MDCCLXII jusqu'à nos jours*, 36 vols. (London, 1780–89; rpt. Westmead, Eng., 1970), 12 and 14 April 1772.

CHAPTER 1

The Rise of the State: The Republic of Letters and the Monarchy of France

C'est la liberté, qui règne dans la République de Lettres. Cette République est un état extrêmement libre. On n'y reconnait que l'empire de la vérité et de la raison.

—PIERRE BAYLE

Heureux au moins les gens de lettres, s'ils reconnaissent enfin que le moyen le plus sûr de se faire respecter, est de vivre unis . . . et presque renfermés entre eux; que par cette union ils parviendront sans peine à donner la loi au reste de la nation sur les matières de goût et de philosophie.

—JEAN LE ROND D'ALEMBERT

Over the course of the seventeenth and eighteenth centuries, the growth of the Republic of Letters paralleled that of the French monarchy. Each polity had its own constitution, but the constituencies of the two states overlapped and so did their goals. Thus the history of the Republic of Letters is interwoven with that of the monarchy from its consolidation after the Wars of Religion until its downfall in the French Revolution. Whereas the history of the monarchy has been narrated many times over, that of the Republic of Letters has not. Here, then, is a history of the Republic of Letters, from its founding in the seventeenth century as an apolitical community of discourse through its transformation in the eighteenth century into a very political community whose project of Enlightenment challenged the monarchy from a new public space carved out of French society.

In the Middle Ages, according to Jürgen Habermas, there was no public sphere, "in the sense of a separate realm distinguished from the private sphere." Publicity was simply a kind of "status attribute" of those with power; it represented the power of the person rather than a

[handwritten margin note: Accepts w/out question Habermas as a canonical text]

sphere of social action.[1] Indeed, it follows that there was no private
sphere either. Rather, the whole notion of public and private emerged
and was contested over the course of the early modern period.[2] Public
and private spheres emerged in the early seventeenth century when the
resolution of the religious wars included the beginnings of both the
administrative state and the idea of freedom of conscience. As freedom
of conscience began to define private autonomy, the administrative
state began to demarcate the private holdings of the prince from the
public budget (11–12).

At first glance, this scenario suggests a simple dichotomy opposing
public and private, the French monarchy and the Republic of Letters,
the power-based state and the conscience-centered individual. Habermas, however, contends that it was the zone of interaction between the
state and the individual that formed the ground of an authentic public
sphere, the realm of civil society and the public. The Republic of Letters was at the dynamic heart of this authentic public sphere. The
"structural transformation of the public sphere" occurred because the
public was not simply a collection of autonomous individuals defined
by conscience but the object of state power (18). "In this stratum,"
Habermas explains, "the state authorities evoked a resonance leading
the *publicum* . . . into an awareness of itself as the latter's opponent, that
is, as the public of the now emerging *public sphere of civil society*" (23).

Criticism, the discursive mode of the Republic of Letters, developed

1. Habermas, *Structural Transformation*, p. 7, hereafter cited parenthetically in the
text. Recent examinations of Habermas's analysis of the emergence of the public sphere
include Keith Michael Baker, "Defining the Public Sphere in Eighteenth-Century
France: Variations on a Theme by Habermas," in *Habermas and the Public Sphere*, ed.
Craig Calhoun (Cambridge, Mass., 1992), pp. 181–211; Anthony J. La Vopa, "Conceiving a Public: Ideas and Society in Eighteenth-Century Europe," *Journal of Modern History*
64 (March 1992): 79–116. Also of great interest are Habermas's own reflections on his
early work and the recent interpretations of it: "Further Reflections on the Public
Sphere" and "Concluding Remarks," both in *Habermas and the Public Sphere*, pp. 421–79.
The following discussion draws on my "Public Sphere and Private Life: Toward a Synthesis of Current Historiographical Approaches to the Old Regime," *History and Theory* 31,
no. 1 (1992): 1–20.
    On Immanuel Kant's notions of criticism and publicity, elaborated primarily in the
1780s, which clearly underlie Habermas's vision of the public sphere, see Onora O'Neill,
Constructions of Reason: Explorations of Kant's Practical Philosophy (Cambridge, 1989);
O'Neill, "Enlightenment as Autonomy: Kant's Vindication of Reason," in *The Enlightenment and Its Shadows*, ed. Peter Hulme and Ludmilla Jordanova (London, 1990), pp. 186–
98; John Christian Laursen, "The Subversive Kant: The Vocabulary of 'Public' and
'Publicity,'" *Political Theory* 14 (November 1986): 584–603; Laursen, "Scepticism and
Intellectual Freedom: The Philosophical Foundations of Kant's Politics of Publicity,"
History of Political Thought 10 (Autumn 1989): 439–55.
2. The same argument is made from the other side of the coin in Roger Chartier,
ed., *Passions of the Renaissance*, trans. Arthur Goldhammer, vol. 3 of *A History of Private
Life*, ed. Philippe Ariès and Georges Duby (Cambridge, Mass., 1989).

"in the zone of continuous administrative contact" between the state and its subjects (24). As private persons, subjects of the state found certain of their activities to be the objects of public policy and thus were provoked into making critical judgments. One such subject was Pierre Bayle, who fled France in the wake of Louis XIV's persecution of the Huguenots and founded in Rotterdam a journal called *Nouvelles de la République des Lettres*. Criticism was the characteristic discourse of a new and authentic public sphere in which private people came together as a public to use their reason publicly (24–27). Above all, the new public was a reading public, a public constructed by the Republic of Letters (29–30).

In Paris, the new public sphere was structured by the salon, the press, and other institutions of sociability and publicity which were developed to counter the courtly institutions of the absolutist state (31–43).[3] In these "forums for discussion," private individuals formed civil society, creating a new public sphere to challenge and eventually to appropriate the old, inauthentic public sphere of the monarchy (51). The great virtue of these institutions was their underlying "principle of publicity," which came to challenge "the practice of secrets of state" (52). This new public sphere was authentic precisely because it was open; its publicity revealed as illegitimate the monarchy's claims to represent the public opaquely, rather than with the openness of critical reason.

The new public sphere, though broader than the Republic of Letters, developed from it and continued to be structured by its institutions of publicity and sociability.[4] The landscape was urban and discursive; the mode of discourse was the criticism of the Republic of Letters. By the middle of the eighteenth century, the cosmopolitan Republic of Letters had become centered in Paris, the major locus of the zone of confrontation between territorial monarchy and the republic. By 1770 the leading citizens of the French Republic of Letters were the self-proclaimed arbiters of the public opinion that was the defining feature of the new public sphere (89–102).

The Republic of Letters was the very center of the public sphere in

3. This opposition between salon and court contrasts with Norbert Elias's argument that the "nobles' and financiers' *salon* of the eighteenth century is a descendant of the royal *salon* of the second half of the seventeenth": *The Court Society*, trans. Edmund Jephcott (New York, 1983), p. 79. For a critique of Elias, see Daniel Gordon, "'Public Opinion' and the Civilizing Process in France: The Example of Morellet," *Eighteenth-Century Studies* 22 (Spring 1989): 318–19.

4. On the identification of the Republic of Letters with the public in the seventeenth century, see Paul Dibon, "Communication in the Respublica Literaria of the 17th Century," *Res Publica Litterarum* 1 (1978): 47; and Françoise Waquet, "Qu'est-ce que la République des Lettres?: Essai de sémantique historique," *Bibliothèque de l'Ecole des Chartes* 147 (1989): 480–81.

which private persons learned to use their reason publicly: the republic's institutions of sociability were its institutions; the republic's modes
and practices of communication structured the discourse of the public
and its sphere of action. In France the Republic of Letters was at the
heart of the new and authentic sphere that emerged as the twin of the
absolutist state in the seventeenth century.

Habermas stuff seems badly integrated

The Republic of Letters in the Seventeenth Century

Like the French monarchy, the Republic of Letters is a modern phenomenon with an ancient history. References to the *Respublica literaria*
have been found as early as 1417.[5] Nevertheless, the *concept* of the
Republic of Letters emerged only in the early seventeenth century and
became widespread only at the end of that century. Paul Dibon defines
the Republic of Letters as it was conceived in the seventeenth century as
"an intellectual community transcending space and time, [but] recognizing as such differences in respect to the diversity of languages, sects,
and countries. . . . This state, ideal as it may be, is in no way utopian,
but . . . takes form in [good] old human flesh where good and evil
mix."[6] According to Annie Barnes, it was based on "the conscious notion of international intellectual cooperation," translated not into "the
creation of a commission or an institute, but [into] the founding of an
ideal state, the Republic of Letters."[7] Françoise Waquet, who has done
the most thorough investigation of the use of the term, emphasizes that
its political implications cannot be separated from the intellectual community and sociability that defined the practices of its citizenry. "The
Republic of Letters is very much a reality," she writes. "At the same
time, it does not any less appear as 'a chimaera.' . . . This double character, real and ideal, endures; we find it today in the expression 'scientific community.'"[8] State building was the order of the day in the seventeenth century, and men of letters participated in it in their own
fashion.

Once the concept of the Republic of Letters was in general use, it
generated its own history, as citizens of the new republic traced their
ancestry back to ancient Greece and Rome. Thus Vigneul-Marville
could write in 1699: "The Republic of Letters is of very ancient ori-

5. Elizabeth L. Eisenstein, *The Printing Press as an Agent of Change: Communications
and Cultural Transformations in Early Modern Europe*, 2 vols. (Cambridge, 1979), 1:137 n.
287.
6. Paul Dibon, "L'Université de Leyde et la République des Lettres au 17e siècle,"
Quaerendo 5 (1975): 26.
7. Quoted in Dibon, "Communication in the Respublica Literaria," p. 44.
8. Waquet, "Qu'est-ce que la République des Lettres?" pp. 494–95.

gin. . . . Never has it been so great, so populous, so free or so glorious. It embraces the whole world and is composed of all nationalities, all social classes [*conditions*], all ages, and both sexes."[9] The Republic of Letters must thus be understood as having both historical specificity and ideal universality—like the pre-Reformation church. Having gradually superseded the church as the home of European intellectual life, the *Respublica literaria et christiana* became simply the *Respublica literaria*.[10]

If the French monarchy under Louis XIV also sought to become universal like the church, it was never cosmopolitan like the Republic of Letters. As the republic created a history for itself that extended it back in time, it also extended itself through space, transcending the hardening national boundaries of the political world. This cosmopolitanism was also projected into the future as an ideal to be realized through expanded communication across the temporal bounds of generations and the spatial bounds of political geography.[11] This communication depended on two fundamental inventions of the modern world—the printing press and the postal system—which together made possible the cosmopolitan polity of the Republic of Letters.[12]

Words—oral, written, and printed—were the medium of the Republic of Letters. Since the sixteenth century, printers, so instrumental to the communication of ideas, had been central to intellectual life.[13] The accuracy of editions made possible by printing fulfilled some of the intellectual aims of humanists and reformers. Moreover, printers and writers, forming part of the same small world, often exchanged roles, and printshops served as early centers of intellectual sociability. At the end of the fifteenth century, for example, an Italian named Aldus published a monumental edition of the works of Aristotle. "In order to complete this task," Lucien Febvre and Henri-Jean Martin explain, "he associated himself with the best scholars . . . in all Europe. This was the foundation of the Aldine Academy . . . . Scholars met in his home at a fixed time each day to decide which texts were to be printed and which manuscripts to adopt."[14] The tradition of printshop sociability was re-

9. Quoted in Dibon, "Communication in the Respublica Literaria," p. 43.
10. Ibid., p. 45.
11. Ibid., pp. 42–55; Waquet, "Qu'est-ce que la République des Lettres?" pp. 491–93.
12. Habermas notes the importance of the simultaneous development of the post and the press for commerce in *Structural Transformation*, p. 16.
13. Eisenstein, *Printing Press*.
14. Lucien Febvre and Henri-Jean Martin, *The Coming of the Book: The Impact of Printing, 1450–1800*, ed. Geoffrey Nowell-Smith and David Wooton, trans. David Gerard (London, 1984), p. 145.

newed in the eighteenth century by the Prosper Marchand circle in The Hague.[15]

The Republic of Letters was unquestionably indebted to the invention of movable type, but another sort of regular movement was necessary for its functioning as well: the circulation of letters. "The role of epistolary exchanges," writes Daniel Roche, "is one of the traditions that organizes most strongly the very notion of 'Republic of Letters.'" According to Dibon, "it was the strict duty of each citizen of the Respublica literaria to establish, maintain, and encourage communication, primarily by personal correspondence or contact."[16] All citizens of the seventeenth-century Republic of Letters were corresponding members, and Cicero and Erasmus were their models. Moreover, citizens considered it their duty to bring others into the republic through the expansion of their correspondence. These expanding networks of epistolary exchange, according to Dibon, "remained—at least until the flourishing of journals in the last years of the century—the primary means of coordinating the life of the Respublica literaria, of making its activities known to its citizens, of heralding the appearance of books . . . , and of spreading news about research in progress."[17]

Correspondence was also integral to establishing a reputation and remained as its mark. "Nothing is better for nourishing . . . the reputation of a man of letters, and sometimes even for establishing it, at least for a time," wrote d'Alembert in an article about the academician President Jean Bouhier, "than a large epistolary commerce." Bouhier, explains Hélène Monod-Cassidy, formed in his library a private academy of men and women, young and old, professors and students, who conversed and shared books freely. From this group constituted by hospitality and the exchange of ideas Bouhier created "a whole stable of correspondents who wrote from the provinces, abroad, and Paris; looked for rare books that he wanted, exchanged Latin citations in order to debate their meaning, or consulted the président on questions of jurisprudence or the translation of a Ciceronian verse."[18] Corre-

15. Margaret C. Jacob, *The Radical Enlightenment: Pantheists, Freemasons, and Republicans* (London, 1981), pp. 182–214.

16. Daniel Roche, "Correspondance et voyage au XVIIIᵉ siècle: Le Réseau des sociabilités d'un académicien provincial, Séguier de Nîmes," in *Les Républicains des lettres: Gens de culture et Lumières au XVIIIᵉ siècle* (Paris, 1988), p. 264; Dibon, "Communication in the Respublica Literaria," p. 52.

17. Dibon, "Communication in the Respublica Literaria," pp. 46–47.

18. Hélène Monod-Cassidy, "De la lettre à la revue: La Correspondance de l'abbé Le Blanc et du président Bouhier; essai sur l'étiologie de la *Correspondance littéraire*," in *La Correspondance littéraire de Grimm et de Meister (1754–1813)*, ed. Bernard Bray, Jochen Schlobach, and Jean Varloot (Paris, 1976), pp. 135–36.

spondence in the Republic of Letters ranged from short notes and
letters of introduction to lengthy newsletters and scientific reports,
from the personal and private to the public and published. It could
complement printed matter, go into print, or enclose what was printed.
"Letters," writes Maarten Ultee, "were at the heart of the republic of
letters."[19]

Reciprocity is the distinctive feature of correspondence as a mode of
communication. Certainly individual letters can be structured by deference (and often were in the Old Regime), but correspondence is a
continuing and reciprocal exchange of letters. The reciprocity of correspondence both reflected and strengthened the sense of equality that
structured relations among citizens of the Republic of Letters. Reciprocity was the fundamental virtue of the republic.[20]

Although, as Dibon points out, there were several ways to send letters, from the traveler's pocket to the diplomatic pouch, it is nonetheless significant that in France the history of the postal service parallels
that of the Republic of Letters. Actually, they are intertwined, and it is
perhaps the post which best marks the intersection of the histories of
the Republic of Letters and the French monarchy.

Eugène Vaillé dates the origin of the French postal service precisely
to 16 November 1603: the date on which Henri IV commissioned his
controller general, Guillaume Fouquet, le sieur de LaVarenne, to allow
royal couriers to accept, transport, and distribute letters for the public.[21] As the Republic of Letters had its antecedents in the world of the
humanists, the post descended from earlier messenger services, both
royal and corporate. The postal service as an institution, however, was
the creation of Henri IV and La Varenne. By first instituting a system
of overland relays that covered the entire territory of the realm and
then taking over the administration of horse rentals, the crown managed to restrict and control freedom of overland movement and set up
its eventual control over the circulation of letters.[22] By 1608, La Varenne had been named postmaster general by letters patent and the
French had something that fits Vaillé's definition of a postal service:
"an organism assuring, according to fixed schedules and itineraries,
and in the shortest amount of time, taking into account what was then

19. Maarten Ultee, "The Republic of Letters: Learned Correspondence, 1680–
1720," *Seventeenth Century* 2 (January 1987): 98.
20. On reciprocity as a moral virtue, see Lawrence C. Becker, *Reciprocity* (London,
1986), esp. chap. 4.
21. Eugène Vaillé, *Histoire des postes françaises jusqu'à la Révolution* (Paris, 1946),
pp. 45–46.
22. Ibid., p. 41. On monopoly as definitive of monarchy, see Elias, *Power and Civility*,
chap. 2.

possible, the transport of correspondences in the service not only of the State, but also of individuals, for which service the latter must pay the cost."[23]

The new postal service marked the growing power of the monarchy and its increasing control over the realm; it was also a service demanded by a growing literate and commercial public of which the citizens of the Republic of Letters were a significant part. The monarchy and the republic would both benefit from the creation of a unified system by which written and printed words could circulate freely and securely. If this new system tightened the monarchy's control over its subjects, it also strengthened the bonds among them and among the citizens of the Republic of Letters.

The tension between state control and public service was at the very heart of the postal system, just as it was at the heart of the state itself. Because this tension not only persisted but intensified as the state and its institutions grew stronger, the public increasingly demanded both better service and less control. In the case of the post, the public wanted faster and more dependable service, on the one hand, and, on the other, absolute privacy of the letters that passed through the mails and freedom of movement for printed goods—journals in particular. Not surprisingly, too, since the public had to bear the cost for this service directly, they did everything they could to avoid paying. Thus, while the postal system supported the Republic of Letters and was supported by it, the relationship between the monarchy and the republic defined by the post was problematic and fraught with tension.[24]

By the middle of the seventeenth century, the cosmopolitan Republic of Letters had also come to a more direct understanding with the monarchies of which its citizens were also subjects. By mutual agreement based on self-interest, the leading citizens of the republic and the leaders of the monarchies founded academies for the advancement of knowledge and the glory of kings. Nowhere was this compact stronger than in France, where the Republic of Letters now found its home not in the printshops of humanists and reformers but in court circles. This was so in part because of a change in the terms and status of printing itself. By the seventeenth century, printers had been incorporated into the guild system of the Old Regime. The trade was overcrowded, and printers were less interested in being a part of the Republic of Letters than in guaranteeing sales. Moreover, the triumph of authority—both

23. Vaillé, *Histoire des postes*, p. 45.
24. Dena Goodman, "Epistolary Property: Michel de Servan and the Plight of Letters on the Eve of the French Revolution," in *Conceptions of Property in Early Modern Europe*, ed. John Brewer and Susan Staves (London, forthcoming).

the monarchy and the Counter-Reformation church—had brought about the subjection of publishing. "Writers and scholars no longer gathered in printers' houses or workshops but in the literary salons of high society, or in the libraries of the aristocracy, at the invitation of learned librarians and under the patronage of powerful individuals, or even monasteries," write Febvre and Martin. Although some printers continued to serve the republic, "they were now like servants in relation to their customers, not their equals or even their protectors as they had been in the sixteenth century."[25] The socially undifferentiated sixteenth-century world of humanist writers and printers was shattered as printers entered the old establishment of corporate society and men of letters turned for support to the new monarchy.

In the academies, the Republic of Letters would gain financial support and social status. With their institution, the monarchy would subordinate a competitive basis of authority to itself while appropriating the rival's achievements. The cosmopolitan basis of the republic was maintained by the correspondences of citizen-academicians and the exchange of academic memoirs and transactions. Universal correspondence was the ideal attempted by such leading citizens of the Republic of Letters as Père Marin Mersenne, of whom a contemporary wrote: "He had become the center of the world of letters, owing to the contact he maintained with all, and all with him, . . . serving a function in the Republic of Letters similar to that of the heart in the circulation of blood within the human body."[26] Corresponding memberships further strengthened the bonds between academies; thus, for example, a member of the French Academy might be named a corresponding member of the Royal Society in London. "One saw established imperceptibly in Europe a literary republic," wrote Voltaire in his *Siècle de Louis XIV*,

> despite the wars and despite different religions. All the sciences, all the arts, thus received mutual assistance in this way: the academies formed this republic. . . . True scholars in each field drew closer the bonds of this great society of minds, spread everywhere and everywhere independent. This correspondence still remains; it is one of the consolations for the evils that ambition and politics spread across the earth.[27]

There were, of course, strains on this new relationship. Times of war, for example, which disrupted both travel and the postal system, also made it politically difficult to be both an active citizen of the cos-

25. Febvre and Martin, *Coming of the Book*, p. 153.
26. Quoted in Dibon, "Communication in the Respublica Literaria," p. 50.
27. [François Marie Arouet de] Voltaire, *Siècle de Louis XIV*, in *Oeuvres complètes*, 52 vols. (Paris, 1877–85), 14:563–64.

mopolitan republic and a loyal subject of one's king.[28] And since virtually the entire reign of Louis XIV was a time of war, the inconvenience was more than occasional. Closer to home, the king's role in admitting members to the academy could always create difficulties, since the notion of merit as the basis of selection and advancement was central to the Republic of Letters. While scholars sought patronage and prestige in allying themselves with the monarchy, they needed to maintain their independence in certain crucial ways if the republic was to survive. Finally, the goal of the republic, the pursuit of knowledge, could always lead to conflicts with church and state. While the monarchy asserted itself as the sole authority—as absolute—and hoped that the creation of academies would force the Republic of Letters to assist it in doing so, the academies maintained enough autonomy to continue to challenge the monarchy at times.[29] Just as the *parlements* in which the French aristocracy increasingly contested the sovereignty of the monarchy were never fully tamed, neither were the academies.

If not utterly subjugated, however, they were compromised. When the Republic of Letters settled into the academies, it entered the service of the state, and in so doing it was forced to betray its independence, if not its cosmopolitan ideals. For example, as part of its inheritance from the church, the language of the early republic was Latin. Gradually, however, French replaced Latin in a shift that reflected not only the secularization of the republic but a French political and military dominance out of which cultural dominance developed only later. By the eighteenth century the triumph of French as the language of the Republic of Letters was universally acknowledged. It was praised even by those citizens of the republic, such as Benjamin Franklin, who were neither French nor francophone.[30]

The transformation of the *Respublica literaria* into the *République des Lettres* also reflected the diaspora of learned French Calvinists to the Protestant North as a result of Louis XIV's revocation of the Edict of Nantes in 1685. As Voltaire summed up the situation in the *Siècle de Louis XIV*, "The French have been scattered farther abroad than the

28. Maarten Ultee, "Res Publica Litteraria and War, 1680–1715," in *Res Publica Litteraria: Die Institutionen der Gelehrtsamkeit in der frühen Neuzeit*, ed. Conrad Wiedemann and Sebastian Neumeister, 2 vols. (Wiesbaden, 1987), 2:535–46. A century later, Jean-Baptiste-Antoine Suard remarked on the same problem in a letter to John Wilkes in England, 22 March 1780, in "Lettres inédites de Suard à Wilkes," ed. Gabriel Bonno, *University of California Publications in Modern Philology* 15 (1932).

29. Waquet, "Qu'est-ce que la République des Lettres?" p. 494.

30. Elizabeth L. Eisenstein, *Print Culture and Enlightenment Thought* (Chapel Hill, 1986), p. 10; Thomas J. Schlereth, *The Cosmopolitan Ideal in Enlightenment Thought: Its Form and Function in the Ideas of Franklin, Hume, and Voltaire, 1694–1790* (Notre Dame, 1977), p. 4.

Jews."[31] Francophone journals, both learned ones such as the *Journal Littéraire* and political ones such as the *Gazette de Leyde* and the *Gazette d'Amsterdam*, dated from the arrival of the refugees in the Low Countries.[32] The presses of the Protestant Reformation became the printing centers of the "French" Enlightenment in the eighteenth century. Indeed, as a continuation of the critical and oppositional tradition of Protestant publishing, and because of increasingly tight controls on publishing in Paris by the printers' guild and the church (also the monarchy and the parlements), the publishers of the Enlightenment Republic of Letters were located for the most part just beyond France's borders.[33]

As Elizabeth Eisenstein points out, Latin continued to be used for scientific and scholarly—that is, academic—exchange in the eighteenth century, but it was no longer the language of the Republic of Letters,[34] for by then the republic had moved out of the academies. The passage from the Latin *respublica* to the French *république* was ideological, in both the epistemological and political senses: as the idea of the Republic of Letters changed, so did its politics. Bayle himself signaled the shift in an article in his *Dictionnaire historique et critique*. "The study of the new philosophy and of living languages," he wrote, "has determined an intellectual change and inaugurated a more enlightened century."[35] The academic savants of the old *Respublica literaria* were being challenged by the men of letters of the new *république*. This challenge was acted out in the academies themselves over the course of the eighteenth century, but the reconstitution of the Republic of Letters was only secondarily a struggle for control of the academies.

In France the Academy occupied itself primarily with the national concern of defining and preserving the French language. Indeed, according to Janet Altman, the founding of the Academy "institutionalized a Republic of Letters whose dominant and increasingly exclusive concern was the governance of language." The publications of its members, Altman continues, "bear clear traces of the alliance be-

---

31. Voltaire, *Oeuvres complètes* 15:29.

32. Jeremy D. Popkin, "The *Gazette de Leyde* and French Politics under Louis XVI," in *Press and Politics in Pre-revolutionary France*, ed. Jack R. Censer and Jeremy D. Popkin (Berkeley, 1987), p. 76.

33. Febvre and Martin, *Coming of the Book*, pp. 143–59; Élizabeth L. Eisenstein, *Grub Street Abroad: Aspects of the French Cosmopolitan Press from the Age of Louis XIV to the French Revolution* (Oxford, 1992); Eisenstein, *Print Culture and Enlightenment Thought*. Important exceptions to this rule were the printers of the *Encyclopédie*, Le Breton and Panckoucke, both of whom operated in Paris.

34. Eisenstein, *Print Culture and Enlightenment Thought*, p. 10; Eisenstein, *Grub Street Abroad*, pp. 38–39.

35. Quoted in Dibon, "Université de Leyde," p. 28.

tween letters and state leaders, showing the extent to which the former depend on the latter."[36]

Because it tied itself to the monarchy, the Academy suffered the fate of the monarchy. The excesses of Louis XIV eventually called forth accusations of despotism, and the Academy, too, was criticized. By the time Louis XV took the throne in 1723, the French Academy was already an object of satire if not scorn. "I have heard talk of a kind of tribunal called the *French Academy*," wrote Rica, one of Montesquieu's fictional Persian visitors. "There is not a less respected one in the whole world." The Academy's corporative existence defined it to such an extent that Rica could go on to describe it as a body with "forty heads all filled with figures, metaphors, and antitheses."[37]

The "Encyclopédie" and the Project of Enlightenment

After nearly a hundred years in the academies, the French Republic of Letters needed a new home. Since the Huguenot refugees provided models of independence and a new critical spirit, the printshops in which they gathered might have appealed to their descendants in the Republic of Letters. Although eighteenth-century men of letters took advantage of the old Reformation printshops, however, now located in what Robert Darnton has called the "fertile crescent" around the borders of France and reinvigorated by the arrival of French Huguenot émigrés, the republic did not simply settle into them. The new citizens were different from their ancestors. They had a greater sense of national identity, a greater sense of their own autonomy and high status within their society, and a new sense of their own authority over and independence from the state. Even as they struggled to free the Republic of Letters from the French monarchy, they asserted their rightful place within French society.

After a hundred years of state service and life at the top, French men of letters had come to conceive of themselves as a *corps*, a status group within French society. This new French identity was overlaid upon the fundamental principles of the Republic of Letters: reciprocity, cosmopolitanism, status based on merit, and fidelity to truth. The republic, moreover, was an urban phenomenon, and Paris was the biggest city in

36. Janet Gurkin Altman, "The Letter Book as a Literary Institution, 1539–1789: Toward a Cultural History of Published Correspondences in France," in *Men/Women of Letters*, ed. Charles A. Porter, *Yale French Studies*, no. 71 (1986): 39.

37. Charles-Louis de Secondat, baron de Montesquieu, *Lettres persanes*, ed. Paul Vernière (Paris, 1975), letter LXXIII.

Europe. Indeed, over the course of the eighteenth century, aspiring young men of letters would pour into Paris from the provinces, and visitors from other countries would come calling. French men of letters were in no hurry to leave Paris. Even as Louis XIV moved the capital of France to Versailles, Paris was becoming the capital of a new Republic of Letters, which would assert its place on the international scene as the equal of the greatest state in political Europe and, by that token, would challenge the authority of France itself. By 1755, Diderot could write of his age as a time "when Philosophy advances by great strides; when it submits to its empire all the objects within its jurisdiction; when its tone is the dominant tone; and when one begins to shake off the yoke of authority and example to abide by the laws of reason."[38]

Those Frenchmen interested in joining the Republic of Letters still sought admission to the academies, but they no longer identified the aims of the republic with those of the academic establishment, just as they had left the printshops when printers became part of the corporative establishment. Autonomy, which men of letters were now able to assert more strongly than ever, was crucial to the constitution of the republic, and that autonomy could not be maintained in a state-sponsored institution any better than it could in a corporative one.

When Denis Diderot and Jean Le Rond d'Alembert were hired by an entrepreneurial printer to translate and expand Ephraim Chambers's *Cyclopaedia*, they used the opportunity to make of their project an embodiment of the new Republic of Letters which would challenge the one represented by the French Academy. They saw as their forebears not the academicians of the seventeenth century but two quite different men of letters: the visionary English statesman Francis Bacon and the Huguenot émigré Pierre Bayle. Bacon had first articulated the collaborative basis of knowledge in his *Great Instauration* and *Advancement of Learning* at the turn of the sixteenth century, before the Republic of Letters had settled into the academies. He also stood for the usefulness of knowledge and against the isolated rationalism of Descartes. Bayle's was the name most identified in the eighteenth century with the Republic of Letters, the *patrie* he had adopted when he fled France in 1684. Bayle may have resided in Rotterdam, but his *Nouvelles* were issued from "la République des Lettres," and from that home he undertook the same task that the French Academy had set for itself earlier in the seventeenth century: the creation of a dictionary. Whereas Bacon preceded the academic Republic of Letters, Bayle challenged, criticized, and opposed it. To Bacon the editors of the *Encyclopédie*

---

38. [Denis] Diderot and [Jean Le Rond] d'Alembert, eds., *Encyclopédie, ou Dictionnaire raisonné des sciences, des arts, et des métiers*, 17 vols. (Paris, 1751–65), 5:636a.

owed, among other things, their tree of knowledge, or "système des connaissances humaines," which appeared in volume 1, at the end of d'Alembert's "Discours préliminaire." Diderot acknowledged his debt to Bayle in, among other articles, "Pyrrhonienne," in volume 8.

In his article "Encyclopédie," Diderot explained why neither the French Academy nor any other existing intellectual institution was adequate to the project at hand. First, he argued, academies were inefficient. After all, it had taken the French Academy sixty years to complete its dictionary. Second, the Academy was too restricted in its membership to embrace all the specialists needed to compile a complete dictionary. In fact, he continued, none of the existing intellectual institutions—academies, learned societies, or universities—was capable of undertaking such a task.

> Each occupied with a particular subject which could doubtless be the basis of a universal dictionary, they neglect an infinity of others that ought to enter into it; and you will not find any that will furnish you with the breadth of knowledge that you need. . . . You will be forced to seek assistance from a great number of men from all classes of society, men of value, but to whom the doors of the academies are no less closed because of their status. There are too many members of these learned societies if one's goal is simply human knowledge; there are not enough in all these societies for a general science of man.[39]

In declaring that there were too many people for the simple task of compiling *human* knowledge, Diderot was suggesting that the academies were full of men dedicated to "divine" knowledge rather than the empirical science of man. At the same time, people with the real, valuable knowledge needed for the completion of the project were closed out of the academies for reasons of social status. In sum, the academic establishment—the academies and the universities—did not represent the Republic of Letters whose knowledge and whose conception of knowledge Diderot wanted to embody in his encyclopedia.[40]

Diderot's conception of knowledge was Baconian rather than Cartesian. That is, he saw knowledge as useful, as empirical as well as rational, and as inductive rather than deductive. But above all, Bacon and Diderot saw knowledge as emerging from association and collaboration rather than from the mind of the isolated reasoner. Thus Bacon had concluded the preface to his *Great Instauration* with *requests* of his readers, rather than assertions of truths or even arguments. He asked first

---

39. Ibid., 5:635a.
40. Diderot had already made this critique in the *Lettre sur les aveugles*, ed. Robert Niklaus (Geneva, 1963), p. 48.

that they "not conceive we here deliver an opinion, but a work; and assure themselves we attempt not to found any sect or particular doctrine, but to fix an extensive basis for the service of human nature." Second, he asked them to participate in the great project of building knowledge on a new foundation. He asked that, "for their own sakes, they lay aside the zeal and prejudices of opinions, and endeavor the common good; and that being, by our assistance, freed and kept clear from the errors and hindrances of the way, they would themselves also take part of the task."[41]

For Diderot and his fellow editor d'Alembert, the communication of ideas was the basis of human society, and human association was the basis of knowledge. Sociability was fundamental to both the political and the epistemological in human affairs. In the "Discours préliminaire," d'Alembert traced the origin of society to the recognition by individuals of the similarity between themselves and other human beings, to the realization that they must all have the same needs and thus a common interest in meeting them. "Whence we conclude that we should find it advantageous to join with them in finding out what can be beneficial to us and what can be detrimental to us in Nature. The communication of ideas is the principle and support of this union, and necessarily requires the invention of signs—such is the source of the formation of societies, with which must have come the birth of languages."[42] Human beings joined together in societies in order to engage in collective endeavors for the satisfaction of their common needs. Human society derived from the meeting of common needs through the communication of ideas.

The exchange of ideas (d'Alembert used the word *commerce*) was thus central to both individual utility and human society. By the same token and conversely, human society and the notion of utility were central to the exchange of ideas that was the basis of human knowledge. Indeed, the human being was at the center of all knowledge, as Diderot asserted in explaining the organization of the *Encyclopédie* according to human faculties, rather than some proposed divine order. "Man is the single term from which one must begin, and to which all must be brought back, if one wishes to please, to interest, to touch [the reader], even in the most arid considerations, the driest details. Make an abstraction of

41. Francis Bacon, *The Great Instauration*, in *Advancement of Learning*, ed. Joseph Devey (New York, 1902), p. 19. Kant used this same passage from Bacon as a motto with which to open the second edition of his *Critique of Pure Reason*. See O'Neill, *Constructions of Reason*, pp. 6–9.

42. Jean Le Rond d'Alembert, *Preliminary Discourse to the Encyclopedia of Diderot*, trans. Richard N. Schwab (Indianapolis, 1963), p. 11.

my existence and of the happiness of my fellow beings, and what will the rest of nature matter to me?"[43]

The editors of the *Encyclopédie* both affirmed the necessity of association for the production of knowledge and challenged the ability of existing intellectual institutions to represent and support such association. They affirmed the Republic of Letters but denied the academic establishment as its home. The *Encyclopédie* would be the work of an independent "society of men of letters and artisans, spread out, each occupied with his own part and linked together solely by the general interest of the human race and by a feeling of reciprocal benevolence."[44] The *Encyclopédie* would itself embody the republic by, for example, becoming the center of the universal correspondence across the ages. "The ultimate perfection of an encyclopedia is the work of centuries," Diderot wrote in his prospectus. "It took centuries to make a beginning; it will take centuries to bring it to an end."[45]

The critique voiced in the *Encyclopédie* extended to the very form of academic association. Diderot wanted association, but he was wary of meetings, where much was said and little was accomplished.[46] Equally important was the idea that this new society of men of letters would be bound together only by mutual ties of goodwill and a common concern for the good of humanity, rather than any particular interest. Not only were academies particularistic bodies, legal corps, but they were tied to the interest of the monarchy. "If the government gets involved in such a work," Diderot wrote, "it will never get done."[47] A monarch may have been able to order a palace to be built in the fields of Versailles, but men of letters were not manual laborers and their work could not be commanded in the same way. An encyclopedia could not be simply another monument to the glory of the king.

43. *Encyclopédie* 5:641.

44. Ibid., 5:636.

45. D'Alembert, *Preliminary Discourse*, p. 127. Part 3 of the "Discours préliminaire" was a revised version of Diderot's prospectus. This sentence appeared in both versions. Diderot's claim again echoes Bacon's in the preface to *The Great Instauration*: "As our state is mortal, and human, a full accomplishment cannot be expected in a single age, and must therefore be commended to posterity" (p. 19).

46. *Encyclopédie* 5:636.

47. Ibid. Diderot had good reason for this criticism. In 1750, when the *Encyclopédie* was getting under way, another project of comparable scale was begun with royal patronage. In 1747 Louis XV had promised funding for the Cassini survey of France, whose aim was to produce a triangulation map of the entire realm. The project was begun in 1750, but funds ran out after only six years. An association of fifty persons was then formed, each of whom signed on for 1,600 livres per year. Public subscriptions were then opened at around 500 livres for the projected 180 maps. The set was not completed until 1818. See Mary Sponberg Pedley, "The Subscription List of the *Atlas Universel* (1757): A Study in Cartographic Dissemination," *Imago Mundi* 31 (1979): 77 n. 32.

With the *Encyclopédie* Diderot was proposing a reformation of the Republic of Letters which would inaugurate a new era in its history. It had begun among men who were spread out across Europe and held together by an epistolary network and, with Latin, a common language. The academies provided a way to bring scholars together in small groups, each of which would communicate with the others. As corps, the academies also gave the Republic of Letters a place within the order of the Old Regime. Diderot was now suggesting not only that the republic was no longer contained within the bounds of the academies but that the structure of the academy was not conducive to its work. He saw a new basis of unity in a new universal: not the academic language of Latin but the universal concern for the good of humanity. And that concern would only be undermined by the limited interest of any corporative body. Although the monarchy might claim that it had no particularistic interest, that it stood above all such limited interests, Diderot was clearly unmoved. Only the Republic of Letters was truly universal, and therefore it could not be contained in or represented by any constituted body, academic or political.[48]

How then was the Republic of Letters to be constituted? It was to retain the same principles of equality and reciprocity among its members on which the academies stood, but instead of gathering people together in the interests of knowledge, it would gather knowledge together in the interests of humanity. The *Encyclopédie* would represent the associative basis of knowledge; it would become the place where ideas were exchanged, preserved, and diffused. It would replace the academies as the meeting ground of the Republic of Letters.

The *Encyclopédie* was to be, and in fact did become, a sort of central bureau, where men of letters could send in their written contributions and have them coordinated and made public. This grand scheme was what distinguished the editors' aspirations from those of the publisher, who simply wanted to translate, print, and sell a book. As a grand scheme, however, the *Encyclopédie* was not unique; it was just the sort of project that men of letters increasingly concocted to improve the republic and make their own places in it. Indeed, in 1747, the same year in which Diderot and d'Alembert accepted the joint editorship of the *Encyclopédie*, another "bureau général de la République des Lettres" was proposed by an anonymous citizen of the Republic. The proposal appeared in a letter printed in a francophone journal published in Amsterdam. The services offered were those fundamental to the ethos

48. Waquet finds the same argument in a German dissertation of 1708. "Qu'est-ce que la République des Lettres?" p. 486.

of reciprocity and traditionally provided by the citizens of the Republic of Letters for one another. By the end of the seventeenth century, entrepreneurial citizens of the republic had started journals that formalized these services by announcing discoveries, publishing requests for data, announcing and reviewing new publications, and taking orders for them.[49] The proposed bureau would be more efficient yet than the journals, which had by then proliferated.

The author began by stating clearly that he intended no new literary journal to add to the glut of existing ones.[50] After naming the various services that would be performed by the *bureau général*, he concluded: "Here, then, is a great need in the Republic of Letters, which everyone is well aware of, and which we hope to fill. There is not a single realm, republic, or even the smallest state, that does not have a supreme court [*tribunal suprême*], to which reports and from which springs, all the business of the state. . . . It is, in a word, the center of unity so necessary to any well-ordered state" (204–5). Despite the energy and goodwill of the citizenry, the Republic of Letters was "in a sort of anarchy, having neither archives, nor chancellery, nor center of unity" (205). The bureau général would fill this void, create this center of unity. The operation would be simple. Letters would be sent to the bureau by scholars who wished to inform the public of anything in the way of news, from "curiosities" to "personal and literary quarrels" (203). The bureau would collate these letters and petitions and report on them to the public (205).

Because this bureau was designed by a citizen of the Republic of Letters as an institution of that republic, the correspondents would not be paid servants of the state but would include "the least citizen," who was encouraged to contribute "his small share to the public treasury of this Republic." Such participation would bring individuals out of obscurity, and the bureau would create for them "a sort of community of goods or network of assistance" by mediating a correspondence between the greatest and the least of the scholar-citizens. Each contributor could thus profit from all the resources of the republic and its most illustrious citizens. Each individual member would benefit, and so would the community as a whole (209).

The author worked within the paradigms of contemporary state building and publishing. He asserted that the project must have hegemony if it was to work. It had to be unique, had to have a protected

---

49. Jean Sgard, "La Multiplication des périodiques," in *Histoire de l'édition française*, ed. Henri-Jean Martin and Roger Chartier (Paris, 1984), 2:198–200.

50. "Projet pour l'établissement d'un bureau général de la République des Lettres," *Bibliothèque Raisonné des Ouvrages des Savans de l'Europe* 39 (July–September 1747): 202, hereafter cited parenthetically in the text.

monopoly or copyright on the publication of its report. But since the republic existed within and across the territories of other states, these requirements of modern political institutions could be achieved only with the authorization and protection of all the powers of Europe (211–13). The author wanted an international *privilège* for his enterprise.

The bureau général, like the *Encyclopédie*, was intended as the center for an independent Republic of Letters, but even before it got off the ground, it was forced to entangle itself with not one but all the states of Europe. It had to seek protection, just as the *Encyclopédie* did. To reassure the would-be protectors of the bureau, its author reminded "les pouvoirs" that this "institute" would be concerned only with the advancement of sciences and literature, and he promised that strict regulation would ensure its "innocence." In particular, all matters political and any other topics that might cause these powers the least umbrage would be proscribed. For even greater security, the author promised that during times of war, neither the letters sent to the bureau nor the loose sheets that emanated from it would be sealed, "and packages [would be] sent thus to the Post Office, where they may be freely opened, so that there will be no suspicion of fraud, or any suspect or illicit correspondence" (213). There were further assurances of fidelity, discretion, and impartiality and, finally, the promise that "all disputes or controversies odious in matters of religion, and all partiality in regard to different peoples or nations . . . , [and] all that might shock or offend or wrong anyone" would be scrupulously avoided (214). To create a "center of unity" for the Republic of Letters, it was necessary to seek protection from the state(s), and to gain that protection, it was necessary not to offend anyone, either politically or personally.

At the end of the letter, the editor of the *Bibliothèque Raisonnée* noted that he supported the project but worried about the difficulty of achieving it and would maintain the anonymity of its author (221). He thus implied that the plan was not only utopian but potentially dangerous for its author. He was probably right. In any case, the project was never realized.

The *Encyclopédie*, of course, did get off the ground and did function as a bureau général for the Republic of Letters. Perhaps coincidentally, perhaps not, the French monarchy chose 1766, shortly after Diderot finished the last volumes of the *Encyclopédie*, to open its own bureau général. In the same year that the government prohibited the distribution of the final volumes of the *Encyclopédie* in Paris, it also closed down by *arrêt du conseil* three private *bureaux de correspondance générale* which had been operating in Paris and united them into a single bureau under an administrator with a royal privilege. This "public" bureau received the title of "general bureau of correspondence, of the exchange of commodities by subjects of the entire extent of the realm."[51] Although the main business of the bureau (like that of its predecessors) was business—collecting *rentes* and other revenues, following through on cases in the courts, making and sending purchases—it was also taking over some of the services of both the French state and the Republic of Letters.

In addition to helping people in the provinces with commercial transactions in Paris, the bureau was charged with "the search for, collection, and delivery of all certificates of baptism, marriage, [and] death, and of all acts and titles in Paris, in all parts of the realm, in the colonies, and abroad." It was also to keep registers of all sorts of property transactions and "of public academies, of public courses in the sciences and the arts, of all objects and jewelry lost and found, [and] of the daily course of public and foreign affairs." It was authorized, further, to send to its patrons, either by subscription or on individual request, "edicts, declarations, ordinances, and regulations."[52] The Bureau de correspondance générale was a public record office for France. Not surprisingly, the government confided the responsibility of *correspondant* to its own officers, the royal intendants. The bureau was to be a public service and thus part of the public trust. Confiding its responsibilities to the state's most trustworthy servants assured that "this well-organized establishment will have the right to expect the confidence of the public and the protection of the ministry."[53]

At the same time as it was to serve the French public and the French state, the bureau also tried to take over some of the services provided in the Republic of Letters. It was charged with the purchase and sending of books and, as already noted, with keeping a register of academic sessions and public courses.[54] Although hardly a threat to the existence of the Republic of Letters, the monarchy's creation of the bureau can be seen as an attempt to invade its public space. As the republic challenged the monarchy for hegemony in the public sphere, the state tried to monopolize the delivery of the republic's services, just as it had created a legal monopoly on the delivery of letters in the seventeenth century through the creation of the postal service.

By providing a "center of unity" the *Encyclopédie* contributed to the establishment of the Republic of Letters as an association—a real society of men of letters—with Paris as its capital. Whereas the French

51. Henri Sée, "La Création d'un bureau de correspondance générale en 1766," *Revue d'Histoire Moderne*, no. 7 (January–February 1927): 51.

52. *Instruction pour les correspondants*, quoted ibid., p. 52.

53. Ibid., pp. 53–54.

54. Ibid., p. 52.

Academy had taken as its mission to compile a dictionary of the French language, Diderot reversed the priorities, making his dictionary the basis of an intellectual association that would challenge the Academy. The result of this reversal was to broaden the Republic of Letters itself, to include as its citizens all who had a contribution to make to the *Encyclopédie*. By the time the project was completed, the number of contributors named in the prospectus had quadrupled.[55] Because the center of the encyclopedic association was a book, the Republic of Letters so conceived could expand further to include the readership of the *Encyclopédie* as well.

The very means by which the *Encyclopédie* was marketed to the public brought together the notions of readership and association. Public subscription was a novel practice recently imported from England, just like Chambers's *Cyclopaedia*. Diderot discussed it with great enthusiasm in the article "Souscription." Those who decided to subscribe to the *Encyclopédie* were joining an association just as the contributors were, a voluntary association of contributors and subscribers, writers and readers; the *Encyclopédie* was the mark of their common commitment to its principles. Their commitment was not, of course, equal, and certainly many of the subscribers would deny any allegiance to the encyclopedists. Implicitly, however, publisher, editors, contributors, and subscribers were bound together in this special way through the project of the book, and therefore, the project took on public meaning and public value.

"It is for the reading public to judge us," d'Alembert wrote at the end of the "Discours préliminaire," adding, "We believe we ought to distinguish that public which reads from the one which only speaks."[56] With this call to judgment, the editors associated the writers of the Republic of Letters with the reading public as their legitimate judges. The reading public would expand both the republic's citizenry and its mission. Not only would the *Encyclopédie* "contribute to the certitude and progress of human knowledge," Diderot had proclaimed at the end of the prospectus, but "by multiplying the number of true scholars, distinguished artisans, and enlightened amateurs, it [would] contribute new advantages to society as a whole."[57] The *Encyclopédie* became the source of a collective identity for those who chose to see themselves as citizens of a regenerated Republic of Letters whose purpose was to improve the larger society of which it was a part.

55. Jacques Proust, "Postface," in *Diderot et l'Encyclopédie* (Paris, 1962; rpt. Geneva, 1982); and John Lough, *The Contributors to the "Encyclopédie"* (London, 1973).
56. D'Alembert, *Preliminary Discourse*, p. 140.
57. Ibid., p. 128.

The editors of the *Encyclopédie* declared the independence of the Republic of Letters from the academies by asserting that their intellectual association was constituted not by the king but by a project dedicated to gathering knowledge in the interest of society and humanity. Political autonomy fostered regeneration because it permitted expansion beyond a narrow corps and infused the republic with a larger purpose. "The purpose of an encyclopedia," wrote Diderot,

> is to bring together knowledge dispersed over the surface of the earth; to expose its general system to those among whom we live; and to transmit it to those who will come after us; in order that the work of past centuries will not have been useless for those of the future; in order that our grandchildren, becoming more knowledgeable will become at the same time more virtuous and happier, and that we will not have died without having deserved well of the human race.[58]

The search for knowledge was now subordinated to the higher good of society, even of humanity as a whole. Thus the service of humanity replaced the service of truth as the ultimate goal of the Republic of Letters, and the quest for knowledge was transformed into the project of Enlightenment. In carrying out this new project, the citizens of the Republic of Letters had to bear in mind, as Diderot reminded his readers, that making people better was at least as important as making them less ignorant.[59] The two goals were interrelated as two aspects of the project of Enlightenment.

This newly conceived Republic of Letters looked outward to the world of human society rather than upward to absolute truth. Its justification lay in its service to humanity rather than in a pure concept of knowledge. Only because the Republic of Letters was particularly concerned with knowledge, however, could it serve humanity in the way that it did. Only because of its connection to a universal knowledge of nature and its laws did it have the responsibility to serve humanity. The universality of the Republic of Letters as uniquely dedicated to a knowledge that transcended particular interests was what gave its citizens both the right and the responsibility to represent and to serve the public.

58. *Encyclopédie* 5:635. Bacon had stated this same goal in *The Great Instauration*: "We advise all mankind to think of the true ends of knowledge, and that they endeavor not after it for curiosity, contention, or the sake of despising others, nor yet for profit, reputation, power, or any such inferior consideration, but solely for the occasions and uses of life" (pp. 18–19).

59. *Encyclopédie* 5:645a. In 1750 Charles Pinot Duclos asked "that men be taught to love one another, that the necessity of this for their happiness be proved to them. . . . In order to make them better, it is necessary only to enlighten them": *Considérations sur les moeurs de ce siècle*, ed. F. C. Green (Cambridge, 1939), pp. 10–11.

Citizenship and the Enlightenment Republic of Letters

chronology
✗

The Republic of Letters and the monarchy came of age together in
the seventeenth century, but by the middle of the eighteenth century
there was a clear conflict between them, generated by the respective
forms of the two polities, as well as by their competing claims to represent and serve France. Keith Baker identifies several ways in which the
monarchy claimed to represent the nation: the king acted as God's
vicegerent on earth; the realm was made visible, thus literally represented to the people in his person; and most fundamentally, "in the
strong sense that a multiplicity can indeed be made one only in the
unity of his person."[60] Over the course of the eighteenth century, other
groups also claimed to represent the nation. The parlements, for example, asserted that their role was to represent the king to the nation
and the nation to the king.[61] In the multiplication of these claims to
represent the nation which culminated in the French Revolution, the
Republic of Letters, too, made its voice heard.

Like the parlements, the Republic of Letters claimed to serve a mediating role. It stood between the universality of knowledge and the
nation. It therefore stood for knowledge, representing it to the nation.
It could also claim to represent the nation to itself because of its self-
assigned role as the arbiter of public opinion.[62] This privileged, if not
unique, position, gave the French citizens of the cosmopolitan Republic
of Letters their particular responsibility as, at the same time, subjects of
the French monarchy. As Voltaire wrote in the *Siècle de Louis XIV*: "One
would not believe that sovereigns would be under any obligation to
philosophers. Yet it is true that the philosophic spirit . . . has contributed a lot to promote the rights of sovereigns. . . . If it has been said
that peoples would be happy when they have philosophers for kings, it
is quite true to say that kings are even happier when many of their
subjects are philosophers.[63]

And yet, much as the citizens of this newly useful Republic of Letters
may have felt that they were serving the monarchy and the nation by
serving humanity and truth, their loyalty to the republic called into
question their loyalty to France. As the *Encyclopédie* reconstituted it, the
republic became the basis of an identity that those opposed to it consid-

60. Baker, *Inventing the French Revolution*, p. 225.
61. Ibid., p. 228.
62. Mona Ozouf, "'Public Opinion' at the End of the Old Regime," *Journal of Modern
History* 60 (September 1988): S6–7. Ozouf notes that the same actors in the competition
to represent public opinion were claiming to represent the nation: the parlements, the
monarchy, and the Republic of Letters.
63. Voltaire, *Oeuvres complètes* 14:538–39.

ered unpatriotic to the core. Arthur Wilson cites Condorcet's recollection that "during the Seven Years' War anyone who could be called an Encyclopedist or a *philosophe* was by that very token imputed to be a bad citizen."[64] After the attempt to assassinate him in January 1757, Louis XV worried that writers were putting dangerous ideas in the heads of the public. He issued a royal declaration holding out stiff penalties for those convicted of writing, publishing, or selling any "writing tending to attack religion, to rouse opinion, to impair Our authority, and to trouble the order and tranquillity of Our States."[65] While those who identified themselves as citizens of the encyclopedic Republic of Letters saw themselves as good citizens of the French state, their opponents decried them as being against everything French: antireligion, antimonarchy, anti-*moeurs*.

The culmination of these competing interpretations came in 1759, when the sale of the *Encyclopédie* was first suspended by the Parlement of Paris and then suppressed entirely by the monarchy under pressure also from the church.[66] Diderot and his publishers, however, refused to abandon the project. The capital investment that was at stake certainly influenced their thinking, but they saw their responsibility to the public as more than financial: having solicited subscribers for their project, they were obliged to follow through. The decision was made to take the *Encyclopédie* underground.

Between 1749 and 1759, morever, there occurred a struggle that was perhaps the most frustrating of all, because it took place within the Republic of Letters itself. As work on the *Encyclopédie* progressed, the public was treated to the spectacle of Jean-Jacques Rousseau, Diderot's closest friend and one of the contributors to the *Encyclopédie*, attacking the moral legitimacy of the project and questioning the integrity of those dedicated to it.

In 1750 Rousseau made his name in the Republic of Letters by winning the annual prize competition sponsored by the Academy of Dijon for his response to the question of whether the establishment of the arts and sciences had contributed to the purification of morals. Rousseau argued that the arts and sciences had contributed rather to their corruption. The publication of the essay stimulated a lively debate on an issue that was central to the Republic of Letters itself: whether the work of its citizens was beneficial or harmful to society. Rousseau rejected not just the association of the republic with the monarchy, as the

64. Arthur Wilson, *Diderot* (New York, 1972), p. 275.

65. Quoted ibid., p. 276. See also Dale K. Van Kley, *The Damiens Affair and the Unraveling of the Ancien Régime, 1750–1770* (Princeton, 1984); and Pierre Rétat, ed., *L'Attentat de Damiens: Discours sur l'événement au XVIIIᵉ siècle* (Paris, 1979).

66. Wilson, *Diderot*, pp. 333–36.

editors of the *Encyclopédie* did, but its association with everything that
defined civilization: luxury, sociability, peace, and women.

Rousseau did not disagree with his friends and fellow citizens of the
Republic of Letters about the definition of civilization; rather, he maintained that what they saw as natural and good was in fact unnatural and
bad. Where they saw good in the ascendancy of gentleness over brute
force, for example, Rousseau saw a weakening of the warrior spirit.[67]
Whereas both Rousseau and his contemporaries saw women as a "civilizing force" that contributed to both sociability and enlightenment,
Rousseau saw civilization itself as corrupting and unnatural. In revers-
ing the argument, he challenged the very basis of the Republic of
Letters, and he threatened the standing men of letters claimed was due
them as useful citizens of the monarchy. No wonder the pages of journals were filled with responses to Rousseau's discourse.

Rousseau had launched a debate with the encyclopedists which
would end in his complete rejection of them and their Republic of
Letters. In 1753 d'Alembert opened his "Essai sur la société des gens de
lettres et des grands" with the statement: "There is no people that has
not been for a long time in barbarism, or rather in ignorance, because
it has not been determined if these words are synonymous." France
had been in this condition for many centuries, although "it had not had
much to complain about, if we believe some philosophers, who claim
that human nature becomes depraved as a result of enlightenment."[68]
D'Alembert's essay was a response to Rousseau's rejection of the sociable Republic of Letters as the basis of intellectual life and inquiry.
"Diogenes did not reproach [Aristippes] for not living among men," he
wrote, "but for paying court to a tyrant" (359). D'Alembert argued for
the possibility—indeed the necessity—of the republic's autonomy in
relation to both the monarchy and the aristocracy. The problem was
not that the arts and sciences to which the Republic of Letters was
dedicated corrupted human beings; rather it was that the citizenry
could not pursue the arts and sciences unless the republic established
itself as independent not only of the monarchy but of the newly "civilized" nobility, eager to "protect" it in the image of the monarchy.

Whereas Rousseau had argued against the social constitution of
knowledge by saying that men of letters ought not to be guided by the
esteem of others, d'Alembert focused on the question of whose esteem
mattered: that of other men of letters and the public guided by them or

---

67. Jean-Jacques Rousseau, *Discours sur les sciences et les arts*, in *Oeuvres complètes*, ed.
Bernard Gagnebin and Marcel Raymond, 4 vols. (Paris, 1959–69), 3:24.
68. Jean Le Rond d'Alembert, "Essai sur la société des gens de lettres et des grands,
sur la réputation, sur les mécènes, et sur les récompenses littéraires," in *Oeuvres complètes*
(Paris, 1822), 4:337, hereafter cited in the text.

that of superficially educated noblemen (340–47). In addition, d'Alembert distinguished between the vanity and sensitivity to insult which generated pointless and damaging *querelles* among men of letters and the natural insecurity about the worth of their cultural productions which inspired them to seek the esteem of others. "Write, one can say to men of letters, as if you loved glory; conduct yourselves as if you were indifferent to it" (348).

Reputation was one sort of esteem that men of letters sought through their relations with *les grands*; consideration was the other. If the need for reputation was based on intellectual insecurity, the need for consideration had a social basis: the unavoidable inequality of conditions in contemporary society. Although human beings were equal in their need to live together in society, the fact of social inequality made it necessary that "the difference between some and others be assured and peaceable, that it not be supported by advantages that can be either disputed or denied."

D'Alembert argued that of the three determinants of inequality—talent, birth, and fortune—talent was the most important but was given least consideration because of uncertainty about intellectual merit: it was a lot easier to know who was the richest or whose birth was most exalted than it was to determine who had the greatest talent. Social harmony thus favored birth and wealth as the bases of hierarchy. But men of letters were nevertheless wrong to seek consideration from their social betters, who ought to be seeking it from them. Men of talent should show "exterior respect" for men with titles, but nobles should show a "more real" respect for the talented (353–57). If men of letters did not demand this respect, they would lose doubly. Not only would they accept unwarranted subordination, but this false position would foster the kind of misunderstandings that would destroy sociable relations altogether. "Thus the intimate commerce of *les grands* with men of letters only too often ends with some dramatic rupture; a rupture that almost always comes from forgetting the reciprocal respect in which one party or the other, or perhaps both sides, have failed" (358). The reciprocity and mutual regard that defined relations in the Republic of Letters could not be sustained on the basis of a false hierarchy. "Let us then conclude," wrote d'Alembert, "that the only great *seigneurs* with whom a man of letters ought to wish commerce are those whom he can treat and regard in all security as his equals and his friends" (359). Equality and friendship had to be the basis of all relationships not only among men of letters but between them and others. The republic and not the monarchy or corporative society would define all social relations in which men of letters would engage and into which they would draw others who sought their company for their true merit, their talent. Men of letters and not the king or *les grands* would define society.

In the first two parts of his essay, d'Alembert tried to convince his fellow citizens of the Republic of Letters that the reasons for which they courted *les grands* were specious or inadequate; in the third part he tried to boost their self-esteem, the lack of which sent them to *les grands* for the rewards they truly deserved and could find within their own republic. "Despite the general enlightenment that glorifies our century," he wrote,

> there are still many people . . . for whom the quality of author or of man of letters is not a very noble title. It must be admitted that the French nation has much difficulty in throwing off the yoke of barbarism which it has carried for so long. This ought not to be surprising; birth being an advantage that is given by chance, it is natural not only to wish to enjoy it but even more to subordinate to it all those [advantages] whose acquisition is more difficult. Laziness and egoism result equally from this.
>
> I know that the majority of *les grands* would protest such a reproach; let them but question their conscience, let them but examine their discourse, and we will remain convinced that the name man of letters is regarded by them as a subaltern title that can only be the share of an inferior *Etat*, as if the art of instructing and enlightening men were not, after the rare art of governing well, the most noble attribute of the human condition. (360)

D'Alembert urged his fellow citizens to take pride in themselves and their work, to see their own nobility as men of letters instead of chasing after those of birth and wealth. Then *les grands* would chase after them, as they ought. The Republic of Letters could establish its autonomy and, on its basis, real power if men of letters realized their worth as its citizens and as the first order in France. They needed to start acting like the noble beings they were, first, by not toadying to those whose value was inferior to theirs, and second, by treating one another with respect and politeness. They needed to stop providing cheap entertainment for *les grands* with their interminable *querelles* and to band together to stop others from insulting them with impunity. "In a country where the press is not free," he wrote, "the license to insult men of letters by satires is only a proof of the little real consideration that people have for them, of the very pleasure taken in seeing them insulted" (365). *Les grands* would give men of letters the consideration they deserved only if they stood together with dignity as citizens of their own commonwealth, "if they finally recognized that the surest means of making themselves respected, is to live united (if it is possible for them) and practically enclosed amongst themselves" (372). D'Alembert's response to Rousseau was not to abandon the Republic of Letters but to strengthen it by making it not just sociable but a true community.

Rousseau's response (although of course it was more than that, just as d'Alembert's essay was more than a response to Rousseau) was the *Discours sur l'inégalité*, written for another prize competition in 1754 and published the following year. In his first discourse Rousseau had reversed the argument about civilization which gave the Republic of Letters and its citizens the basis for their claims to status and autonomy within France; in the second discourse he went even further, questioning the naturalness of the sociability on which the history of civilization, and thus the Republic of Letters, was based. Men, according to the Rousseau of the second discourse, were not only equal by nature (as d'Alembert himself declared) but unsociable by nature. With this double attack, Rousseau challenged both the French society of orders and the sociable Republic of Letters as unnatural.

Two years later (1757) d'Alembert took up the cause again in an article on the city of Geneva which appeared in the seventh volume of the *Encyclopédie*—the last to appear before it went underground. D'Alembert blamed the prohibition of the theater by the Calvinist fathers of that city on a "barbarous" prejudice against actors. With good laws, he argued, "Geneva would have theater and *moeurs*, and would enjoy the advantages of both."[69] Culture and morality were not opposed to each other, and Rousseau's own Geneva could demonstrate that they were not. Rousseau responded with the *Lettre à M. d'Alembert sur les spectacles*, published the following year, 1758. In it he described the pernicious effects that French theater would have on the *moeurs* of the pure Swiss, and he traced these effects to a specific cause: the influence of women on French culture and the sway they held over men of letters. Rousseau had made this point in a footnote in his first discourse,[70] but the power of women over men, especially of salonnières over men of letters, became the unstated theme of his response to d'Alembert and the rest of his erstwhile friends—especially Diderot—engaged on the *Encyclopédie*. The *Lettre à d'Alembert* was Rousseau's philosophical break with the Enlightenment Republic of Letters and his personal break with his friends who constituted it and battled for it against the monarchy, the church, the parlements, *les grands*, and now himself. Rousseau, who had argued that man was by nature unsociable, rejected the society of the Republic of Letters and began to create his own myth of the solitary seeker of truth, the lone man of virtue in a corrupt world.[71]

69. Quoted by Rousseau in *Lettre à M. d'Alembert sur les spectacles*, p. 4. All citations are from Jean-Jacques Rousseau, *Politics and the Arts: Letter to M. d'Alembert on the Theatre*, ed. and trans. Allan Bloom (Ithaca, 1968).

70. Rousseau, *Oeuvres complètes* 3:21.

71. The passage in which Rousseau broke with Diderot is found on p. 7 of the *Lettre à d'Alembert*. For Rousseau's account of this whole period and the break see books 9 and 10

By the late 1750s, a confused marquis de Castries could write of
Diderot and Rousseau: "It's incredible. People don't talk of anything
but of those fellows. Persons without an establishment, who don't have
a house, who are lodged in a garret. One just can't get used to all
that."[72] The public did get used to "all that" because "those fellows"
took them seriously and asked for their judgment. By 1766, the philosophes had created a new public space for the Republic of Letters by
making it the center of public opinion. They had done so by taking
d'Alembert's advice and inviting the public (including *les grands*) to join
them first as readers and then as writers. By volunteering to submit to
the tribunal of public opinion, men of letters made that tribunal an
institution of their republic. At the same time, they activated their
readership, gave the public a role to play. Open-ended and interactive
forms of writing, such as letters, correspondences, and dialogues, encouraged an active readership; literary journals counted on their readers' contributions.

Readers appreciated the opportunity to become active citizens of the
Republic of Letters and to enjoy the new respect thus accorded them in
a France that excluded them from official politics. They took up their
responsibilities eagerly and with a sense of self-importance.[73] Before
the second half of the eighteenth century, public opinion was a tribunal
only for *le monde*; eventually even the monarchy found itself forced to
submit.[74] When men of letters sought to establish themselves as the
arbiters of public opinion, they did so because they recognized its power. At the same time, they were empowered by the public, or at least
they arrogated to themselves the power they claimed the public had
vested in them. In 1769, for example, André Morellet wrote:

> If the ministers and the placemen have their accomplices, the public has
> its as well, although few. I call accomplices of the public those who *se*

---

of his *Confessions*, in *Oeuvres complètes*, vol. 1. For an alternative, if fictionalized, contemporary account, see [Louise-Florence-Petronille Tardieu d'Esclavelles, marquise] d'Epinay,
Histoire de Madame de Montbrillant, ed. Georges Roth, 3 vols. (Paris, 1951), esp. vol. 3. For
more recent accounts, see Wilson, *Diderot*, chaps. 19, 21–22; and Maurice Cranston, *The
Noble Savage: Jean-Jacques Rousseau, 1754–1762* (Chicago, 1991).

72. Quoted in Wilson, *Diderot*, p. 306.

73. Certainly the readership drawn into the Republic of Letters included many
members of the governing elite; nevertheless, the representation of politics by the monarchy and its organs continued to be centered around the king and the court. The *Gazette
de France*, for example, still represented politics in the terms of Habermas's representational public sphere. See Jeremy Popkin, "The Prerevolutionary Origins of Political
Journalism," in *The Political Culture of the Old Regime*, ed. Keith Michael Baker, vol. 2
of *The French Revolution and the Creation of Modern Political Culture* (Oxford, 1987),
pp. 206–7.

74. Baker, *Inventing the French Revolution*, chap. 8.

chargent with defending its interests, with enlightening it, and with making known that it is neither as stupid nor as evil as it is said to be. These are the people who are the enthusiasts of certain phantoms known as "liberty," "happiness of nations," "tolerance," "reason." They are known by the name of philosophes: their job has always been dangerous.[75]

Morellet, who tended to see the world in black-and-white terms, painted a heroic portrait of the philosophe, champion of the public and foe of the royal government with its paid hirelings.[76]

When the *Encyclopédie* reemerged at the end of 1765, it was to a new world: the Republic of Letters had now established itself in the well-governed precincts of the Parisian salons and had become the very center of public opinion. By then, Diderot found that it was possible, for example, to get the *Encyclopédie* to his subscribers despite a government prohibition on its distribution in Paris.[77] By the summer of 1766, besides distribution of the last volumes of the *Encyclopédie*, three major events in the Republic of Letters occupied Parisian circles: Rousseau's public falling out with David Hume, with whom he had sought refuge in England in December 1765, only to accuse him of treachery six months letter; the salonnière Marie-Thérèse Geoffrin's trip to Poland to visit Stanislas Poniatowski, the new king and her adoptive son; and the La Barre case championed by Voltaire.

From July through September 1766, letters between Hume and Rousseau, and from the two principals to people strategically placed in Parisian salons, were a major subject of both conversations and letters.[78] In October, at the urging of d'Alembert and the salonnière Julie de Lespinasse, French and English editions of an account of the Hume-Rousseau affair were published, based on all the letters compiled by Hume and with an introduction by another philosophe, Suard. Over the next few months readers responded with letters to the editors of French journals and English papers and with a wave of pamphlets, mostly in the form of letters. The reading public was taking up Suard's challenge to act in their capacity as public tribunal. "The facts are all

75. André Morellet, "Les Marionnettes," in *Mémoires sur le dix-huitième siècle et sur la Révolution*, 2 vols. (Paris, 1821), 2:364. There is a telling ambiguity in the term *se chargent*, which can mean either "charge themselves" or "are charged." Later, Morellet contrasts the "accomplices of the public" to the French Academy, which Richelieu founded only "in order to have a permanent corps of accomplices" (p. 362).

76. The portrait is somewhat blurred when one learns that the following year Morellet wrote a refutation of his friend and fellow philosophe Galiani under orders from the ministry of finance, which paid him.

77. Wilson, *Diderot*, pp. 502–4.

78. I treat this affair at length in "The Hume-Rousseau Affair: From Private *Querelle* to Public *Procès*," *Eighteenth-Century Studies* 25 (Winter 1991–92): 171–201.

laid before the public," he had written, "and Mr. Hume submits his cause to the determination of every man of sense and probity."[79]

Meanwhile, reports were coming in from the east: Geoffrin had left Paris on 21 May 1766 and arrived in Warsaw on 24 June, after a stop in Vienna to see Empress Maria Theresa. She returned to Paris on 10 October, having occupied Parisians, Viennese, and Poles for months with this adventure and the letters in which it was inscribed. As Friedrich-Melchior Grimm wrote in November to the royal and noble subscribers to his manuscript *Correspondance Littéraire*, which sent news of the Republic of Letters throughout Europe: "Mme Geoffrin's trip to Warsaw has been the subject of conversation and of curiosity by the public throughout the summer."[80] Geoffrin herself had written to her daughter in June: "If people are talking about my trip in Paris, I assure you that it is even more talked about in Vienna."[81] In July even Voltaire had written to Geoffrin from his home in Ferney, near the Swiss border. He flattered her profusely, then asked her to read and pass along to Stanislas a petition to support the Sirven family, Protestant victims of French Catholic persecution, whose cause he had been pursuing for three years. "We ask only to see our list honored by names that will encourage the public," he explained. "The affair in question is of concern to the human race, and it is in its name that we address you, madame. We will owe you the honor and the pleasure of seeing a good and great king come to the aid of virtue against a village judge, and to contribute to the extirpation of the most horrible superstition."[82]

Voltaire was now using the public arena to launch his political campaigns. In addition to the Sirven case, which had begun in 1762 and still was not resolved, 1766 saw through the La Barre affair, a new case of *l'infâme*, which Peter Gay has called "the source of Voltaire's greatest fright and greatest fury in his Ferney years."[83] The affairs of Jean Calas and Elizabeth Sirven both involved the persecution of Protestants by French Catholic authorities. The La Barre case was different. The chevalier de La Barre was a French Catholic youth who aroused the wrath of local authorities by mutilating a public crucifix. The local court condemned him to be burned, at the stake for sacrilege, but only after he did public penance and had his tongue cut out and his right

79. *A Concise and Genuine Account of the Dispute between Mr. Hume and Mr. Rousseau . . .* (London, 1766), p. viii.

80. *Correspondance Littéraire*, 1 November 1766.

81. Quoted in [Pierre Marie Maurice Henri,] le marquis de Ségur, *Le Royaume de la rue Saint-Honoré: Madame Geoffrin et sa fille* (Paris, 1897), p. 265.

82. Voltaire to Geoffrin, 5 July 1766, in Voltaire, *Correspondence*, 51 vols. of *The Complete Works*, ed. Theodore Besterman, 107 vols. (Geneva, 1968–77), D13392.

83. Peter Gay, *Voltaire's Politics: The Poet as Realist* (New York, 1965), p. 278.

hand cut off. After a vain appeal to the Parlement of Paris, La Barre was in fact beheaded in July 1766. His corpse was then publicly burned, and a copy of Voltaire's *Dictionnaire philosophique* was thrown into the fire along with it. For part of the prosecution's case against the nineteen-year-old La Barre rested on proof that he had read this and other impious works by Voltaire.[84]

On 6 August the *Mémoires secrets pour servir à l'histoire de la République des Lettres en France* (a manuscript newsletter emanating from Paris) reported:

> Three manuscript letters, dated from 6 July, concerning the affair and execution of M. de la Barre, Gentleman burnt at Abbeville for sacrilege, are circulating. These three epistles are being attributed to M. de Voltaire: they are worthy of him by the cry of humanity that he makes heard everywhere, and by the delicate sarcasm with which he seasons everything that he says.
>
> The *Parlement* is furious about these letters and we are assured that the first president has complained to the king.[85]

Voltaire's reaction to threats was always to flee: after his forced exile to England in 1726, he fled to Cirey in 1734, to Les Délices outside Geneva in 1755, and finally to Ferney in 1758. In the summer of 1766 he panicked again, crossed the border to Switzerland, and came up with a plan of founding a colony in Clèves under the protection of Frederick the Great.[86] In July he sent a letter to Diderot, asking him to pack up his *Encyclopédie* and join him:

> A man such as you can look only with horror upon the country in which you have the misfortune to live. You really ought to come to a land where you would have complete liberty, not only to print as you wish, but to preach openly against superstitions as outrageous as [they are] bloody. You would not be alone, you would have companions and disciples. . . . You would . . . leave slavery for liberty. I cannot understand how a sensitive heart and a just mind can live in the land of monkeys transformed into tigers. If this proposal satisfies your indignation and pleases your wisdom, say the word, and we will hasten to arrange everything in a manner worthy of you, with the greatest secrecy, and without compromising you. . . . Believe me, wise men with a sense of humanity must gather together far from the senseless barbarians.[87]

84. Ibid., pp. 278–80.
85. *Mémoires Secrets* 3:61.
86. Gay, *Voltaire's Politics*, p. 280.
87. Voltaire to Diderot, July 1766, D13442.

This letter was among a dozen written by Voltaire that summer and inserted by Grimm in the September issue of the *Correspondance Littéraire* as the "Suite de la Correspondance du Patriarche." In them Voltaire railed about the La Barre case and about Jean-Jacques and revealed his own sense of panic. Diderot, however, was no more eager to leave Paris now than he had been in 1749, when he spent the summer locked up in a royal prison rather than follow Voltaire's example and gained his freedom by agreeing not to make any more trouble. Unlike Voltaire and Rousseau, who hovered around the edges of France, dreaming of a safe haven where they could control their own lives, and perhaps more lives than just their own, Diderot stayed put. In the preface he wrote in September 1765 for the last ten volumes of the *Encyclopédie*, he had reaffirmed his commitment to France:

> In the space of twenty consecutive years, we have scarcely been able to count a few minutes of rest. After whole days consumed by an ungrateful and continuous labor, how many nights were passed in waiting for the troubles that malice tried to attract to us! How many times did we awake uncertain if, giving in to the cries of calumny, we would be torn from our families, our friends, our fellow citizens, to flee beneath a foreign sky in search of the tranquillity that we needed, and the protection we were offered there! But our *patrie* was dear to us, and we always expected that prejudice would give way to justice.[88]

This little preface was a direct stab both at those who had persecuted the *Encyclopédie*, its editors, and its contributors for the last twenty years and at Rousseau: Rousseau, who, after attracting more heat to the philosophes by attacking them, just left the country; Rousseau, whose published response to d'Alembert's article "Genève" not only included a personal attack on Diderot but also contributed significantly to the official suppression of the *Encyclopédie* and d'Alembert's decision to quit the project. It was also a factor in Diderot's subsequent decision to continue the work, but to hold off publication of further volumes until the whole thing was complete.[89] The preface to volume 8, which came out in the fall of 1765, was thus the first page of the *Encyclopédie* to appear since d'Alembert's "Genève" and Rousseau's response to it.

88. *Encyclopédie* 8:i; Wilson, *Diderot*, pp. 479–80. Justifying Voltaire's actions, while trying to argue for the patriotism of men of letters, d'Alembert had written in the *Essai sur les gens de lettres*: "The only motives that can authorize a man of letters to renounce his country, are the cries of superstition raised against his works, and the persecutions, sometimes deaf, sometimes open, that it [*sic*] rouses towards him. Although indebted for his talents to his compatriots, he is even more so to himself for his happiness" (p. 352).

89. Wilson, *Diderot*, chaps. 21–22, 25, and 35.

"The world has certainly grown older," Diderot wrote in the preface, with the author of the *Discours sur l'inégalité* in mind. "It does not change; it is possible that the individual improves, but the mass of the species becomes neither better nor worse."[90] This was hardly a reflection of Diderot's care and hard work toward changing the common way of thinking; it was an expression of his frustration and, as Arthur Wilson notes, his fatigue.[91] When Diderot asserted his patriotism and explained it by saying that "the man of goodwill is susceptible to an enthusiasm that the evil person does not feel,"[92] he was reminding the public that Rousseau was not the only man of letters who could claim to be a patriotic citizen and a virtuous man.

Rousseau had written the *Lettre à d'Alembert* in the voice of a good citizen of Geneva, establishing his authority by identifying himself on the title page as "Citizen of Geneva" and d'Alembert as a member of "the French Academy, the Royal Academy of Sciences of Paris," and four other academies. Rousseau then went on in his preface, addressed directly to d'Alembert, to explain how patriotism, rather than personal animosity, forced him to write:

> With what avidity will the young of Geneva, swept away by so weighty an authority, give themselves to ideas for which they already have only too great a penchant? Since the publication of this volume, how many young Genevans, otherwise good citizens, are waiting for the moment to promote the establishment of a theatre, believing that they are rendering a service to their country and, almost, to humankind? This is the subject of my alarm; this is the ill that I would fend off. I do justice to the intentions of M. d'Alembert; I hope he will do the same in regard to mine. I have no more desire to displease him than he to do us injury. But, finally, even if I am mistaken, must I not act and speak according to my conscience and my lights? Ought I to have remained silent? Could I have, without betraying my duty and my country?[93]

Having captured the space of public opinion by deferring to it, Diderot and the rest of the philosophes were able to answer this and other

---

90. *Encyclopédie* 8:i. The relevant passage in Rousseau's *Discours* reads: "But while the difficulties that surround all these questions would leave some room for dispute on this difference between man and animal, there is another very specific quality that distinguishes them, and upon which there can be no disagreement: this is the faculty of perfectibility; a faculty which, with the aid of circumstances, successively develops all the others, and resides within us as much in the species as in the individual": *Oeuvres complètes* 3:142.

91. Wilson, *Diderot*, p. 480.

92. *Encyclopédie* 8:i.

93. Rousseau, *Politics and the Arts*, p. 5.

challenges. They at last had a forum in which to contest both Rousseau's claim to the high ground of patriotism and the attacks on their own loyalty coming from other quarters. In his preface to the last volumes of the *Encyclopédie*, Diderot addressed not Rousseau but the reading public, invoking them as a tribunal. "The public has judged the first seven volumes," he reminded them; "we only ask the same indulgence for these."[94] In the salons of Paris the Republic of Letters constituted itself as the subject matter of conversation and correspondence and of the newsletters, pamphlets, and journals that developed from them. "Today everything is philosophe, philosophic, and philosophy in France," Grimm informed his subscribers in February 1767.[95] Because the philosophes took the public seriously, the public reciprocated with a mutual respect that increased its own self-respect as a recognized tribunal.

From the salons of Paris, the philosophes and their Republic of Letters could now wage a campaign to capture the academies on their own terms. Having rejected the academy as a base, they now turned to it as a field to be conquered. The French Academy and the Academy of Sciences, in particular, would be incorporated into a new salon-based Republic of Letters, just as the tribunal of public opinion had been. The academies would be taken back from the monarchy.[96]

When the ballots were cast in his favor at the end of 1766, Antoine-Léonard Thomas was the first man to be elected to the French Academy since 1764. His election was to be followed over the next few years by those of three more members of the *parti encyclopédique*: Etienne Bonnot de Condillac, Jean-François de Saint-Lambert, and Etienne de Loménie de Brienne.[97] In his "Discours de reception," delivered in January 1767, Thomas tackled the issue of patriotism head on. In the wake of 1766, when the Republic of Letters had conquered and defined the space of public opinion and its leading citizens were the center of public debate, Thomas addressed the members of the Academy and the public on the subject of "the man of letters as citizen."

When a man reaches the age of reason, said Thomas, the *patrie* asks of him, as of every citizen: "What will you do for me?" The man of letters replies: "I will consecrate my life to the truth." Thomas then went on to explain why the state needs truth and why a particular group must be responsible for it.

94. *Encyclopédie* 8:i.
95. *Correspondance Littéraire*, 1 February 1767.
96. Keith Baker argues that the conquest of the academies was d'Alembert's strategic response to the suppression of the *Encyclopédie*, to which he eventually won Voltaire over. See *Condorcet: From Natural Philosophy to Social Mathematics* (Chicago, 1975), p. 22.
97. François-Albert Buisson, *Les Quarante au temps des Lumières* (Paris, 1960), p. 44.

Those who govern men cannot at the same time enlighten them. Busy with action, they are always on the move, and their souls do not have the time to reflect. A class of men has thus been established—and protected everywhere—whose *état* is to use their minds in peace, and whose duty is to activate those minds for the public good; men who . . . pull together the enlightenment of all countries and centuries, and whose ideas must . . . as it were, represent to the *patrie* the ideas of the whole human race.[98]

According to Thomas, the man of letters was the intermediary between the Republic of Letters, which was of all times and places, and the *patrie*. He served the *patrie* by representing the Republic of Letters to it. Speaking to his fellow "immortals" of the Academy, whom he was now joining, Thomas declared that the role of the man of letters was no longer simply ornamental; nor did his achievements serve primarily to glorify the state and its prince, as they had for Richelieu and Louis XIV. Now, according to Thomas, the man of letters was to be useful not primarily as a royal subject but as a patriotic citizen. By spreading enlightenment he would serve the *patrie* rather than simply the king. Only by maintaining his independence and his primary loyalty to truth—that is, his citizenship in the Republic of Letters—could the man of letters fulfill his duties as a citizen of the *patrie*. At the heart of intellectual service was not personal fidelity to the king but an independent loyalty to truth which made a man both a citizen of the Republic of Letters and useful to the *patrie*.[99]

Both Voltaire and Grimm believed Thomas was referring to d'Alembert's refusal to join the court of Frederick the Great when he wrote: "A King calls Socrates to his Court, and Socrates remains poor in Athens. In the world, simple and without pomp, he will speak to men without either flattering or fearing them."[100] D'Alembert had already established his position on the necessary independence of men of letters; now he was being presented to the members of the Academy as the model citizen of the Republic of Letters.

Although Thomas did speak at some length about how the various branches of learning corresponded to branches of government, the role he defined for the man of letters went far beyond advising on legislation and other aspects of public policy. "The glory of the man

98. [Antoine-Léonard Thomas], *Discours prononcés dans l'Académie françoise, le jeudi, 22 janvier 1767, la reception de M. Thomas* (Paris, 1767), pp. 4–5.

99. On the contemporary discourse of citizenship and professionalism, see Colin Jones, "Bourgeois Revolution Revivified: 1789 and Social Change," in *Rewriting the French Revolution*, ed. Colin Lucas (Oxford, 1991), pp. 96–103.

100. [Thomas], *Discours*, p. 13. Voltaire discussed this passage in a letter to d'Alembert, 28 January [1767], D13884; Grimm discussed it in *Correspondance Littéraire*, 1 February 1767.

who writes," said Thomas, "is thus to prepare useful materials for the man who governs. [But] he does more; in enlightening the people, he makes authority more secure."[101] He does not, of course, enhance authority in the same way as the church would, by strengthening faith and obedience; rather, he teaches his compatriots the foundations of law, the meaning of the general will, and the value of conventions: "With an enlightened populace, the force of power does not lie in power itself, it is in the soul of him who is ruled. The more one knows the source of authority, the more one respects it.[102]

Despite the case Thomas made for the utility of the man of letters in bringing the wisdom of the ages to bear on matters of legislation, it is easy to see that the roles of citizen and subject might not be as harmonious as he suggested. Perhaps this is why the prince de Rohan said in his official response to Thomas for the Academy: "It is no doubt lovely to spread the enlightenment of one's century and to improve *les moeurs*; but this interesting and sublime role is confided only to those rare men for whom the Supreme Being has reserved the gift of genius. Letters have a less striking but more universal merit, that of making those who cultivate them happy."[103]

In contrast to Thomas's image of a company of men of letters marching out to do their patriotic duty by enlightening the multitudes, Rohan, whose primary loyalty seems to have been less to truth than to the order of the French monarchy, would reserve this power for the select few. The cultivation of letters, Rohan implied, was really just a private pleasure, although a few geniuses might be called upon to raise the general level of culture.

Thomas, however, was explicit about the public nature of knowledge. Only because knowledge was public could men of letters from all over France, Europe, and (potentially) the world share a common citizenry. Knowledge was thus *the* public thing, the *res publica* that constituted the Republic of Letters.[104] And whereas public knowledge was the basis of the republic, public opinion was one of its primary spheres of action, for the activity of spreading enlightenment, which Thomas attributed to men of letters as their public duty, required the dissipation of shadows as well. This is the aspect of Thomas's speech on which Grimm

101. [Thomas], *Discours*, p. 7.

102. Ibid., p. 8.

103. Louis de Rohan, "Réponse au discours de M. Thomas," in [Thomas], *Discours*, p. 20.

104. [Thomas], *Discours*, p. 7. This is how Immanuel Kant was to talk about the "public use of reason" in 1784. Kant, "An Answer to the Question What Is Enlightenment?" in *Perpetual Peace and Other Essays*, trans. Ted Humphrey (Indianapolis, 1983), pp. 41–48.

elaborated in his report to the subscribers of the *Correspondance Lit-téraire*:

> The man of genius has really become the arbiter of public thinking, opinions, and prejudices; the impulsion he gives to other minds is transmitted from nation to nation, is perpetuated from century to century, since printing and the ability to write have established the communication of enlightenment and the commerce in thought which extend from one end of Europe to the other, and which will without fail change the face of the human race in the long run.[105]

The Republic of Letters was a kind of public space, but it was not the same space as that occupied by the territorial state. It was the heart of the new public sphere whose history Habermas has written. It was the public forum that the French monarchy lacked. The "politics of contestation," Keith Baker argues, had no place in absolutist political theory, because "the process by which competing claims and policies are transformed into authoritative definitions of the general good . . . occurs, in ideal terms, only in the mind and person of the king." The government could thus be referred to as the "secret du roi," and open discussion "by unauthorized persons without explicit permission, of matters pertaining to governmental policy or public order" was made illegal. "The politics of absolutism," he concludes, "was not a public politics."[106] From the perspective of the Republic of Letters, one could even argue that the monarchy was a private sphere, since its relationships were governed not by publicly accessible reason but by privately contracted obedience and fidelity: the extension of particularism, not its true opposite.[107]

Thomas maintained that the man of letters was not just capable of being a good citizen but had a crucial role to play in public service and the obligation to accept it. Indeed, it was as a philosophe that the man of letters would be the most loyal citizen because he would be most

---

105. *Correspondance Littéraire*, 1 February 1767.
106. Baker, *Inventing the French Revolution*, pp. 169–70.
107. On the monarchy as a system of fidelities, see Roland Mousnier, *The Institutions of France under the Absolute Monarchy, 1598–1789: Society and the State*, trans. Brian Pearce (Chicago, 1974), pp. 99–111; and the volume dedicated to him, *Hommage à Roland Mousnier: Clientèles et fidélités en Europe à l'époque moderne*, ed. Yves Durand (Paris, 1981). See also my *Criticism in Action: Enlightenment Experiments in Political Writing* (Ithaca, 1989), pp. 75–78. Mona Ozouf argues that the "public" was opposed not to the private sphere but to the particular in eighteenth-century France. Ozouf, "'Public Opinion,'" p. S2. Philippe Ariès acknowledges this second meaning of the public in Chartier, *Passions of the Renaissance*, p. 9.

useful to his *patrie*. In making his case Thomas used as models precisely those members of the Academy whose loyalty to the monarchy was most obviously in question: Voltaire and d'Alembert. He did not appeal to the luminaries of the past or to the most old-fashioned and devout of contemporary academicians. Voltaire and d'Alembert were members of the Academy, but they also represented the new Republic of Letters. Voltaire was already considered its patriarch. Three years later his compatriots in the republic were opening a subscription to pay for a statue of him, just as French cities raised money to erect statues of the king.[108] D'Alembert not only was associated with the *Encyclopédie* but was generally considered to be Voltaire's man in Paris.

In arguing for the patriotism of men of letters, Thomas used the figures of Voltaire and d'Alembert as models to emulate because they represented the new Republic of Letters of the philosophes, which was now in a position to assert itself as *the* Republic of Letters. In so doing he blatantly ignored a good portion of the academicians whom he was addressing. As Grimm remarked at the time: "If the picture painted by M. Thomas of the man of letters does not match all the Forty whom immortality assembles at the Louvre; if the abbé Batteux and the abbé Trublet, and so many others, do not have the right to recognize themselves there, who would dare dispute the influence of the man of genius on the public spirit, and the revolutions that result from it?"[109]

Many years later, Stéphanie de Genlis still remembered an exchange of letters between Voltaire and d'Alembert which must have gone the rounds in Paris in 1766 and which she invoked to demonstrate their lack of patriotism. "One of the things for which I least pardon the philosophes is their disparagement of France," she wrote.

> In 1766 [Voltaire] wrote to d'Alembert: "I will die soon, *and it will be in detesting the land of monkeys and tigers*, where I was born through my mother's folly almost seventy-three years ago." Could contempt and hatred be expressed with any more animosity? D'Alembert replied: "France is really odious to me; and, if my reason is for her, surely my heart is not."[110]

108. Dena Goodman, "Pigalle's *Voltaire Nu*: The Republic of Letters Represents Itself to the World," *Representations* 16 (Fall 1986): 86–109.

109. *Correspondance Littéraire*, 1 February 1767.

110. [Stéphanie Félicité Ducrest de Saint-Aubin,] la comtesse de Genlis, *Dictionnaire critique et raisonné des étiquettes de la cour*, 2 vols. (Paris, 1818), s.v. "Patrie." The version of this letter in Voltaire's *Correspondence* is slightly different. In a previous letter to d'Alembert (18 July 1766), Voltaire had referred to France as "a country of monkeys who so often become tigers." In the letter Genlis quotes, tentatively dated by Besterman 10 August 1766, he writes: "You have the connections, the pensions, you are connected. As for me, I will die soon, and it will be in detesting the country of monkeys and tigers where the madness of my mother had me born almost seventy-three years ago." Voltaire's "lack

When Voltaire called France the "land of monkeys and tigers," the monkey was Rousseau, and the tigers were the provincial courts run by nobles made ferocious by religious fanaticism. Voltaire wanted to wrest France and the French from them, and he appealed to public opinion in order to do so. In trying to shape that opinion he was taking up his responsibility as a Frenchman and as the leading citizen of the Republic of Letters by combatting the foes of both France and the republic. In his own terms and those of his compatriots in the French Republic of Letters, Voltaire was expressing his patriotism by engaging in the project of Enlightenment. Like Thomas, he was displaying a new commitment on the part of French men of letters to identify patriotism with philosophy, the good of France with that of the Republic of Letters. No longer would Grimm, for example, have cause to complain that candidates for the French Academy were selected only for their love of the king and *la patrie*; patriotic feelings, as now defined by Thomas and Voltaire, were expressed in the commitment to philosophy itself.[111]

By 1778 Louis-Sébastien Mercier could write of "the man of letters–citizen" as the "avenger of the public cause." Eric Walter sees this figure as emerging from a process of linguistic transformation over the course of the eighteenth century. In 1730 the term *philosophe* evoked the figure of the sage or the scholar; over the course of the years 1740–1770, it became a defensive term within a conflict between those who called themselves true philosophes and those who attacked them as "so-called philosophes." At the same time, the meaning of *man of letters* shifted from the educated amateur to the newly defined, newly militant philosophe who was proud to declare his independence. In a third key, the term *author* was devalued and *writer* rose. When Thomas spoke of the "man of letters" at the French Academy in 1767, the term resonated with the associated terms *philosophe* and *writer*. It was this man of letters whom he identified with the good citizen, and it was this identification that Mercier could use uncritically eleven years later.[112]

---

of patriotism" was thus based on both his disgust with the French judicial system and his sense of being cut off by the state from its system of patronage. In 1822 Genlis referred to this same letter in again indicting Voltaire: "As you assure us that you are all *eminently French*, you ought to detest the writer who was *eminently anti-French*; the writer who ceaselessly elevated the English nation above our own; the writer who called his compatriots *des Welches*, and France, the country of *monkeys* and *tigers*; the writer who a thousand times mocked openly *the love of the patrie*, and who says, in his *Dictionnaire* . . . that one ought not to become any more attached to one's *patrie* than the gambler can be to the gaming table at which he has so much to gain, and that he leaves with regret as soon as he loses" (*Les Dîners du baron d'Holbach* [Paris, 1822], pp. x–xi).

111. See Karlis Racevskis, "L'Académie française vue par Grimm," in Bray, et al., *Correspondance littéraire de Grimm*, pp. 248–49.

112. Eric Walter, "Les Auteurs et le champ littéraire," in Martin and Chartier, *Histoire de l'édition française* 2:392–94.

In his speech to the Academy, Thomas redefined the man of letters as a citizen by redefining him as a philosophe. The message to the assembled academicians was that if they wanted to claim that the Academy represented the Republic of Letters, they would have to reshape themselves according to the model of Voltaire and d'Alembert. But even that would not be enough. For although the academic structure was internally egalitarian, it was by definition limited to a small elite and constrained by its connection with the monarchy. It could never attain either the independence or the openness—the publicity—that the Republic of Letters required. It could not expand enough to carry out the project of Enlightenment. The Republic of Letters might incorporate the academy, but it would not again return to it as its social base. That base was now established in the Parisian salons, from which networks of social and intellectual exchange were being developed to connect the capital with the four corners of France and the cosmopolitan republic. This new home better represented and better supported the new Republic of Letters, whose aim was to serve humanity and whose project was Enlightenment.

How was Enlightenment defined? Another big word thrown around —

CHAPTER 2

Philosophes and Salonnières:
A Critique of
Enlightenment Historiography

Rousseau accorde tant aux femmes, qu'on ne peut
être fâché de ce qu'il leur refuse.

—SUZANNE NECKER

As men of letters gave over to the public the authority to judge them (claiming for themselves, of course, the right and responsibility to represent public opinion), they found in a few women who cultivated it the ability to govern their discourse by enforcing the accepted rules of polite conversation. As governors, rather than judges, salonnières provided the ground for the philosophes' serious work by shaping and controlling the discourse to which men of letters were dedicated and which constituted their project of Enlightenment. In so doing, they transformed the salon from a leisure institution of the nobility into an institution of Enlightenment.

The identification of the Enlightenment with the Parisian salons and the women who led them has never been viewed as a positive collaboration, however. Although historians have generally acknowledged that salonnières did more than decorate the rooms in which the philosophes met, they have consistently taken a negative view of the role these women played in shaping the Enlightenment. Rather than see salonnières as the philosophes did—as the legitimate governors of a potentially unruly discourse—historians have viewed them through Rousseau's eyes, as the unqualified judges of male cultural performance and production. They have perpetuated Rousseau's critique, accepting without question his basic premise: that women undermine seriousness.

Under the guidance of Marie-Thérèse Geoffrin, Julie de Lespinasse, and Suzanne Necker, Parisian salons became the civil working spaces of the project of Enlightenment. The seriousness of that project was matched and supported by the seriousness with which the salonnières approached their own métier. Their definition of utility was the same as that of the philosophes: they contributed to the good of humanity by joining the Enlightenment Republic of Letters, and furthering its work.

In Chapter 3 I show how the salonnières governed the Republic of Letters by enforcing the rules of polite conversation. For now I want to trace the historiography of the Enlightenment in the twentieth century as it has addressed the role of the salonnière. Only after recognizing the Rousseauian thread that runs through our understanding of the Enlightenment can we begin to question it, and then to reconsider the meaning and function of the salonnière in the Enlightenment Republic of Letters.

Rousseau's Critique of Salons and Philosophes

In the same *Lettre à d'Alembert* in which Rousseau identified himself as the virtuous citizen and d'Alembert and Diderot as the corrupt pawns of kings, Rousseau also clearly set out his position on Parisian salons and the women who led them. The French, he wrote, showed a lack of respect for women in general by admiring those who least deserved it.

> The most esteemed woman is the one who has the greatest renown, about whom the most is said, who is the most often seen in society, at whose home one dines the most, who most imperiously sets the tone, who judges, resolves, decides, pronounces, assigns talents, merit, and virtues their degrees and places, and whose favor is most ignominiously begged for by humble, learned men. . . . In society they do not know anything, although they judge everything.[1]

What bothered Rousseau was not so much that good women did not get the respect they deserved but that men lowered themselves to earn the admiration of (bad) salon women. The problem with salons was that in them men fell into error by aiming solely to please women. Worse, they became effeminate, womanish. "Unable to make themselves into men, the women make us into women," he wrote. What distinguished ancient Greek and rustic Swiss men from the corrupt French was not only their integration with nature but their separation from women. Platonic academies and male clubs provided a form of sociability upon which male virtue could be built. "As for us," wrote Rousseau,

1. Rousseau, *Politics and the Arts*, p. 49.

we have taken on entirely contrary ways; meanly devoted to the wills of the sex which we ought to protect and not serve, we have learned to despise it in obeying it, to insult it by our derisive attentions; and every woman in Paris gathers in her apartment a harem of men more womanish than she . . . . But observe these same men, always constrained in these voluntary prisons, get up, sit down, pace continually back and forth to the fireplace, to the window . . . , while the idol, stretched out motionlessly on her couch has only her eyes and her tongue active.[2]

The active, feral nature of men was constrained in these gilded prisons under the unnatural domination of salon women. "Imagine," Rousseau asked, "what can be the temper of the soul of a man who is uniquely occupied with the important business of amusing women, and who spends his entire life doing for them what they ought to do for us?"[3] If, as Rousseau believed, society had originated out of men's need to be judged by others, then the epitome of that corruption was to seek the judgment of women.

Here Rousseau placed himself, alone among his peers, above the traps set by manipulating women. He presented himself as the only man who could speak honestly, like a man; the only spokesman of his age for truth and virtue; indeed, the only man left in an effeminate and therefore false society.[4] He constructed a polar opposition between the man Rousseau and the philosophes, dominated by and transformed into a horde of scheming women. Rousseau's later paranoid delusions of a philosophe conspiracy against him were an extension of this fear of women, with whom he had already identified the philosophes in the Lettre à d'Alembert.[5]

2. Ibid., pp. 100–101, and see 61 and 71–72.
3. Ibid., p. 103.
4. Rousseau was not alone for long, for he easily attracted admirers who shared his feelings. One of the earliest was Louis-Sébastien Mercier. In Le Bonheur des gens de lettres (London [Paris], 1766), the young Mercier adopted a Rousseauean rhetoric to warn "men of genius who have learned how to meditate" to protect themselves against the "enslavement of [their] masculine talents by the taste of sociétés," which threatened to "corrupt [their] eloquence, [their] bold and sublime vision, [their] virtuous heroism" (21–22). Mercier's recommendation, blending the lessons of the Lettre à d'Alembert and La Nouvelle Héloïse, was to educate women so that, instead of being frivolous and thus lowering men, they could elevate them properly (32–33). By the 1780s, however, Mercier had, by his own account, outgrown his youthful Rousseauean enthusiasm and become an advocate of cities and sociétés as the only world for gens de lettres. He was less than consistent, however, on what role he thought women should play in urban intellectual sociability. See chap. 6.
5. In his response to Rousseau, d'Alembert wrote: "You are at least, Sir, more accurate [juste] or more consistent than the public; your attack on our Actresses is equivalent to an even more violent one against other women. I do not know if you are one of the small number of sages whom they have sometimes been able to make unhappy, and if by

My point here, however, is not to rail against Rousseau or to discuss the origin and meaning of his fear of women. That subject has been amply explored by others.[6] Rather, I would like to show how Rousseau's joint indictment of salonnières and philosophes has been implicitly taken up by historians in the twentieth century and what its implications are for our understanding of the Enlightenment and the women who shaped it. For Rousseau's contention that salonnières undermined seriousness still underlies Enlightenment scholarship today.

Rousseau's Critique and Twentieth-Century Historiography

In 1914 the French historian Daniel Mornet opened a lecture on the salons with a quotation from Saint-Preux, the hero of Rousseau's novel *La Nouvelle Héloïse*. Further quotations from *La Nouvelle Héloïse* are strewn throughout the piece. With Rousseau as his guide, Mornet identified himself (through the use of the indeterminate *on*) with the plight of the thinking man forced to submit to the rule of women. He concluded that

---

the evil that you say of them, you have wished to give back to them that which they have done to you": *Lettre de M. d'Alembert à M. J. J. Rousseau sur l'article "Genève".* . . (Amsterdam, 1759), pp. 125–26.

Rousseau's autobiographical works are steeped in paranoia. I quote the following passage from the third dialogue of *Rousseau, Juge de Jean-Jacques* because of the explanation of it given by Rousseau's twentieth-century editor. "Since the philosophe sect has been united into a corps under its leaders, these leaders, by the art of intrigue to which they have applied themselves, have become the arbiters of public opinion, and by its means, of reputation, even of the destiny of individuals and by them of that of the State. Their attempt was made upon J. J. and the greatness of the success, which must have astonished even them, made them feel the extent to which their credit could reach. Thus they would think to associate themselves with powerful men in order to become with them the arbiters of society, those above all who, disposed like them to secret intrigues and to subterreanean looks, could not fail to meet and often to fan the flames of their own. . . . See how the century in which we live has become the century of hatred and of secret conspiracies" (*Oeuvres complètes* 1:965). The term "powerful men" in Rousseau's text generates the following note from the editor, Robert Osmont: "There are particular understandings such as that which allies Voltaire and Choiseul by the intermediary of Mme Du Deffand; there are the relations which are formed in the salons, Monday and Wednesday *chez* Mme Geoffrin, Tuesday *chez* Helvétius, Thursday and Sunday *chez* d'Holbach, later on Fridays *chez* Mme Necker." Rousseau did not even need to mention the centrality of the salons in the conspiracies he saw as pervasive; his readers make the connection for him.

6. See, e.g., Susan Moller Okin, *Women in Western Political Thought* (Princeton, 1979), pp. 99–194; Schwartz, *Sexual Politics*; Carol Blum, *Rousseau and the Republic of Virtue: The Language of Politics in the French Revolution* (Ithaca, 1986), esp. chap. 6; Joan B. Landes, *Women and the Public Sphere in the Age of the French Revolution* (Ithaca, 1988), chap. 3.

it is the worldly life which makes fashionable a disdain for the serious life and for the scruples of work and meditation. . . . In the most serious of these salons, one submits to the imperious necessities of the worldly life. Obviously, one assembles only in order to please, and to please requires accommodation. One must think constantly not of that which is true or that which is right [*juste*], but of that which will neither shock nor surprise.[7]

According to Mornet, those who wished to think or feel deeply and seriously avoided the "dangerous prestige" of the Parisian salons. In the salons, lesser men could find safe haven from the storms of publishers and polemical journals in "the smiles of women, the eagerness of guests, the headiness of pleasing." The result? Classical literature was (merely) sociable literature. Clarity and elegance were gained in this socializing of literature, but the sacrifice of substance for style was clearly not a fair trade, and Mornet suggested that French literature had been permanently marked by this shift in emphasis.[8]

In *French Liberal Thought in the Eighteenth Century* (1929), the British historian Kingsley Martin took a different approach: he regretted the greatness the philosophes might have achieved had they not been held back by the women in whose salons they were forced to perform. "If the philosophe had to disguise his argument to placate his enemies he had also to modulate it to please his friends," he wrote. Salonnières, the "arbiters of taste," were thus simply another class of censors to whose despotic authority the philosophes were forced to submit. "The patronage of literary women," Martin went on, "did corrupt the philosopher: he was compelled to adjust his style according to the intellectual fashion; he had always to be alert to please his hostess, to write so that she could talk about his book without having read the part which cost the greatest effort and which would constitute its permanent value."[9]

In this passage Martin was doing little more than repeating what might be called a "sympathetic" attack on Voltaire made by Rousseau in the *Discours sur les sciences et les arts*. There Rousseau had acknowledged the need for praise but claimed that in his own time great art was being sacrificed for it. What will the artist do to win it, he asked, "if he has the misfortune to be born among a people and at a time when scholars, having become fashionable, have put frivolous youth in a position to set the tone; when men have sacrificed their taste to the tyrants of their

7. Daniel Mornet, *La Vie parisienne au XVIIIe siècle: Leçons faites à l'Ecole des hautes études sociales* (Paris, 1914), p. 133.

8. Ibid., pp. 134, 138, 141–43.

9. Kingsley Martin, *French Liberal Thought in the Eighteenth Century: A Study of Political Ideas from Bayle to Condorcet* (New York, 1963), pp. 103, 105.

liberty [women]; . . . What will he do, gentlemen? He will lower his genius to the level of his century." Then, addressing himself directly to Voltaire, he demanded: "Tell us, famed Aroüet, how many strong and masculine beauties have you sacrificed to our false delicacy, and how much has the spirit of gallantry, so fertile in small things, cost you in great ones?"[10] This sacrifice of greatness in the eyes of posterity for the praise of female contemporaries was precisely what Kingsley Martin would regret in discussing the philosophes in our own century.

Without having to mention Rousseau, without suggesting that his defense of the philosophes against the tyranny of salonnières was supported principally by the very person who grouped the philosophes in a conspiracy with women against him, Martin reiterated Rousseau's indictment. "Solemnity was impossible . . . ; sincerity and seriousness were also difficult. . . . If the conversation in the *salon* had been too serious, the less intelligent would have been slighted," he wrote.[11]

Like Mornet, Martin concluded that "the really important work of the century was done away from the *salons*."[12] He claimed further that in the 1760s the philosophes broke away from the female-dominated salons to form their own male "salons"—those of Claude Dupin, Alexandre de La Poupelinière, and Paul Henri Dietrich, baron d'Holbach— just as Rousseau had suggested they should do in the *Lettre à d'Alembert*. He acknowledged that the philosophes continued to frequent the "old" salons but maintained that they did so simply for form's sake; the real work went on in these new salons, which "accepted the new doctrines, permitted freedom of conversation, and themselves provided good dinners and good music."[13] One wonders, then, why the names of Geoffrin, Lespinasse, and Necker were recorded and praised again and again in the letters and works of the philosophes, while Dupin and Poupelinière are all but forgotten.

It is not surprising that the only scholarly study of Enlightenment sociability in Paris is Alan Kors's *D'Holbach's Coterie: An Enlightenment in Paris* (1976). In order to distinguish the "circle" that met regularly at

---

10. Rousseau, *Oeuvres complètes* 3:21.

11. Martin, *French Liberal Thought*, pp. 106–7.

12. Ibid., p. 108.

13. Ibid. Martin's chronology does not hold up. By the mid-1760s, d'Holbach was retrenching his "salon" because, after more than a decade, it had gotten so big that it had lost its intimacy. It was at that moment, in 1764, that Julie de Lespinasse opened her salon, and the same year that Suzanne Curchod arrived in Paris from Lausanne. Her salon did not open until after her marriage to Jacques Necker the following year. The salon of Julie de Lespinasse flourished until her death in 1776, and Necker's was still going in 1789. See Alan Charles Kors, *D'Holbach's Coterie: An Enlightenment in Paris* (Princeton, 1976), p. 10; and Marguerite Glotz and Madeleine Maire, *Salons du XVIIIème siècle* (Paris, 1949), pp. 223 and 296.

the baron's from a mere salon, Kors adopted the term *coterie*, though he acknowledged that Rousseau had used it pejoratively.[14] Like the Genevan circles glorified by Rousseau in the *Lettre à d'Alembert*, the all-male "coterie d'Holbachique" allowed the philosophes to get serious. "By themselves," Rousseau had written of the Genevans, "the men, exempted from having to lower their ideas to the range of women and to clothe reason in gallantry, can devote themselves to grave and serious discourse without fear of ridicule."[15] Implicitly following Rousseau and Martin, Kors argued that the "coterie d'Holbachique" offered the philosophes a haven from the judgment of women and the conflict between the female-imposed rules of the salons and the philosophes' own thoughts, convictions, and enthusiasms. These rules, according to Kors, placed limits on free speech, limits on truth telling, limits on debate itself. "It was impolite to challenge the vague religiosity of the ladies; it was impolite to be pessimistic," he charged. "In addition, there were limits to the *forms* of expression tolerated at these gatherings; it was impolite to quarrel and, above all, to quarrel sincerely and doggedly."[16]

According to Kors, the salonnières instituted these rules of polite conversation in the selfish pursuit of their own pleasure and to protect that respectability which the philosophes would have liked to challenge. Thus, while salonnières might act scandalously, taking lovers, they demanded propriety—and thus dishonesty—in speech. "These hostesses insisted upon the rules of polite conversation, and the philosophes adapted as best they could. The women repaid them by intriguing for them to obtain places in the Académies, taking their sides in various feuds, and flattering their vanities."[17]

In his review of *D'Holbach's Coterie*, the French historian Daniel Roche seconded Kors's evaluation of the differences between the d'Holbach circle and the salon. "What was the real role of the Parisian salons and of sociability in the formation and expansion of philosophe ideas?" he asked. The answer was clear:

> Authors admit too easily the coincidence of a structure of sociability with the adhesion to new values, without seeing that the form of the gathering itself dictates the limits that cannot be crossed, the subjects about which one is silent, the choices that are made. Worldly discussion is at the same time a brake upon a certain audacity of thought, the encouragement to paradox more than to sincerity. The space of the salon is that of a highly

14. Kors, *D'Holbach's Coterie*, pp. 9–10.
15. Rousseau, *Politics and the Arts*, p. 105.
16. Kors, *D'Holbach's Coterie*, p. 92.
17. Ibid., p. 93.

codified social ritual, regularized by the female presence, where one knows what one must say and when. It has its Maître Jacques, but this is neither *disputatio* nor the debate of ideas, firm and frank.[18]

What characterized the d'Holbach circle, according to Roche, was precisely the partial refusal of "salon self-censorship." Observers, he wrote, were struck by "the freedom, the open-hearted discussion, the provocative audacity, the true dialogue, and the jokes." At a time when the dominant sites of sociability and discourse were the Academy, constrained by political power, and the salon, constrained by social conformity, only the d'Holbach circle was truly free and honest.[19]

Alan Kors, however, went beyond romanticizing the d'Holbach circle as the space of male freedom and honesty; he questioned the integrity of salonnières and, like Rousseau, attacked their morals. Blind to the paradox in his own argument that salonnières at the same time stifled honest debate out of concern for their respectability and lowered the intellectual tone with their promiscuity, he simply added the charge of hypocrisy. Thus he displaced a charge brought against the philosophes by a long historiographical tradition critical of the Enlightenment: it was the salonnières, not the philosophes, who were the real hypocrites.[20] And yet, of the three major salonnières—Geoffrin, Lespinasse, and Necker (and Kors mentioned them by name)—only Lespinasse took a lover, and by the time she did, she was already beyond the bounds of respectability. As an unmarried woman of dubious parentage, living on her own in Paris but sharing a house with her friend d'Alembert, she was hardly attempting to assert herself as a model of respectable gentility.

The language of Kors's critique of the salons was straight out of Rousseau, but he used it to defend the philosophes against Rousseau's attack on their masculinity. He contrasted liberty, content, sincerity, rigor, thoughtfulness, earnestness, honesty (and quarreling!), on the one hand, to politeness, pleasure, charm, wit, form, respectability, duty, intrigue, flattery, and vanity, on the other. In the paragraph in which he described what the philosophes were really like, their "private

18. Roche, "Salons, Lumières, engagement politique: La Côterie d'Holbach dévoilée," reprinted in *Républicains des lettres*, pp. 247–48.

19. Ibid., p. 248.

20. Marxists found the philosophes hypocritical because they used universalist language to further the interests of a single class, the bourgeoisie; some feminists now make the same kind of argument in relation to gender. Perhaps the most intriguing version today is Reinhart Koselleck's. "Criticism gave birth to hypocrisy," he writes. "What for Voltaire was still tactical camouflage became habitual practice in the hands of his successors. They became the victims of their own mystification. Strategy became mendacity": *Critique and Crisis*, p. 117.

world," which the "elegant ladies" who fed them did not understand, each sentence was punctuated with the word "man" or "men." "They were men who examined in their minds the whole fabric of the traditions and givens of the culture . . . . They were men whose minds were increasingly unfettered . . . . They consciously saw themselves as men whose ideas represented a major period of transition."[21] The message is clear: Rousseau was wrong; the philosophes really were men, and they proved it by forming their own circle, where they and their ideas could not be emasculated by salonnières. Kors had fleshed out the argument that Kingsley Martin only suggested.

Not long after Martin tried to associate the serious work of the Enlightenment with male-only social gatherings by dissociating it from the salons, the German philosopher Ernst Cassirer entered the lists in this effort of rehabilitation. In *The Philosophy of the Enlightenment* (1932), Cassirer removed the Enlightenment from any social context whatsoever. The aim of his book, he said, was to place "the philosophy of the Enlightenment against the background of another and broader historical and philosophical theme. . . . For the movement to be described . . . forms but a part and a special phase of that whole intellectual development through which modern philosophic thought gained its characteristic self-confidence and self-consciousness."[22] The context within which the Enlightenment was to be understood was not the social context of salons but the rationalist and idealist intellectual context that began with the Greeks and continued through the French Enlightenment to Kant, Hegel, and Cassirer himself. Cassirer's Enlightenment was no longer Rousseau's Enlightenment of men and women but a movement of the "spirit struggling with purely objective problems, [which] achieves clarity and depth in its understanding of its own nature and destiny, and of its own fundamental character and mission" (vi).

And yet, looked at more closely, it was Rousseau's Enlightenment after all. In his discussion of the political philosophy of the Enlightenment, Cassirer came to the startling conclusion that "Rousseau is a true son of the Enlightenment, even when he attacks it and triumphs over it" (273). The site of this contest, the "clash of doctrines" Cassirer identified as "Rousseau's passionate quarrel with his epoch" (273), was very simply a quarrel between the sociable and the unsociable. What set Rousseau apart from and above his contemporaries, according to Cassirer, was his realization that "the very intellectual and sociable culture

21. Kors, *D'Holbach's Coterie*, pp. 93–94. Like Martin, Kors also argued that "real" philosophes (such as Diderot) avoided the salons or were kept out of them (92).

22. Ernst Cassirer, *The Philosophy of the Enlightenment*, trans. Fritz C. A. Koelln and James P. Pettegrove (Boston, 1955), pp. v–vi, hereafter cited in the text.

which the eighteenth century looks upon as the height of real humanity . . . [was its] greatest peril" (270). Rousseau had revealed as problematic what the philosophes accepted "naively and credulously." The
philosophes' "faith" that "the refinement of manners and the growth
and extension of knowledge will and must finally transform morality
and give it a firmer foundation" was so strong, Cassirer wrote, that "for
most of these thinkers the concept of the community which they are
endeavoring to formulate and justify becomes synonymous not only
with the concept of society but even with that of sociability" (268–69).
Rousseau, however, was able to see "as if in a sudden vision . . . the vast
abyss before him which had remained veiled from his contemporaries,
and on whose edge they had moved with no idea of the threatening
danger" (270).

What was this danger from which Rousseau, the brother who had
been cast out from the family of philosophes, was saving them? No
mere logical perils or philosophical traps but the emasculation of philosophy itself. "Not only political, but also theoretical, ethical and aesthetic ideals are formed by and for the salons," Cassirer explained.
"Urbanity becomes a criterion of real insight in science. Only that
which can be expressed in the language of such urbanity has stood the
test of clarity and distinctness" (268).

Rousseau's tremendous achievement, according to Cassirer, was to
save the Enlightenment from itself and thereby to express its essential
meaning. The *Discours sur l'inégalité* was Rousseau's attempt to raise
man from his depraved condition in order to start "social existence all
over again." Society would be destroyed, and this time man "shall not
succumb to the power of his appetites and passions but he shall himself
choose and direct. He shall grasp the helm himself and determine both
his course and his destination." Cassirer's "man," like Rousseau's, is
implicitly male: he fears the power of women as the object of his own
appetites and passions. Only when he has freed himself from the confines of a female-directed social world can he forge his own direction.
He will begin by finding a "firm law within himself, before he seeks the
laws of external objects." Only after he has achieved true freedom in
this way can he "with confidence devote himself to the freedom of
intellectual inquiry." Only then will knowledge avoid becoming "a victim of mere 'hair-splitting,'" he wrote, "nor will it render man effeminate and indolent" (272–73).

Cassirer, like Mornet, Martin, and Kors, viewed the Enlightenment
through a Rousseauean lens. He accepted the charge that the philosophes were less than men, less than philosophers. He was able to
recuperate the Enlightenment by idealizing it and by making Rousseau
the symbol of the "true inner spiritual unity of the age" (273). Naive

and credulous, "none of the Encyclopaedists doubted that man can live otherwise than in fellowship and sociability, or that he could realize his destiny under other conditions" (266). Rousseau disabused them of this notion. In so doing, according to Cassirer, he "did not overthrow the world of the Enlightenment; he only transferred its center of gravity to another position" (274). True enough. What Rousseau did, after all, was to displace the project of Enlightenment from the salons.

Cassirer did more than anyone else to make the Enlightenment the subject of serious scholarship. Indeed, it was he who established the very existence of a "philosophy of the Enlightenment," he who integrated it into the mainstream of the history of Western thought as a crucial component in its development. After Cassirer, the Enlightenment could no longer be written off as the mere plaything of amateurs (philosophes, not philosophers) wrapped around the little fingers of silly but sly women.[23] But what happened to the women? They had disappeared. Cassirer made the Enlightenment serious by freeing it from the complex and problematic social reality of which salonnières were an important part, and he used Rousseau to help him do it. His index lists forty-seven references to Kant but none to Geoffrin, Lespinasse, or Necker.

Historians of the Enlightenment since Cassirer have criticized him for ignoring the social dimension of intellectual history. That strategy derived from his belief that the Enlightenment was misguided in its assumption that sociability, and not masculine reason, was the basis of ethical, political, and intellectual activity. Peter Gay and, after him, Robert Darnton, called for a "social history of ideas" in direct response to the limitations of Cassirer's approach.[24] French historians reacted similarly to their own tradition of Enlightenment historiography as the domain of literary scholars whose "siècle des Lumières" was either a pendant to or a moment of "l'âge classique."[25] Coming out of the

23. Peter Gay, *The Enlightenment: An Interpretation*, 2 vols. (New York, 1966–69), 1:ix.

24. Robert Darnton, "In Search of Enlightenment: Recent Attempts to Create a Social History of Ideas," *Journal of Modern History* 43 (March 1971): 113–32. See Darnton's references to Gay, esp. notes 1 and 2. The call for a social history of ideas issued by the Italian historian, Franco Venturi, in *Utopia and Reform in the Enlightenment*, reached anglophone ears at the same time, as Margaret C. Jacob notes in "The Enlightenment Redefined: The Formation of Modern Civil Society," *Social Research* 58 (Summer 1991): 475.

25. Most important in this tradition were Gustave Lanson and Paul Hazard. More recent scholars include Robert Mauzi, Jean Ehrard, Jacques Chouillet, and the group associated with the journal *Dix-huitième Siècle*. British historiography followed the French model, as represented by Theodore Besterman and his legacy in *Studies on Voltaire and the Eighteenth Century*. Thomas E. Kaiser makes the same point more broadly in "This Strange Offspring of *Philosophie*: Recent Historiographical Problems in Relating the Enlightenment to the French Revolution," *French Historical Studies* 15 (Spring 1988): 551.

tradition of social history associated with the journal *Annales* and taking
Mornet as their spiritual founder, they also moved in the direction of a
social history of ideas.[26] The recent work of Daniel Roche and Roger
Chartier thus converges with that of Darnton—even as they disagree—
in resituating the Enlightenment in a particularly French social context.

What is this new social history of the Enlightenment, and what role
do salonnières play in it? It is, first of all, a serious history, a history of
work rather than of play. But to the degree that it is serious, it continues to exclude salonnières. While there is considerable disagreement
about the nature of the Enlightenment—who is to be included in it and
what they are thought to have accomplished as part of it—there is
implicit agreement that whoever was doing important things, they were
doing them outside the salons and beyond the reach of salonnières. Not
only does Rousseau's assumption that salonnières undermined Enlightenment seriousness remain unchallenged, but his critique is reestablished on "firmer" ground.

The first attempt at a social history of the Enlightenment—Peter
Gay's two-volume work *The Enlightenment: An Interpretation* (1966–
1969)—was immediately criticized by Darnton as merely a reshuffling
of canonical texts. True social history, said Darnton, requires the historian to get underneath the published writings of the dominant philosophes to the social bottom of things, through archival research.[27] Although Darnton's wholesale attack on the reading of texts as central to
intellectual history is more than questionable,[28] it is certainly true that
Gay's textual approach effectively marginalized the salonnières. In this
sense, Gay did simply extend Cassirer's idealism. He situated Enlightenment ideas, as expressed in texts, in a rich social and political context
(rather than Cassirer's intellectual one), but it was the ideas themselves,
and the philosophes who expressed them, which were the actors in his
drama. Salonnières played at best a supporting role.

An examination of the indexes of Gay's two volumes yields two references to women who ran salons, but in neither case is Gay interested in
them as salonnières. Suzanne Curchod was only "the girl whom Gibbon
loved so tepidly and yielded up so readily."[29] Gay does not note that this

26. See Lynn Hunt, "French History in the Last Twenty Years: The Rise and Fall of
the *Annales* Paradigm," *Journal of Contemporary History* 21 (1986): 209–24.

27. Darnton, "In Search of Enlightenment," p. 122; Darnton, "The High Enlighten-
ment and the Low-Life of Literature in Prerevolutionary France," *Past and Present*, no. 51
(May 1971), reprinted as "The High Enlightenment and the Low-Life of Literature," in
The Literary Underground of the Old Regime (Cambridge, Mass., 1982), p. 1.

28. See Dominick LaCapra, *History and Criticism* (Ithaca, 1985), pp. 87–94.

29. Gay, *Enlightenment* 1:117, also 2:260 n. 7.

"girl" later married Jacques Necker and led one of the most important salons of the Enlightenment. It was Suzanne Curchod, the woman scorned, not Suzanne Necker, the salonnière, who fit into Gay's picture of the Enlightenment. For Gay, women entered into the Enlightenment only as the objects of (male) philosophes—of their affections or of their thoughts. The salonnières as a group remained nameless, referred to only as "the cultivated Parisian ladies who played hostess to philosophes from all over the world." And while they *played* hostess, the men they served earned Gay's esteem for attempting "to treat them as equals, as well as an item on the agenda of reform."[30] Gay's Enlightenment was a reflection of well-meaning but ultimately sexist 1960s liberalism: a liberalism that denied women a voice by speaking for them in a universal voice identified with the men of the Enlightenment.

Like Cassirer's intellectual history, Gay's social history continued to maintain the seriousness of the philosophes only by abstracting it from the cultural practice of the salon. What of Gay's critics? Have they done any differently?

By the 1970s there was an "establishment" in Enlightenment scholarship to be overthrown, represented in the United States by Cassirer and Gay and identified with its subject matter: the "establishment" of the Parisian philosophes and the salonnières who were associated with them. In France, Roche and Chartier have looked beyond the Parisian elite, first to the provinces, then to the people, to resituate the Enlightenment in eighteenth-century French culture. In America, Darnton has attempted to dethrone the philosophes of Cassirer and Gay by reasserting the Rousseauean position that the philosophes, under the sway of salonnières, represented the frivolity and corruption of the Old Regime as a whole. For the new social historians of ideas, the Enlightenment was a serious business only when it lay outside—and especially when it challenged—the salons where women and philosophes conspired to maintain their hold on the privileged social institutions of Old Regime intellectual life.[31]

In 1978 Daniel Roche published his monumental work *Le Siècle des lumières en province: Académies et académiciens provinciaux, 1680–1789.* For Roche, the real Enlightenment happened in the provinces, where local elites operated in a social and intellectual network of which their

---

30. Ibid., 2:33 and 201–2.

31. Thomas Kaiser sees historiographical progress in a general agreement that "the *philosophes* cannot be dismissed as salon intellectuals." He acknowledges Darnton's contribution to this consensus by providing "fresh evidence . . . not only that the *philosophes* toadied to supposedly 'enlightened' monarchs on occasion, but also that their general political goal was to reinforce the Old Regime rather than subvert it": "This Strange Offspring of *Philosophie*," pp. 556 and 558.

provincial academies were the center. The Parisian philosophes, en-
trenched in their own academies, no longer in a position to sustain the
critical project they had defined, became its object. "The transformations of society and of ideas support a sharper and sharper critique of
academism. The little world of authors reveals itself to be profoundly
agitated, but the philosophes are in power."[32] Committed to decentering the Parisian intellectual establishment, Roche ignored the salons
entirely in his lengthy chapter on "The Institutions of the 'Republic of
Letters.'" Masonic lodges; literary, agricultural, and medical societies;
national and provincial academies; correspondences; periodicals—all
have a place here, but the salons do not. The "Republic of Ideas,"
whose institutions Roche identified, "incarnated in voluntary mani-
festations of participation and collective responsibility,"[33] was an entirely male affair, for its institutions did not include the salons that had
so diminished the reputation of the Enlightenment in earlier scholarship. Indeed, Roche was described on the back cover of a collection of
his articles published in 1988 as a historian who, "not satisfied with
clichés and commonplaces, decided early on to examine the Enlightenment from close up—no longer simply in the salons of the Parisian
elites, but in the farthest provinces."[34]

While maintaining the suspicions of Parisian philosophes which
Mornet had inherited from Rousseau, Roche continued the trend toward rehabilitation of the Enlightenment as a serious affair by leaving
salonnières out of it altogether. His new constitution of the Republic of
Letters, like Kingsley Martin's, was founded on the same kind of male
institutions for which Rousseau yearned in the *Lettre à d'Alembert*. The
article in the 1988 collection *Les Républicains des lettres* which is titled
"Salons, Lumières, engagement politique," is in fact the review of
D'Holbach's Coterie mentioned earlier, in which salons are dismissed and
the d'Holbach circle put in their place.

Until recently, Roger Chartier has similarly omitted salons from his
discussions of Enlightenment sociability. In *Passions of the Renaissance*,
volume 3 of *A History of Private Life* (French edition, 1986), Chartier
identified "literary societies, Masonic lodges, clubs, and cafés" as the
centers of a new "practice of intellectual association" but excluded
salons from the litany.[35] In *Lectures et lecteurs dans la France d'Ancien
Régime* (1987), he attempted to sketch out the culture of the Old Re-

32. Daniel Roche, *Le Siècle des lumières en province: Académies et académiciens provinciaux,
1680–1789*, 2 vols. (The Hague, 1978), 1:290.
33. Ibid., 1:256.
34. Roche, *Républicains des lettres*.
35. Chartier, *History of Private Life* 3:17. For a critique of Chartier on this point, see
Gordon, "'Public Opinion' and the Civilizing Process," p. 305.

gime. Here, in one short section devoted to the reading practices of the elite, Chartier discussed first a father and a son reading together, then two male friends doing the same, then a reading in a provincial academy. For contrast, he closed with a description of readings *en famille* supported by Jean-François de Troy's painting *La Lecture de Molière* (Figure 1). As Chartier described the scene,

> In a richly furnished rococo *salon,* an aristocratic company of two men and five women listen to one of the men read Molière. The women, in house dress, are comfortably installed in *bergère* armchairs, and one of them leans toward the reader to look at the text he is reading. . . . The reader has stopped for a moment, and the gazes of the various members of the group meet or avoid the others' gazes, as though the pleasures of society that had brought them together to read aloud have sent each one back to his or her own thoughts and desires.[36]

Whereas men read Cicero together and, according to a contemporary letter, bewail "public ignorance, . . . the lack of taste among our young people, who amuse themselves reading new books that are often frivolous and superficial, and who neglect the great models from which they could learn to think properly,"[37] the mixed company in de Troy's painting are reading the less-than-serious Molière, indulging in the pleasure of society, which brings them in the end to their own desires rather than to clear thinking, the aim of Enlightenment. "Salon reading," declares the legend given this painting in *Passions of the Renaissance,* "gathered a select company but did not fully absorb everyone's attention, as is evident from the glances exchanged or avoided, signs of desire and complicity."[38]

Like Roche, Chartier omitted Enlightenment salons from the institutions of Old Regime culture. He presented male-only gatherings as serious centers of elite culture, and mixed-company family gatherings as their opposite. But which was the Enlightenment? Since the location

36. Roger Chartier, *Lectures et lecteurs dans la France d'Ancien Régime* (Paris, 1987), p. 209. This essay has been translated as "Urban Reading Practices, 1660–1780," in *Cultural Uses of Print.* I quote from the translation, p. 233.

37. Président Dugas to Bottu de Saint-Fonds, 27 March 1731, in ibid., p. 232.

38. Chartier, *History of Private Life* 3:151. The art historian Michael Fried views Troy's work differently. He identifies him as one of a few painters in the early eighteenth century "who now and then produced work whose absorptive character is undeniable." This painting is one of those works: Fried, *Absorption and Theatricality: Painting and Beholder in the Age of Diderot* (Chicago, 1980), p. 44. Molière was one of the objects of Rousseau's attack on French culture in the *Lettre à d'Alembert.* Not surprisingly, Rousseau saw Molière as a threat to the natural patriarchal order of society and a representative of the hypocrisy of polite society: *Politics and the Arts,* pp. 34–47.

Figure 1. Jean-François de Troy, *La Lecture de Molière* (1728). Courtesy of the Marquess of Cholmondeley.

of the Enlightenment in eighteenth-century culture was never the focus of Chartier's picture, this glimpse of elite culture suggests that for him it was either the serious business of men or the pleasant affair of mixed company. Again, if it was serious, it was the work of men; if it was not, it included (salon) women. The Enlightenment as a phenomenon was so marginalized that it was impossible to know which position Chartier might take.[39]

In *The Cultural Origins of the French Revolution* (1991) Chartier has attempted to integrate popular and elite culture, on the one hand, and private life and political culture, on the other. The result is a cultural history that owes as much to Habermas as it does to Philippe Ariès and the *Annales* tradition, and that goes significantly beyond the limitations of his previous work. Salons now figure in Chartier's cultural history as one of the institutions of the new political culture of the Old Regime. Following Habermas, he associates the salons with "the public literary sphere" and characterizes them "as places where works and cultural actors could find independent intellectual consecration outside rule-bound institutions and established cultural bodies." He identifies the salons as the first institutions "to encourage the new public literary sphere born in the eighteenth century and emancipated from the tutelage of the court and the Académie française."[40]

And yet, although he now gives salons an important role, Chartier's characterization of salonnières is more old than new. "There were subtle filiations and rivalries between the various social sets, each of which was dominated by a woman," he writes. "A fierce rivalry for the highest distinction thus reigned in the society of the Parisian salons. In the last analysis, what was at stake was control of an intellectual life that had been emancipated from the tutelage of the monarchy and the court."[41]

In contrast to this female rivalry for the attention of men was, once again, the male friendship of the d'Holbach circle. Whereas the philosophes connived *together* at d'Holbach's, factions formed in the salons based on "the preferences of the women who were their hostesses." Salonnières were thus intriguing women who substituted their own power for that of the monarchy and the court. The emancipation of male intellectual life was threatened by the rivalries and ambitions of the salon women who now sought to control it. Their interests were

---

39. One reason it is difficult to identify the Enlightenment in Chartier's eighteenth-century culture is that the general aim of his work has been to collapse the distinction between elite and popular culture. See, e.g., "Culture as Appropriation: Popular Cultural Uses in Early Modern France," in *Understanding Popular Culture: Europe from the Middle Ages to the Nineteenth Century*, ed. Steven L. Kaplan (Berlin, 1984), pp. 229–53.

40. Chartier, *Cultural Origins*, pp. 154–57.

41. Ibid., pp. 155–56.

defined solely in terms of their relationships to men: to dominate them, to attract them, or to intrigue for them.[42]

Even more revealing than the old contrast between the d'Holbach circle and the salons is a new one posed by Chartier's juxtaposition of salons and literary journalism. The rivalry that was a negative characteristic in salonnières becomes a form of healthy competition when Chartier discusses (male) journalists. "Even though they vied with one another to dictate, through their choices and decrees, the 'correct' interpretation of works," he writes, "the very fact that there were a number of periodicals in circulation fueled critical debate and lively discussion."[43] Salonnières, however, did not compete for guests; rather, they shared them: they established their salons on different days of the week so that they and their guests could attend multiple salons. Journalists, by contrast, needed to compete for subscribers, whose financial resources were limited. The short life spans of eighteenth-century periodicals testify to the cutthroat competition to which they inevitably succumbed.[44] The material base of the salon in private wealth made it possible for salonnières to support one another; the material base of journalism did not. Gender was not the determining factor here; economics was.

Chartier's most recent work thus demonstrates a new understanding of the importance of the salons in the cultural history of the Enlightenment, but it is tempered by old stereotypes of women and power. In Robert Darnton's picture of eighteenth-century French culture, however, there is no tension between the role of salons and that of salonnières. Nor is there any attempt to dissociate the philosophes from the salons. Rather, Darnton's social history of the Enlightenment resituates the philosophes squarely in the centers of gravity from which Cassirer tried to abstract them. In fact, Darnton has given us the most Rousseauean representation of the Enlightenment Republic of Letters to date.

"Except for men like Condorcet," wrote Darnton in his 1971 review of Gay's *Enlightenment*, "the last of the philosophes fit in perfectly with the Sèvres porcelain and *chinoiserie* of the salons; the High Enlightenment served as frosting for France's crumbling upper crust."[45] Beneath this "High Enlightenment," however, lay a low one whose depths Darnton has sought to plumb, "to get to the bottom of the Enlightenment and even to penetrate into its underworld, where the Enlighten-

42. Ibid.
43. Ibid., p. 159.
44. Sgard, "Multiplication des périodiques," in Martin and Chartier, *Histoire de l'édition française* 3:200.
45. Darnton, "In Search of Enlightenment," p. 119.

ment may be examined as the Revolution has been studied recently—
from below."[46]

Darnton's purpose has been to give the Enlightenment its clay feet, to
show that the philosophes were not truly noble by exposing their co-
optation by the aristocratic society of the Old Regime (2–3). His language is full of disdain for the philosophe, who, "formerly a fringe
character picked up for amusement by the salons and readily turned
out into the street for drubbings, begging, and *embastillement*, . . . was
becoming respectable, domesticated, and assimilated into that most
conservative of institutions, the family" (5). It is hard to tell which is
more despicable: to be the plaything of the salons or to be domesticated
in the family.

To make his case, Darnton focuses on a "typical" philosophe, J. B. A.
Suard, the person who edited the *Exposé succinct* of the Hume-Rousseau
affair. Suard was also instrumental in introducing the works of the
Scottish Enlightenment into France.[47] Darnton, however, presents him
as a man of little talent who "made it" in the Republic of Letters by
passing the test of *le monde*. As Darnton tells his story, Suard

> met and captivated the Abbé Raynal, who functioned as a sort of recruit-
> ing agent for the sociocultural elite known as *le monde*. Raynal got Suard
> jobs tutoring the well-born, encouraged him to write little essays on the
> heroes of the day . . . and guided him through the salons. Suard com-
> peted for the essay prizes offered by provincial academies. He published
> literary snippets in the *Mercure*; and having passed at Mme. Geoffrin's, he
> began to make frequent appearances in *le monde*. . . . With doors opening
> for him in the salons . . . , Suard walked into a job at the *Gazette de France*;
> lodging, heating, lighting, and 2,500 livres a year for putting polish on
> the materials provided every week by the ministry of foreign affairs. (4)

Suard's success, we learn, was due to a new kind of protection, which,
in contrast to court patronage, "involved knowing the right people,
pulling the right strings . . . . Older, established writers, wealthy bourgeois, and nobles all participated in this process of co-opting young
men with the right style, the perfect pitch of bon ton, into the salons,
academies, privileged journals, and honorific posts" (6–7). Suard, in
other words, breezed through the doorway where Rousseau had

46. Darnton, *Literary Underground*, p. 1, hereafter cited in the text. Darnton's agenda
has not changed significantly in the last twenty years. See "The Facts of Literary Life in
Eighteenth-Century France," in Baker, *Political Culture of the Old Regime*, pp. 261–91; and
"The Brissot Dossier," *French Historical Studies* 17 (Spring 1991): 191–205.

47. Gordon, "Idea of Sociability," chap. 5.

turned on his heel and, with virtue and integrity intact, walked nobly away, slamming the door behind him.

The Enlightenment may have been radical, and thus serious, at the start, Darnton maintains, but by the 1770s it was merely a prop to the social order, "domesticated" by *le monde*. Darnton calls this fall into comfort "the establishment of the Enlightenment" (6–7), associating it in the contemporary reader's mind with the historical "establishment" of Darnton's own day. And in case there is any doubt as to whose point of view Darnton is taking, he reminds us that "to the outsiders, the whole process looked rotten. . . . Seen from the perspective of Grub Street, the republic of letters was a lie" (23).

Darnton admits that those he identifies as "outsiders" were not inclined to attribute their failures to any lack of talent, but he takes up their position by condemning the "Suard generation of philosophes" as at least equally untalented and certainly less radical:

> There was nothing shockingly new at all in the works of [Voltaire's] successors, for *they* had been absorbed, fully integrated into *le monde*. . . . And while they grew fat in Voltaire's church, the revolutionary spirit passed to the lean and hungry men of Grub Street, to the cultural pariahs who, through poverty and humiliation, produced the Jacobinical version of Rousseauism. . . . It was from such visceral hatred, not from the refined abstractions of the contented cultural elite, that the extreme Jacobin revolution found its authentic voice. (40)

Darnton's attack on the philosophes is simply Rousseau's attack as it was taken up by those who identified with him in the 1770s and 1780s.[48] Rousseau had created the image of himself as outsider, as the only man who was able to withstand the feminizing pressure of the salons. He had created the image of the philosophes as feminized pussycats, rather than roaring lions, under the sway of dominating salonnières. Some of those who found themselves frustrated in a Republic of Letters that remained under political, social, and economic constraints found in this self-image of Rousseau a hero, and in his image of a female-dominated world of favors and forbidden pleasures a comforting explanation of why they were unable to achieve their aspirations to be the philosophes that Voltaire and the *Encyclopédie* called on them to be.

Darnton has legitimated Rousseau's attack on philosophes as the playthings of salon women in an extremely attractive way.[49] In the

48. See Blum, *Rousseau and the Republic of Virtue.*
49. Darnton's interpretation continues to shape the general understanding of the Enlightenment, but recently historians have begun to challenge the "Darnton thesis." See

name of the disenfranchised he has discredited the enemies Rousseau created for himself, just as Rousseau and his followers did, but now with the authority and credibility of the historian whose aim is simply "to argue for a broadening of intellectual history, and to suggest that a mixed genre, the social history of ideas, could contribute to a fresh assessment of the age of the Enlightenment."[50]

Darnton's broadening of intellectual history falls short because it remains trapped within masculinist assumptions that mask the role of women in the cultural practices of the French Enlightenment. In this crucial respect, his "fresh assessment" is as old as the Enlightenment itself. It originated with Rousseau and has been at the center of Enlightenment historiography throughout this century. It is time that it was challenged.

The Enlightenment Salonnière

Only the Romantics of the nineteenth century seem to have appreciated the salons of the late eighteenth century, but what they found in them to love only reinforces the views of men before and after them. Sainte-Beuve called Geoffrin's salon "one of the premiere institutions of Europe," but he located Lespinasse's greatness in her love letters rather than in her work as a salonnière. These letters, he wrote, are "one of the most curious and most memorable monuments to passion"; the principal claim of their author is "the glory of a loving woman."[51]

Over the course of the nineteenth century, the illustrious women of the eighteenth century, including the major salonnières, found biographers among aristocratic amateurs nostalgic for a world now vanished, and salons became the subject of *petite histoire*.[52] From the rubble of the Revolution, memoirs and correspondences of ladies and philosophes were found and published in elegant editions. At the center of this flush of attention was Edmond and Jules de Goncourt's contribution, *La Femme au dix-huitième siècle* (1862).

Jeremy Popkin, "Pamphlet Journalism at the End of the Old Regime," *Eighteenth-Century Studies* 22 (Spring 1989): 351–67; Gordon, "Idea of Sociability," chap. 5; and Eisenstein, *Grub Street Abroad*.

50. Darnton, *Literary Underground*, p. viii.

51. Charles Augustin Sainte-Beuve, Introduction to *Letters of Mlle de Lespinasse*, trans. Katharine Prescott Wormeley (Boston, 1903), pp. 1 and 7.

52. The comte d'Haussonville published *Le Salon de Mme Necker* (Paris, 1882); the marquis de Ségur published *Le Royaume de la rue Saint-Honoré: Madame Geoffrin et sa fille* (Paris, 1897) and *Julie de Lespinasse* (Paris, 1905). In this continuing tradition, the duc de Castries has recently published *Julie de Lespinasse: Le Drame d'un double amour* (Paris, 1985) and *La Scandaleuse Madame de Tencin* (Paris, 1986).

again—
more context is necessary

According to the Goncourts, Enlightenment salons were indeed serious, but this seriousness was a sign of decadence, the first stage in the destruction of all that was beautiful and good. "Between [the] salon of the time of Louis XV and [that] of the time of Louis XVI," they wrote, "is the difference between the two reigns. The salon of the time of Louis XV seemed to open onto the present, the salon of the time of Louis XVI opens onto the future. Its walls, its architecture are saddened like the court and like society, by reform, seriousness, rigidity. . . . This is still society, but it is no longer pleasure."[53] The Goncourts were right to say that pleasure was not the aim of Enlightenment salons. Indeed, salonnières were as critical as Rousseau of those who sought merely to please. But it was not because they and their guests were planning the Revolution; rather, they were conducting the Enlightenment.

Again,
unexamined

Enlightenment salons were working spaces, unlike other eighteenth-century social gatherings, which took play as their model. Certainly wit was valued in all social gatherings of the period, but wit for wit's sake was not encouraged in the salons frequented by the philosophes. *Le jeu* in all its forms—word games, social games (*jeux de société*), and especially gambling—was virtually absent. The Enlightenment was not a game, and the salonnières were not simply ladies of leisure killing time. On the contrary, Enlightenment salonnières were precisely those women who fought the general malaise of the period by taking up their métier.[54] Like the philosophes who gathered in their homes, the salonnières were practical people who worked at tasks they considered productive and useful. They took themselves, their salons, and their guests very seriously.

The salonnières of the Enlightenment were a small number of elite women who knew and admired one another, lived lives of regularity rather than dissipation, and were committed both to their own education and to the philosophes' project of Enlightenment. During the first decades of the eighteenth century, Claudine-Alexandrine Guérin de Tencin and Anne-Thérèse de Marguenat de Courcelles, the marquise de Lambert, paved the way for the great salonnières of the high Enlightenment: Marie-Thérèse Geoffrin, whose salon flourished from about 1749, when her mentor Tencin died, until her own fatal illness began in 1776; Julie de Lespinasse, who broke out on her own from the

53. Edmond and Jules de Goncourt, *La Femme au dix-huitième siècle* (Paris, 1982), p. 77.
54. See Elisabeth Badinter, *Emilie, Emilie, ou L'Ambition féminine au XVIIIème siècle* (Paris, 1983), pp. 34–35. Nina Rattner Gelbart argues that this same energy was channeled into journalism by the female editors of and subscribers and contributors to the *Journal des Dames*. See *Feminine and Opposition Journalism in Old Regime France: "Le Journal des Dames"* (Berkeley, 1987), pp. 91 and 134.

salon of her mentor, Marie Du Deffand, in 1764 and received regularly from 1765 until her death, also in 1776; and Suzanne Necker, who formed her salon at about the same time as Lespinasse and continued at least until her husband's fall from power in 1781.

There were other women whose names should be mentioned as well: Anne-Catherine Helvétius, who led a salon with her philosophe husband until his death in 1771 and then continued it afterward on her own; Elisabeth-Josèphe de La Borde, baronne de Marchais, whose salon gave the physiocrats a home; Du Deffand, who first brought Lespinasse to Paris to assist her, then drove the younger woman out—and the philosophes with her. Two other women have already been mentioned through their writings: Epinay, whose home was a haven for her philosophe friends but never a salon in the formal sense; and Genlis, who was neither a salonnière nor a friend of the philosophes but a writer whose lengthy memoirs are a window on their world. By all accounts, the salons of Geoffrin, Lespinasse, and Necker formed the social base of the Enlightenment Republic of Letters. What follows is a composite portrait of the Enlightenment salonnière drawn from the words of and about these three women especially, but supplemented by glimpses of the other women I have mentioned. This composite portrait is meant to contribute to our understanding of the salonnière as a historical phenomenon while at the same time acknowledging the individuality of the women of whom it is composed.

The Enlightenment salonnières did not form salons to gain fame and power through association with brilliant and powerful men. This is the sort of explanation that assumes the centrality of men to the actions of women. It is what the men who frequented the salons sometimes liked to think and what historians of the salon have continued to write. It is embedded in all the books on the salons which are little more than collections of anecdotes and bons mots of these same brilliant and powerful men. In his praise of Geoffrin, for example, Morellet wrote that her purpose in forming a salon was to achieve celebrity by "procuring the means to serve men of letters and artists, to whom her ambition was to be useful in bringing them together with men of power and position."[55]

Certainly Geoffrin did aim to be useful, just as it is clear that she achieved celebrity by doing so; yet the noble "service ideal" so often attributed to women does not provide a satisfactory explanation of her actions. Fame and glory were virtues of the old male nobility, the by-products of more complex and individual ambitions sought by men at a

55. André Morellet [ed.], *Eloges de Madame Geoffrin, contemporaine de Madame Du Deffand* (Paris, 1812), pp. v–vi.

time when, as Elisabeth Badinter notes, ambition was a dubious virtue in a woman.[56] The salonnières were not social climbers but intelligent, self-educated, and educating women who adopted and implemented the values of the Enlightenment Republic of Letters and used them to reshape the salon to their own social, intellectual, and educational needs. The initial and primary purpose of Enlightenment salons was to satisfy the self-determined educational needs of the women who started them.

In an age when many women worked but few pursued careers, the salon was just that: a career based on a long apprenticeship and careful study, resulting in the independence of a mastership. It was a career open to talent but it also required significant capital to launch and support. Unlike the men who shaped themselves and made their mark in the world through careers, the salonnière reaped no material reward from her labor. The economics of her career consisted of pure outlay.

The women who became salonnières always apprenticed in an established salon before breaking out on their own. The primary relationship that underlay the salon as a continuing social institution was thus between female mentors and students, rather than between a single woman and a group of men. Such was the case of Marie Du Deffand, who in her youth, according to one observer, practically lived at the private court of Sceaux, dominated by the duchesse de Maine. Geoffrin frequented Tencin's salon for almost twenty years. Only at the older woman's death in 1749 did she formalize her own salon. Necker then "studied" under Geoffrin, and Lespinasse, who served as Du Deffand's companion for twelve years, also dined regularly at Geoffrin's.[57]

I can only suggest here the variety and complexity of motivations that might explain why particular women established salons in the eighteenth century. Lambert, for example, wanted to provide for herself a social space and time free from gambling, which had taken on epidemic proportions by the early years of the century. As an alternative to this form of social life, she regularly invited a wide assortment of men and women to her home, where they were enjoined to "speak to one another reasonably and even wittily, when the occasion merited."[58]

56. Badinter, *Emilie, Emilie*, pp. 7–37.

57. The best general studies of the salons are Glotz and Maire, *Salons du XVIIIème siècle*; Marie Gougy-François, *Les Grands Salons féminins* (Paris, 1965); and Roger Picard, *Les Salons littéraires et la société française, 1610–1789* (New York, 1943). For a discussion of the phenomenon of "surrogate motherhood" among salonnières, see my "Filial Rebellion in the Salon: Madame Geoffrin and Her Daughter," *French Historical Studies* 16 (Spring 1989): 27–47.

58. Suzanne Delorme, "Le Salon de la marquise de Lambert, berceau de l'*Encyclopédie*," in *L'"Encyclopédie" et le progrès des sciences et des techniques*, ed. Suzanne Delorme and René Taton (Paris, 1952), p. 20. Necker also distinguished between gambling and the

A different sort of motivation must be ascribed to Geoffrin, who was moving in the opposite direction when she attended Tencin's salon and eventually established her own. Whereas Lambert was trying to upgrade a social life characterized by dissipation, Geoffrin made a daring step for a devout young wife and mother when, at the age of eighteen, she began to frequent the afternoon gatherings at the home of her neighbor.[59] It was well known that Tencin in her youth had escaped from a convent and forced vows, then produced an illegitimate child who grew up to be d'Alembert. By the time she moved into Geoffrin's neighborhood in 1730, Tencin was considerably more sober but still must have seemed dazzling to a young woman who had been raised by her grandmother and married off at fourteen to a man five times her age. Nevertheless, the enticement of Tencin's salon for Geoffrin was not the titillation of the older woman's past but the stimulation of her present intellectual company: men such as Fontenelle, Marivaux, and Montesquieu, the most important and daring writers of their day. For Geoffrin was not only young and devout, she was also as ignorant as she was bold and curious. As she wrote later to Catherine the Great of the grandmother who had raised her, "She was so happy with her lot that she regarded knowledge as superfluous for a woman. She said: 'I've gotten along so well that I've never felt the need for it.'"[60] Following these principles, Mme Chemineau taught her granddaughter to read but not to write, trusted her to neither a convent nor a tutor, and personally gave her an education that was for the most part religious.

Two years after her grandmother's death, Geoffrin began her own course of studies with the men who gathered at the home of Tencin, a course she continued for the rest of her life. For Geoffrin, the salon was a socially acceptable substitute for the formal education denied her not just by her grandmother but more generally by a society that agreed with Mme Chemineau's position. Years later, Genlis wrote that as a child she had had the opportunity to attend her brother's Latin lessons regularly for seven months, but when he went back to school and she asked to continue the lessons herself, her mother said no.[61] Most parents saw no purpose in educating their daughters, and even when they did, there were no institutions in which to do so. The convents to which young girls were often sent performed primarily a social and moral

---

activities she encouraged. See *Nouveaux mélanges extraits des manuscrits de Mme Necker*, ed. Jacques Necker, 2 vols. (Paris, 1801), 1:281–82.

59. Ségur, *Royaume de la rue Saint-Honoré*, pp. 23–24.

60. Quoted ibid., pp. 6–7.

61. [Stéphanie Félicité Ducrest de Saint-Aubin], la comtesse de Genlis, *Mémoires inédites . . . sur le dix-huitième siècle et la Révolution française depuis 1756 jusqu'à nos jours*, 10 vols. (Paris, 1825), 1:77–78.

function and only secondarily a pedagogical one.[62] Emilie Du Châtelet's father had no recourse but to provide her with a battery of tutors in the early years of the century, and fifty years later Diderot was struggling to do the same on a much more limited budget for his daughter, Angélique.[63]

Genlis educated herself haphazardly, reading whatever books she could find, learning from anyone who would teach her. After her marriage she devoured her husband's library. "I had a great desire to educate myself," she wrote in her memoirs;

> the library at Genlis was quite considerable. The late marquis de Genlis, a very serious and pious man, had made one-half of it, and my brother-in-law had made the other, entirely composed of novels. . . . As to history, I was so ignorant that I did not know where to begin. . . . I should have started with ancient history, but lacking a guide, I gave no order to my readings which, at this beginning of a course of studies, lost me a lot of time.[64]

Genlis did not grow up to be a salonnière. The disorderliness with which she attacked the problem of her education perhaps explains why. It was a talent for and dedication to organization that made salonnières successful at what they did, and made the salon an institution of the Enlightenment. Morellet noted that the regularity of her life contributed significantly to Geoffrin's ability to attract guests.[65] Like Du Deffand and Lespinasse, she traveled rarely, in contrast to the almost frenetic movement that characterized her contemporaries, of whom Genlis was more typical. The regularity of her habits was part of a larger sense of organization that defined all aspects of Geoffrin's life and every hour of her day, from a five o'clock rising, through a morning of domestic duties, letter writing, and errands, to the afternoons she devoted twice a week to her salons.[66] Even on her trip to Warsaw in 1766 she wrote to her daughter:

> I live here as in Paris. I rise every day at five o'clock; I drink my two large glasses of hot water; I take my coffee; I write when I am alone, which is

62. Samia I. Spencer, "Women and Education," in *French Women and the Age of Enlightenment*, ed. Spencer (Bloomington, 1984), p. 86; François Furet and Jacques Ozouf, *Reading and Writing: Literacy in France from Calvin to Jules Ferry* (Cambridge, 1982), pp. 72–73; and Martine Sonnet, *L'Education des filles au temps des Lumières* (Paris, 1987).

63. On Châtelet, see Gougy-François, *Grands salons féminins*, pp. 80–81. Diderot refers to his problems in educating his daughter in *Le Neveu de Rameau*. See also Wilson, *Diderot*, p. 455.

64. Genlis, *Mémoires* 1:201–2.

65. Morellet, *Eloges de Mme Geoffrin*, pp. 56–57.

66. Ségur, *Royaume de la rue Saint-Honoré*, pp. 102–3.

rare; I do my hair in company; I dine every day with the king, *chez lui*, or with him and *les seigneurs*. I make calls after dinner; I go to the theater; I return to my place at ten o'clock; I drink my hot water, and I go to bed. And in the morning I begin all over again. I eat so little at these great dinners that I am often obliged to drink a third glass of water to appease my hunger. I owe to the severity of this diet my good health. I will be faithful to it until I die.[67]

For twelve years, Lespinasse was home every evening from five until nine o'clock to receive.[68] Necker has left evidence of her preparations for her weekly salon. The chevalier de Chastellux is said to have once leafed through a notebook in which she had written: "Preparation for today's dinner: I will speak to the Chevalier de Chastellux about [his books] *Félicité publique* and *Agathe*, to Mme d'Angiviller about love." She had also noted her intention to start a literary discussion between Jean-François Marmontel and the comte de Guibert. The comte d'Angiviller relates that one evening he and Jacques Necker were awaiting other guests for supper in Suzanne Necker's salon when the husband came across his wife's "agenda" for the day, in which she had written: "Praise M. Thomas again for his poem about Jumonville."[69] The development of such an agenda is not surprising in a woman who wrote in her journal: "One must take care of one's cleaning, one's toilette, and above all the maintenance of order in one's domestic interior before going into society; but once one is in the world, one must not think about all these little things, nor let them penetrate that which occupies one."[70] And in contrast to Geoffrin's grandmother, who believed that conversation could be a substitute for learning in a world where women could and should get along on wit rather than knowledge,[71] Necker prepared herself thoroughly for her weekly performances. "One is most ready for conversation when one has written and thought about things before going into society," she wrote in her journal.[72]

Necker's seriousness, and that of the salon whose discourse she shaped, is revealed most clearly in the concern she displayed in all things for paying attention. The word *attention* dominates the five vol-

---

67. Geoffrin to Marie-Thérèse, marquise de La Ferté-Imbault, 8 July [1766], in Geoffrin papers, Etampes family papers (private collection, Paris).

68. Picard, *Salons littéraires*, p. 263.

69. All three anecdotes are related in Glotz and Maire, *Salons du XVIIIème siècle*, pp. 300–301; the third comes from Charles Claude Flahaut, comte de La Billarderie d'Angiviller, *Mémoires: Notes sur les Mémoires de Marmontel*, ed. Louis Bobé (Copenhagen, 1933), p. 70.

70. [Suzanne Curchod] Necker, *Mélanges extraits des manuscrits de Mme Necker*, ed. Jacques Necker, 3 vols. (Paris, 1798), 1:223.

71. Ségur, *Royaume de la rue Saint-Honoré*, p.6

72. Necker, *Mélanges* 1:300.

umes of her journals published after her death by her husband. One
must pay attention, she reminded herself repeatedly, not get distracted. Her purpose in life was not to distract men from their serious
business but rather to discipline herself and her guests so that that
business might be carried out. Her concern was to concentrate her own
attention and to focus that of the philosophes (her guests); her intent
was to be a serious contributor to the social and intellectual project of
Enlightenment through the shaping of its discourse in her salon.

Here are just a few examples drawn from the many instances in
which *attention* occurs in Necker's journals:

> Attention allows one to find new ideas in the most common things: one
> cannot read aloud well without fixing one's attention; in a word, distrac-
> tion kills, negates all the intellectual faculties.

> One gets used to inattention in letting one's mind wander when one is
> alone.

> As soon as the attention of men gathered together is distracted for a
> single moment, one cannot fix it again.

> The great secret of conversation is continual attention.

> Virtue, health, talent, happiness, are the fruits of patience and atten-
> tion.[73]

Condillac had made attention central to his epistemology in his *Essai
sur l'origine des connaissances humaines* (1746). Attention, he said,
brought different ideas together, "engendering" imagination, contem-
plation, and memory. In the *Encyclopédie*, Diderot had defined *distraction* as "a libertinage of the mind" and *attention* as its opposite; Morellet
identified attention as the first principle of conversation.[74] For Necker,
it was the key to all the activities in which she engaged and to the goods
to which she aspired, from personal happiness and virtue to success as
a salonnière. The business of a salonnière, according to Necker, was to
fix the attention of her guests, to keep them from getting distracted.

Like other salonnières, however, Necker was first concerned with her
own education. It was to this end that she first applied the principle of

73. Necker, *Nouveaux mélanges* 1:49–50 and 190; *Mélanges* 3:297; *Nouveaux mélanges*
1:34 and 320.
74. Etienne Bonnot de Condillac, *Essai sur l'origine des connaissances humaines* (Paris,
1973), pp. 125–28; Diderot, "Distraction," in *Encyclopédie* 4:1061; André Morellet, "De la
conversation," in *Mélanges de littérature et de philosophie du 18e siècle*, 4 vols. (Paris, 1818),
4:82–83.

paying attention, but she was not simply trying to learn enough to keep up with the men in her salon. Rather, education was the end, and salon guests—her own and those of other women whose salons she frequented—the means to attaining it. Like other salonnières whose model she tried to follow, Necker attended salons, and later formed her own, primarily to educate herself and then to play an active role in shaping an evolving discourse and discursive space of increasing political importance.

Necker's self-education is chronicled in the journals that form a significant part of it. They are what she calls a "spectateur intérieur," a new form of journal, modeled on the *Spectator* of Joseph Addison and Richard Steele but containing the thoughts and impressions of the individual. In her journal she could study and improve herself rather than society.[75] Thus she wrote that "when one makes it a law to write down everything that one hears and all that one reads that deserves to be retained, one's attention is fixed involuntarily much more than by aimless effort."[76] Paying attention was both the means and the end of a program of self-education, a discipline that applied to life in general.[77]

For Necker, education began with reading, and with reflecting on and writing about what she had read.[78] Reading also became the basis for conversation in the salon, where she could learn from those who were gathered only by paying close attention to what they said. Necker's journals are filled with the words of her guests, since from the thoughts of others her own developed, and they too were carefully worked out and recorded.

Necker's salon was more than a self-constructed private school. In pursuing a personal goal, Necker also created a serious discursive space in which others could develop and exchange ideas, share and criticize one another's work, collaborate on the collective projects characteristic of the Enlightenment. The construction of this regular discursive space required just as much attention as did reading and writing. To lead the conversation effectively, to fix the attention of her guests, to keep them from getting distracted, the salonnière had to pay equally close attention to her own words.

Necker did not create her salon out of whole cloth. She saw the parallels between her own work as a salonnière and that of her husband as a royal adminstrator, but she found more direct models and guidance in other women, especially Geoffrin, in whose salon she "appren-

75. Necker, *Nouveaux mélanges* 1:62–70.

76. Ibid., 1:188.

77. Paying attention was also a discipline that informed Necker's education of her daughter: ibid., 2:185–86.

78. Necker, *Mélanges* 1:177–83; *Nouveaux mélanges* 2:150–58.

ticed" before forming her own.[79] Necker's "Pensées" are strewn with precepts learned from her mentor, and the *Mélanges* include a portrait of her.[80] From Geoffrin she learned that "all the evils of this world, except death, . . . come from a lack of firmness" and that "the taste for pleasure . . . puts you continually in a [state of] dependence."[81] She did not always agree with Geoffrin, however, nor did she follow her precepts blindly. She remarked, for example, "Mme Geoffrin believed that one must not prepare what one has to say in certain delicate situations; it would, she said, nullify simplicity and naturalness." But Necker countered: "This observation does not apply to all *gens d'esprit*."[82] In refusing to follow Geoffrin's precepts uncritically, Necker resembled her mentor all the more, for self-education of the sort she pursued was a critical project. Her admiration for the older woman was no more clearly expressed than when she wrote: "It is more valuable to imitate Mme Geoffrin in her conduct than in the principles of her conduct. . . . She was in the end the true *philosophe* of women."[83] Necker learned from the men and women of the salons (including her own), but that learning always developed out of the reflection in which she engaged in her journals. She was paying attention to what others said, did, and wrote, but she was also shaping what she heard, saw, and read in her own way by attentively reflecting on her observations.

The attention Necker paid to the written and the spoken word, and to books and people through them, was also the principle by which she conducted her salon and which she strove to instill in others. Thus a conversation was effective when everyone's attention was fixed; a good reading fixed the attention of the listeners. "This precept of permanent attention to a single object," she wrote, "is applicable to business, to study, and to conversation."[84]

Catherine the Great, herself an admirer and correspondent of Geoffrin, was for Necker the model woman of the century. "She never had a taste for pleasure," Necker commented, "and this characteristic was one of the causes of her greatness; it is the taste for pleasure which undermines the consideration for all women."[85] In one way or another, all the Enlightenment salonnières were trying to establish centers of gravity in a society and an age generally characterized, then and now, as frivolous and licentious.[86]

79. Necker, *Mélanges* 2:1–3; Haussonville, *Salon de Mme Necker* 1:214–15.
80. Necker, *Mélanges* 3:241–72.
81. Ibid., 2:238; Necker, *Nouveaux mélanges* 1:103.
82. Necker, *Nouveaux mélanges*, 1:314–15.
83. Ibid., 1:291–92.
84. Necker, *Mélanges* 2:147–48.
85. Ibid., 1:298.
86. Jean-François de La Harpe, for example, wrote of "la légèreté française" as the

One final need that the salon may have fulfilled for the women whose lives were shaped by it is suggested by a letter that Julie de Lespinasse wrote to Condorcet in 1773. For Lespinasse, a woman whose birth denied her a legitimate place in the order of the Old Regime, the Republic of Letters provided an alternative community founded on the mutuality of friendship. It was an imperfect refuge from a society, the violation of whose norms underlay her very existence. The salon was not a new family for a woman whose family did not want her and whose illegitimacy constrained her from starting her own family; no, the Enlightenment salon was a community of friends whose relations were as much opposed to the patriarchal relations of the family as they were to the absolutist relations of the monarchy. Thus, she wrote to her friend Condorcet:

> I, who have known only pain and suffering, I, who have been the victim of viciousness and tyranny for ten years, I, finally, who am without fortune, who have lost my health, and who have experienced only atrocities from people from whom I should have been able to expect comfort, and who, by means of a singularity unheard of, have had a childhood agitated by the very care that was taken to exercise and exalt my sensibility, I knew terror, fright, before having been able to think and judge. Consider, my good Condorcet, if I am justified in my small degree of attachment for life and if my disgust for all that men hold dear, the pleasures of dissipation and of vanity, cannot be justified. I know only one pleasure, I have but one interest, that of friendship; that supports me and consoles me; but more often I am torn apart. There, for speaking to you a lot about myself, I would ask your pardon, if it were not to prove to you my friendship.[87]

The Republic of Letters, unlike the monarchy, the family, and *le monde*, was based on friendship, marked by its epistolary relations and its values of reciprocity and exchange. By establishing a salon in and for the Enlightenment Republic of Letters, Lespinasse created a space not only for philosophes but also for herself in the world of friendship which had traditionally been thought to be the preserve of men. Like Geoffrin and Necker, she found in the Enlightenment Republic of

---

major threat to the success of the Lycée de Paris, when it opened in 1784: La Harpe, *Correspondance littéraire*, 5 vols. (Paris, 1801–1807), 5:102. But this was a commonplace of the age.

87. Lespinasse to Condorcet, 19 October 1773, in [Jeanne-Julie-Eléanore de] Lespinasse, *Lettres inédites de Mademoiselle de Lespinasse*, ed. Charles Henry (Paris, 1887). On the way in which the family and the state reinforced each other in early modern France, see Sarah Hanley, "Engendering the State: Family Formation and State Building in Early Modern France," *French Historical Studies* 16 (Spring 1989): 4–27.

Letters a sort of relationship with men and women which was both an alternative to the romantic love and patriarchy of the dominant social and political orders and a challenge to traditional assumptions about women.[88]

The conventional image of the salon as a frivolous place in which earnest philosophes were distracted from their work by foolish but seductive women can no longer be sustained. This reevaluation of the salon, moreover, is supported by recent interpretations of the rococo, the style in architecture and the fine and decorative arts which characterized the Age of Enlightenment. Like the salon, the rococo has generally been viewed as light and frivolous, as merely decorative—as feminine.[89] Architecturally, the *salon* and *salle de compagnie*—and the dining room, where most salon conversation took place over lengthy dinners—were novelties in the new style of private residence favored by the Parisian elite in the eighteenth century: the rococo *hôtel* (Figure 2). As a reaction against Versailles, the hôtels were self-consciously private buildings, but as Michael Dennis points out, they were not designed simply for "private events contained behind a facade, as in medieval or early Renaissance houses." Characterized spatially by a new articulation of public and private areas, the rococo hôtel was both public and private, in the manner of the Republic of Letters.[90] The discursive space of the salon was located within the public architectural space of these new private homes. It was because the salon was located within private homes that salonnières could figure in the public discourse articulated within them.[91]

88. The belief in women's incapacity for friendship goes back at least to Cicero; its most important articulation in French was by Michel de Montaigne in "De l'amitié," in *Essais*, ed. Maurice Rat, 2 vols. (Paris, 1962), 1:197–212. In an unpublished manuscript, Paula Radisich notes that Geoffrin always referred to the artists she patronized and who attended her salon as her friends. Necker formed close friendships especially with Buffon and Thomas; Epinay's friendship with Galiani, maintained in their regular correspondence after his departure from Paris in 1769 until her death in 1783, is the subject of a book by Francis Steegmuller, *A Woman, a Man, and Two Kingdoms: The Story of Madame d'Epinay and the Abbé Galiani* (New York, 1991); the word *amitié* is a recurring theme in the correspondence of Amélie Suard and Condorcet. See *Correspondance inédite de Condorcet et Madame Suard, 1771–1791*, ed. Elisabeth Badinter (Paris, 1988). Through letters, the salonnières also maintained their friendships with other women; for example, Geoffrin and Catherine wrote to each other, as did Necker and Geoffrin. The attendance of the salonnières at one another's salons was also a sign of their friendships, although patronage was a dimension of both salon attendance and letter writing.

89. Mary D. Sheriff, *Fragonard: Art and Eroticism* (Chicago, 1990), pp. 1–29.

90. Michael Dennis, *Court and Garden: From the French Hôtel to the City of Modern Architecture* (Cambridge, Mass., 1986), pp. 91–117.

91. Goodman, "Public Sphere and Private Life," p. 18.

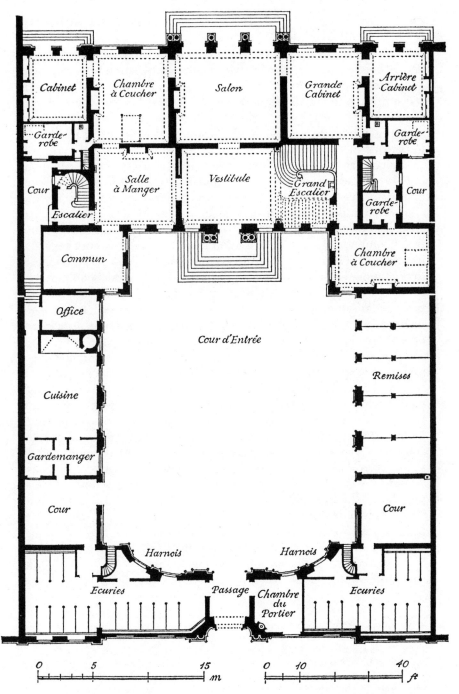

Cabinet

Chambre
à Coucher

Salon

Grande
Cabinet

Arrière
Cabinet

Garde-
robe

Garde-
robe

Cour

Salle
à Manger

Vestibule

Grand
Escalier

Garde-
robe

Cour

Escalier

Commun

Chambre
à Coucher

Office

Cour d'Entrée

Remises

Cuisine

Gardemanger

Cour

Cour

Harnois

Harnois

Ecuries

Passage

Chambre
du
Portier

Ecuries

0   5   15
                                m

0   10   40
                              ft

Figure 2. Plan of the ground floor of the Hôtel Desmarets, Paris (1704), by Lassurance.
Reproduced courtesy of Yale University Press from Wend Graf Kalnein and Michael Levey,
eds., *Art and Architecture of the Eighteenth Century in France* (1972) in the Pelican History
of Art.

The architectural space of the Enlightenment salon was designed and decorated in the rococo style. Paintings by contemporary artists alternated with mirrors that expanded the salon beyond the limits of its walls through the play of light that figured the discourse within them.[92] Geoffrin was the most prominent collector of contemporary French painting of her age, and she held a Monday salon for artists in addition to the one on Wednesdays for men of letters.[93]

Michael Fried has shown that from at least midcentury, French painting was just as serious as I have argued salons and salonnières were. The principle of paying attention which pervades Necker's writings and which underlay her life may be seen as identical to the principle of absorption which Fried finds in painting from 1750 on.[94] Absorption, Fried contends, developed as a good in and of itself, without regard to its occasion. The absorption of the painter in his work was transferred to the painted subject and, through the painting, to the beholder. This transfer of the principle of absorption is parallel to the transfer of the principle of attention to the guest in the work of the salonnière. The painter, like the salonnière, transferred his own guiding principle to others through the principled creation of a shared space.

Of the many examples Fried gives of absorption, one stands out as the perfect illustration of the identity between the principle of attention, which made salons serious places, and that of absorption, which made eighteenth-century painting equally serious: a pair of paintings by Carle Van Loo, commissioned by Geoffrin to hang in her salon. *La Lecture espagnole* and *La Conversation espagnole* (Figures 3 and 4), painted about 1754, took as their subjects the two activities that dominated the salon: conversation and reading aloud. These paintings, Fried says, "exemplify Van Loo's ability to infuse the *sujets galants* that remained popular in the *Encyclopédiste* society in which he moved with a seriousness of purpose appropriate to that society." Even more telling is the passage Fried quotes from a contemporary review in the *Journal Encyclopédique* on the occasion of the exhibition of *La Lecture espagnole* in the Salon of 1761. In it the author comments on the "keen attention" with which the young people listen to the reading and the different sort of

92. Annik Pardailhé-Galabrun, *The Birth of Intimacy: Privacy and Domestic Life in Early Modern Paris*, trans. Jocelyn Phelps (Cambridge, 1991), pp. 164–67.

93. Paula Radisich, unpublished ms., p. 7. Geoffrin's husband was the director of and major shareholder in the royal mirror works at Saint-Gobain, which, along with his wife's dowry, was the source of his wealth. Mirrors were thus at the material base of Geoffrin's salon. After her husband's death in 1749, Geoffrin sat on the board of the mirror works and played an active role in its management, including attendance at weekly board meetings: ibid., p. 59 n. 58.

94. Fried, *Absorption and Theatricality*, pp. 7–70.

Figure 3. La Lecture espagnole, engraved by Jacques Firmin Beauvarlet after the painting by Carle Van Loo (c. 1754). Courtesy of Bibliothèque Nationale, Paris, Cabinet des Estampes.

Figure 4. La Conversation espagnole, engraved by Beauvarlet after the painting by Van Loo (c. 1754). Courtesy of Bibliothèque Nationale, Paris, Cabinet des Estampes.

"attention" paid to the reading by the mother or governess who is keeping an eye on her charges.[95] What Fried calls absorption is clearly the principle of attention that guided Necker. This painting and its pendant can thus be seen as representations of the guiding principle of the Enlightenment salon and its characteristic activities. They stand in sharp contrast to de Troy's *Lecture de Molière*, as it is interpreted by Chartier.

The connection between the Van Loo paintings and the salon does not end with Geoffrin's commission of them. In 1772 Geoffrin sold the paintings to Catherine the Great; the profit she realized from the sale went to furnish the new lodgings of Julie de Lespinasse and to provide her with an annuity. The Van Loos then reappeared in the form of engravings adorning the walls of Lespinasse's salon. By hanging the engravings on the walls of her own salon, Lespinasse not only acknowledged the generosity of her friend, mentor, and patron but placed herself and her guests under the sign of seriousness established by Geoffrin.[96]

Each for her own reasons, Geoffrin, Lespinasse, and Necker gathered around them people eager to socialize in a serious fashion, and they established regular, structured occasions for doing so. It was the seriousness and regularity of these salons, not their lightness, that distinguished them from those of the seventeenth century and from other social gatherings of their own time. After he left Paris, Galiani thought often about the difference between these salons and the gatherings available to him in Naples. In 1771 he wrote to Epinay, thanking her for a manuscript she had sent him and noting that he would present it on one of the "Fridays" when he met with friends who were trying to recreate their Parisian experience. "But our Fridays are becoming Neopolitan Fridays," he wrote, "and are getting farther away from the character and tone of those of France, despite all [our] efforts. . . . There is no way to make Naples resemble Paris unless we find a woman to guide us, organize us, *Geoffrinise* us."[97]

95. Ibid., pp. 25, 27.
96. See *Correspondance Littéraire*, 15 December 1772. This is one of the many legendary stories of Geoffrin's generosity. Paula Radisich suggests that gift giving was part of the "potlatch" continuum of Geoffrin's style of art patronage. The circle of friendship that began with the commission was completed only with the gift to Lespinasse. (Radisich, unpublished ms.) Lespinasse's salon (that is, the room) is described in the inventory made upon her death, quoted in Glotz and Maire, *Salons du XVIIIème siècle*, p. 225.
97. Galiani to Epinay, 13 April 1771, in Ferdinando Galiani, *Correspondance*, ed. Lucien Perey and Gaston Maugras, 2 vols. (Paris, 1890).

CHAPTER 3

Governing the Republic of Letters: Salonnières and the Rule(s) of Polite Conversation

> Ce n'est qu'en se poliçant que les hommes ont ap-
> pris à concilier leur intérêt particulier avec l'intérêt
> commun; qu'ils ont compris que, par cet accord,
> chacun tire plus de la société qu'il n'y peut mettre.
>
> —CHARLES DUCLOS

> Le gouvernement d'une conversation ressemble
> beaucoup à celui d'un Etat; il faut qu'on se doute à
> peine de l'influence qui la conduit.
>
> —SUZANNE NECKER

When the anonymous author wrote to the *Bibliothèque Raison-née* proposing a bureau général for the Republic of Letters in 1747, he was responding to a perceived anarchy in the republic, the result of its growth and its lack of government. Although the Republic of Letters was, in theory, structured by the principles of reciprocal exchange embedded in its epistolary relations, the reality fell far short of this ideal. French men of letters in particular increasingly found themselves engaged in divisive *querelles* rather than constructive debate. As Paris became established as the capital of the republic and French men of letters were drawn together there, they began to meet and to collaborate directly. Their traditional epistolary relations were now enriched by direct verbal ones, but they lost the mediating force provided by the formality of letters. In the Parisian salon they found a new kind of governance for an Enlightenment Republic of letters.

Geoffrin, who acted as mentor and model for other salonnières, was responsible for two innovations that set Enlightenment salons apart from their predecessors and from other social and literary gatherings of the day. She invented the Enlightenment salon. First, she made the one-o'clock dinner rather than the traditional late-night supper the sociable meal of the day, and thus she opened up the whole afternoon for talk. Second, she regularized these dinners, fixing a specific day of the week for them (Monday for artists, Wednesday for men of letters). After Geoffrin launched her weekly dinners, the Parisian salon took on the form that made it the social base of the Enlightenment Republic of Letters: a regular and regulated formal gathering hosted by a woman in her own home which served as a forum and locus of intellectual activity. In the Enlightenment salon, conversation was the primary mode of discourse, but it supported written production of all sorts— from informal letters to the most formal poetry—by circulating it, disseminating it, and reading it. Most salons met weekly and took the form of a dinner that would last all afternoon, but discourse, not dining, was their defining function.

The philosophes adopted the salons as a center for their Republic of Letters and respected the women who led them as governors because they provided the republic with a basis of order. That order could be established only through voluntary submission to the rules of polite discourse and the female governors who enforced them. For much as they groaned about the constraints placed upon them by the salonnières, the men of the Enlightenment sought out and continued to frequent salons to serve their own needs, just as salonnières had formed them to serve theirs. In this chapter, I would like to explain how and why three women who led salons between 1749 and 1776— Geoffrin, Lespinasse, and Necker—shaped the discursive project that was the French Enlightenment through the application of a distinctively republican form of government.

The function of salonnières was to maintain order in the Republic of Letters by enforcing the rules of polite conversation. The rules, and thus the governors, were necessary because eighteenth-century French intellectual practice was both militant and personal. Traditional French scholarly and social behavior and attitudes ran head on into the collective and critical ideals and practices of the cosmopolitan Republic of Letters, generating a social and intellectual crisis and creating a need for governance.

Cultural Practices of the Old Regime

Formal education in the West has always been fundamentally agonistic. From the Greeks through the eighteenth century, education was rooted in oral culture. "What was taught in the formal educational operation," writes Walter Ong, "was to take a stand in favor of a thesis or to attack a thesis that someone else defended." Students "learned subjects largely by fighting over them."[1] The primary form the *agon* took in the education of boys and young men from the Middle Ages on was disputation, a form of ceremonial combat. One contends that male insecurity, although it may not have been the "cause" of the agonistic structure of pedagogical and scholarly practice, was certainly fundamentally related to it.[2]

Since the days of Peter Abelard in the twelfth century, French schools and scholars had been steeped in the language of battle. "I was so carried away by my love of learning," Abelard wrote in his *Historia Calamitatum*, "that I renounced the glory of a soldier's life, made over my inheritance and rights of the eldest son to my brothers, and withdrew from the court of Mars in order to kneel at the feet of Minerva. I preferred the weapons of dialectic to all the other teachings of philosophy, and armed with these I chose the conflicts of disputation instead of the trophies of war."[3] Right up to the end of the Old Regime, the centerpiece of French secondary education was mastery of Aristotelian dialectic through a lengthy training in disputation.[4] Despite the focus on texts and exigesis, on the written word, pedagogy was still overwhelmingly oral. Listening and memorizing were the modes of learning; examinations were always oral and generally disputatious in form.[5]

In the sixteenth century, a reform in the Parisian *collèges* (secondary schools) instituted the *modus parisiensis*, which would become the basis of Jesuit education in the seventeenth and eighteenth centuries. Under their new, broader curriculum, the humanist collèges educated their students in the classics as well as Christian doctrine. They added rheto-

1. Walter J. Ong, *Fighting for Life: Contest, Sexuality, and Consciousness* (Ithaca, 1981), pp. 122–23.

2. Ibid., p. 144. That insecurity need not be construed as fundamentally psychological. In 1672 Thomas Hobbes constructed his life as a writer as a state of war within the social and political state of war of his times. "Everybody was given licence to write what he wished provided he remained within the law of the land," he wrote. "I availed myself of the permitted freedom and wrote my *De Corpore*, which turned out to be a cause of perpetual war against me. *Leviathan* had turned the whole clergy against me. Both nests of theologians were my foes": "The Autobiography of Thomas Hobbes," trans. Benjamin Farrington, *Rationalist Annual*, 1958, p. 28. The translator notes, however, that the "Autobiography," written in Latin verse, was addressed to a friend, and we can thus see it as within the epistolary discourse of friendship of the Republic of Letters (p. 22). I am grateful to Christine Di Stefano for this reference.

3. Peter Abelard, *Historia Calamitatum*, in *The Letters of Abelard and Heloise*, trans. Betty Radice (Harmondsworth, 1974), p. 58.

4. Marie-Madeleine Compère, *Du collège au lycée (1500–1850): Généalogie de l'enseignement secondaire français* (Paris, 1985), p. 26.

5. Ong, *Fighting for Life*, p. 126.

ric, complementing the traditional memory-based training in dialectic with a new discipline that would develop the student's creative potential: eloquence, the art of thinking and speaking well. The graduate of a Parisian collège would be the master of discourse.[6]

Under the leadership of the Paris-trained Ignatius Loyola, the Jesuits brought a renewed militancy to the field of education. One of the underlying principles of the Jesuit *ratio studiorum* was the idea that competition among students would foster individual ambition.[7] "In order to train pupils in intensive formal work which was, however, pretty lacking in substance," explains Emile Durkheim, "it was also necessary to stimulate them. The goad which the Jesuits employed consisted exclusively in competition."[8] Indeed, as Durkheim describes it, the experience of a student at a Jesuit collège was not simply an education but a competitive struggle at every level from the group to the individual. Each class was divided into two camps, Romans and Carthaginians, and each camp was divided into groups of ten students ranked according to their academic merits and led by a captain. Romans and Carthaginians lived "on the brink of war," Durkheim explains, "each striving to outstrip the other."

> Just as the camp as a whole was in competition with the opposite camp, so in each camp each group had its own immediate rival in the other camp at the equivalent level. Finally, individuals themselves were matched, and each soldier in a group had his opposite number in the opposing group. Thus academic work involved a kind of perpetual hand-to-hand combat. . . . It was even possible for any individual to do battle with a pupil from a higher group and, if victorious, to take his place.[9]

The university and the old collèges that replaced the medieval schools had eliminated institutionalized rivalry, preferring, like Thomistic philosophy itself, to reconcile competing visions rather than to pit them against one another. The Jesuits restored competition, recognizing how productive its underlying passions could be, and they succeeded so well that their own competitors found themselves forced to imitate them.

The competitive system devised by the Jesuits characterized the edu-

6. Compère, *Du collège au lycée*, p. 78; François Lebrun, Marc Venard, and Jean Quéniart, eds., *Histoire générale de l'enseignement et de l'éducation en France*, vol. 2: *De Gutenberg aux Lumières (1480–1789)* (Paris, 1981), pp. 321–22.

7. Gay, *Enlightenment* 2:504.

8. Emile Durkheim, *The Evolution of Educational Thought: Lectures on the Formation and Development of Secondary Education in France*, trans. Peter Collins (London, 1977), p. 260.

9. Ibid.

cation of boys in France from collège to university. "I spent about five years at the Sorbonne," wrote the Jesuit-trained Morellet in his memoirs, "forever reading, forever disputing, forever poor, and forever happy."[10] On a rather different note, Durkheim concludes that "the *ancien régime* up to the second half of the eighteenth century . . . really knew only one intellectual ideal, and it was on the basis of this ideal that French youth was moulded for more than two hundred years."[11]

In Walter Ong's view the *agonia* central to education for two hundred years has structured consciousness itself, at least as it has developed through masculine intellectual history. "There is structure in academia deeper than in the Balinese cockfights reported on by Clifford Geertz," he writes. "*Ludus*, the Latin word for school, . . . means also war games." The ludic dimension of schoolwork is pursued not for amusement but as training; students are "playing at" a game in order to learn how to do.[12]

French scholars, steeped in the traditional militancy of learning, were also shaped by the personal character of human relations in the Old Regime. Human relations in the Old Regime were personal relations, and attacks were personal attacks. Disinterestedness was difficult to achieve in a society in which each person was defined by his or her membership in a group, from the family to privileged corps. The social practice that best illustrates the merger of personal human relations with militancy is the duel. Like scholarly disputation, dueling was a form of ceremonial combat that functioned, at least in part, to contain more violent confrontation.[13] Duels were fought to defend honor and reputation, thus as a response to personal attacks. Furthermore, dueling was a privilege of the nobility. Finally, the "dueling mania" that reached its peak in the seventeenth century was rooted in the social chaos called the "confusion of ranks." The duel thus combined the militancy of war with the ethos of personal honor, within a framework of hierarchy and privilege which was threatened with social chaos.[14]

In the early seventeenth century, Richelieu called dueling a plague that all the royal edicts thus far issued had been unable to stop.[15] Even

10. André Morellet, *Mémoires sur le dix-huitième siècle et sur la Révolution* (Paris, 1988), p. 52. Further references to Morellet's memoirs will be to this edition.

11. Durkheim, *Evolution of Educational Thought*, pp. 266–67.

12. Ong, *Fighting for Life*, pp. 140 and 132–33.

13. Ibid., pp. 142–43.

14. Robert A. Schneider, "Swordplay and Statemaking: Aspects of the Campaign against the Duel in Early Modern France," in Charles Bright and Susan Harding, eds., *Statemaking and Social Movements: Essays in History and Theory* (Ann Arbor, 1984), pp. 267–73.

15. [Armand Jean du Plessis, duc de] Richelieu, *The Political Testament of Cardinal Richelieu*, trans. Henry Bertram Hill (Madison, 1961), p. 22.

Louis XIV could not stop the practice, although Voltaire later praised him rather optimistically for having done so.[16] Despite its provision of the death penalty, his 1679 edict proved ineffectual. Louis XV renewed the edict in 1725, but he was equally frustrated. In the *Lettres persanes*, published in 1721, Montesquieu's Usbek observed that the royal edicts only put Frenchmen in a terrible bind: the "laws of honor oblige an *honnête homme* to avenge himself when he is offended; but, on the other hand, justice punishes him most cruelly when he does avenge himself."[17] As late as 1782 we find Danceny, at the end of Choderlos de Laclos's *Liaisons dangereuses*, defending Cécile's honor by challenging Valmont to a duel, and Valmont, to defend his own, forced to accept the challenge.

In the *Lettres persanes*, the behavior of men of letters was described as parallel to that of the nobility. This is not surprising, for men of letters had been learning to behave "nobly" in aristocratic salons throughout the reign of Louis XIV.[18] Usbek's discussion of the *querelle* between the ancients and the moderns, which was preoccupying literary Paris during his fictional visit in 1713, placed disputes in the Republic of Letters within the personal discourse of reputation which characterized the nobility's social relations. In this regard, the French *République des Lettres* was simply continuing the discursive practices of the Latin *Respublica literaria*, for Usbek hastened to point out that those who disputed in Latin were even worse than the worldly men of letters who championed the moderns and the use of French as the language of their republic. The use of this "barbarous tongue," he noted, "seem[ed] to add something to the fury and obstinacy of the combatants."[19]

When d'Alembert wrote a critique of French education in his article "Collège" in the *Encyclopédie*, some thirty years later, he prefaced his remarks in such a way as to highlight this problem:

> It is not against men that I am making war, but against abuses, abuses that shock and afflict the majority of those like myself who contribute to their maintenance because they are afraid to stand up against the torrent. The subject about which I am going to speak concerns the government and religion and well deserves to be spoken of freely, which ought not to offend anyone: with this precaution, I will open the subject.[20]

16. Voltaire, *Siècle de Louis XIV*, in *Oeuvres complètes* 14:507.

17. Montesquieu, *Lettres persanes*, letter xc. Almost a hundred years later, Genlis made the same point in the article "Duel," in her *Dictionnaire critique*. Dueling was uncivilized, but loss of honor, not of life, was the only threat that could discourage men from engaging in it.

18. Lougee, "*Paradis des Femmes*," chap. 3.

19. Montesquieu, *Lettres persanes*, letter xxxvi.

20. *Encyclopédie* 3:635.

D'Alembert was making war, but not against persons, and thus offense ought not to be taken. Because education was a public concern—a matter of government and religion—it needed to be spoken of freely, that is, made the object of criticism. The subject of education thus needed to be distinguished from the persons of those who educate (teachers), the criticism of one not implying a personal attack on the other. The criticism of objects had to be distinguished from the insult to persons. Or as Jean Formey put it in the article "Dispute" in the *Encyclopédie*, the trick was to "beat our adversary, without wounding him."[21]

Although the distinction between personal insult and the criticism of ideas may not have been new, the need to disentangle them in practice took on a new urgency in the Enlightenment Republic of Letters. First, the intellectual training of men of letters was combative and their social behavior was personal. In addition, their epistemology and their ideals told them both that they should be critical and that they needed to work together if they were to advance knowledge and the good of humanity. Finally, the *Encyclopédie* had given them a new sense of collective identity. Now, brought together in Paris, they saw the possibility of working closely together in a variety of new projects. The problem facing the philosophes was deceptively simple: how were they to continue to debate and disagree in person and still remain collaborators and friends?

Until the mid–eighteenth century, this problem had been minimized because relations among the citizens of the Republic of Letters were primarily epistolary. The emphasis on reciprocal service and friendship expressed and embodied in epistolary exchanges was a constant theme throughout the history of the Republic of Letters. Correspondence made collaboration across Europe, and even across the Atlantic, possible and bound the citizens of the republic into a cooperative network of intellectual exchange. Through correspondence, men of letters overcame distances that would otherwise have kept them from fruitful discussion and access to scholarly resources. But distance and the formality of the epistolary means used to overcome it also supported friendship by minimizing direct confrontation while allowing for debate. Oral exchanges, by contrast, were more spontaneous, inherently

---

21. *Encyclopédie* 4:1044. Formey was a French Huguenot scholar whose parents had fled France in the wake of Louis XIV's revocation of the Edict of Nantes. He had good reason to take a critical (Baylean) perspective on disputes, theological and otherwise. Here he sounds strikingly like another political exile to Holland in the 1680s, John Locke, who defined "civility" as "in truth, nothing but a care not to shew any slighting, or contempt, of any one in Conversation": *Some Thoughts concerning Education*, ed. John W. Yolton and Jean S. Yolton (Oxford, 1989), p. 203.

less subject to the control of the speaker than written ones were of the writer. Epistolary relations, based as they are in written, formalized, and therefore highly controlled discourse, could significantly transcend the difficulties of personal interaction in a society where direct verbal acts were always potential challenges.

Correspondence was also a means of counteracting the potential for animosity and strife that arose from cutting across the hierarchical categories of the Old Regime. With their vast correspondences, seventeenth-century men of letters tried to transcend these categories rather than break them down. In Paris the philosophes sought to enrich epistolary relations with personal ones, letters with conversation, and the reciprocal and collaborative ideals that had always characterized the Republic of Letters were put to the test.

Whenever people of different ranks and orders of society mixed and tried to interact on an equal footing—as they had done even in the aristocratic salons of the seventeenth century—the possibility of misunderstanding increased. The risk of insult was particularly great in the Republic of Letters, where the citizenry was drawn from all the orders of French society and yet social distinctions were not recognized.[22] Formal rules of speech and behavior were counted on to minimize the potential for such misunderstandings. If men of letters learned to defend their honor in aristocratic salons in the seventeenth century, they also learned there that formalized, rule-bound discourse was the best way to overcome the problems that social mixing entailed. As Carolyn Lougee points out, the major function of these early salons and the women who led them was to socialize those who wanted to enter—or at least deal with—the nobility.[23] Conversation was meant to replicate the formality of correspondence in order to limit conflict and misunderstanding between people of different social ranks and orders.

An example of the negative consequences of such social mixing when not properly controlled is the well-known story of Voltaire's flight to England in 1726. Because the chevalier de Rohan had publicly "insulted" him, Voltaire challenged the young nobleman to a duel, and Rohan, refusing to lower himself by responding to the challenge, sent

22. Equality in the Republic of Letters had an intellectual basis, as Duclos asserted in *Considérations sur les moeurs*: "It has been said that gambling and love render all conditions equal: I am persuaded that the mind should have been added. . . . Gambling levels by lowering the superior; love, by raising the inferior; and the mind, because true equality comes from that of souls" (p. 138). Evidence of the denial of marks of social distinction in the Enlightenment Republic of Letters is found both in the *Encyclopédie*, where contributors were identified without such marks; and in the Academy. See Duclos to comte de Clermont, 1753, in *Correspondance de Charles Duclos (1704–1772)*, ed. Jacques Brengues (Saint-Brieuc, 1970), letter 33.

23. Lougee, "*Paradis des Femmes*," pp. 41–55.

his servants to beat Voltaire up. To avoid being thrown into the Bastille and with the connivance of the French government, Voltaire fled to England. The conflict arose because within Old Regime social categories a person of Voltaire's status could not be insulted by a member of the nobility. Nor could Rohan accept Voltaire's challenge, which was itself an insult—if not a threat—since it denied these social categories. Peter Gay presents the conflict from Voltaire's point of view. "At thirty," he writes, "Voltaire was the successor of Virgil as well as Racine—truly an eminent citizen in the Republic of Letters." And yet, "all his friendships with the great, all his brilliant successes, had availed nothing before the insults of the cowardly and brutal nonentity, Rohan, whose sole merit was to have a cardinal for a cousin."[24] An eminent citizen of the Republic of Letters ought to be equal to, if not better than, even the highest-ranking subject of the French monarchy, but French society and the Republic of Letters operated with different sets of social categories.[25] Voltaire's status in the Republic of Letters could not be directly translated into status in French society, nor could the chevalier be ranked by the Republic of Letters. Rohan and Voltaire came into conflict because each acted according to his proper status in a society whose categories the other did not acknowledge.

Charles Duclos, who bridged the generation of Voltaire and that of Diderot and d'Alembert—he was born in 1704 and preceded d'Alembert as perpetual secretary of the French Academy in 1755—tried to build a bridge between le monde and the Republic of Letters as well. In his Considérations sur les moeurs de ce siècle, published in 1750, he indicated why men of letters found it difficult to converse with others: "If a man gives us to understand that he is intelligent, and that moreover he has reason to think so, it is as if he were warning us that we ought not to impose on him by means of false virtues, or to hide any of our faults from him, and that he will view us as we are, and will judge us with justice. Such an announcement already resembles an act of hostility."[26] Men of letters came into conflict—with each other and with le monde — because they based status on intelligence and discourse on truth telling. Identifying oneself as a man of letters was thus a challenge to a social order maintained by politeness and deference, whose principles the Republic of Letters opposed.

Upon entering the Republic of Letters, the philosophes did not leave Old Regime France. Even on their own ground, they still found them-

24. Gay, Voltaire's Politics, p. 39.

25. For the social categories that organized the Republic of Letters, see Duclos, Considérations sur les moeurs, pp. 136–37; and Jean-François Marmontel, Mémoires, ed. John Renwick, 2 vols. (Clermont-Ferrand, 1972), 1:158.

26. Duclos, Considérations sur les moeurs, p. 142.

selves acting and speaking like Old Regime Frenchmen. After all, it was not for insulting someone but for responding to a perceived insult that Voltaire got into trouble. Even leaving aside the risk that men of letters might insult someone outside the republic in criticizing a belief or practice, it was even more disturbing that they risked insulting one another. How could they be properly critical and collaborate on the project of Enlightenment without stepping on one another's toes? Or as the author of one of the many letter-pamphlets generated by the Hume-Rousseau affair put it, "The opinions of men, about which they quarrel most, concern each other least. Every man has, and ever will have, his own; and if difference of opinion is a sufficient cause of quarrelling, no two speculating men can come to an *éclaircissement*, and continue friends."[27] Perhaps Diderot had been right to say that an encyclopedia was best written by coordination of written contributions through a central bureau, rather than in *séances encyclopédiques*.[28]

But the *Encyclopédie* went underground in 1759, not ten years after the first volume appeared. It could not serve as the meeting ground of the Republic of Letters as its editors had hoped it would. And in any case, the project of Enlightenment was bigger than the writing of an encyclopedia. Eighteenth-century men of letters needed to establish their republic on a broader and more stable base. The Parisian salon, in which seventeenth-century men of letters had learned to participate in a discourse that cut across social lines, became for the philosophes the central institution of their republic.

Republican Governance in the Salons

The salon gave the Republic of Letters a social base, but even more important, it provided the republic with a source of political order in the person of the salonnière. She gave order both to social relations among salon guests and to the discourse in which they engaged. The salonnière had always been crucial to the functioning of the salon; now she became crucial to the project of Enlightenment carried out in and through it.

From 1765 until 1776, men of letters and those who wanted to be counted among the citizens of their republic could meet in Parisian salons every day of the week. Some, such as Marmontel and Morellet, went every day. Not coincidentally, these years correspond to the height

27. [Ralph Heathcote], *A Letter to the Honorable Mr. Horace Walpole, concerning the Dispute between Mr. Hume and Mr. Rousseau* (London, 1767), p. 23.

28. *Encyclopédie* 5:636.

of the Enlightenment, when the philosophes were both highly productive and highly visible. It was also during this decade that they came closest to their goal of establishing themselves as the arbiters of public opinion and captured significant positions in both the royal administration and the royal academies.[29]

By 1777, however, Jacques-Henri Meister, now the editor of the *Correspondance Littéraire*, was forced to describe the sorry state of the Republic of Letters after it had lost two of its leading salonnières: "The disorder and anarchy that have reigned in this party since the death of Mlle de Lespinasse and the paralysis of Mme Geoffrin prove how much the wisdom of their government had averted evils, how much it had dissipated storms, and above all how much it had rescued it from ridicule."[30] Meister was not alone in using political language to describe the work of the salonnière. Suzanne Necker, whose husband rose to be finance minister under Louis XVI, saw the parallel between her own work and his: "The government of a conversation very much resembles that of a State," she wrote; "one can scarcely doubt its influence."[31] A community in discourse and of discourse, the Republic of Letters was governed through the government of conversation, and the salonnières were its governors.

The eulogies of Geoffrin and Lespinasse stressed their ability to govern conversation by harmonizing both discordant voices and unruly egos. Of Lespinasse, Marmontel wrote:

> She found [her guests] here and there in the world, but [they] were so well matched that, when they were [with her], they found themselves in harmony like the strings of an instrument played by an able hand. Following this comparison, I could say that she played this instrument with an art that resembled genius; she seemed to know which sound the string she had touched would make; I would say that she knew our minds and our characters so well that, to put them in play, she had only to say a word.[32]

Of salons in general and Geoffrin in particular, Thomas wrote:

> These sorts of societies that, in order to survive, cannot be too constrained, but that, with the liberty of democracies, are sometimes beset

---

29. Baker, *Condorcet*, pp. 23 and 40.

30. *Correspondance Littéraire*, July 1777. Meister wrote in the midst of the *querelle* between the Gluckistes and Piccinistes which split the philosophes in 1774 and continued into the next decade. "Never, under their respectable administration," he continues, referring to Geoffrin and Lespinasse, "would we have seen all the scenes which the musical war has brought about; never."

31. Necker, *Mélanges* 2:1.

32. Marmontel, *Mémoires* 1:220.

with agitations and movement, require a certain power to temper them. It seems that this power is no better held than in the hands of a woman. She has a natural right that no one disputes and that, in order to be felt, has only to be shown. Madame Geoffrin used this advantage. [In her salon], the reunion of all ranks, like that of all types of minds, prevented any one tone from dominating.[33]

Finally, Suzanne Necker wrote to Grimm in 1777:

Mlle de l'Espinasse is no more; the movement that she gave to her society has slowed down greatly. M. d'Alembert, who was its soul, is having trouble becoming its motor [organe]: he brings his friends together three days a week; but everyone in these assemblies is [now] convinced that women fill the intervals of conversation and of life, like the padding that one inserts in cases of china; they are valued at nothing, and [yet] everything breaks without them.[34]

Philosophes and salonnières agreed that the salonnière achieved success by balancing and blending voices into a harmonious whole. On one level, this was the rococo aesthetic of order and variety applied to the discursive space of the salon: the salonnière brought order to the variety of views expressed by her guests.[35] Such harmonizing was necessary both because different views were expressed, and because strong egos were involved. Because social and intellectual identities could not be easily separated when philosophes interacted directly, it was essential that the salonnière bring them into harmony. Her function was political as well as aesthetic. As both Thomas and Necker indicate, women were thought to be particularly suited to effecting this much-needed harmony. In the eighteenth century the ideal woman was characterized by a lack of ego which enabled her to direct her attention to coordinating the egos of the men around her. The qualities that defined the successful salonnière were thus thought to be gender-specific.

In the seventeenth century, François Poulain de La Barre had inscribed this definition of the female in a history of human society.[36] Poulain began his history with a prepolitical state of nature. The peace and equality of this orginal state were broken by an increasing division of labor between men and women, as the expansion of societies brought about the creation of hierarchy and authority. Since government at this

---

33. Antoine-Léonard Thomas, "A la mémoire de Madame Geoffrin," in Morellet, *Eloges de Mme Geoffrin*, p. 89.

34. Necker to Grimm, 16 January 1777, in Necker, *Mélanges* 1:344–45.

35. Jean Starobinski, *The Invention of Liberty, 1700–1789*, trans. Bernard C. Swift (Geneva, 1964), pp. 39–41.

36. I here follow Lougee's reading of Poulain de La Barre, *Egalité des deux sexes*, in "*Paradis des Femmes*," p. 20.

stage simply meant military defense, men were entrusted with it on the basis of their physical strength. But order having been reestablished through the institution of this first form of government, military governors were no longer needed. Now, when this third stage had been reached, women should become preeminent, since government would no longer be a matter of force but of the humanity and discernment that were women's strengths.

Poulain ascribed the virtues of the salonnière to woman's nature; they can perhaps better be explained by the exclusion of women from the educational system in which men, particularly men of letters, were formed. Walter Ong has called the Latinate educational system of the West a male puberty rite. Latin, used only by males, was the key that unlocked the door to the tribal wisdom of academe. "The academic world," Ong concludes, "was strictly a male world, even though most males were not in fact a part of it. It was profoundly agonistic, and its agonistic structures registered masculine needs."[37] When the philosophes rejected the academy and the university as the institutional bases for their Republic of Letters and instead adopted the Parisian salon, they moved out of that male world, but they brought with them the mentality and practices learned during their initiation into the culture against which they were trying to rebel. Salonnières helped to save them from themselves.

The salonnières developed neither the combative, disputatious spirit nor the direct mastery of the word which came from a training in dialectic and rhetoric.[38] The salonnière was thus able to stand apart from the disputants and outside the dispute, controlling the collective discourse of those who, as citizens of a republic, did not want their mastery of the word to become the basis of mastery over persons. The salonnière's art was thus based on selflessness, which allowed her to manage the egos of others without imposing her own upon them. Her virtues were negative virtues, "female" virtues, such as modesty.

Geoffrin once received a letter from an admirer who told her that she was known and praised throughout Europe for her modesty. "I am humble because I cannot do anything," she responded—in all modesty. At the same time, however, she did not deny the virtues that earned her this praise:

37. Ong, *Fighting for Life*, pp. 129–30, 135. Ong goes on to point out that as women entered academia in the nineteenth and twentieth centuries, the following practices were dropped: Latin as both a subject and a means of instruction, the agonistic teaching method; public oral disputations and examinations, physical punishment.

38. It is significant in this regard that an eighteenth-century rhetoric aimed at young women taught them how to appreciate style rather than how to use it. See [Gabriel-Henri Gaillard], *La Rhétorique françoise à l'usage des jeunes demoiselles* (Paris, 1787). I am grateful to Françoise Douay for this reference.

Do not believe that my nothingness which I recognize in regard to others negates me in regard to myself. I sense in myself an elevated soul, reason, and virtues. The knowledge of these advantages, in making me satisfied with myself, makes me see and feel clearly that they are useful only for my personal happiness.

I remain, then, humble, but I am so with dignity. That is to say, even in lowering myself, I would not suffer to be lowered by anyone.[39]

Maintaining the tension between inner satisfaction and outer negation which made Geoffrin the model salonnière was not easy. In his eulogy of Lespinasse, the comte de Guibert wrote:

I have tried to understand the principle of that charm which no one possessed as she did, and here is what it seems to me to consist in: she was always devoid of ego [*personnalité*], and always natural. . . . She knew that the great secret of how to please lay in forgetting oneself in order to become occupied with others, and she thus forgot herself constantly. She was the soul of conversation, and she thus never made herself its object. Her great art was to show to advantage the minds of others, and she enjoyed doing that more than revealing her own.[40]

Guibert was the recipient of love letters written by Lespinasse late in the night, after her friends and guests had gone home. "In the midst of all these *bad writers* and all the *prigs, fools, pedants* with whom I spent my day, I thought only of you and your foolishness, I missed you," she wrote one night. For Lespinasse, passion and its expression in letters and music mirrored the emptiness of her selflessness; hers was a vain attempt to fill that emptiness, expressed in a desire for love often figured as death.[41]

In his eulogy of Geoffrin, Morellet emphasized how she allowed others to speak of what interested them without herself making substantive contributions to the conversation. She knew how to "let them chat without interruption."[42] This did not mean, however, that the salonnière was passive. Interaction, as sociolinguist Pamela Fishman points out, is work, and women do the bulk of it. "As with work in its usual sense," she writes, "there appears to be a division of labor in conversation." Women's work in conversation, she argues, is relative to

39. Letter in the hand of Geoffrin to [?], undated, Geoffrin papers.

40. [Jacques-Antoine-Hippolyte, comte de] Guibert, "Eloge d'Eliza," in *Lettres de Mlle de Lespinasse*, ed. Eugène Asse (Paris, n.d.), p. 360.

41. Lespinasse to Guibert, dated Tuesday, 1774, in *Lettres de Lespinasse*. See Dena Goodman, "Julie de Lespinasse: A Mirror for the Enlightenment," in *Eighteenth-Century Women and the Arts*, ed. Frederick M. Keener and Susan E. Lorsch (New York, 1988), pp. 3–10.

42. Morellet, "Portrait de Madame Geoffrin," in *Eloges de Geoffrin*, p. 11.

[handwritten annotation: no real effort to contextualize sources — many of which are eulogies]

men's needs. Sometimes the silence of a "good listener" might be required; at other times silences need to be filled to keep conversation going. Conversational work is not the same as talking. Although Fishman draws her conclusions from a study of household conversations among American married couples, they resonate strikingly with contemporary perceptions of the salonnière's role in the more formal conversations of eighteenth-century Paris.[43]

The salonnière's attentiveness to others, her silence even, was as much a conscious action as was the loquacity of her male guests. According to Necker, the salonnière's métier consisted in actively attending to others. "As long as one is in society," she wrote, "one must occupy oneself with others, never keeping silent out of laziness or from distraction, but only in order to listen or to let others speak." This attention to others implied a denial of the self, since, again according to Necker, "the greatest attack of distraction and inattention is an attack of ego, because one sees and focuses only on oneself."[44]

The eulogies of the three great Enlightenment salonnières, together with their own understanding of themselves and of one another, add up to the definition of a *maîtresse de maison* in Genlis's *Dictionnaire des étiquettes*. "In order to do well the honors of a home," she wrote,

> it is necessary to have in one's character tact, finesse, excellent breeding, great equanimity [*égalité d'humeur*], calmness, and the ability to be obliging. One must, when one receives people, forget oneself, feel absolutely no desire to shine, and put kindness in the place of the desire to please; one must occupy oneself with others, without agitation, without affectation, and know how to set them off to advantage without appearing to protect them; one must, finally, encourage the timid, put them at their ease, maintaining the conversation by directing it with skill rather than keeping it up oneself, such that each person gets the reception that can and ought to satisfy him.[45]

Published in 1818, after the great salons had passed into memory, Genlis's *Dictionnaire* presented an ideal based on the distinctive features of the women who had shaped that institution in the eighteenth century.

Enlightenment salons were places where male egos were brought into harmony through the agency of female selflessness. Men such as

---

43. Pamela M. Fishman, "Interaction: The Work Women Do," in *Language, Gender, and Society*, ed. Barrie Thorne, Cheris Kramarae, and Nancy Henley (Rowley, Mass., 1969), p. 99.

44. Necker, *Nouveaux mélanges* 1:188–89, 302.

45. Genlis, *Dictionnaire critique*, s.v., "Maîtresses de maison."

Morellet, whom Diderot called "the most egoistic [*personnel*] man I know,"[46] could meet together every day to collaborate on the project of Enlightenment only if women kept them from dominating and insulting one another, kept them within the bounds of polite conversation and civil society.

"Politeness," wrote Suzanne Necker, "has been regarded as a [kind of] servitude; while its origin, on the contrary, is found in the consideration that force has given to weakness, to age, to women, to children . . . . Politeness conforms to the principle of equality that is so often spoken of; it is the rampart of those who cannot defend themselves, and that as well on which their praise and their merit are based."[47] Politeness was a female attribute because it derived from weakness rather than strength. But it was also a principle of equality, since it redressed the balance between strong and weak, male and female. The government of salonnières was thus appropriate for a Republic of Letters whose relations were structured by reciprocity and the equality it implied. In this crucial respect, the government of salonnières was just the opposite of the government of kings, although both were the sources of order in their respective polities.

According to contemporary theories of absolute monarchy, the king was the source of unity and order in a particularistic society. His role was to impose order authoritatively by reconciling the competing claims of the different groups from a position above them all.[48] While the salonnière, too, created order in an otherwise disorderly society, she did so not with an authority imposed from above and sanctioned by God and history but in republican fashion, by consent of the governed —exactly as John Locke had defined legitimate political authority. American colonists looked to Locke for a theory of republican government in the eighteenth century; the citizens of the Republic of Letters experienced its practice in the Parisian salon. Like the president the Americans would later elect, and unlike the French king, the salonnière was neither the source of law nor above it; she was neither a legislator nor an absolute ruler. She brought about order in society by embodying and enforcing the rule of law to which each member of the republic consented.

Because the Republic of Letters was not defined territorially, it was perhaps the only republic in history about which it can be truly said that consent defined citizenship. One could not be born in the Republic of Letters; one could not even move to it. One chose to become a citizen

46. Diderot, *Apologie de l'abbé Galiani*, in *Oeuvres politiques*, ed. Paul Vernière (Paris, 1963), p. 71.

47. Necker, *Nouveaux mélanges* 2:291.

48. Baker, *Inventing the French Revolution*, p. 169.

by affirming its values, sharing in its practices, and consenting to the rules of polite discourse by which those values and practices could be realized. Government by salonnières was government by consent.

And yet, one should not assume that the citizens of the Republic of Letters submitted to the rule of law and the government of women without a struggle. Although it made sense to submit to women because of their ability to suppress their egos and harmonize those of men, it also went completely against male notions of natural gender relations for men to place themselves under the control of women. Women, after all, were traditionally viewed as the source of disorder in society. As Rousseau wrote in the *Lettre à d'Alembert*, "Never has a people perished from an excess of wine; all perish from the disorder of women."[49] In the traditional view, it was not women who established order among men by enforcing the rule of law but law that created order by subjecting wives to their husbands.[50] It is thus easy to understand why Rousseau feared government by women above all. "Do you think, Sir," he asked d'Alembert, "that this order is without its difficulties; and that, in taking so much effort to increase the ascendancy of women, men will be the better governed for it?"[51]

Whereas Rousseau was consistent in advocating the domestication of women and rejecting the salonnière as a corrupter of men,[52] the philosophes were not. They were caught in the web of conflicting paradigms of the female, seen as at once the source of both order and disorder.[53] This difficult position resulted in part from the location of the salon in the home, the locus of the family. Women, understood to be the source of disorder in society, were the source of order in the "natural" unit of the family. "Within the shelter of domestic life women [are thought to] impose an order, a social pattern, and thus give meaning to the natural world of birth and death and other physical processes," Carol Pateman explains.[54] When the Republic of Letters made a home for itself within the safe precincts of the Parisian *hôtel*, a space beyond the ordinary limits of the state, it accepted the governance of women and the type of order a woman could legitimately impose.

---

49. Rousseau, *Politics and the Arts*, p. 109. Carol Pateman uses this quotation to open her very insightful article "'The Disorder of Women': Women, Love, and the Sense of Justice," in *The Disorder of Women* (Stanford, 1989), pp. 17–32.

50. Natalie Zemon Davis, *Society and Culture in Early Modern France* (Stanford, 1965), pp. 124–26. See also Lougee, *"Paradis des Femmes,"* pp. 11–14.

51. Rousseau, *Politics and the Arts*, p. 47.

52. "There are no good [*moeurs*] for women outside of a withdrawn and domestic life": *Politics and the Arts*, p. 82. Rousseau continues this theme in *Emile* and *La Nouvelle Héloïse*; it is the focus of scholarship on Rousseau and women.

53. See Simone de Beauvoir, *The Second Sex*, trans. H. M. Parshley (New York, 1974), p. 162.

54. Pateman, *Disorder of Women*, p. 25.

Men had seen themselves as women's natural rulers for so long, however, that it was difficult for them to feel comfortable with the situation reversed, even if it was with their consent and not through tyranny that the reversal had come about. The resistance to the rule of salonnières is best expressed in the memoirs of Marmontel and Morellet, written soon after the salon-centered Republic of Letters had passed into memory. In the masculine world that emerged from the French Revolution, these men who had submitted themselves to the rule of women in that earlier age were perhaps wondering if such submission had been necessary.

In his memoirs, Marmontel, who not only spent part of each day in one salon or another throughout the 1760s and 1770s but also lodged for a number of years in Geoffrin's house, expressed his frustration. After asserting that he had never become one of Geoffrin's friends, though he had always retained her respect, he found himself forced to say also that "the society of Mme Geoffrin lacked one of the pleasures that I value most, freedom of thought. With her soft 'voilà, that's fine,' she did not fail to keep our minds as on a leash; and I had dinners elsewhere where one was more at ease."[55]

Morellet made a similar criticism of Geoffrin in his memoirs. "She was, in fact, a little meticulous and timid," he complained, "obsequious towards the government, deferential to royal officials and court society; feelings quite excusable and quite natural in an elderly woman, who, with reason, looked after her own life, and did not wish to compromise its ease and tranquillity." Morellet recalled that after long dinners, during which Geoffrin controlled the conversation, the philosophes would walk over to the Tuilleries, where they would meet friends and "learn the news, subvert [fronder] the government, and philosophize at our ease. We would make a circle, seated at the foot of a tree in the main path, and abandon ourselves to conversation animated and free like the air that we breathed."[56]

Only Necker, who was herself criticized in similar terms by her guests, saw no constraint in Geoffrin's practice as a salonnière. "Mme Geoffrin permits herself to hear and to say everything," the younger woman wrote admiringly, "and yet she is never indecent."[57] Of Necker's salon, Morellet wrote: "The conversation was good there, although a little constrained by the severity of madame Necker, around whom many subjects could not be touched, and who suffered above all from the liberty of religious opinions."[58] Necker's descriptions of Geoffrin

---

55. Marmontel, *Mémoires* 1:170.
56. Morellet, *Mémoires*, pp. 98, 97.
57. Necker, *Mélanges* 3:245.
58. Morellet, *Mémoires*, p. 144.

are free of Morellet's patronizing tone when he portrays her as a timid, elderly lady who is primarily concerned for her own well-being. That image is undermined by Geoffrin's actions; she did not hesitate to go out on a limb to help her philosophe friends, such as Morellet and Marmontel. Surely, it is not fair to accuse a woman of excessive timidity when she could write to a friend in these terms: "Here is the *Mémoire* written in your hand. It has never left mine. I have had it copied in my bedroom by a man who does not know your handwriting at all, and who certainly does not know about whom you wish to speak. I have omitted from yours whatever I thought was not useful. I will say in my letter whatever is necessary. I am sending it to you for a reading."[59]

As we have seen, however, historians have perpetuated the view that the salonnières, out of their own self-interest and fear, constrained the philosophes despotically. They have responded sympathetically, even instinctively, to the feelings expressed by men such as Marmontel and Morellet, taking them at face value without asking why these men would continue to frequent salons that were prisons to them. Perhaps we can answer that question by taking a closer look at one particular philosophe: Morellet.

André Morellet, who, like Marmontel, could be found in the salons every day of the week, best embodied the conflict between the old ethos of scholastic dueling and the new ethos of the Enlightenment Republic of Letters. Educated by the Jesuits in Lyon and then at the Sorbonne in Paris, Morellet was universally regarded as the most disputatious of the philosophes.[60] Voltaire took to referring to him in letters as "Mord-les" or "Bite-'em."[61] Galiani wrote of him to Epinay: "He is a man whose heart is in his head, and whose head is in his heart. He reasons by passion and acts on principles."[62] Dominique-Joseph Garat recalled that when Morellet and the Italian economist Pietro Verri met, "although the conformity of their principles made dispute almost impossible, these conversations would have felt like an eternity to them without the resource of dispute."[63] Morellet wrote of himself in his *Mémoires*: "I was . . . violent in dispute, but my antagonist could never reproach me for the least insult. My warmth was only for my opinion, and never against my adversary; and I sometimes spit blood after a dispute in which I had not let escape a single personal remark."[64]

59. Autograph letter in the hand of Geoffrin to [?], n.d., Geoffrin papers.
60. Morellet, *Mémoires*, chaps. 1–2.
61. Wilson, *Diderot*, p. 495.
62. Galiani to Epinay, 27 [January] 1770.
63. Dominique-Joseph Garat, *Mémoires historiques sur la vie de M. Suard*, 2 vols. (Paris, 1820), 2:203.
64. Morellet, *Mémoires*, p. 51.

And yet, although Morellet defended his disputatious spirit, he also wrote that the most valuable part of his university education was his membership in a residential student club, the Society of the Sorbonne. There he not only made life-long friendships with progressive members of the elite such as the future royal ministers Turgot and Loménie de Brienne, who helped advance him in his career, but also learned to value sociability and comradeship as fundamental to intellectual life. It was in the dining hall with his fellow students that Morellet argued theology and philosophy for five years and made lasting friendships.

In 1805, when he wrote his memoirs, Morellet looked back to the Society of the Sorbonne as the model of social and intellectual life in which disputation and friendship went hand in hand. The social and intellectual world that was destroyed by the upheavals of the French Revolution was not the hazily remembered club of Morellet's student days, however, but the salon world in which he and his fellow philosophes ate, drank, and argued under the guidance of salonnières every afternoon and evening for more than ten years.

In Morellet's memoirs, the constraint of the salons was contrasted to freedom and natural harmony in three different all-male social and discursive settings: first, the Society of the Sorbonne; then, the meetings under the tree in the Tuilleries, which recall those of the mythical Germanic barons of France idealized as the founders of the state by aristocratic historians in the eighteenth century; and finally, the weekly dinners at the home of d'Holbach. "It was there," wrote Morellet, "that one was forced to listen to the freest, the most animated, and the most instructive conversation that ever was."[65] Marmontel, too, remarked on the contrast: "I will not speak at all of those of our friends whom you have just seen under the eye of madame Geoffrin, and submitted to her discipline," he wrote. "*Chez* baron d'Holbach and *chez* Helvétius, they were at their ease, and even more likable, because the mind, in its movements, can deploy its strength and its grace well only when nothing hinders it."[66]

Like Rousseau, like the men who founded political clubs during the French Revolution and extolled fraternity as a fundamental political value, Morellet dreamed of an idyllic world of male companionship in which discordant voices were naturally harmonized.[67] In the real world

65. Ibid., p. 130. Kors writes of d'Holbach that "it is perhaps to the Baron's remembrances of his student milieu and its pleasures, and not to a Parisian tradition of salon life, that the coterie holbachique owed its inspiration": *D'Holbach's Coterie*, pp. 11–12.

66. Marmontel, *Mémoires* 1:227.

67. Rousseau, *Politics and the Arts*, pp. 98–99; Blum, *Rousseau and the Republic of Virtue*, p. 210.

*whose
voice
here?*

of eighteenth-century France, however, this natural harmony had never existed. Government was necessary precisely because it did not exist in civil society. In the Republic of Letters, too, government was necessary if harmony was to reign.

A 1774 letter reveals Morellet's ability to believe men to be self-governing, even in the face of an admission to the contrary. In response to a letter from Lord Shelburne, Morellet wrote: "Mme Geoffrin believes . . . that there is a bit of flattery in what you say about her being the only person 'whom you like to be governed by,' and when I had explained this English to her, we agreed that for you there is no such thing as 'governed by,' that you would always govern yourself, and that you would never let yourself be governed by anyone."[68] Perhaps Geoffrin decided to agree with Morellet's argument, but Shelburne's testimony and recognition remain.

Another glance at Morellet's memoirs and Necker's journals suggests that the underlying tensions in the salons were the product of the combative spirit among men of letters and their resistance to putting into practice their own republican values: values they counted on the salonnières to support and uphold by enforcing the rules of polite discourse. In describing the freedom of conversation at d'Holbach's, Morellet wrote that "often a single person took the floor and proposed his theory peacefully and without interruption. Other times, it took the form of hand-to-hand combat, of which the rest of the group were silent spectators: a manner of listening that I found only rarely elsewhere."[69] Here Morellet claimed to value a discursive setting in which the speaker—conceptualized either in individualistic or traditional terms—had the greatest freedom, but without regard for the group. Necker, on the other hand, showed a different principle to be at work in the salon, where the salonnière's "great art . . . is to prevent anyone of her society from taking up too much room at the expense of others."[70] Indeed, she noted that the salonnière, far from letting men drone on, "must adroitly interrupt those people who get bogged down in private arrangements: it is wrong to say that it suffices for a salonnière to let things run along; her role is always to take up the shuttlecock when it falls from the racquet."[71]

If the philosophes could talk at length without interruption only at d'Holbach's, it was indeed because there was no salonnière to control them. But we ought not to assume that such discursive license constitut-

68. Morellet to Shelburne, 13 December 1774, in *Lettres de l'abbé Morellet à Lord Shelburne,* ed. Edmond Fitzmaurice (Paris, 1898).
69. Morellet, *Mémoires,* p. 130.
70. Necker, *Nouveaux mélanges* 1:100–101.
71. Necker, *Mélanges* 2:85.

ed liberty in the Republic of Letters. True liberty rested on acceptance of the equal right of each to speak, on mutual respect for the rules of discourse by which such rights were guaranteed, and on acceptance of the salonnière's role in enforcing them. "The freedom of men under government," Locke had written, "is to have a standing rule to live by, common to every one of that society and made by the legislative power erected in it." "Where there is no law," he declared, "there is no freedom."[72] Montesquieu, too, had grounded political liberty in law. "In a state, that is to say, in a society where there are laws, liberty can only consist in doing what one ought to do, and in not being forced to do that which one ought not," he wrote in *De l'esprit des lois.* "Liberty is the right to do all that the laws permit; and if a citizen were allowed to do what they forbid, he would no longer have any liberty, because the others would all have the same power."[73]

What were the rules of polite conversation? What were these laws that the salonnières were empowered to enforce? More fundamentally, what was the political order instantiated in and articulated by the rules of polite conversation?

Polite Conversation and Enlightenment Discourse

Polite conversation originated in the civic and socially mobile atmosphere of sixteenth-century Italian courts as a noble and nobilizing discourse. It was normalized in courtesy books, which "offered a growing number of readers a system of rules, methods, and techniques for making social interaction both agreeable and lasting."[74] In seventeenth-century Paris, polite conversation became situated within the new architectural space of the *hôtel.* It was first located in the *alcôve* or *ruelle* carved out in the bedroom for intimate conversation between a guest and a sick person or a woman in childbed; in the eighteenth century it moved to newer, more public spaces within the *hôtel*: the dining room and salon.[75] The localizing of noble interactions in what we now call the "salon" and their characterization as discursive marked the domestication of the nobility and its resistance to absorption by the royal court.

French nobles turned to polite conversation as a way to preserve their social identity. Such a move obviously had more than psychological importance in a culture in which social definition was the basis of

---

72. John Locke, *The Second Treatise of Government* (Indianapolis, 1952), pp. 15, 32.
73. Montesquieu, *Oeuvres complètes*, p. 586.
74. Elizabeth C. Goldsmith, *Exclusive Conversations: The Art of Interaction in Seventeenth-Century France* (Philadelphia, 1988), p. 4.
75. Pardailhé-Galabrun, *Birth of Intimacy*, pp. 59–63 and 101–2.

status, order, and power. Politeness gave the nobility a new definition to replace their old military values and practices. Politeness could also distinguish the noble from the nonnoble in a new way. To live and act nobly continued to imply a disdain for the practical and the material and for work even more than for the wealth it produced. If the members of the second estate could no longer justify their privileged status as "those who fight," they could at least make clear that they were not to be confused with "those who work." Nobility thus became identified with leisure. The nobles' attempt to reconstitute themselves as a group served as a reaffirmation of their autonomy vis-à-vis the monarchy, especially since this new definition, being behavioral, discursive, and moral, excluded not only working and fighting but service as well.

The monarchy unceasingly tried to co-opt politeness by making it a function of hierarchy and subordination to royal authority, but its success was only partial. Orest Ranum has interpreted the Fronde as the ultimate breach of politeness, when "princes insulted other princes, judges other judges, gentlemen other gentlemen in a melee of social disorder."[76] In this case the monarchy asserted its authority by showing that it alone was capable of resolving such disputes within a particularistic and hierarchical society. The king was the implied author of the ultimate conduct book.

And yet, although one can see the king as master of the master discourse of the French political order, the monarchy was still not able to absorb the nobility into itself. On the contrary, society (*le monde*) became more strongly defined even as the monarchy did. "The social milieu of the salon was increasingly viewed as the more hospitable environment for perfect sociability," writes Elizabeth Goldsmith. *Le monde* "suggests a notion of restricted exclusivity that is at the same time all-encompassing, it encloses everything (of any importance) within its boundaries."[77] When Louis XIV moved the court to Versailles, he succeeded in drawing the old nobility out of their country strongholds, but he also opened the way for Paris to become identified with a world beyond his control. This independent Paris was not only the site of bread riots that threatened civil order from below, but of the salons in which an autonomous nobility strengthened itself with a unifying discourse. Over the course of the seventeenth and eighteenth centuries, this polite discourse posed as great a threat to the monarchy as did the discordant voices of the bread rioters.

76. Orest Ranum, "Courtesy, Absolutism, and the Rise of the French State, 1630–1660," *Journal of Modern History* 52 (September 1980): 446.

77. Goldsmith, *Exclusive Conversations*, pp. 6–7. See also France, *Politeness and Its Discontents*, p. 64.

The larger social order was hierarchical, and the king's authority placed him at the top of that hierarchy politically, but the social structure within the salon was egalitarian. As an exclusive group, Goldsmith notes, the nobles could counterbalance their "collective sense of superiority with the conviction that they themselves [were] a community of equals." In the seventeenth century, polite conversation instantiated equality in noble salons, just as epistolary exchange did in the Republic of Letters. "Communication among the members of the group [was] based on the principle of reciprocity," Goldsmith writes, "with each speaker contributing to the equanimity of the circle as a whole."[78]

Goldsmith has interpreted conversational exchange in the noble salons as analogous to the potlatch principle of pure reciprocity explored by anthropologists Marcel Mauss and Marshall Sahlins, in which the constant circulation of gifts simultaneously binds a society together and animates it.[79] The same analogy can be drawn to the epistolary exchanges of the Republic of Letters. What the salon nobility, the Republic of Letters, and the Trobriand Islanders had in common was a sense of community and commerce based on a set of values distinct from trade and individual profit. In these groups, exchange was not trade, and profit accrued to the group first, and to the individual only through it. All three cultures assumed the pretense, at least, of unlimited resources, an assumption not that difficult to sustain if the currency is verbal.

If polite conversation served first as a way of redefining the nobility as a social group at a time when its existence was threatened from above, below, and within, it also permitted more flexibility than had been possible before. Politeness allowed the nobility defined by it to respond to a social topography that, thanks to the monarchy, could no longer be viewed as terra firma. It came to function as a substitute not only for the martial definition of nobility but for birth itself. As the seventeenth century proceeded, Carolyn Lougee shows, "behavior superseded birth as the criterion of status. The *honnête homme* was the man of whatever social origin who appropriated to himself noble *civilité*. The ideology of the salons rested on this substitution of behavior for birth."[80] In the salons, it was polite conversation that constituted civility, and women who taught upwardly mobile men how to practice it. As Poulain de La Barre wrote, "If [men] wish to enter *le monde* and play well their role in it, they are obliged to go to the school of ladies in order to learn there the politeness, affability, and all the exterior which

78. Goldsmith, *Exclusive Conversations*, p. 10.
79. Ibid., p. 11.
80. Lougee, "*Paradis des Femmes*," p. 52.

today makes up the essence of *honnêtes gens*."[81] From the point of view
of the less intransigent segments of the nobility, politeness gave them
control over entry into an elite that could no longer be based on either
birth or might but was not simply going to roll over and die.

Politeness may thus be understood as a response to the monarchy's
attempt to appropriate the definition of nobility to itself, rather than as
the mere capitulation of a warrior elite. Even Voltaire, who claimed
that it was Louis XIV who "succeeded in transforming a hitherto tur-
bulent people into a peaceable people," went on to speak of "the houses
which all the great nobles built or bought in Paris and their wives who
lived there with dignity" as forming "schools of politeness" that im-
proved *les moeurs*. "Decency," he wrote, "which was due principally to
the women who gathered society in their homes, made minds more
agreeable, and reading made them more solid in the long run."[82]

Politeness could function as a bastion of the nobility, even as it let
new people in, by maintaining exclusivity. The equality among participants in a polite conversation signified not a leveling of society but the
exclusivity of the group to which the newcomer was being admitted.
The salons may have been schools of politeness, but they were very
exclusive schools nonetheless. Only with the proper education, which
depended on admission in the first place, could one make the grade.
And yet, a certain amount of leveling did take place, because the shift
from birth to behavior as the criterion of nobility facilitated social mobility. Moreover, the emphasis on appearance made it impossible to
make a distinction between the truly (essentially) noble and the cheap
imitation because, simply, there was none. As Roger Chartier notes,
"the concept of civility is in fact situated at the very heart of the tension
between appearance and essence that defines Baroque sensibility and
etiquette."[83] Voltaire could thus claim with satisfaction, that "the houses,
the theaters, the public promenades, where people began to assemble
in order to partake of a more gentle life, rendered little by little the
exterior of all citizens almost the same. Today one notices how politeness has invaded all *conditions*, to the very counter [*fond*] of a shop."[84]
By the time of the Revolution, Germaine de Staël could look back on
the society of the Old Regime as highly flexible and a function of
conversation. "The relationships of the different classes among themselves were well suited to develop in France the sagacity, moderation
[*mesure*], and propriety of the spirit of society," she wrote. "The ranks
were not at all well defined, and pretentions were constantly stirring

81. Quoted ibid., p. 54. See also Goldsmith, *Exclusive Conversations*, p. 20.
82. Voltaire, *Siècle de Louis XIV*, in *Oeuvres complètes* 14:516.
83. Chartier, *Lectures et lecteurs*, p. 60.
84. Voltaire, *Siècle de Louis XIV*, in *Oeuvres complètes* 14:517.

things up in the uncertain space that each person could by turns conquer or lose. The rights of the third estate, the parlements, the nobility, the power of the king himself, nothing was determined in any invariable way; everything happened, so to speak, by skill in conversation."[85]

If politeness could be learned only in salons, how could it invade all stations of life? Clearly, there must have been another way. In fact there were two: publication and imitation. While conduct books opened nobility to the literate, direct imitation was possible for anyone who could read a manner and a mien. Certainly imitation was at work if Voltaire was correct in his observation that even shopgirls were polite. Since the behavior learned within the walls of the salon was not to be confined to it, like some secret ritual, it became visible to anyone who had the opportunity to observe it.[86] The very necessity to act out one's nobility to prove that one had it made nobility possible to imitate.

The publicity of the conduct books was the publicity of noble conduct itself. Those who read them learned not simply to imitate nobility but to attain it through spoken and written discourse: conversation and correspondence. From the conduct books we learn how the idea and the ideal of conversation, like nobility itself, developed over the course of the seventeenth century.[87]

In Nicolas Pasquier's book Le Gentilhomme, published in 1611, social interactions were still conceived in combative terms: words were weapons, and discourse was understood as a means of resolving disputes while retaining one's reputation. Conversation was dueling translated into discourse. At the same time, the term conversation, referred in these early years not to discourse but to those who engaged in it. The art of conversation was the art of surrounding oneself with the right people. Reputation remained the key to nobility: to be defended by the new verbal weapons and to be established by the company one kept.

By 1730 Nicolas Faret could declare in L'Honnête homme that too much attention was given to quarrels and confrontation and that sociability was, as a consequence, too combative. Faret did not question the importance of reputation, but he rejected the rhetoric of combat and the image of the noble as warrior which had supported it. At the same time, he granted even more importance to sociability itself as a

85. [Germaine] de Staël-Holstein, "De l'Allemagne," in Oeuvres, 3 vols. (Paris, 1858), 3:50.

86. Daniel Roche discusses this sort of urban "reading" in The People of Paris: An Essay in Popular Culture in the Eighteenth Century, trans. Mark Evans and Gwynne Lewis (Berkeley, 1987). Peter France notes that "the discovery of polite society by a person from another world is a common theme in eighteenth-century literature": Politeness and Its Discontents, p. 67.

87. The following discussion of seventeenth-century conduct books is based on Goldsmith, Exclusive Conversations, chap. 1.

defining feature of the new nobility. Discourse and sociability—the two poles of reputation—were coming together. A good reputation, according to Faret, was not something whose defense required constant vigilance but something to be nurtured and cultivated with constant care and attention. Association with people whose public image one wanted for one's own was the basis of reputation; continued association, moreover, was the only way to protect a reputation once won. "The isolated individual is unprotected," wrote Faret, "because having given nothing to the group he can expect nothing in return."[88] Polite conversation, as a function of sociability first and of language only secondarily, gave priority to the dynamics of the group over the performance of the individual.

The centrality of association to reputation and, through reputation, to nobility placed the emphasis on appearance, that is, how one appeared to others and how one's association reflected on oneself. The aspiring noble needed to choose his associates wisely, both as models to emulate (to reflect them in himself) and so that they might reflect well on him. It was necessary to choose company in which one felt in harmony with the reflection of oneself in the eyes of others; otherwise, conversation would be nothing but constraint. Conversation became positive and harmonious rather than combative when those who engaged in it saw themselves in each other and saw their discursive interactions as mutual generosity or balanced reciprocity. The reputation of each was supported by association in and with the group.

But if the conduct books were telling people simply to associate with the right people, and the right people were those with whom one was already in harmony, how could this "conduct" be practiced by a larger public and politeness become a learned behavior? Well, if politeness referred to a proper ordering of things, to correct association, then it could become the art by which such ordering was effected. In 1671 Antoine de Courtin published the *Nouveau traité de la civilité qui se pratique en France* and with it transformed the conduct book into a taxonomy of social actions and a set of rules for interactions, particularly those between people of unequal status. He defined civility as "a science that teaches [how] to put in its correct place what we must do or say."[89] Rather than assume an identity among speakers as a prerequisite for polite conversation, Courtin made conversation the basis for establishing equity: a set of just relations among those who are not equal. With Courtin, the focus shifted back to the individual, not, however, as combatant but as a locus within the socially differentiated space

88. Ibid., p. 21.
89. Quoted ibid., p. 22 (my translation).

of society. That differentiated space would be transcended (but not transformed) by an art of conversation that would give a place to all speakers by recognizing the relationship of each to the others.

Correspondence was the written equivalent of polite conversation understood in this way. Seventeenth-century epistolary manuals stressed the balance to be achieved in the exchange of letters. More so even than conversation, correspondence was an exchange of gifts, especially when the letters contained news. Like conversation as well, letter writing required the individual to think always in terms of the other. A good letter writer would adapt style to situation and to his or her relationship to the recipient. "Most expedient is to do with one's pen what Proteus did with his person," wrote Paul Jacob in *Le Parfait secrétaire* (1646), "changing it into all possible forms, diversifying it according to the needs of the subject, the quality of the person."[90] Like conversation, the epistolary exchange maintained an ideal of harmony and reciprocity, while remaining always potentially unbalanced, since it rested on no stable foundation. The balance of conversation and correspondence had to be established with each verbal act and its response.[91] The epistolary manual, like the conduct book, taught the letter writer how to write and respond in order to maintain balance through proper ordering.

The development of the conduct book into a taxonomy and a set of rules marked a significant stage in the nobility's process of redefinition, which had begun with demilitarization. With demilitarization exclusivity became valorized as the means of nobility, but now it was threatened by the monarchy's continuing creation of new nobles. Exclusivity had to be defined in new ways rather than simply taken for granted. Politeness, as a criterion by which *le monde* could determine nobility independently of the king's designation, became the means of identifying the truly noble, those to be admitted to the exclusive circle of *le monde*. To make politeness the basis of nobility, the site of polite conversation had to be both exclusive and autonomous vis-à-vis the monarchy. It was thus located in the salon and not in the court, where competition for status was orchestrated and adjudicated by the king. In place of a taxonomy of social status represented most graphically by seating arrangements in the court—who sat on what before whom—was a taxonomy of discursive acts for those who would sit in a circle of equals.[92] To

90. Quoted ibid., p. 30 (my translation).

91. "A correspondence is a joint endeavor in which meaning is the product of collaboration," Mireille Bossis reminds us in "Methodological Journeys through Correspondences," in Porter, *Men/Women of Letters*, p. 68. Not only meaning but the correspondence itself as an ongoing endeavor depends upon collaboration.

say the right thing to each person in one's circle was the mark of polite conversation. Politeness demonstrated that one belonged in the circle of interlocutors. This circular reasoning maintained the exclusivity of a circle that was in fact open.

Emulation of proper models, upon which the freedom and harmony of Faret's associations were based, came into play again as model conversations and letters became the preferred means of teaching politeness. By providing models rather than rules in their writings, the chevalier de Méré and Madeleine de Scudéry steered polite conversation away from scholastic dialogue and the legalistic classicism that informed academic discourse in particular. They also relocated the definition of conversation in those who engaged in it by making the art of conversation an art of imitation.

By the end of the century, François de Callières could complain that conversation no longer reflected those who engaged in it since it was nothing but a game of mirrors in which all speech and gestures were borrowed. Like the noble titles that the rich could now buy from the king, polite conversation had become a commodity that could be acquired and displayed as a sign of noble status. Another writer, Morvan de Bellegard, wrote that "many people pass for polite who have only the bark [*écorce*] of politeness: they hide themselves, but beneath borrowed exteriors that dazzle. . . . Thus one must not make too much of this purely external politeness that consists only in certain contrived manners. . . . It must have its roots in the heart and be based on true feelings.[93]

Common sense was invoked as the only principle by which true politeness could be distinguished from the false. Unlike rules, which could be published and thus made public, this notion of common sense would not undermine *le monde*'s ability to define itself, since it amounted to an internalization of the rules expressed as the consensus of public opinion. The consensual definition of public opinion restored the ideal of harmony which had fallen out of the meaning of conversation when it was distinguished from association. Once conversation was identified with discourse alone, harmony had to be established: government was necessary. Public opinion took on increasing importance as the tribunal by which *le monde* governed itself.

Politeness thus became the defining characteristic of a nobility that

92. See Emmanuel Le Roy Ladurie, "Rangs et hiérarchie dans la vie de cour," in Baker, *Political Culture of the Old Regime*, pp. 61–75.
93. Quoted in Goldsmith, *Exclusive Conversations*, p. 27 (my translation). This is what Peter France calls "la politesse du coeur," which he sees as an "enlightened" development of politeness in the work of La Bruyère, Marivaux, and later writers. *Politeness and Its Discontents*, p. 66.

needed to reassert its autonomy and exclusivity while accepting the reality of social mobility. Polite conversation, because it connoted both verbal art and association, replaced the martial art and adversarial stance of combat as the defining characteristic of a modern nobility. Publicity was a crucial aspect of politeness, manifested in the publication of conduct books and epistolary manuals, in the elevation of common sense to public opinion as the moral tribunal by which *le monde* could maintain its autonomy and exclusivity, and in the need for display which made imitation possible. Both politeness and publicity were related to reputation, which remained central to nobility even as its martial basis was abandoned and harmonious cooperation was valorized. What made the whole thing hang together was a shift from the essence of birth to the appearance of behavior as the only way to judge nobility and establish and protect reputation. Social mobility was made possible through learning, but so was hypocrisy, the result of mere imitation, and thus judgment and discernment became important. Set loose from the moorings of birth and social function, and resistant to entering the safe harbor of the monarchy, the nobility rocked unsteadily and increasingly counted on reciprocal relations of verbal exchange and consensus to maintain its necessary balance in a changing world.

Autonomy, exclusivity, social mobility, and *reputation*, the key terms in *le monde*, were key terms in the Republic of Letters as well. There, too, exclusivity and social mobility were in tension, and the desire for autonomy drove the citizenry into the realm of public opinion, where reputations were won and lost. The Republic of Letters shared with the polite nobility the ideal of reciprocal exchange, the equity of relations defined by conversation and correspondence, and the very practice of constructing social relations by means of correspondence. Most significant, the Republic of Letters used the practice of polite conversation invented by the nobility to transform itself from a combative to a collaborative group and to assert its autonomy vis-à-vis the state. Whereas the nobility had its chivalric martial tradition, men of letters had the scholastic and Jesuit tradition of disputation to overcome; whereas the nobility needed to assert its power to define itself in the face of a monarchy intent on absorbing it in a hierarchical court, men of letters needed to assert the autonomy of their republic and their own control over citizenship within it in the face of royal academies.

If the association of the Republic of Letters with the monarchy in the academies threatened autonomy, however, so did association with the nobility. Was it any better, after all, to be judged by *le monde* than by the king? That was the question d'Alembert had asked in his *Essai sur les gens de lettres.* In addition, politeness had two drawbacks as a discursive base for the Republic of Letters. First, polite society was a society of leisure rather than work. Second, politeness put the emphasis on appearance rather than substance and raised the problem of imitation, of sham and posing. It could, in literary terms, valorize mere wit.

Thus polite conversation might not have been taken up as the appropriate mode of discourse for the Republic of Letters had it not had compelling advantages, not least of which were the institution of the salon and the services of the salonnière. But there was another dimension of politeness that gave it substance and thus made it more attractive, if still troublesome. This was the relationship of politeness to a new urbanity that developed in England in the early years of the eighteenth century.[94]

When seventeenth-century French conduct books were translated into English they found a very different readership and a whole new social context. In England, politeness became the mark not of nobility but of a civil and civic urbanity. Good company extended beyond the domestic and even intimate space of seventeenth-century Parisian salons to the public social space of coffeehouses. And yet, as a social practice, English politeness displayed the familiar character of its French origins. "*Politenesse,*" wrote Abel Boyer in *The English Theophrastus* in 1702, "may be defined as dextrous management of our words and actions, whereby we make other people have better opinion of us and themselves."[95] Here were discourse and association as the defining terms of conversation; here, too, was Faret's mirror game of appearance and opinion. As a code of conduct and an art of self-presentation, however, English politeness was not a substitute for some older definition of nobility but the complement to and completion of social virtues. It was still appearance, but the appearance of virtue: politeness was the form that made virtue visible and attractive in the world. The value of politeness lay not in its ability to define an elite that had lost its social and political function but in its quite different ability to socialize and politicize private virtue by making it public and civic.

The possibility of sham was still a risk, as Boyer himself noted: "Politeness or good-breeding, does not always inspire a man with humanity, justice, complaisance and gratitude, but yet it gives him the outside of these virtues, and makes him in appearance what he should be in

94. The following discussion of politeness in England is derived primarily from Lawrence E. Klein, "The Third Earl of Shaftesbury and the Progress of Politeness," *Eighteenth-Century Studies* 18 (Winter 1984–85): 186–214. See also his "Berkeley, Shaftesbury, and the Meaning of Politeness," *Studies in Eighteenth-Century Culture* 16 (1986): 57–68.

95. Quoted in Klein, "Third Earl of Shaftesbury," p. 190.

reality."[96] Because virtue, like nobility, was a hidden quality for which politeness was taken to be the visible sign, it could be counterfeited by the cultivation of the sign alone.

The third earl of Shaftesbury, who was fully aware of the potential of politeness to be not a sign of virtue but a cover for moral license, nevertheless campaigned for it. He believed that it was necessary to rescue morality and philosophy from pedantry and make them sociable and thus useful in the modern, civic, and urbane world of the eighteenth century.[97] He saw politeness as the matrix whereby philosophy and morality could be reintegrated into society according to the model of the ancients. Rather than the leisure ideal of the French nobility, politeness signified a civilization that, like ancient Greece, made virtue the object of public discourse and public life the subject of philosophy.

The conversational form of polite discourse would be the model for a polite writing. In the form of dialogue, philosophy would once again become a worldly discourse, a discourse of civic virtue for a modern urban society. "The social ambience of 'politeness' was thus urban and urbane," writes Lawrence Klein. "Its political conditions were freedom, legality, and equality. Its key trait, however, was publicity: the openness of public spaces to which men came to talk, where the noise of public discourse mingled with that of philosophical discourse."[98]

This English, more public form of polite conversation was practiced primarily in the coffeehouse, which by the early 1700s, Klein has shown, was championed by Whig writers as "a site for a conversable sociability conducive to the improvement of society." This is not to say that conversation was invariably polite there, but the urban space of London was represented as "a field in which opportunities for politeness were both won and lost. The coffeehouse was a particular arena in the struggle for politeness." In an increasingly voluble urban world, threatened with discursive (and thus social and political) anarchy, the coffeehouse as an institution and polite conversation as a discursive practice disciplined by the rules imported from across the channel could be used to construct a new sort of order to replace the authorities of church and state.[99]

96. Quoted ibid., pp. 190–91.

97. Shaftesbury's critique of pedantry echoes Locke's critique of disputation, which, in contrast to civil conversation, he found uncivil in society and counterproductive in the search for truth: Locke, *Some Thoughts concerning Education*, pp. 240–41; Peter Walmsley, "Civil Conversation in Locke's *Essay*," *Studies on Voltaire and the Eighteenth Century* 303 (1992): 411–17.

98. Klein, "Third Earl of Shaftesbury," p. 211. See also Nancy S. Streuver, "The Conversable World: Eighteenth-Century Transformations of the Relation of Rhetoric and Truth," in *Rhetoric and the Pursuit of Truth: Language Change in the Seventeenth and Eighteenth Centuries* (Los Angeles, 1985), pp. 84–88.

99. Lawrence E. Klein, "Coffee Clashes: The Politics of Conversation in Seventeenth- and Eighteenth-Century England," unpublished paper.

Within the walls of the coffeehouse, polite conversation could create the illusion of social equality by suspending distinctions of rank. Whereas in the Parisian salon equality was a function of exclusivity whose purpose was to create a harmonious, cohesive group, in the London coffeehouse the social identity of complete strangers could be created by conversation itself. "In the urban society of the 18th Century," Richard Sennett has observed, "the initial social bond was established by forms of courtesy based on a recognition that people were 'unknown quantities.'" The cardinal rule governing coffeehouse conversation was that "anyone sitting in the coffeehouse had a right to talk to anyone else, to enter into any conversation, whether he knew the other people or not, whether he was bidden to speak or not. It was bad form even to touch on the social origins of other persons when talking to them in the coffeehouse, because the free flow of talk might then be impeded."[100]

The discipline of polite conversation produced an ideal of liberty without, however, governance, for the Whig conversational ideal emphasized freedom from external constraint and submission to politeness as an internalized discipline. Coffeehouse conversation was good if it flowed freely and no one controlled it. Entry was open to anyone willing to pay the penny admission fee. In a sense, the penny took the place of the salonnière, for its payment signified tacit consent to submit to the rules of polite conversation. These rules were posted at the door and elaborated in conduct books such as *The Conversation of Gentlemen Considered*, published by John Constable in 1738. Constable acknowledged his debt to the French but then set out rules of discourse in the English idiom appropriate to the London coffeehouse. "Different opinions, and a measurable liberty of declaring them, is necessary to enliven conversation, and to improve it," he wrote. Yet such liberty of opinion ought not to compromise the harmony of the conversation by turning into violent opposition; therefore, men must develop "the talent of contradicting without displeasing."[101] Personal restraint sufficed to maintain a free and harmonious discourse that was nonetheless always threatened by individual expression.

Another threat to conversation was reading. Whereas in the Parisian salons spoken and written discourse (conversation and correspondence) had been treated as interchangeable, Englishmen were not agreed as to the proper relationship between the two in their joint

100. Richard Sennett, *The Fall of Public Man: On the Social Psychology of Capitalism* (New York, 1978), pp. 62 and 81.

101. Quoted in Daniel Gordon, "The Art of Conversation, or The Concept of Society in the British Enlightenment," unpublished paper.

relation to a more public ideal of sociability. Constable and other writers of conduct books saw reading as a solitary pursuit and thus a threat to sociability, but writers with a broader vision, such as Shaftesbury, Addison, and Steele, advocated an integration of speaking and reading as part of the larger project of integrating learning with life and, especially, moral philosophy with public life and discourse.

Coffeehouse owners encouraged the integration of reading and conversation by providing newspapers to their customers. They took this aspect of their trade seriously enough to apply for a monopoly on it in 1729.[102] Newspapers became the occasions and topics of the conversations that took place in the coffeehouse, filling the same role as letters did for salon conversation. The privacy of letters and the publicity of newspapers as vehicles of news marked a significant difference between the seventeenth-century Parisian salon and the eighteenth-century London coffeehouse, but the integration of the written and spoken word in an economy of discursive exchange constituted the common ground of polite conversation.

Addison and Steele's *Spectator* and *Tatler* made conversations the model and the subject matter of the printed word. They presented themselves as emanating from clubs associated with the London coffeehouses, integrated the letters of habitués into their texts, and thus recreated the essay as a form that both represented coffeehouse sociability and stimulated it.[103] If Shaftesbury saw polite conversation as the model for a polite writing that would bring philosophy into the world, Addison wanted to bring polite writing into the coffeehouse and its conversational public sphere. "It was said of *Socrates*, that he brought Philosophy down from Heaven, to inhabit among Men," he proclaimed, "and I shall be ambitious to have it said of me, that I have brought Philosophy out of Closets and Libraries, Schools and Colleges, to dwell in Clubs and Assemblies, at Tea-tables, and in Coffee-Houses."[104]

Shaftesbury's vision of polite conversation was homosocial, but the sociable world of Addison and Steele, which included assemblies and tea tables, was mixed-gender. "In addition to amalgamating good breeding and philosophy," Klein writes, "good conversation was premised on the co-operation of the sexes."[105] This English version of polite sociability did not, however, assign women the governing role they had

---

102. Sennett, *Fall of Public Man*, p. 81.

103. France, *Politeness and Its Discontents*, pp. 75–77.

104. Quoted in Lawrence E. Klein, "Gender, Conversation, and the Public Sphere in Early Eighteenth-Century England," in *Textuality and Sexuality: Reading Theories and Practices*, ed. Judith Still and Michael Worton (Manchester, 1993), p. 100.

105. Ibid., pp. 109–10.

in France. Indeed, David Hume, the foremost British citizen of the French Republic of Letters, was to express concern about the sovereignty of women in the united kingdoms of learning and conversation he found across the Channel.

In an essay on essay writing published in 1742, Hume contrasted the "conversible" to the "learned" world and defined the essay as a conversation piece. "The Separation of the Learned from the conversible World seem[s] to have been the great Defect of the last Age," he wrote, "and must have had a very bad Influence both on Books and Company: For what Possibility is there of finding Topics of Conversation fit for the Entertainment of rational Creatures, without having Recourse sometimes to History, Poetry, Politics, and the more obvious Principles, at least of Philosophy?"[106] Both learning and society had been the losers in an age in which they had been kept apart. What brought them together were two discursive forms: conversation and the essay. The topoi of the one were the genres of the other.

Hume presented himself as the "ambassador" from the "dominions" of learning to those of conversation and then acknowledged the diplomatic (and polite) necessity of "paying his respects" to the "Sovereign of the state where he is commission'd to reside." The sovereigns of the dominion of conversation, according to Hume, were women, and though men of letters ought to seek good relations with that empire, they could not grant it authority over their republic. "As the Case stands," he wrote diplomatically, "my Commission extends no farther, than to desire a League, offensive and defensive, against our common Enemies, against the Enemies of Reason and Beauty, People of dull Heads and cold hearts." To unite the conversable and learned worlds under the governance of women, however, seemed to him quite another matter.[107]

In France, Hume noted with some discomfort, "the Ladies are, in a Manner, the Sovereigns of the *learned* World, as well as of the *conversible*; and no polite Writer pretends to venture upon the Public without the Approbation of some celebrated Judges of that Sex." He acknowledged that women of "sense and education" were indeed better judges of polite writing than their male counterparts and unworthy of the ridicule heaped on "learned ladies." Nevertheless, he felt compelled to add that in France "their verdict is, indeed, sometimes complain'd of." He concluded his essay with advice to women on how to correct their "false taste" in areas where their judgment was clouded. "Let them accustom themselves to Books of all Kinds," he advised. "Let them give

106. David Hume, *Essays Moral, Political, and Literary*, ed. Eugene F. Miller (Indianapolis, 1985), pp. 533–34.
107. Ibid., pp. 535–36.

Encouragement to Men of Sense and Knowledge to frequent their Company."[108]

For Hume, as Nancy Streuver argues, the conversable world was "the site of serious investigative projects" because it generated "the sense of a common interest that is the sense of 'humanity.'" It was the realm not only of the agreeable but also of the useful, and the learned had thus to "prove" and "recruit" themselves there, where freedom was defined by the "constraints of community." And if Hume himself held back from accepting the legitimacy of the authority of women in that world, Streuver concludes, Jane Austen eventually appropriated it. She took up "Hume's thesis that the conversable world is a site of serious inquiry but reject[ed] his satiric description of 'female sovereigns.'"[109] So, too, did the French philosophes when they brought the serious and civic English ideal of polite conversation back to France.

The nobilizing discourse of seventeenth-century Paris underwent a sea change when it crossed the Channel and became the Whig discourse of the London coffeehouse. When men of letters entered the Parisian salon in the eighteenth century, they brought with them a notion of polite conversation which owed as much to contemporary English models as to the French tradition. They saw themselves as French Shaftesburys, Addisons, and Steeles and helped transform Parisian salons into centers of this new style of conversation.[110] A portrait of Diderot written by his friend Baculard d'Arnaud in 1742 reveals the aspiring man of letters in this new light:

> Philosophe by taste and not by habit,
>   With virtue mixing gentle pleasure,
> Enemy of vain study,
>   Flying from desire to desire,
> Learned censor, equitable judge,
> Master of his mind, more the master of his heart,
> Lover of Iris, among the pleasures of the table,
> Everywhere a sincere friend, and never a vile flatterer.
>   Licidas in this painting,
> You will easily recognize your portrait,

108. Ibid., pp. 536–37.

109. Streuver, "Conversable World," in *Rhetoric and the Pursuit of Truth*, pp. 91–94.

110. Marivaux's *Spectateur français* was one of a dozen French periodicals modeled on that of Addison and Steele, and the *Spectator* has long been recognized as one of the formal sources of Montesquieu's *Lettres persanes*, published at the same time. See France, *Politeness and Its Discontents*, pp. 74–96; Chartier, *Cultural Origins*, p. 158; and Vernière, Introduction to *Lettres persanes*, p. vii.

> I have only lent my hand to Nature,
> Nature, in her turn, has lent me her brush.[111]

This was the young Diderot who, three years later, would publish his first major work, a rather free translation of Shaftesbury's *Inquiry concerning Virtue or Merit*. In the first footnote of the translation, Diderot quotes his mentor directly on the sorry state of philosophy and comments on how well his words express the contemporary situation in France.

> You must allow me, Palemon, thus to bemoan *Philosophy*; since you have forced me to engage with her at a time when her credit runs so low. She is no longer *active* in the world; nor can she hardly, with any advantage be brought upon the public *Stage*. We have immured her (poor Lady!) in colleges and cells; and have set her servilely to such works as those in the mines. Empirics, and pedant sophists are her chief pupils. . . . So far is she from producing statesmen as of old, that hardly any man of note in the public cares to own the least obligation to her.[112]

When Morellet turned to the subject of conversation later in the century, he, too, took an Englishman for his model and guide. His "De la conversation" began as a translation for the *Mercure de France* of Jonathan Swift's "Hints toward an Essay on Conversation." Two years later, Morellet developed this piece into a much fuller treatment, explaining that his goal was to carry out the plan Swift had merely sketched. He acknowledged Swift as a master of the subject by noting that he associated with Addison and others and that his conversation was sought after by all.[113] Morellet accorded far more importance to conversation, however, than even the English model. He extended the ethical and public roles that English theorists of civic virtue had given conversation to even greater intellectual and political goals as the discursive base of the French project of Enlightenment.

Morellet's interest in the theory of conversation derived from the problems posed by disputation and criticism in a collaborative Republic of Letters. His translation of Swift, which appeared in the *Mercure* at the end of 1778, followed by only a few months his original essay "De l'esprit de contradiction," which had run in the same journal in the summer of that year.[114] The expanded version of "De la conversation"

---

111. "Réplique de Baculard d'Arnaud: Le Portrait de M. D***," in Denis Diderot, *Oeuvres complètes*, ed. Roger Lewinter, 15 vols. (Paris, 1970), 1:6–7.

112. Diderot, *Oeuvres complètes* 1:20.

113. Morellet, "De la conversation," in *Mélanges* 4:71.

114. Morellet, "De l'esprit de contradiction," *Mercure de France*, 15 August 1778, pp. 138–52, and 25 August 1778, pp. 258–78; "Essai sur la conversation," *Mercure de France*, 5 November 1778, pp. 5–22.

was accompanied by "De l'esprit de contradiction" and a response to it by Loménie de Brienne in two collections Morellet published after the Revolution: a *mélanges* of his own work and the volume of *éloges* of Geoffrin.

What Morellet called the spirit of contradiction was the critical spirit of the Enlightenment Republic of Letters: "It is that which leads the human race unconsciously to enlightenment and to happiness by the successive destruction of all errors. In exciting minds to combat the false opinions that have been set forth on all sorts of subjects, it gives birth to discussion and to the discovery of the truths that oppose them." The spirit of contradiction, Morellet declared, was not simply a product of amour propre or self-interest but the manifestation of the love of liberty, which was its principle.[115]

In his response to Morellet's argument, Loménie de Brienne acknowledged that truth could indeed emerge only out of the "clash of ideas." He located the source of the critical spirit, however, not in a love of liberty but in the relativity of judgments and the imperfection of human beings:

> It comes from objects that have many faces, and of which everyone sees the side that pleases him; it comes from people who do not have the same interests, the same eyes, the same principles, the same knowledge; it comes above all from expressions that are not widely enough shared, particular enough, to be accurate; such that almost everything that one says or writes being susceptible to contradiction, we need not be surprised to find this sort of opposition.[116]

Morellet, responding to Brienne, acknowledged that these were all good reasons for particular contradictions. Nevertheless, he maintained the validity of the pure critical spirit as the expression of liberty. While there were certainly those, like Brienne, who argued in the interest of truth, there were others who argued simply in order to argue, without reason or self-interest, and they were proof of a pure spirit of criticism.[117]

Morellet found it important to establish this pure spirit of criticism, independent of any interest, even truth, for the same reason that modern thinkers argue in favor of basic research. The activity itself must be promoted and defended regardless of the practical applications that may derive from it, for if one depends upon application to validate

---

115. Morellet, *Mélanges* 4:161–62, 153, and 147. Here Morellet's argument parallels that of Formey in his article "Dispute," in *Encyclopédie* 4:1044–45.

116. [Etienne de] Loménie de Brienne, "Critique des réflexions précédentes," in Morellet, *Mélanges* 4:171–72.

117. Morellet, "Réponse aux réflexions précédentes," in *Mélanges* 4:173–74.

research, bad applications can equally well be used to invalidate it. As
Morellet put it in his conclusion:

> Let us look at man as he is; let us not lend him perfections that he does
> not have any more than defects of which he is free. Let us recognize the
> real motives of his actions, which are neither good nor bad in themselves,
> but only such by the direction that we give them: such are the spirit of
> contradiction and the love of liberty that is its principle. The first has
> advantages and disadvantages that balance each other; the second is the
> source of action, human activity itself, indifferent to good or evil, but
> without which nothing useful, good, or great would ever be accom-
> plished, or rather, without which man would no longer be man. Let us
> enjoy them both, and take care to use them for our happiness and that of
> our fellow men, in turning them away from the baneful uses which pas-
> sions and ignorance too often make them serve.[118]

For Morellet, the spirit of criticism had to be dissociated from its results
not only to protect the right to criticize, regardless of the implications
of particular criticisms, but also because criticism could be directed
toward good and useful ends only if its neutrality was recognized.

Like Rousseau in his *Discours sur l'inégalité*, Morellet defined man as
naturally free and declared that freedom to be morally neutral: man
was by nature neither good nor evil; he became so only by the way in
which he used his nature. For Rousseau, *pitié* and amour propre defined human nature; for Morellet, it was the critical spirit. Both Rousseau and Morellet believed that human freedom was manifested in the
ability to use one's natural attributes toward either good or evil. Both
thought that in most cases history displayed poor use of that freedom,
and enlightenment showed how to redirect it toward good ends.[119] In
defining the critical spirit as the expression of liberty, however, Morellet was rejecting both pitié and amour propre. If in "De l'esprit de
contradiction" he had made clear that the critical spirit was not a product of amour propre, in "De la conversation" he implicitly posited
conversation as an alternative to pitié as the solution to the problems
raised by the critical spirit in society.

In his critique, Brienne had cautioned his friend that "criticism must
be gentle and without bile, falling on things, and not on persons."[120]
Both men realized that it was not enough to disengage criticism from
personnalité in theory. Morellet, however, was not satisfied simply to ask
people to be nice to one another. Rather, he sought to elaborate a

118. Morellet, "De l'esprit de contradiction," in *Mélanges* 4:164.
119. Rousseau, *Oeuvres complètes* 3:125–26 and 131–33.
120. Loménie de Brienne, "Critique," in Morellet, *Mélanges* 4:172.

theory of conversation that would articulate a structure of social and discursive relations within which the spirit of criticism—the human spirit, as he saw it—could truly and fully function. Like Locke, Morellet believed that government was the proper means of both protecting and restraining individual freedom in society.

"Conversation," Morellet wrote, "is the great school of the mind, not only in the sense that it enriches the knowledge gained with difficulty from other sources but in making it more vigorous, more accurate, more penetrating, more profound." In addition, conversation trained the intellectual faculties of mind, memory, and judgment and strengthened the attention of both speakers and listeners. This last skill, which was to become central for Suzanne Necker, Morellet considered crucial for all the rest, and the result of conversation rather than reading, as might otherwise be assumed. "In the majority of men, reading is not accompanied by this strong attention that is precisely the instrument of all our knowledge," he wrote. "This attention becomes easy in conversation." Finally, "a no less interesting effect of conversation is to improve man's morality and sociability."[121] Morality and sociability were functions of each other since *les moeurs*, according to Morellet, were fundamentally social. Because they conversed the most, the French had the highest degree of sociability and thus the greatest morality. Morellet did not mean that their morals were the best—simply that they were the most highly developed.[122]

In his *Considérations sur les moeurs*, Duclos, too, had observed that although the French were the most polite nation, they were not necessarily the most virtuous. He went on to argue that a *peuple policé* was worth more than a *peuple poli* and that *les moeurs*, enforced by public opinion, performed this policing function.[123] Duclos had made reputation, which was central to seventeenth-century French conceptions of nobility and conversation, the principle behind society more broadly conceived. "Men are destined to live in society," he wrote;

> moreover, they are obliged to by the need they have for each other: they are in this regard in a [state of] mutual dependence. But it is not only material needs that bind them; they also have a moral existence that depends on the opinion they have of one another. . . . The desire to occupy a place in the opinion of men gave birth to reputation, celebrity, and renown, powerful springs of society which derive from the same principle.[124]

121. Morellet, *Mélanges* 4:73–76.
122. Ibid., 4:76–77.
123. Duclos, *Considérations sur les moeurs*, pp. 12 and 44–45.
124. Ibid., p. 64.

Duclos was applying the French tradition of conversation to the larger ends of enlightenment. For him, conversation was not only the basis of politeness, although it was that. Polite conversation was also well-governed conversation, the basis of good thinking and good social order. Morellet, by adapting the English conception of conversation as the mark and motor of civic virtue to the French social context embodied in the salon, arrived at a similar position, for the salon differed from the coffeehouse in being governed rather than anarchic. And it was women who took on the policing function in this microcosm of French society.

"The free commerce of the two sexes [is] one of the most powerful principles of civilization," wrote Morellet, "and of the improvement of sociability. This effect occurs by means of conversation."[125] What distinguished France from other nations was its extreme sociability; what distinguished French sociability from its English form in particular was the role women played in it. Women were thus central to the definition of France's national character and its greatness.

Morellet spelled out the rules of polite conversation as he had learned them from Swift by enumerating the vices to be avoided: inattention; interrupting or speaking all at once; overeagerness; egoism; despotism or the spirit of domination; pedantry; illogic; the spirit of pleasantry; the spirit of contradiction; dispute; and personal conversation substituted for general conversation.[126] But the necessary harmony of conversation, against which all these vices operated, did not depend simply on their avoidance. The free atmosphere of the coffeehouse, where men voluntarily excercised the necessary restraint, was not invoked. Rather, Morellet explained that in France the most effective conversation was held in small groups of ten to twelve people around a natural center. "To be frank," he wrote, "I have never seen consistently good conversation except where a salonnière [*maîtresse de maison*] was, if not the only woman, at least a sort of center of the society." His point was not that there ought to be only one woman in the group of men but that the natural role of women was to be a center around which men gathered, and if more than one woman played this role, the conversation would not function properly. Groups that included educated women or those who desired instruction could generate excellent conversation just as well as those that were all male. Such women were, however, uncommon.[127]

The issue of whether or not women contributed to good conversa-

125. Morellet, "De la conversation," in *Mélanges* 4:77.
126. Ibid., 4:82–83.
127. Ibid., 4:129–30.

tion was fundamentally political. Although he granted that women could in theory contribute to good conversation in the same way as men, the point was of only marginal interest to Morellet because so few women were disposed to make this sort of contribution. He did not, of course, ask why they should be so little interested in learning, but that is not my point here. Rather, I would like to focus on the issue that was central for Morellet: the effect of women on conversation when they acted according to their nature. Because Morellet saw women as naturally attracting men to themselves and thereby uniting them, he held that one woman exerted a positive force in conversation, but additional women exerted a negative one. Because woman's natural role was to create a circle around herself as center, she became a governor of men. More women would mean more circles, more societies, and inevitable conflict, since there was no higher authority to adjudicate among them. No women, however, would surely mean anarchy.

In his essay on conversation, Morellet articulated what might be called the salonnière function. As a man of his age, he used the discourse by which gender differences were articulated in the eighteenth century: the discourse of nature.[128] And yet, in acknowledging that a conversational circle could include several women as long as there was only one salonnière, he identified the salonnière with a feminine function and dissociated her from biological woman. In the terms of twentieth-century feminism, Morellet's definition of the salonnière was not essentialist, even though Morellet was himself constrained by the essentialist discourse of nature.[129] Because of this constraint, Morellet was not able to make the more radical claim that men could be salonnières. And indeed, such a claim would require a lot of imagination in the eighteenth century, when men were less likely to switch roles than were women.[130] Furthermore, Morellet was only secondarily interested

128. Thomas, Diderot, and Galiani all couched their essays on women in the discourse of nature. Indeed, the discourse on women was bound up with the discourse of nature in the eighteenth century, just as nature was understood in terms of contemporary notions of gender. See, e.g., Jeffrey Merrick, "Royal Bees: The Gender Politics of the Beehive in Early Modern Europe," *Studies in Eighteenth-Century Culture* 18 (1988): 7–37; Maurice Bloch and Jean H. Bloch, "Women and the Dialectics of Nature in Eighteenth-Century French Thought," in *Nature, Culture, and Gender,* ed. Carol MacCormack and Marilyn Strathern (Cambridge, 1980), pp. 25–41.

129. See Diana Fuss, *Essentially Speaking: Feminism, Nature, and Difference* (New York, 1989).

130. One could argue, however, that d'Holbach did just that. Not only did he lead a "salon," but he published all his work anonymously, on the model of female writers. A more radical case is that of the chevalier d'Eon, a French diplomat, who in 1772 asserted that he was a woman and maintained that identity until his death in 1810. See Gary Kates, "D'Eon Returns to France: Gender and Power in 1777," in *Bodyguards: The Cultural Politics of Gender Ambiguity,* ed. Julia Epstein and Kristina Straub (New York, 1991), pp. 167–94.

in the question of gender roles; his primary concern was the government of conversation, and the conversation that interested him was that of men.

Morellet's ambivalence toward salonnières was based on the assumption, first, that serious conversation was male conversation and, second, that the work women did to enable it was natural to them. As conversation was gendered male, women disappeared from the definition of it, even as their centrality to its functioning was acknowledged. "The work [of conversation] is not seen as what women do," writes Pamela Fishman, "but as part of what they are. . . . It is too often seen as an aspect of gender identity rather than of gender activity.[131]

Michel Serres's analysis of how systems function is the most powerful statement of the paradox of women's role in conversation. What we call interference or static and the French call *le parasite* is the sign of the functioning of the system of communication. "Systems work because they do not work," Serres declares, and "nonfunctioning remains essential for functioning." A successful transmission obliterates the channel of communication, presenting its success as immediacy, transparency. If a relation is "perfect, optimum, and immediate, it disappears as a relation." The parasite is the mark of communication, but if it is visible or audible, then it indicates a failure of perfect communication. The paradox of the parasite is the paradox of the salonnière. "It is very simple but has great import. The parasite is the essence of relation. It is necessary for the relation and ineluctable by the overturning of the force that tries to exclude it. But this relation is nonrelation. . . . The parasite is being and nonbeing, relation and nonrelation."[132] The salonnière is the "parasite" in Enlightenment conversation; she is being and nonbeing in the discourse of and about salon conversation.

By acknowledging the central role of women in shaping good conversation, Morellet synthesized the French tradition of the noble salon and the English Whig conception of conversation, advocating the rules of the latter and the government of the former. Underlying both were the values they shared: political autonomy, publicity, and worldliness of the society defined by conversation; reciprocity, mutual respect, and equality among members of it; and unity of spoken and written discourse in it. In his essay on conversation, written just a year after his eulogy of Geoffrin and later published in the same volume with it, Morellet reintegrated the French and English idioms in the service of a project of Enlightenment which required both order and freedom, women and men, to achieve its end of advancing the good of society and humanity.

131. Fishman, "Interaction," in Thorne et al., *Language, Gender, and Society*, pp. 99–100.

132. Michel Serres, *The Parasite*, trans. Lawrence R. Schehr (Baltimore, 1982), p. 79.

In the end, whether they liked to admit it or not (and sometimes they did), it was salonnière-directed conversation that saved the philosophes from themselves, to the degree it was possible to do so. Perhaps the best way to understand the mixed signals they gave out is to appreciate how attractive the myth of harmony was for men of the eighteenth century, even as they experienced, again and again, the antagonism and divisiveness that characterized their lived reality. They liked to think that they could achieve such harmony naturally, despite all evidence to the contrary. The physiocratic economic theories were predicated on such a hope; so was the appeal to public opinion as consensus. As Suard explained, "The agreement of opinions alone gives the springs of public order a mild and easy force. Once this agreement is found, obedience anticipates the law, and the political spheres are subject to harmony, just like the celestial spheres."[133] In the chapters that follow I describe the challenges to natural harmony which developed once Enlightenment discourse escaped the regulated bounds of the salon. For now, I would like to explore one expression of the myth and dream of natural harmony as an idealized representation of salon conversation itself: Jacques Delille's long poem La Conversation.

First published in 1812, Delille's poem was the product of many years of salon-going in the two decades before the Revolution. "A society of spiritual and polite people, united in order to converse together and to instruct one another in an agreeable conversation by the mutual communication of their ideas and their feelings," he wrote in a lengthy prose preface, "has always seemed to me the best representation of the human race and of social perfection." "There," he continued, "without regulation, without constraint, is exercised a gentle police, founded on the respect the assembled men inspire in one another." Those evils that had traditionally characterized the Republic of Letters and still disturbed society at large were absent from this highest form of sociability. "There," Delille proclaimed, "the mind exercised by observation and experience reads in the eyes, in the mien, in the bearing of each person that which his amour propre fears or desires to hear and, assuring to the society the equilibrium of opposing pretensions and rival vanities, forms out of all that could degenerate into struggles and combats the most harmonious accord."[134]

Delille represented conversation as a self-regulating system that produced social harmony through the mutual regard of men for one another. He contrasted it to the ancient form, which merely transported the partisan debate of the forum into the private home, transforming

133. Quoted by Garat in Mémoires historiques 2:94–95. See also Baker, Inventing the French Revolution, pp. 197–99.
134. J[acques] Delille, La Conversation (Paris, 1812), pp. 7–8.

the salon into a battlefield. "What a difference between those tumultuous assemblies and these pleasant societies!" he exclaimed.[135] Eighteenth-century conversation would form a model of harmony to be transported into the public forum, rather than the other way around, creating what Keith Baker has called "a politics without politics."[136]

Delille invested his poetic treatment of conversation with language as political as Meister's and Morellet's. The society defined by polite conversation was a form of republic in which not only despotism but even monarchy had no place.

> They know arbitrary power not at all.
> Conversations are the popular state:
> > No one there wants to be dominated;
> One displeases there in trying too hard to please,
> And he who wishes to rule alone is soon
> > dethroned.[137]

Delille's anonymous editor commented on this verse, explaining that "this society is always in a perfect order, and no one is charged with policing it."[138] The editor would seem to have been justified in drawing such a conclusion, but Delille, in the end, belied it. Having begun by setting out conversation as an ideal society whose perfect harmony was achieved without rules or police, he ended by giving credit where credit was due: to Geoffrin, the premier salonnière of the age:

> In her, reason could still charm us;
> > She was flattered, she was revered,
> And the art of governing replaced the art of pleasing.

> In days gone by, this is how, in her brilliant decline,
> > I saw the celebrated Geoffrin,
> With what art, above all, in her sovereign hands
> Did she take hold of the reins of conversations! . . .

> With advanced age, middle age and childhood,
> > From her useful experience
> > Kept the old authority,
> At the very onset stifled dispute,
> Or encouraging the struggle of opinions,
> Made issue from our debates the truth.[139]

135. Ibid., pp. 20–22.
136. Baker, *Inventing the French Revolution*, p. 196.
137. Delille, *Conversation*, p. 135.
138. Editor's note, ibid., pp. 214–15.
139. Delille, *Conversation*, pp. 159–60.

In the end, although Delille expressed in the most lyrical terms the perfect harmony that sprang naturally from conversation, he also remembered the salonnière as the person who made of conversation a medium by which discordant views could be shaped into harmonious, consensual truth. In the end, it was the salonnière, and not nature, who made the dream of social and intellectual harmony come true.

The restraining force of the salonnières in the Republic of Letters, the control they tried to maintain over the citizens of the republic and their discourse, was sometimes denied, sometimes resisted by the citizenry, but it was nonetheless necessary and legitimate and in no way arbitrary or despotic. Like all laws, the rules of Enlightenment discourse aimed, in Locke's words, "not to abolish or restrain but to preserve and enlarge freedom."[140] If philosophes such as Morellet and Delille sometimes suggested otherwise, their complaints are undermined not only by the conversational theory they admired and elaborated but by the regularity of their attendance at salons in the 1760s and 1770s, the praise they lavished on the salonnières whose services they valued, and the anarchy that did indeed beset the Republic of Letters when the philosophes ventured from the well-governed confines of the Parisian salons.

140. Locke, *Second Treatise*, p. 32.

CHAPTER 4

Into Writing:
Epistolary Commerce in
the Republic of Letters

La lumière de l'esprit peut changer de climat, mais
elle est aussi impérissable que celle du soleil. Il y a
deux grandes inventions: la poste qui porte presque
en six semaines une découverte de l'équateur au
pôle, et l'imprimerie qui la fixe à jamais.

— DIDEROT TO FALCONET

Although conversation was the governing discourse of the salon-
based Republic of Letters, it was not the only form of discourse. Rather, it was the matrix within which and out of which
the written word flowed. If conversation shaped the discursive space
within the boundaries of the salon, writing moved the Enlightenment
out of that circumscribed world and into the public world beyond it.
The public was first a reading public, and the philosophes both created
and represented that public by writing for it. What they wrote took
many forms—as many forms as there were, and then some, for when
the old forms seemed inadequate, they simply invented new ones. The
drame and the epistolary novel were such novel genres. Sometimes it
was only in retrospect that eighteenth-century writers realized the extent of their own creativity, as when Montesquieu wrote in 1754 that his
Lettres persanes was "a kind of novel."[1] As the Republic of Letters expanded to include people from a broad stratum of the elite, some of
these new citizens used genres at hand, such as the lawyer's *mémoire
judiciaire*, for purposes of enlightenment. The Enlightenment Republic
of Letters was true to its name, for there was no hierarchy of genres, no
queen of the arts, in a republic whose citizens engaged in all the variety
of literary practices, stretching the limits of the literary itself. What else

1. Montesquieu, "Quelques réflexions sur les *Lettres persanes*," in *Lettres persanes*,
p. 3.

could one expect from a community whose guiding text was an encyclopedic dictionary?

The problem posed in this chapter concerns the link between the narrowly circumscribed world of salon conversation and the expanding reading public. How did the philosophes, from their base in the salons, reach out to (create) that public discursively? What forms of writing allowed them to break out of the circle of conversation without betraying its values? Indeed, how could those values be represented and promulgated through writing? For only through the translation of salon values into writing and then into print could enlightenment be spread.

The key to answering these questions is the letter, the dominant form of writing in the eighteenth century. The philosophes increasingly and creatively used letters to bridge the gap between the private circles in which they gathered and the public arena that they sought to shape and conquer. Was this a turning backward? Salon governance, after all, was a solution to the problem of anarchy in a Republic of Letters which no longer depended solely on epistolary exchanges. The philosophes, however, did not simply return to the seventeenth-century epistolary mode of learned exchange between scholars and academies. They did not simply write letters. Instead, they employed and deployed an epistolary genre in the public sphere; they transformed letters and correspondences into a variety of public media, which, because they were extensions of epistolary commerce, retained the crucial reciprocity that made their readers members of a community. Through the circulation of letters, philosophes and salonnières established a network of intellectual exchange which was the first circle of expansion beyond the walls of the salons. As letters and correspondences became the bases and models for print media of broader circulation, this network expanded to become fully public. The letter was transformed into the newsletter and then into the journal. The pamphlet wars of the eighteenth century were letter exchanges, correspondences, often initiated by men of letters but continued by the public itself. The epistolary genre became the dominant medium for creating an active and interactive reading public.[2]

From Montesquieu's *Lettres persanes* to Diderot's *Lettre sur les aveugles* and Rousseau's *Lettre à d'Alembert*, the letter was already prevalent by 1760 as the form of writing that brought writers and readers together

2. Bernard Bray has identified approximately 475 works whose titles indicate they are epistolary which are discussed in the pages of the *Correspondance Littéraire* between 1747 and 1793. And this figure does not include letters inserted in the text itself! See "La CL témoin du goût pour la forme épistolaire," in Bray et al., *Correspondance littéraire de Grimm*, pp. 213–14.

to interact on a footing of equality—just as conversation did in the salons. By the end of the century, the copied and circulated letter, the open letter, the published letter, and the letter to the editor were uniting a vast web of readers into a network of intellectual exchanges that often began in the salons of Paris but spread outward from them to the four corners of Europe and the New World. This vibrant epistolary network was a two-way street, as readers responded to writers, becoming writers themselves in pamphlets and in the columns of an emerging periodical press that was itself an institutional extension of the epistolary network. The reciprocal exchange crucial to the Republic of Letters from its inception became the means of expanding a scholarly republic into what Habermas has called a "critically debating public," a "public engaged in rational-critical debate."[3]

The philosophes named themselves the representatives of this new public, acting as intermediaries among its members and between the public and the state. They also submitted themselves to the tribunal of public opinion constituted by their own readership. Eric Walter has interpreted Voltaire's vast network of correspondence on the model of Habermas's public sphere, as the "tribunal of reason" constituted by individuals to whom Voltaire addressed himself as to a "vast court of appeal, anonymous but active."[4] Thus Voltaire could write in a letter to the lawyer Jean-Baptiste Elie de Beaumont: "I know only one fair judge, and even it only in the long run: it's the public. Only at its tribunal do I plan to win the Sirven proceeding."[5] In all the cases he prosecuted, Voltaire used epistolary networks as the means of achieving publicity, for publicity, he had already realized in 1762, when the Calas case came to his attention, was the only thing that could stop fanaticism.[6] By the time of the La Barre affair, he was an absolute master of these networks. Walter uses the language of high-speed communication to describe Voltaire's correspondence during that summer of 1766, when he

> accelerates the flux of information, short-circuits the different networks, intensifies and prolongs the resonance of an event that has been propelled into the public sphere by the gazettes. Private letters, semi-public letters, letters that are public but apocryphal, this correspondence jams the limits between public and private, so much and so well that it func-

3. Habermas, *Structural Transformation*, pp. 73 and 83.
4. Eric Walter, "L'Affaire La Barre et le concept d'opinion publique," in *Le Journalisme d'Ancien Régime: Questions et propositions* (Lyon, 1982), p. 369; see also Walter, "Les Auteurs et le champ littéraire," in Martin and Chartier, *Histoire de l'édition française* 2:397.
5. Voltaire to Elie de Beaumont, 19 August 1766 (D13501).
6. Voltaire to d'Alembert, 15 May 1762 (D10414).

tions as a sort of news bureau that includes its sources of information, its editorial elaboration, its networks for transmission, its different readings [*lectorats*].[7]

The seventeenth-century citizens of the Republic of Letters had used correspondence primarily for communication among themselves and only secondarily to expand the republic. For the philosophes, the expansion of the Republic of Letters through epistolary exchange was enlightenment itself. Their project was to create a readership in their own image and in so doing to transform society in the image of the republic. In creating through epistolary means a public that was an extension of the Republic of Letters, they challenged the monarchy and its ability to shape society according to its own notions of authority and hierarchy.

Letters in the Enlightenment Republic of Letters

Correspondence and conversation were complementary discursive modes in the salon and equally important to it. Since the seventeenth century, letters had always been defined with reference to the oral exchange of conversation.[8] Salonnières and philosophes alike engaged in correspondences that extended salon membership beyond its spatial and temporal limits. Horace Walpole, for example, was a corresponding member of Du Deffand's salon, and Galiani, who had been a major figure in all the Parisian salons during his ten years as secretary to the Neapolitan ambassador, kept up a weekly correspondence with Epinay (who shared his letters with the rest of her circle) for fifteen years after his departure. Catherine the Great and Stanislas Poniatowski (king of Poland) both corresponded regularly with Geoffrin.[9] Catherine and Frederick the Great also maintained correspondences with Voltaire which could be relayed to Paris via letters to well-placed people there, such as d'Alembert and Du Deffand.

Maintaining a correspondence was not a casual activity. "We have established a correspondence, the Prince of Gotha and I," wrote Galiani to Epinay in 1772, in a letter that forms a part of their regular, numbered, weekly correspondence.[10] After some hesitation, resulting

7. Walter, "Affaire La Barre," pp. 372–73.

8. Mireille Gérard, "Art épistolaire et art de la conversation: Les Vertus de la familiarité," *Revue de l'Histoire Littéraire de la France* 78 (1978): 959–60.

9. *Correspondance inédite du roi Stanislas-Auguste Poniatowski et de Madame Geoffrin (1764–1777)*, ed. Charles de Mouÿ (Paris, 1875). Catherine's letters to Geoffrin are published in Ségur, *Royaume de la rue Saint-Honoré*, pp. 431–62.

10. Galiani to Epinay, 14 March 1772.

from the too-wide circulation and eventual publication of her first letter, Catherine entered into what the eighteenth century called "epistolary commerce" with Geoffrin. The agreement to correspond was a formal engagement implying reciprocal responsibilities. If one of the correspondents failed to carry out those responsibilities, the other ended the relationship, generally, as in the contemporary epistolary novel, by asking that all previous letters be either returned or burned.

A letter is not a solitary act of communication: letters follow one another, imply one another, respond to one another, following a circular rhythm based on chronological continuity.[11] Moreover, the communications network that kept the Republic of letters going was not autonomous. It remained dependent on the communications apparatus of the state, which gave it yet another rhythm: the rhythm of the post. Just as verbal exchanges were structured by the rules of polite conversation, epistolary ones were structured by the post. The private time of reading and writing was inscribed within the public time of arrivals and departures.

The royal monopoly on postal service created a public out of those who sent and received letters, a reading public that was dependent on the post and whose reading and writing were structured by it. If eighteenth-century letter writers often complained about missing or lost letters, it was because the dominant principle of mail delivery was regularity and predictability, rather than, for example, speed or volume. Expectations of regularity and reliability were raised by the annual official publication, beginning in 1699, of the *Almanach Royal*, which listed the schedule of postal couriers. By 1763 the post had become big enough business that a M. Guyot could begin annual publication of the *Guide des Lettres*, devoted solely to the comings and goings of the post. By means of this publication, its author explained, "one can easily know, in whatever city one may be, the days and hours of the departure of letters and those of their arrival at their place of destination. . . . A useful work for all those engaged in epistolary commerce."[12]

Already in 1761, twelve years after the *petite poste* was inaugurated to provide local service in Paris, the *Almanach de la Poste de Paris* had begun annual production. It was distributed by postmen to their regular customers as a New Year's gift. Both postmen and clientele could be understood, in their different ways, as the "société des gens de lettres"

11. Alain Pagès, "La Communication circulaire," in *Ecrire, Publier, Lire: Les Correspondances (Problématique et économie d'un "genre littéraire")*, ed. Jean-Louis Bonnat and Mireille Bossis (Nantes, 1983), pp. 345 and 350.

12. Quoted in Eugène Vaillé, "Guides et livres de poste sous l'Ancien Régime," *Bulletin d'Informations, de Documentation, et de Statistique*, no. 12 (December 1934): 50–52.

mentioned on its title page, which mimicked that of the *Encyclopédie.*
Each year the postal patron could open his or her little almanac to a
New Year's greeting from the trusty postman, such as the following
from the *Almanach* of 1772:

> The renewal of the year
> Imposes on me the duty
> Of proving to you my zeal
> Both morning and evening:
> Never does foul weather
> Find me stopped,
> To serve and to please you
> Are what make me happy.

Or this one from 1774:

> Receive the pure homage
> Of an open and honest heart,
> The feeling that commits me
> To you grows each day;
> Last year, I remember
> That you surpassed my wishes:
> Can one have too much zeal,
> For a heart so generous![13]

The almanac allowed correspondents to predict the arrival of news,
but it also attuned their lives to the rhythms of arrivals and departures.
The testimony of epistolary novels such as *La Nouvelle Héloïse* is supported by the correspondences of Rousseau's contemporaries. From
Warsaw, for example, Geoffrin wrote to her daughter: "I arrived here
the twenty-second, around five o'clock in the evening. Naturally, I
wanted to write to you immediately, but that would have been useless.
The post does not go out until tomorrow."[14] From Naples, Galiani
wrote to Epinay that he had scheduled his weekly "salons" with a friend
from his Paris days for the day the post arrived from France. "We thus
share with each other our treasures," he explained.[15] Condorcet maintained two regular correspondences, one with Amélie Suard and one
with Turgot. He and Turgot both counted on correspondence for keeping in touch with the Parisian center: Condorcet when he was in the

---

13. *Almanach de la Poste de Paris par une Société des Gens de Lettres* (n.p., 1772, 1774). See
also Vaillé, "Guides et livres de poste," pp. 56–57.

14. Geoffrin to La Ferté-Imbault, 24 June [1766], in Geoffrin papers.

15. Galiani to Epinay, 27 August 1774.

country for long spells visiting his mother; Turgot when he was away at his intendant's post in Limoges. One summer they discovered the limits of regular epistolary exchange. "I wrote to you about Givet," Condorcet began; "since then I have returned here from lands where reading and writing are unknown, so that letters only go out once a week: that's what has interrupted our commerce."[16] The correspondence with Suard reveals a friendship more in the style of Julie and St. Preux. Condorcet's letters to her are accordingly more passionate in relation to the comings and goings of the post:

> I am, Madame, in a small provincial city where we only get letters only twice a week and where a drunken messenger brings them several hours and sometimes a day later than he should. On these days I have no common sense, at every moment I ask if this man has arrived, I do not speak of anything else, my heart beats when I see him and the cold people who surround me think that the tone of *le monde* and the mania of wit have turned my head.[17]

Lovers awaited the arrival of letters impatiently, but everyone in the eighteenth century counted on the post—to maintain friendships, to keep in touch with the capital, to conduct business. Writers needed to communicate with printers, and readers often responded to writers by writing to them directly.[18] Fundamentally and originally, however, letters were the primary means for the transmission and circulation of news. If by the end of the eighteenth century the letter increasingly became the expression of the individual and the correspondence the communion of hearts and souls, this separate function of the letter did not take the place of reporting the news. As Alain Pagès notes, the eighteenth-century letter "transmits a public content—open to everyone—as much as it does a private content—for the use of a single addressee." The origin of periodicals lies in this narrating and news function of letters. "The 'gazette' of the eighteenth century," Pagès reminds us, "is simply a collection of 'correspondences.'"[19] Habermas, too, emphasizes the news function of correspondences when he writes of a "traffic in news" that articulated the horizontal relations of com-

16. Condorcet to Turgot, 11 August 1772, in *Correspondance inédite de Condorcet et de Turgot*, ed. Charles Henry (Paris, 1883).

17. Condorcet to Suard, [April 1771], in *Correspondance inédite de Condorcet et Madame Suard*.

18. The best-documented example of this phenomenon is the torrent of correspondence Rousseau received in response to *La Nouvelle Héloïse*. See Robert Darnton, "Readers Respond to Rousseau: The Fabrication of Romantic Sensitivity," in *The Great Cat Massacre and Other Episodes in French Cultural History* (New York, 1984), pp. 215–52.

19. Pagès, "Communication circulaire," in Bonnat and Bossis, *Ecrire*, p. 344.

mercial exchange. In the seventeenth century, these horizontal relations were assimilated into the vertical order of the monarchy with the royal post and formalized into newsletters or *nouvelles*.[20]

Letters were primarily transmitters of news, but they also embodied the writer and thus, on another level, functioned as a substitute for conversation, an absence made present. In the seventeenth century, Scudéry had defined the *lettre galante* as "a conversation between absent persons." A century later, Galiani wrote to Epinay: "You know that I would love for my letters to be read and viewed by all my friends. This is not out of vanity: it is to preserve me in their memory; it is because I would love to talk to them, and I no longer can."[21] Ultimately, the absence represented by letters was the relationship between correspondents itself, since the letter implies both partners and the correspondence binds them together. As Pierre Dumonceaux suggests, the letter is thus a *relation* in two senses of the term: it defines a relationship between correspondents in relating its content. The *Relations* of the Jesuit missionaries captured both meanings as the authors used the accounts they related to shape and solidify their relationship to their sponsors back home.[22]

Reflecting these two dimensions of the letter, the correspondence maintained and shaped a broader membership in the eighteenth-century salon than conversation allowed and also supplied substance for that conversation. If letters were a substitute for conversation, conversation "prolonged and completed readings and epistolary relations."[23] Incoming mail was quarried for news, gossip, information, ideas. Outgoing mail, too, was central to salon life. The salon was the distribution point, the nexus of intellectual exchange. Letters were shared, read aloud, passed around, and generally inserted into the discourse of the salon. Geoffrin, for example, wrote to Marmontel:

20. Habermas, *Structural Transformation*, pp. 15–16. See also Pierre Dumonceaux, "Le XVIIIᵉ siècle: Aux origines de la lettre intime et du genre épistolaire," in Bonnat and Bossis, *Ecrire*, pp. 290–91.

21. Scudéry quoted in Gérard, "Art épistolaire et art de conversation," p. 966; Galiani to Epinay, 30 October 1772. The idea of the letter as an absence made present is no doubt as old as letters themselves. It was the theme of Heloise's first letter to Abelard, in which she quoted from one of Seneca's epistles to Lucilius: "Thank you for writing to me often, the one way in which you can make your presence felt, for I never have a letter from you without the immediate feeling that we are together. If pictures of absent friends give us pleasure, renewing our memories and relieving the pain of separation even if they cheat us with empty comfort, how much more welcome is a letter which comes to us in the very handwriting of an absent friend": *Letters of Abelard and Heloise*, p. 110. See also Janet Gurkin Altman, *Epistolarity: Approaches to a Form* (Columbus, 1982), p. 14.

22. Dumonceaux, "XVIIIᵉ siècle," in Bonnat and Bossis, *Ecrire*, p. 291.

23. Roche, *Républicains des lettres*, p. 278.

"Your letter will be, today, Wednesday, a very agreeable reading at dinner and at supper." And Galiani wrote to J. B. A. Suard: "My letters are like those of Saint Paul, *Ecclesiae quoe est Parisiis*. Read them, then, to my friends."[24] The practice was so common that it was necessary to state explicitly if one wanted a particular letter to remain confidential. Galiani wrote to d'Holbach, for example, "Will you really take care of delivering the two enclosed letters to the persons to whom they are addressed? I send to you unsealed the one to the abbé Morellet; you will see that it is not made to be read to the whole world. *Pusillus grex electorum* should read it. No one must take a copy. Think of the position I occupy and the country I inhabit."[25]

Galiani, who had spent much of his time in Paris in the salons, knew that to write to one of their regulars was to enter the communications network. The salon spread manuscripts, news, gossip, information, and ideas through the Parisian center and beyond; it transmitted messages in the fashion of a bureau général; and it also reported on happenings in the salon itself. In April 1773, for example, Lespinasse sent Condorcet an account of the reading of a new play by its author; in April of the following year, she asked him in a letter if he had received one of three copies of a certain dialogue that had been sent out; in October 1774 she sent extracts of a letter on the death of the pope addressed to the Swedish ambassador to both Condorcet and Guibert.[26]

Galiani's correspondence reveals how fast and how far letters could travel. Even he was surprised when he learned through a third party that the letters he had been sending to Paris were being read in the king's palace in Warsaw! In 1773 he wrote to Epinay:

A man among my friends has received a letter here from the papal nuncio in Warsaw, who informs him that his Very Polish Majesty, in order

24. Geoffrin to Marmontel, 29 July 1767, in Jean-François Marmontel, *Correspondance*, ed. John Renwick, 2 vols. (Clermont-Ferrand, 1974); and Galiani to Suard, 30 June 1770.

25. Galiani to d'Holbach, 7 April 1770. The same day, Galiani wrote to Epinay, telling her that d'Holbach would show her the letter but that he did not want copies to circulate. On 24–27 April, however, Epinay wrote that d'Holbach had forwarded the letter to Morellet without showing it to anyone. When Epinay next wrote she informed Galiani that "Panurge does not breathe a word of the letter you have written him." She also passed on the news that Morellet had read the letter to d'Alembert and Lespinasse; in her next letter she reported that Marmontel, too, had heard the letter and admired it (Epinay to Galiani, 5–7 May 1770, and 12–13 May 1770). On 26 May, Galiani wrote to Epinay: "I am in despair that you have not read my letter to Panurge." He had just written a reply, he said, and hoped that this time Morellet would "communicate my letter to the honorable company. If he does not do so, however, I have kept a copy, and I will send it to you in the next post. In the meantime, commit all the crimes and all the mischief possible, including murder, to obtain a copy of my first [letter]."

26. All in *Lettres inédites de Lespinasse*.

to relieve himself of boredom (of which he has great need), has been passing his time reading a collection of my letters to my friends in France which someone had sent him a short time ago, and that he had the clemency and the discretion to communicate to his Holiness's nuncio.

Voilà, the strangest and most unexpected blow that I have ever received. My letters in Warsaw! My letters communicated to a nuncio, not of the Diet, but of the pope! . . . It's true that I wanted my letters to be shown to some of my friends, but I have never had among my friends either kings or nuncios. Never have I agreed to have copies of my letters handed out. . . .

What letters has he received? Are they mine? Have they been attributed to me? First of all, I disavow all of them.[27]

Eventually, Galiani calmed down, remembering that the king was a philosophe king and that the nuncio was a friend of his. "Nothing is so true," he wrote in his next letter, "as that I would love like crazy for people to see and read my letters, provided that those who show them remember that I am in Naples, that I am an abbé, and that there are still enough Jesuits in the world with enough life in them to seek revenge." A few weeks later, he put the affair in an even broader perspective: "Scholars are a race of fools rather difficult to handle. They aspire to celebrity, and at the same time do not want to be compromised; but you can't have one without the other . . . . I am a scholar, and I am thus a fool. I want two incompatible things. I am like the poet who did not want to be identified as the author of certain verses, but who could not stand that they be found bad."[28]

A wide range of manuscript materials passed through the salons—many on their way to eventual publication. Some manuscripts, such as poems, were enclosed with letters or were letters themselves: *epîtres*, or epistles in verse. Other works, such as Guillaume Thomas François Raynal's *Histoire des deux Indes*, were composed collectively in the salon, generated by it.[29] And this work may have emerged from an earlier, uncompleted project, conceived by Raynal, Suard, and two or three other young men newly arrived in Paris in the 1750s, a collectively written general history of voyages.[30] Morellet said of Claude Adrien Helvétius that he "continually wrote his book in company."[31] His wife's salon provided the social base for his writing and supported that of others.

The salon also provided a forum in which manuscripts could be read

27. Galiani to Epinay, 3 July 1773.
28. Galiani to Epinay, 14 August and 4 September 1773.
29. Glotz and Maire, *Salons du XVIIIème siècle*, p. 329.
30. Garat, *Mémoires historiques* 2:63–64.
31. Morellet, *Mémoires*, p. 135; see also Garat, *Mémoires historiques* 1:229–30.

aloud. Here a young author could find an audience of established and influential writers and sympathetic amateurs who, if they were impressed with his work, might back him and it. With this aim in mind, writers would go to more than one salon with poem or play in hand. Delille, for example, read parts of his translation of Virgil's *Georgics* in salons for nine years before publishing it. Such activity could advance the career of a young writer and the hopes for publication or production of his work. It also introduced new citizens into the Republic of Letters, and the philosophes already established there, who saw virtue in numbers, encouraged the entry of talented new people who were sympathetic to their aims. The opportunity to read manuscripts aloud in the salons served the salon's function as meeting ground, of the expanding space for the expanding republic.[32]

In his *correspondance littéraire* with the Russian Count Showaloff, Jean-François de La Harpe frequently reported on salon readings because, "as everything is fashion in this country, that of readings is currently very much in vogue."[33] La Harpe knew that better than anyone else. He read his play the *Barmécides* in salons as early as 1767 but did not see it staged until 1778.[34] In 1770 he appeared with another tragedy, *Mélanie, ou La Religieuse*. With it he became the most sought-after guest in all the salons of Paris. On 15 February Grimm reported on the phenomenon in his own *Correspondance Littéraire*. A year or so previously, he explained, a story had gone around Paris of a girl who had hanged herself in the parlor of a convent on the day she was to take her vows against her will and after many protests. This was the subject of La Harpe's tragedy. The young poet had written it, according to Grimm, not with any hope of seeing it staged, "for we are a long way

32. On the popularity of readings of manuscripts, see Genlis, *Dictionnaire critique*, s.v. "Lectures." Not all readings, of course, achieved their author's aims. In 1754 a young curé read his work at d'Holbach's. It was so bad that everyone made fun of him—everyone, that is, except Rousseau, who, according to one person who was present, "got up like a madman, and, throwing himself at the curé, grabbed his manuscript, threw it to the ground, and said to the frightened author: Your play is worthless; your discourse is an extravagance; all these gentlemen are making fun of you; get out of here, and go back to vicaring in your village": Letter from Jean-Antoine-Joachim Cérutti to the editor of the *Journal de Paris*, [end of November 1789], in Rousseau, *Correspondance complète*, ed. R. A. Leigh, 50 vols. (Geneva, 1965–1985), 46:99–101. See also *Correspondance Littéraire*, 1 August 1755.

33. La Harpe, *Correspondance littéraire*, letter 17 [1775?], 1:142. He had reported on readings of new poems by Delille and Roucher in his letter 14 (1:116–19), and in letter 18 (1:147–49) the discussions of the grain trade.

34. Glotz and Maire, *Salons du XVIIIème siècle*, p. 314. La Harpe's readings are mentioned in the following letters: Lespinasse to Condorcet, 25 [June 1774], in *Lettres inédites de Lespinasse*; Condorcet to Turgot, 10 December 1770, in *Correspondance inédite de Condorcet et Turgot*; and Condorcet to Amélie Suard, [April 1771], in *Correspondance inédite de Condorcet et Madame Suard*.

from using our theaters for the great and noble end of reforming moeurs." Undaunted, however, La Harpe wrote his tragedy and began to read it in various salons. "For the last two weeks," wrote Grimm,

> he has read it to fifteen different circles; the least of these circles was composed of twenty people, there were some with thirty or forty; it is said that M. de La Harpe still has commitments for three more weeks; thus, twenty or so circles still remain for him to meet. Fashion is mixed up in this, everyone wants to have attended one of these readings; after matters of finance, it's the most important matter of the day.[35]

The real surprise was yet to come, however. Two weeks later, Grimm reported that *Mélanie* had just been published. "The commotion made in Paris by the readings from circle to circle, and the reputation that they have given the work, have caused it to sell 2,000 copies in three times twenty-four hours," he wrote. La Harpe, he reflected, had been smart to give readings of his play, for they gave it a vogue it could not otherwise have had and attracted protectors among those who heard it. By contrast, Grimm reminded his readers, the year before an unknown playwright named Fontanelle had written a tragedy that made some cautious allusions to the cloister, and his work had been banned, its distributor sent to the galleys.[36]

Reading one's manuscripts aloud in salons could be an alternative to publication or a stepping-stone to it or, as La Harpe learned, both. In any case, the author hoped to profit from submitting his work to the critical discourse of the salon. There were manuscripts that were read in or circulated through salons and never published, such as Gentil-Bernard's "Art d'Aimer," which went the rounds for years, and Guibert's "Eloge du Chancelier de l'Hospital."[37] Jacques-André Naigeon claimed that "the town and the court read almost all of Diderot's manuscripts."[38] Habermas sees salon readings as a crucial forum for the philosophes. "There was scarcely a great writer in the eighteenth century who would not have first submitted his essential ideas for discussion in such discourse, in lectures before the *académies* and especially in the *salons*," he writes. "The *salon* held the monopoly of first publication:

35. *Correspondance Littéraire*, 15 February 1770.
36. Ibid., 1 March 1770; see also *Mémoires Secrets*, 24 February 1770. On 3 April the *Mémoires* printed both a poem in praise of La Harpe's tragedy and a parody of the poem.
37. Glotz and Maire, *Salons du XVIIIème siècle*, pp. 27 and 313; Picard, *Salons littéraires*, p. 334.
38. Jacques-André Naigeon, *Mémoires historiques et philosophiques sur la vie et les ouvrages de D. Diderot* (Paris, 1821), pp. 410–11.

a new work, even a musical one, had to legitimate itself first in this forum.[39]

Circulating manuscripts read aloud in the salon to those not present extended the benefits of salon participation to absent members. Turgot, for example, depended on Condorcet to include him in the discourse of Lespinasse's salon. "I am sending you the little verse from M. de La Harpe to M. de Marchais," Condorcet wrote. "Wednesday, he will read some long ones *chez* Mademoiselle de l'Espinasse. Sunday I will send you a *précis* of the play and some verses."[40]

Salon readings were not merely a second-best alternative mandated by strict censorship, nor do these private readings simply reflect the elitism of eighteenth-century intellectual life. Although publication was certainly risky, and it was more dangerous than these "private" readings or the "private" circulation of manuscripts, there was nothing clandestine about the salons, and one could also get into trouble with unpublished work, or even speech. A police report of 1751, for example, described Geoffrin's salon as follows:

> There assembles every afternoon at this lady's house a circle of wits, among whom are especially M. de Fontenelle and Helvétius, Farmer General, who are her friends.
>   She often provides meals.
>   Also she sells the rarest new books; that is to say, the authors send her a dozen copies and she takes pleasure in making her friends buy them.[41]

Not satisfied with infiltrating established salons, moreover, the Parisian police came up with the novel idea of establishing their own. Their salonnière, according to Lieutenant of Police Jean Charles Pierre Lenoir, "was received into the best homes in Paris," and, in turn,

> entertained in her own home, several times a week, courtiers, men of letters, socialites, and these idle persons one sees everywhere and who meddle in everything. She served, on days she entertained, a tea the cost of which the police paid. Her house, where persons of all conditions and of good and bad company gathered, was not regarded as completely open; only a few women attended; there were no games; people spoke there with complete freedom.[42]

39. Habermas, *Structural Transformation*, p. 34.

40. Condorcet to Turgot, 10 December 1770, in *Correspondance inédite de Condorcet et de Turgot*. The play is probably the *Barmécides*.

41. Quoted in Wilson, *Diderot*, p. 223.

42. Quoted in Alan Williams, *The Police of Paris, 1718–89* (Baton Rouge, 1979), p. 108.

Through the establishment of this phony salon, Lenoir claimed to have learned more of importance than he did through his inspectors and other contacts. Obviously, there can be no simple distinction between "safe" salon activity and "unsafe" publication.

The insecurity of salon discourse, both oral and written, moreover, lay precisely in the salon's position as a center of intellectual exchange open to new recruits. Salonnières such as Geoffrin, whose reputation extended from Russia to America, had to make difficult decisions about whom to include and whom to exclude. They depended on letters of introduction from those they trusted, opening their doors gladly to young men duly armed with such a letter in one hand and, not infrequently, a poem or play in the other. In one such letter to Geoffrin from the papal nuncio in Warsaw, the author, after flattering her at some length, finally got around to introducing his nephew: "It is he, madame, who will have the honor to present this letter to you, who will ask to be admitted into your charming society, who will be proud of the advantage he is taking of his uncle."[43]

Despite the requirement of a letter of introduction, there were occasional problems. In Geoffrin's career, the greatest one occurred early on. In 1754 she forcibly ejected from her house one abbé de Guasco who had been introduced to her by Montesquieu, one of her oldest friends. The protegé was admitted and invited back more than once, but eventually rumors that he was a spy for some powerful political figure caused her to close her doors to him, as had other women before her. In this case, however, Guasco wrote to Montesquieu, who responded in terms sympathetic to the abbé:

> I am quite astonished, my dear friend, by the behavior of *la Geoffrin*: I had not expected of her such dishonorable treatment towards a friend whom I esteem, whom I cherish, and whose acquaintance she owes to me.

43. [Antonio Eugenio] Visconti to Geoffrin, n.d., Geoffrin papers. Toward the end of her life, Geoffrin found the demands of this constant stream of introductions too great, as she explained in a letter to Grimm: "I reproach myself for having too brusquely turned down the offer, very honorable and very flattering for me, you made me of receiving Monsieur the Baron de Wreech; I am going to write down the reasons I should have spoken to you: I hope that they will excuse me to you and to Monsieur le Baron. I am seventy-one years old. New acquaintances tire my head a lot; I forget the names, titles, qualities; I make mistakes concerning identities that too often make me feel my approaching end. Moreover, when foreigners just pass through, only confused ideas of them stay with me. If they stay long enough for me to get to know them well, if they are nice, I get attached to them, and their departure grieves me. . . . You told me, my dear Grimm, that Monsieur le Baron was very nice and full of merit; this is one more reason to fortify myself in my resolution not to make new acquaintances any longer, neither foreigners nor even among my fellow citizens. The barrier is closed" (copy of a letter from Geoffrin to Grimm, 17 December 1770, Geoffrin papers).

I reproach myself for not having warned you not to go to her house any more. What has happened to hospitality? What has happened to morality? What men of letters will be secure in this house, if things there depend thus upon caprice?[44]

Two more damning letters followed, and thirteen years later, in November 1767, Guasco sought his revenge by publishing his correspondence with Montesquieu, by then long dead. As Geoffrin's daughter later noted in her account of the scandal, the timing of the publication was not fortuitous: Montesquieu's letters questioning Geoffrin's hospitality and morality reached the public at the very height of her celebrity in the wake of her trip to Poland.[45] News of Montesquieu's words, carried by the press, spread quickly. The *Gazette d'Utrecht* broke the story, making sure to quote the most insulting epithets. Geoffrin, outraged and concerned for her reputation, responded by writing to the duc de Choiseul, Louis XV's minister, with whom she had entered into delicate negotiations on behalf of Stanislas when he had sought recognition as king of Poland two years earlier. Now she asked him to step in and get a retraction from the *Gazette*, whose distribution in France depended upon the compliance of the French postal authorities and the foreign ministry.[46] Through pressure on the government of Holland, Choiseul had a retraction written by France's chargé d'affaires in The Hague placed in the next issue of the *Gazette*. Declaring that the references to Geoffrin were "entirely false and slanderous," the article added: "No more is needed to convince us that the letters attributed to the late M. de Montesquieu are spurious. We hereby retract. This is a homage that we owe to the truth, and that we render moreover with pleasure to the personal merit of madame de Geoffrin." For good measure, the government-controlled *Gazette de France* printed an article, also at the direction of Choiseul and at Geoffrin's request, displaying outrage both at Guasco and at the foreign competition:

These letters, printed without permission and published less to honor the memory of the great man under whose name they appear than to serve private hatred, have just been announced in a foreign Gazette in the most indecent manner, that most capable of disturbing the repose of citizens.

One cannot see without indignation the writers of certain public pa-

---

44. Montesquieu to Guasco, 8 December 1754, in Ségur, *Royaume de la rue Saint-Honoré,* p. 467. Ségur discusses the affair on pp. 293–95.

45. "Voilà l'histoire qui a donné lieu à cette lettre," in La Ferté-Imbault's hand and dated 15 March 1783, in Geoffrin papers.

46. On the Dutch francophone press, see Jeremy Popkin, *News and Politics in the Age of Revolution: Jean Luzac's "Gazette de Leyde"* (Ithaca, 1989).

pers lend themselves to hidden and outrageous animosities without measure or prudence against people who, by their conduct and their estimable qualities, enjoy the consideration that the public never confers without just cause.[47]

The French diplomat showed no particular regard for "truth" when he directed the *Gazette d'Utrecht* to declare the Montesquieu letters spurious, but his concern for reputation and his tough attitude toward slander were not at all out of line with that of his contemporaries in the Republic of Letters and among the public at large. Just as the commitment to truth could be overpowered by the uncontrolled egos of philosophes it could be tempered by concern for reputation.

The Guasco affair is a perfect example of a problem that plagued an age in which laws and edicts multiplied to control publications that were offensive to the state, the church, individuals, or some combination of the three, such as the rash of pornographic pamphlets about Marie Antoinette in the 1780s which cast doubt on the virility of the king while portraying the queen as a promiscuous sex fiend.[48] The very proliferation of such pamphlets shows that the French government was more successful in harassing and intimidating legitimate authors than it was in stopping the tide of slanders or *libelles*.[49]

One person who addressed the problem of unauthorized publication, which could damage reputations and thus disturb public tranquillity, was Michel de Servan, a lawyer from Grenoble and active citizen in the Republic of Letters. In 1782 Servan published "Réflexions sur la publication des lettres de Rousseau et des lettres en général," in which he urged that letters be considered the legal property of both sender and receiver and thus unpublishable without the express permission of both. The unpublished writings of deceased authors should remain that way, unless heirs had been directed otherwise. Echoing the concern voiced in the *Gazette de France* fifteen years earlier, Servan pointed out that since the French did not govern themselves and had not sought their happiness in a "stormy liberty," they at least had to be able to find happiness in "civil peace and the *douceurs* of society." The

47. Des Rivaux, chargé d'affaires, to Choiseul, 24 November 1767, in Ségur, *Royaume de la rue Saint-Honoré*, pp. 472–73; *Gazette de France*, [18, 19, or 20] November 1767. A copy of Choiseul's letter of 4 December 1767 telling Geoffrin of its publication is in the Geoffrin papers and is mistranscribed by Ségur in *Royaume*, p. 474.

48. See Chantal Thomas, *La Reine scélérate: Marie-Antoinette dans les pamphlets* (Paris, 1989); Sarah Maza, "The Diamond Necklace Affair Revisited (1785–1786): The Case of the Missing Queen," pp. 63–89, and Lynn Hunt, "The Many Bodies of Marie Antoinette: Political Pornography and the Problem of the Feminine in the French Revolution," pp. 108–30, both in *Eroticism and the Body Politic*, ed. Lynn Hunt (Baltimore, 1990).

49. On the *libelles*, see Darnton, *Literary Underground*, chaps. 4–6.

privacy of letters was obviously essential to this civil peace and quiet and therefore should not be abused.[50]

The press was both friend and enemy of the citizens of the Republic of Letters, just as it was both friend and enemy of all public persons and entities in the Old Regime. If the philosophes could use gazettes and pamphlets to their own ends, so could the monarchy; if the monarchy could complain about the abuse of the press, so could philosophes and salonnières.[51] Simply put, discourse could not be controlled once it moved out of the well-governed precincts of the salons any more than it could be outside the confines of the court. As circulation increased and the public reached and shaped by the Republic of Letters expanded, the men and women at the Parisian center discovered they had less and less control over discourse that originated there, either its destination or, more important, its interpretation and reactions to it. The networks of intellectual exchange centered in the Parisian salons and strengthened by the philosophes for the purpose of spreading enlightenment became independent structures of communication as they became more extensive and expeditious. The farther and faster news traveled, the more autonomous it became.

Nouvelles à la Main *and*
Correspondances Littéraires

The networks of intellectual exchange defined by epistolary commerce were formalized, strengthened, and expanded first through manuscript newsletters, whose editors were well established in the Parisian salons. The newsletters they edited were both derived from and devoted much of their space to letters and pieces in the form of letters.

Robert Tate traces the origins of the *nouvelles à la main* to the letters the provincial nobility used to keep in touch with the capital and the court. In an alternative but parallel explanation, Habermas ascribes this development to provincial merchants' need for news, and Hélène Monod-Cassidy reminds us that the letters that Jean de Valincour wrote regularly to Président Bouhier from Paris in the 1720s formed a

50. [Antoine-Joseph] Michel de Servan, *Oeuvres choisies*, ed. [St.-Xavier] de Portets, 5 vols. (Paris, 1822), 2:409. At the time of the Guasco affair, Grimm had expressed a similar response, remarking in the *Correspondance Littéraire* on the difficulty of protecting the posthumous image of a great man. He accused the editor of falsifying the portrait of Montesquieu for his own ends. See Bray, "*CL* témoin du goût," in Bray et al., *Correspondance littéraire de Grimm*, p. 215.

51. On the ways in which the monarchy used the press, see Baker, *Inventing the French Revolution*; and Popkin, *News and Politics*.

sort of "private gazette" or "epistolary gazette."[52] The epistolary origins of newsletters are thus found in three overlapping categories of the elite of the Old Regime: aristocracy, commercial bourgeoisie, and men of letters. Perhaps we should add to this list the royal bureaucrats and functionaries whose official correspondence formed the basis of the privileged *Gazette de France*. Eventually two sorts of newsletters would sort themselves out of this general need for news from the capital: those that reported from Paris and Versailles as the center of the French state were called *nouvelles à la main*, and those that reported from Paris as the center of the Republic of Letters were called *correspondances littéraires*. From their epistolary beginnings, these two forms of communication developed into distinct genres of newsletters corresponding to different genres of published periodicals—the *nouvelles* to the gazette or newspaper, the *correspondances* to the *journal* or literary revue. Let us look at the *nouvelles* first.

The first stage in the transformation from personal correspondence to public newsletter occurred when those in the provinces, rather than counting on friends or relatives, began to hire correspondents, or *chasseurs de nouvelles*. The *chasseurs* eventually organized themselves into *bureaux de rédaction* to pool their news resources and enable them to provide multiple copies of newsletters to subscribers on a regular basis. Each bureau, Tate explains, had "its registers for the recording of news, its 'chef de rédaction,' its scribes, and its correspondents in the provinces and abroad. At these centres, manuscript newsletters—called 'nouvelles à la main,' 'feuilles de nouvelles,' 'gazettes secrètes,' or 'gazetins'—were copied and distributed throughout Paris or sent by regular mail service . . . to the provinces."[53] The bureaux de rédaction effected an important change in the dynamics of the newsletter.

52. Robert S. Tate, Jr., *Petit de Bachaumont: His Circle and the "Mémoires Secrets," Studies on Voltaire and the Eighteenth Century* 65 (1968), p. 130; Habermas, *Structural Transformation*, p. 16; Monod-Cassidy, "De la lettre à la revue," in Bray et al., *Correspondance littéraire de Grimm*, p. 137.

53. Tate, *Petit de Bachaumont*, p. 130. Perhaps the abbé Guasco, who was barred from Geoffrin's salon, was one of these *chasseurs*—or at least was suspected of being one. Spies, after all, were writers of newsletters in someone's pay. The genre was fictionalized in *L'Espion turc*, by Jean-Paul Marana, in which the hero sent letters home from the French capital during the reign of Louis XIV. This work became the model not only for Montesquieu's *Lettres persanes* but for a whole slew of more imitative eighteenth-century epistolary "spy" novels, such as *L'Espion chinois* (1745). By the 1770s one set of actual newsletters was published as *L'Espion anglais* (1777–85), possibly by one of the editors of the *Mémoires Secrets*, Pidansat de Mairobert. See Charles E. Kany, *The Beginnings of the Epistolary Novel in France, Italy, and Spain* (Berkeley, 1937), pp. 99–100; and Popkin, *News and Politics*, p. 57. Also by the 1770s, Morellet could refer to himself in one of his newsletters to Lord Shelburne as "your spy in Paris": Morellet to Shelburne, 4 January 1776, in *Lettres de Morellet à Shelburne*.

Whereas the early correspondences had channeled a one-way flow of news from Paris and Versailles to the provinces, the bureaus brought news into the capital as well and provided it to Parisian subscribers along with provincials. They were autonomous centers of information, resembling more the gazettes and newspapers that would develop from them than the simple letters from which they derived.

The development from chasseurs de nouvelles to bureaux de rédaction parallels that of men of letters from patronage to relative autonomy in the eighteenth century. It is not surprising, therefore, to find a major bureau established in a Parisian salon throughout the long reign of Louis XV. From the time that Cardinal Fleury closed down the Club de l'Entresol in 1731 until the death of Marie Anne Legendre Doublet in 1771, men and women met daily in her salon to record and disseminate news. The Club de l'Entresol had been an attempt, inspired by Lord Bolingbroke, to create an English-style center of political sociability in Paris during the Anglophile and relatively tolerant final years of the Regency of the duc d'Orléans. Under the leadership of the abbé Charles Castel de Saint-Pierre, and in the changed political circumstances of Cardinal Fleury's ascendancy with the accession of the young king to the throne, the club attempted to go public by requesting an official authorization to undertake the study of politics. Fleury replied by closing down the club altogether, observing that "as these sorts of matters generally take one farther than desired, it is not fitting that they should make up the subject matter of [these assemblies]."[54] The founding of Doublet's salon coincided with the suppression of the club and shaped its interest in the discussion of political news into its dissemination through a newsletter.[55]

If other Parisian salons functioned as bureaus, Doublet's was one. The members of the group assembled at the same time each day in her *salle de compagnie*. Upon arrival, each person recorded in one of two registers—one for "certain" news and one for "doubtful"—the news he or she had collected that day. The two registers were then scrutinized and their contents verified.[56] Tate notes that this procedure mimicked that of the parlements in registering royal edicts. The right of remonstrance, regained by the parlements under the Regency and used throughout the eighteenth century to assert their autonomy, allowed them to protest to the king and refuse to register any edict that they

54. Quoted in Koselleck, *Critique and Crisis*, p. 67.
55. Tate, *Petit de Bachaumont*, p. 126. According to Tate, in the beginning the members of Doublet's salon were probably all men, reflecting the salon's origins in an English-style club. By the mid-1740s, however, the company was thoroughly mixed. See ibid., p. 119.
56. Ibid., pp. 135–36.

determined did not conform to the fundamental law of the realm. This refusal to register edicts, which repeatedly brought the parlements into conflict with the monarchy, unified them and gave meaning to their claims of independence and authority. The publication of parliamentary remonstrances was the mirror image of the dissemination of news from Doublet's salon, for while the latter "published" only what was verified, the former published the reasons for which verification was refused. The *nouvelles* thus consisted of information and the remonstrances of criticism. This simple distinction, however, is misleading. In the eighteenth century publication was itself a significant contribution to politics, and remonstrances were hot news items.[57] The work done by the members of Doublet's salon thus complemented that of the *parlementaires*. Not surprisingly, there was significant overlap in the personnel of the two groups.[58]

The conversation in Doublet's salon revolved around the news items gathered by her guests. It was enriched by letters sent in by corresponding members such as Voltaire or regular members temporarily away from the capital.[59] Despite the disdain he often expressed for *nouvellistes*, Voltaire was a frequent contributor to Doublet's registers via letters to friends who were among her guests. In the fall of 1742, for example, he reported on military matters. "I have sent this news to M. le président de Meinières to adorn the great book of Mme Doublet," he wrote in a letter to another woman, in which he recounted the same event.[60] Voltaire, however, was no naive reporter; he also generated or contested news in whose circulation he was interested. In September 1750, for example, he wrote to the comte d'Argental, asking him to insert in Doublet's registers a disclaimer in regard to some scandalous verses that, he claimed, a disloyal secretary had written and was attributing to him.[61] In 1764 he sent a similar disclaimer to d'Alembert to disseminate through the salons of Lespinasse and Geoffrin in regard to his authorship of the *Dictionnaire philosophique*. Voltaire found Grimm's

---

57. Ibid., p. 136. On the use and publication of remonstrances, see Baker, *Inventing the French Revolution*, pp. 61–63. On the political importance of news see Censer and Popkin, *Press and Politics*; and Popkin, *News and Politics*.

58. Tate, *Petit de Bachaumont*, pp. 112–17.

59. Ibid., pp. 121 and 137–39. Louis A. Olivier writes that the Doublet manuscripts in the Bibliothèque Nationale consist in large part of "letters forwarded by mme. Doublet without comment. Many of these are letters sent to her from officers at the front during wartime and would be more appropriately called the raw materials for *nouvelles*. Since these are often originals they must have been edited in some sense, even if only copied, before being sent to subscribers": "Bachaumont the Chronicler: A Questionable Renown," *Studies on Voltaire and the Eighteenth Century* 143 (1975), p. 166, n. 13.

60. Quoted in Tate, *Petit de Bachaumont*, p. 138.

61. Ibid., pp. 138–39.

Correspondance Littéraire useful too, as evidenced by the "Correspondance du patriarche" of 1766 concerning the La Barre affair.[62]

As in the Enlightenment salons, mail coming into Doublet's was not only registered but read aloud, and it could include manuscripts enclosed within letters.[63] And as in other salons, the news that came in also went out through the mails. Before there was a newsletter available to subscribers, there was a correspondence between Doublet and her sister in the provinces. And after the manuscript newsletter, there was publication. Starting in 1777, Pidansat de Mairobert began publication of a day-by-day chronicle drawn from the Doublet newsletter. The *Mémoires Secrets* have provided generations of historians with information and anecdotes about the Ancien Régime and the Enlightenment; they provide us with access to what their historian has called "the high point of *nouvelles à la main* in eighteenth-century France."[64]

The manuscript newsletters that originated in Doublet's salon were compiled weekly from the register of "certain" news by her valets, who were authorized by their mistress to copy and sell them for their own profit. They were distributed in Paris and the provinces and even, perhaps, abroad. As with the letters Doublet wrote to her sister, their content, as one historian has put it, "is what most of us would call news. During war-time that news concerns the front. . . . Otherwise, it consists primarily of short entries reporting deaths and marriages, official appointments and miscellaneous public events. Among the latter are occasional reports on the relations between the king and the parlement."[65] Because these newsletters lay midway between personal correspondence and anonymous publication, they could be tailored to individual subscribers. Each "packet of news," as Tate refers to them, varied "according to the tastes and interests of individual recipients, some desiring details on the affairs of the *parlement* . . . , others preferring a heavy dose of anecdotes."[66] As a consequence, it is often impossible to tell the difference between "private" correspondences and "public" newsletters: seemingly personal correspondences, ostensibly destined for a single reader, were often newsletters sent out to many.[67]

---

62. Voltaire to d'Alembert, 19 [September 1764], D12090. Voltaire was frequently newsworthy, and thus one can trace the communication networks of the eighteenth century through reference to him as well as by his use of them. Henri Duranton does so in "Les Circuits de la vie littéraire au XVIIIème siècle: Voltaire et l'opinion publique en 1733," in *Journalisme d'Ancien Régime*, pp. 101–15.

63. Tate, *Petit de Bachaumont*, p. 139.

64. Ibid., pp. 140–41, 162, 204.

65. Olivier, "Bachaumont the Chronicler," pp. 165–66.

66. Tate, *Petit de Bachaumont*, pp. 139–40.

67. Françoise Weil gives two examples of newsletters that appear to have been written for a single reader, but were not, in "Les Gazettes manuscrites avant 1750," in *Journalisme d'Ancien Régime*, pp. 96–97.

The *Mémoires Secrets*, though based on these newsletters, was something other than a print version of a manuscript source.[68] First, the *Mémoires* did not serve the function of timely reportage; it was a retrospective chronicle. With this shift in temporality came a shift in emphasis and in literary goals. As one editor explained, he was trying to write history, and by that he meant "the adventures of society," rather than the "accounts of sieges, battles, negotiations, and public ceremonies amply treated in the gazette"—what he called the "theatre of sovereigns."[69] The emphasis fell on what current historians like to call social and literary news, as opposed to the so-called political news of the *nouvelles à la main* and their true print successors and competitors, the gazettes.

The full title that Pidansat de Mairobert gave to his publication was *Mémoires Secrets pour Servir à l'Histoire de la République des Lettres en France depuis 1762 jusqu'à Nos Jours*. It was specifically intended to serve as a history of the Republic of Letters, and therefore its content reflected the republic's political and social concerns as well as the literary and artistic news that would be central to it. To distinguish between the *nouvelles* and the *Mémoires* in terms of the weight each gave to "news" versus "anecdotes" is to miss the underlying shift in subject matter from the monarchy to the Republic of Letters. The definitive difference between the two texts lay in the polity whose news each was covering: the newsletter was a manuscript gazette of the monarchy; the *Mémoires* was a printed history (or at least a chronicle) of the republic.

Louis Olivier's comparison of the coverage given to the expulsion of the Jesuits by the newsletters and by the *Mémoires* illustrates the difference well. "The *nouvelles* deal with the expulsion of the Jesuits on a day-to-day basis, reporting events as they occur, frequently but not at great length," he explains. "In a three-week period in January and February of 1762 the *nouvelles* contain no fewer than seven entries on the subject." The *Mémoires*, on the other hand, celebrated the expulsion as a watershed in the history of the Republic of Letters: "Here is one of the most famous epochs in the republic of letters! The *arrêts* of the parlement are being executed today, and the Jesuits within its jurisdiction are closing their colleges."[70]

Though *nouvelles* formed the core of the *Mémoires Secrets*, the resulting publication reflects a shift in interest away from the monarchy to

68. Olivier argues that the editors of the *Mémoires Secrets* used mainly the *nouvelles* of Pidansat de Mairobert, which were related but not identical to Doublet's, and that these were only a few of the many manuscript periodical sources they used: "Bachaumont the Chronicler," p. 176.

69. Quoted in Tate, *Petit de Bachaumont*, p. 172.

70. Olivier, "Bachaumont the Chronicler," pp. 173–74.

the Republic of Letters. The reason may lie in the fact that the readership of the *Mémoires* was the public that the philosophes had been
shaping since the 1750s. The *Mémoires* thus reads more like a print
version of the various literary correspondences emanating from the
republic than like the *nouvelles* that reported on the monarchy. It represents an attempt to transform the material of one into the form of the
other.

Like the *nouvelles à la main*, literary correspondences attracted their
readers with anecdotes and transcribed letters, as well as news of political and cultural events. There, however, the similarity ends. Their temporality and periodicity, for example, were different. Whereas the *nouvelles* were issued weekly and aimed, like the gazettes, to be as timely as
possible, the *correspondances* were less frequent, and as Tate points out,
their articles were longer and more "meditative."[71] The reader of a
literary correspondence was asked to reflect and consider more than
the reader of *nouvelles* was. The literary correspondence aimed to enlighten the reader in the style of the Republic of Letters; the *nouvelles*,
by contrast, aimed to inform and, frequently, scandalize (if not
slander). Olivier refers to the "more sober, reportorial approach" of the
nouvelles, in contrast to the *Mémoires Secrets*.[72] The literary correspondence was not so much concerned with breaking stories or providing
"secret information" as it was with creating an informed and critical
readership. As a text of mixed genre, the *Mémoires Secrets* was more
concerned with revealing secrets than were the literary correspondences (witness, again, the title) and yet had the luxury of reflecting
and commenting at greater length on the information conveyed.

According to Tate, however, the "essential" difference between the
two genres is the predominantly literary content implied by the title of
the one, versus the "heavily political (generally *frondeur*)" content of the
other. Here he makes the same distinction as Olivier, but this time the
Mémoires Secrets falls on the side of the *nouvelles*. Again, however, such a
distinction hides as much as it reveals, and so does the assumption that
supports it: that the princely audience of the literary correspondence
constrained political expression, while the audience of "freethinking
Parisian aristocrats" who bought the *nouvelles* imposed no such constraints.[73] At the bottom of this comparison is the improper distinction
between the political and the nonpolitical signaled by the qualifier

71. Tate, *Petit de Bachaumont*, p. 174.
72. Olivier, "Bachaumont the Chronicler," p. 174, n. 34. The implied judgment that
such reportorial neutrality is superior to the "tendentiousness" of the *Mémoires* is
matched by Popkin's condemnation of the *nouvelles* in comparison to the francophone
gazettes in the same terms: *News and Politics*, p. 59.
73. Tate, *Petit de Bachaumont*, p. 174.

frondeur, which resonates with the traditional sense of Old Regime politics represented by the Fronde: a politics whose participants were the nobility and the crown and whose primary concern was a struggle between them for power and authority. By contrast, the new politics of the Republic of Letters included Voltaire and the Calas family, Diderot and the *Encyclopédie*, and these political concerns were reported at length not in the *nouvelles* but in the *correspondances*.

A new politics was emerging in the 1760s, an Enlightenment, encyclopedic, Voltairean politics—the politics of the Republic of Letters—which found expression in the *Correspondance Littéraire* and the *Mémoires Secrets* but not in the *nouvelles* of the Doublet group. The strong link between the Doublet *nouvelles* and the political Jansenism of the parlements uncovered by Tate only confirms their essentially old-fashioned notion of politics as the struggle between the crown and the nobility, in contrast to the newer politics of the public sphere.[74] If both crown and parlements found themselves obliged to participate in the public discourse of this new arena and thus to contribute to its constitution, its novelty did not lie with them.

The public created by the Republic of Letters became the object of crown and nobility only after they, like other playwrights and actors before them, learned to value the power of public opinion. "The public sphere in the political realm evolved from the public sphere in the world of letters," Habermas reminds us; "through the vehicle of public opinion it put the state in touch with the needs of society."[75] When the traditional political actors entered the public sphere created by the Republic of Letters, they did not politicize it; rather, it repoliticized them: they were now compelled to participate in a new kind of politics in which authority, for example, was the subject of criticism and not simply the basis of truth or the object of political struggle, and in which public opinion had replaced traditional authorities as the determinant of public policy.[76]

The *nouvelles à la main* and the gazettes that mirrored them demonstrate the adaptability of traditional political actors to changed circumstances. The *correspondances littéraires*, however, represent the manuscript journalism of the Republic of Letters which defined those circumstances, the new arena, the new public sphere. The hybrid *Mémoires Secrets* represents the shift of interest from the old politics of the

74. On political Jansenism in the parlements see Dale K. Van Kley, *The Jansenists and the Expulsion of the Jesuits from France, 1757–1765* (New Haven, 1975); and Van Kley, "The Jansenist Constitutional Legacy in the French Prerevolution," in Baker, *Political Culture of the Old Regime*, pp. 169–201.

75. Habermas, *Structural Transformation*, pp. 30–31.

76. Baker, *Inventing the French Revolution*.

monarchy to the new one of the Republic of Letters, which was effected over the course of the 1760s and 1770s.

By the middle of the nineteenth century, Charles Nisard felt it necessary to emphasize the popularity of these manuscript journals in the decades before the Revolution. Since only a few literary correspondences had been published, the importance of this practice for the many lesser-known men of letters who wrote them and the princes and aristocrats who subscribed to them could not be appreciated. "What has happened to the others," he wondered, "those of Thiriot, Arnaud de Baculard, Suard, d'Alembert himself . . . and of the *reporters* of a less elevated order who worked at cut rates?"[77] Paule Jansen suggests one reason why literary correspondences were so popular. After comparing the content of Grimm's *Correspondance Littéraire* for one month in 1768 with that of twelve journals published the same year, she concludes that almost everything in the *Correspondance* could be found in one or another of the journals. Some items even appeared earlier in the press than they did in Grimm's manuscript. Grimm, therefore, was a journalist like other journalists; the difference, Jansen concludes, was that he was a better journalist. Whereas items appeared here and there in the public press, Grimm managed to bring them all together to supply his subscribers with the most complete account of what was going on in Paris.[78] Grimm could be such a good journalist because he was well situated in the salons at the center of the Enlightenment Republic of Letters.

J. B. A. Suard's correspondence with John Wilkes reveals another aspect of the interdependency of literary correspondences and periodicals. In October 1772, three months before he began a three-year stint as literary correspondent for the margrave de Bayreuth, Suard wrote to Wilkes on behalf of a "friend." This "man of wit and merit," he explained,

> is very poor and . . . is looking for some means of subsistence. He has been hired, for money, to write to a foreigner all the current news of this country, and he would very much like to multiply his correspondences because this would be an increase of income and not of work. I thought that this might interest one of your printers of gazettes. . . . Finally, one would find in your newspapers an article of Parisian News that would make sense and have some continuity, since now one can find little but nonsensical platitudes, copied and disfigured from the Dutch gazettes.[79]

77. Charles Nisard, *Mémoires et correspondances historiques et littéraires inédits—1726 à 1816* (Paris, 1858), pp. 86–87.

78. Paule Jansen, "La *Correspondance littéraire* et douze périodiques traités par ordinateur," in Bray et al., *Correspondance littéraire de Grimm*, pp. 150–51.

79. Suard to Wilkes, 30 October 1772, in "Lettres inédites de Suard à Wilkes."

Like journalism, literary correspondence was a source of income for the struggling man of letters. It was attractive because the writer had significantly more freedom than he would have in editing a publication that had to run the gauntlet of police and censorship.[80] Suard somehow thought he could double as foreign correspondent for a London newspaper and as literary correspondent for a German prince, supplying both with the same news. The scheme failed, however, because Suard got scared. In the letter just quoted he referred to the "literary inquisition" in France, which obliged living authors to attribute their work to the dead. This situation explains his reference to a "friend," even in a letter that was hand delivered. Suard further cautioned Wilkes to "speak of this object as of a purely literary correspondence" if he replied by the post. By this he meant not that the subject matter would be purely literary but that the arrangement was to send news privately to an individual rather than to publish in a periodical. Wilkes responded enthusiastically, but Suard withdrew his offer. He drew back because Wilkes asked for more than just news: he thought Suard could provide a monthly commentary on the French political scene. Suard had to explain to his English friend the facts of life in France in the 1770s.

> I thought I had made clear to you that the man who offered his services did not wish to compromise himself in any way; that he would send only publicly known facts without commentary, and private adventures the most apt to amuse or interest foreigners. I have communicated and translated your letter for him, but your proposition scared him. . . . It would be impossible for a series of articles of the sort that you desire, printed outright in your papers, not to stimulate investigations, and nothing would be so easy as to get back to the source.[81]

Through this exchange Suard discovered that the formal similarities between foreign and literary correspondence masked the significant gulf that was publicity. Unwilling to take the leap, he gave up his money-making scheme in the interest of security, retreating to the relative safety of the manuscript literary correspondence.

Although the English scheme fell through, Suard still managed to double his profits by signing up another Central European correspondent, the margrave d'Anspach. A letter from the margrave's agent, the comte de Gemmingen, reveals that the literary correspondent had more

---

80. In her *Essais de mémoires sur M. Suard* (Paris, 1820), Amélie Suard recalled that the abbé Jean-François Arnaud "lived . . . off a correspondence with a duke of Wirtemberg, where he could lay out everything that he thought and felt," and for that reason he was inclined to reject an offer to edit the *Gazette de France* because it would constrain him (p. 41).

81. Suard to Wilkes, 9 December 1772, in "Lettres inédites de Suard à Wilkes."

duties than simple reportage: he functioned as a *bureau de correspon-dance*, as the foreigner's agent in Paris in matters cultural. Suard was asked to help the margrave improve his library. "You have seen, sir, by the catalog that Mademoiselle Clairon has shown you, that [the collec-tion] is far from complete, and that much is needed to make it into a well-chosen library," wrote the count. "Your knowledge will supply that, and monseigneur will be charmed to form his collection according to your advice."[82] Morellet, too, assisted his correspondent Lord Shel-burne in forming his library. He also located a French chef for him.[83] And Grimm was constantly employed on behalf of his various royal and noble correspondents. They frequently commissioned him to buy paintings for them. Often Grimm bought pieces on behalf of his clients from Geoffrin, who supported the artists who came to her Monday salons by buying their paintings.

Above all, the *correspondances littéraires*, like the *nouvelles*, formalized the salon function of sending out the mail. They connected Paris with subscribers in the Republic of Letters and served as a medium for the transmission of letters. As in the letters of salonnières and their guests, the salon—its activities and participants—was often itself the subject matter, the place where news happened. The salon took its place beside the academies and other cultural institutions of interest to European readers. The receipt and circulation of a letter by Voltaire or a discus-sion of the politics of the grain trade or the reading of a new poem was news in the Republic of Letters.

"Literary correspondence" is, in a sense, a redundancy, for both words derive from letters. The *correspondances littéraires* thus reiterated their commitment to the dual purpose of the letter in the salon-based Republic of Letters. First, as part of a correspondence, the letter was a form of communication, a link between people who used epistolary commerce as a basis of community and a means of exchanging repre-sentations and interpretations of the world. Second, the letter was spe-cifically "literary"—what we in the twentieth century would call a piece of writing. The letter was a formal genre of writing, its composition an act of creation as well as communication. A good letter was a work of art that communicated. It was also part of the larger whole that was the correspondence. What distinguished literary correspondences from private correspondences such as that between Geoffrin and Catherine or between Voltaire and d'Alembert was not their formality but their lack of reciprocity: literary correspondents only sent letters regularly; they did not regularly receive them.

82. [Le comte de Gemmingen to Suard, 22 May 1773], in Nisard, *Mémoires et corre-spondances*, p. 89.
83. Morellet to Shelburne, 20 October 1774, in *Lettres de Morellet à Shelburne*.

The reports of men such as Grimm, Suard, and La Harpe were valuable because their authors were insiders in the salons. News items that found their way into a *correspondance* but not anywhere else were probably gleaned from salon conversation.[84] Thus, although the *correspondances* could be as collaborative as the *nouvelles*, they were not the product of news bureaus in the Doublet sense, where salon guests were reporters and valets were scribes. Rather, since the salon was perceived to be the center of activity, the collaboration of editors and writers was a representation of the salon itself—its personnel and its activities, as well as its ideology and values. Hélène Monod-Cassidy thus finds the origins of literary correspondences in the private correspondences of Parisian men of letters with their friends and patrons back home in the provinces. She gives the example of abbé Le Blanc, who left his native Dijon at twenty-two to seek fame and fortune in the capital in the 1720s. "Very quickly," she writes,

> he was received in the salons of the epoch. . . . He accumulated a hoard of small bits of news and commentary that he sent to Dijon. And the président [Bouhier] responded, with grace, showing his curiosity about the details of Parisian life, criticizing the poems that he received from Le Blanc. The abbé gave him news of the Academy, commented on the speeches that he heard; when he met Voltaire, or Crébillon *fils*, for example, he communicated to the président the observations, the confidences they gave him.[85]

A literary correspondent was, in one way or another, less than equal to the person with whom he corresponded. If he was originally a young protégé like Le Blanc, in the heyday of such correspondents (the 1770s and 1780s) he was more likely the paid agent of a foreign prince or noble. Morellet, who was not above this sort of work himself, as his correspondence with Lord Shelburne demonstrates, nevertheless displayed in a critique of Grimm's *Correspondance Littéraire* the unease of men of letters of the Old Regime when faced both with the necessity of making a living and the personal cast of intellectual discourse. At the end of his life, when he was rewriting the history of Enlightenment sociability, he had the rare opportunity to see the published version of Grimm's *Correspondance Littéraire* and was unhappy with some of what he found written about himself. In his "Observations sur la *Correspondance Littéraire* de Grimm," which was published as an appendix to his memoirs in 1821, Morellet sought to set the record straight by defining

84. Jansen identifies one such news item in "*Correspondance littéraire* et douze périodiques," in Bray et al., *Correspondance littéraire de Grimm*, p. 149.
85. Monod-Cassidy, "De la lettre à la revue," ibid., p. 138.

the literary correspondent in rather unflattering terms: "He is a man who, for money, is hired to amuse a foreign prince every week—to whom he belongs—and, with, in general, all literary production that sees the light of day, and that of which he is the author."[86]

The literary correspondent was thus a somewhat problematic figure in the Enlightenment Republic of Letters, even if it was a figure cut by many men of letters out of financial need and because the position offered relatively more freedom than journalism. There was also a certain amount of old-fashioned honor attached to serving a prince or count instead of selling one's literary wares on the open market.

The literary correspondence was in some important ways a false development for the discourse of the Enlightenment Republic of Letters, for the asymmetrical relationship between patron and patronized was inscribed there. Like the letters sent back to his patron in Dijon by the young abbé Le Blanc, Monod-Cassidy argues, Grimm's *Correspondance Littéraire* "responded to a double need for a communication that appeared personal but was, in reality, rather general. This was to recognize the importance of the personnage to whom the letters were addressed—just as one dedicated a tragedy to a nobleman or a great lady." Such a balance between the public and the personal was a sort of "homage rendered . . . to the dignity of [the reader's] person."[87] As long as this sort of privilege characterized discourse that emanated from the Enlightenment Republic of Letters, it could convey ideas and information, but it could not represent the values of the republic as academic and scholarly correspondences had represented them in the seventeenth century.

Thus, while literary correspondences formalized the news-gathering and -disseminating functions of letters, they did not fully represent the ideals of the Republic of Letters as private correspondence had done. Although they were derived from two-way correspondence, they could not provide a model of discourse for an Enlightenment Republic of Letters that as a *republic* was based on the reciprocal communication that defined it as a community; and as a republic of *letters* took the higher aims of literary or artistic creativity as its own; and that as a center of Enlightenment had to reach out to the public. Only with the further extension and transformation of the literary correspondence into the literary journal did the Enlightenment Republic of Letters find an epistolary genre that was both public and reciprocal, and which could thus reach out to become the center of a growing enlightened

86. Morellet, "Observations sur la Correspondance Littéraire de Grimm," in *Mémoires* (1821 ed.), 1:331–32.

87. Monod-Cassidy, "De la lettre à la revue," in Bray et al., *Correspondance littéraire de Grimm*, p. 142.

public. Only with the publication of epistolary texts and the whole field
of discourse generated by that publication, in pamphlets, periodicals,
and letters to editors, was the reciprocity of republican literary discourse achieved and a critically debating public created.

Periodicals

Throughout the eighteenth century, the book review and extract
were the major features of literary journals. And although some men
of letters tended to sneer at journalists and disdain their extracts as
inadequate substitutes for the books themselves, they and their work
were crucial to the Republic of Letters.[88] Editors, writers, and readers
alike could profit from the practice of literary journalism. Not surprisingly, just as the number of books published each year increased
enormously in France over the course of the eighteenth century, so did
the number of journals, more than doubling between 1740 and 1780,
from 64 to 150.[89]

According to Morin d'Hérouville, it was the citizenry who demanded
such publications. In the *avertissement* for his *Annales Typographiques*, he
noted that each country had its own journals and books, but that everybody was not so learned as to speak all their languages. Moreover, the
world was quickly expanding: "We see geographical maps multiply as
new lands are discovered." Thus, for some time, "the citizens of the
Republic of Letters have wished that there was in a universal language
such as French an exact notice of everything that appears in all the
countries of Europe." The resulting publication, which was little more
than an annotated catalog, its editor described as "a sort of universal
library . . . , a great literary map of the world."[90]

Periodicals also published announcements of projects, literary and
otherwise, to which the citizenry of the Republic of Letters could subscribe. Under the rubric, "Nouvelles littéraires," were included not only
announcements and extracts of new books but also announcements of
projects and prospectuses in which readers were invited to participate
through subscription.[91]

---

88. For the *Encyclopédie*'s attitude toward the journals, see Paul Benhamou, "The
Periodical Press in the *Encyclopédie*," *French Review* 59 (February 1986): 410–17.

89. Walter, "Auteurs et le champ littéraire," in Martin and Chartier, *Histoire de
l'édition française* 2:391.

90. Quoted in Claude Labrosse, "Fonctions culturelles du périodique littéraire," in
Labrosse and Pierre Rétat, *L'Instrument périodique: La Fonction de la presse au XVIIIe siècle*
(Lyon, 1985), p. 80.

91. Jacques Wagner, *Marmontel, journaliste, et le "Mercure de France" (1725–1761)*
(Grenoble, 1975), p. 31; Labrosse, "Fonctions culturelles," in Labrosse and Rétat, *Instrument périodique*, p. 9.

Some editors, moreover, defended their work by claiming that the extracts they provided were but the means to a higher goal. The editor of the *Nouvelliste du Parnasse*, for example, declared that the epistolary form of his journal was meant to make his readers think about the novelties of which he informed them: "Our goal . . . has never been to make extracts of new books; our letters are aimed at reflections on intellectual and other works, when they create the occasion to say agreeable or curious things. It is not without reason that we have chosen the epistolary style; beyond the fact that this style is free and relaxed, certain tricks [*tours*] that are common to it give sharpness [*éclat*] and vivacity to reflections."[92] In the same vein, Dominique-Joseph Garat wrote that the editorial team of Suard and Jean-François Arnaud

> conceived and executed under two successive titles, the *Journal étranger* and the *Gazette littéraire*, the project of making known to France, either by analytical extracts or by complete translations, all that would appear in Europe in the arts, in the sciences, in letters, no matter what their success, their *éclat*, or simply the noise they made. . . .
>
> Everyone with an enlightened spirit in Europe was called to the execution of this project and entered into it; what the foreigners did for France, they did also for their own country: never had there been a correspondence so widespread, so varied, and so well maintained solely by the interests, everywhere [else] neglected, in reason, taste, and the enlightenment of peoples.[93]

Garat also discussed the collaborative interrelationship between this French effort and its Italian counterpart. "Two periodical works," he wrote, "contributed powerfully to the opening of new literary and philosophical communications between these two . . . countries: the *Journal étranger* . . . and le *Cafè* [sic], edited in Milan with no less success by the marquis de Beccaria, the marquis de Véry, and . . . their collaborators. Articles from the *Journal étranger* often went into le *Cafè*, those of le *Cafè* into the *Journal étranger*. Never have new ideas had such rapid circulation at long distance."[94]

The journal editor was not simply the "parasite" he was reputed to be, predigesting the work of writers for a lazy reading public. Journals increasingly published short stories, poems, and articles, some even in serial form. The literary journal could be the place of first publication, could fulfill for authors what Robert Favre calls the function of promo-

92. Quoted in Monod-Cassidy, "De la lettre à la revue," in Bray et al., *Correspondance littéraire de Grimm*, p. 141.
93. Garat, *Mémoires historiques* 1:151–52.
94. Ibid., 2:193–94.

tion by opening to them "an intermediate space between the study and the bookshop, between their solitude or their small circle of friends and the large public to whom they seek access."[95] Marmontel played an important role in expanding this function when he edited the *Mercure de France* from 1758 to 1761. There his own stories became a regular feature, along with the contributions of many of his friends and colleagues in the Republic of Letters. A letter from Voltaire suggests that the philosophes welcomed this forum. "When you are short of new work," he wrote to Marmontel, "I can provide you with some foolishness or other that will not appear under my own name and will serve to fill up the volume." Marmontel's response shows that Voltaire was not alone in his enthusiasm.

> My work will be well seconded if the men of letters wish to hold to the promises they have made me with the best grace in the world. Bernard himself, the wise and discreet Bernard will open his portfolio to me. I will have some fragments of *l'Art d'aimer*. I have some pretty pieces from M. de Saint-Lambert, and from M. le comte de Tressan.
>
> M. D'Alembert is going to give me a beautiful piece of philosophy; M. de Vaucanson, the description of a new *métier* he has made for the Gobelins. . . . M. Diderot, this Atlas who holds up the Encyclopédie, has offered to comfort me by giving me some extracts.[96]

The practice of publishing new work in the *Mercure* continued long after Marmontel's tenure, moreover, as the publication in 1778 of Morellet's essays on contradiction and conversation demonstrate. It also extended to other journals. Over the years 1765–1780, for example, Favre has found new poems in eight journals besides the *Mercure de France*.[97]

Journalism thus performed important services for both readers and writers by bringing them together in a variety of ways. It could also be an important source of financial support. When philosophes such as Raynal, Marmontel, Suard, and Arnaud landed editorships of major privileged periodicals such as the *Mercure de France* and the *Gazette de France* they found themselves in relatively comfortable circumstances. Although these positions were sinecures, those who held them could and did use their publications to shape a citizenry for the Republic of Letters, as Garat's praise of Suard and Arnaud makes clear.[98] Whether

95. Robert Favre, "Une Fonction du périodique: Du manuscrit au livre," in *Journalisme d'Ancien Régime*, p. 258.

96. Voltaire to Marmontel, 16 May [1758], and Marmontel to Voltaire, [c. 25 May 1758], in Marmontel, *Correspondance*. See also Wagner, *Marmontel, journaliste*, pp. 271–80.

97. Favre, "Fonction du périodique," in *Journalisme d'Ancien Régime*, p. 261.

98. See also Labrosse, "Fonctions culturelles," in Labrosse and Rétat, *Instrument périodique*.

privileged or not, journals and their editors were important means of shaping a critical reading public.

"As institutionalized art criticism," writes Habermas, "the journals devoted to art and cultural criticism were typical creations of the eighteenth century." They were typical because they were critical, not just mechanical or synthetic. If philosophy and literature were themselves critical, this was not enough: only through the critical form of journalism could the reader learn in a fashion adequate to that which he or she was being taught. "It was only through the critical absorption of philosophy, literature," Habermas explains, "that the public attained enlightenment and realized itself as the latter's living process."[99]

A favorable review, a representative extract, or even a brief description was helpful both to the struggling author and to the provincial reader in facilitating diffusion beyond Paris and beyond France, where people depended on periodicals to let them know what had been published and if it was worth ordering. Norman Fiering writes of the reliance of eighteenth-century Americans on the learned European journals to which they subscribed. James Logan of Philadelphia, for example, "was determined to be a full citizen of the international republic of letters even though an ocean separated him from its capitals." He subscribed to two of these periodicals, the *New Memoirs of Literature* and the *Present State of the Republick of Letters* (an English imitation of Bayle's *Nouvelles*). "His impatience with [the] editing [of the *New Memoirs*] was surely an indication of his desperate sense of dependency upon [it]," writes Fiering. "The man of letters in eighteenth-century America had to struggle hard to overcome mere provincial status."[100]

Americans were not alone in their desire to overcome provincial status in a world of slow communication, unsure and expensive postal service, and difficult transportation, especially across national borders. Daniel Roche reminds us that travel was still an elite phenomenon in eighteenth-century Europe.[101] Arthur Young's *Travels in France* is on one level a detailed account of these difficulties as he experienced them in the 1780s.[102] In his letters to Epinay, too, Galiani was forever complaining about the post and trying to minimize the high cost of keeping in touch.[103] Nor did he ever manage even one trip back to Paris after

99. Habermas, *Structural Transformation*, pp. 41–42.

100. Norman S. Fiering, "The Transatlantic Republic of Letters: A Note on the Circulation of Learned Periodicals to Early Eighteenth-Century America," *William and Mary Quarterly* 33 (October 1976): 659.

101. Roche, *Siècle des lumières en province* 1:321. In a study of a provincial academician in the 1770s, however, Roche notes that his visitors outnumbered his correspondents five to one: Roche, *Républicains des lettres*, p. 275.

102. Arthur Young, *Travels in France during the Years 1787, 1788, 1789*, ed. M[atilda Barbara] Betham-Edwards (London, 1924).

103. E.g., Galiani to Epinay, 5 May 1770.

his hasty departure in 1769. Indeed, he never again managed to get farther from Naples than Rome.

Even Galiani, who could count on personal correspondence to keep him in touch with Paris, also read the gazettes and journals and enjoined Epinay to fill her letters only with news that he would not already have found in these public sources. "In general, save the news that can be found in the gazettes; thus nothing about shallots nor about Chalotais," he wrote, referring to the ongoing story of the Breton lawyer whose defiance provoked a crisis for the French monarchy. "I will read that in the *Courrier d'Avignon* (today of Monaco), which is, in truth, very interesting, but which will not have printed in its entirety Voltaire's *pamphlet*, for which infinite thanks. It has found a lot more readers here than you could have ever imagined."[104]

Starting in the 1760s, there was increased interest in the speed and extent of the circulation of literary news. Claude Labrosse finds that editors no longer felt they could satisfy their subscribers with quarterly publication: every journal he studied came out at least monthly, and many appeared weekly. Also, more attention was paid to news from England and the provinces. He quotes the *avertissement* for the *Avant-coureur*: "In order to infuse more interest in this paper in making it common to the provinces, we propose to draw from the principal cities of the realm all that is of a kind to be included in it, and to get it to the point at which it will become a channel of communication that will carry into the Provinces the knowledge of our literary riches and pour into the capital those that we can gather from all the places where we have established correspondences."[105]

Like letters, however, journals and gazettes circulated by means of the postal system. Mutual dependence on the post bound the writers and readers of letters and periodicals together in relation to an absolutist state that exercised the power to control the written materials that went through its hands by opening letters and restricting the circulation of periodicals or banning them altogether. In addition, because journals and gazettes were distributed through the post, their periodicity was that of private correspondence. Indeed, Eugène Vaillé speculates that "the periodicity of the first papers was a function of the postal couriers, weekly at first, when there was, at the center of information, only one courier per week, to become then bi-weekly and finally daily. . . . In terms of receiving and distribution, the importance of

<hr />

104. Galiani to Epinay, 25 September [1769]. In his letter to her of 5 May 1770, Galiani mentioned the *Gazette de France, Gazette de Naples, Mercure [de France]*, and *Gazette de Florence*. On L. R. Caradeuc de La Chalotais see John Rothney, ed., *The Brittany Affair and the Crisis of the Ancien Régime* (New York, 1969).

105. Labrosse, "Fonctions culturelles," in Labrosse and Rétat, *Instrument périodique*, pp. 73–78, 85–86, and n. 19.

the postal service was as essential as the printing press for multiplication."[106]

It was this periodicity that transformed revolutionary pamphlets into newspapers in 1789, and it was crucial to readers' experience and understanding of the world in which they lived. "With the periodical," writes Labrosse, "reading enters into *the necessity of the event*, it becomes itself a type of event." More specifically, Pierre Rétat sees in the point at which the *Révolutions de Paris* began to publish as a periodical a shift from meaningless chronicle to a sense-making journalism that constituted a "theoretical affirmation of the principles of the Revolution."[107]

If periodicals became events in the lives of their readers, reading them also became habitual. "Unlike the reader of a novel, the reader of *The Spectator* is not carried along by the logic of cause and effect or by the teleology of the plot," writes Michael Ketcham of the London periodical that made the greatest impression on the philosophes. "Instead, he is carried along by habit, and this makes for a very different kind of reading than reading fiction." The *Spectator*, he argues, became the "literary analogue of habit."[108]

Beyond shaping the relationship between the text and the event, therefore, periodicity also shaped the relationship between the text and the reader. Unlike the reader of a book or a pamphlet, the subscriber to a journal or gazette was subject to the rhythms of periodical production and distribution. Jeremy Popkin notes that readers of gazettes set aside time to read them, "regulated by the predictable schedules of publication and mail delivery." Reading groups that formed to share the cost of periodicals also distributed the time of reading them, as each member was given a fixed time to read the paper before handing it on to the next subscriber. "Newspaper readers were thus time-conscious readers; newspaper reading served to integrate them into the broader flow of public time, rather than serving, like book reading, as an escape into a private realm divorced from external constraints."[109]

If periodical reading was thus different from book reading, it was for the same reasons similar to letter reading; subscription to a periodical was a formalized extension of participation in a correspondence. Each number of the journal or gazette was the equivalent of a letter in a

106. Eugène Vaillé, "La Poste et la presse sous l'Ancien Régime," *Bulletin d'Informations, de Documentation, et de Statistique*, no. 5 (May 1936): 34.
107. Labrosse, "Fonctions culturelles," in Labrosse and Rétat, *Instrument périodique*, p. 62; Pierre Rétat, "Forme et discours d'un journal révolutionnaire: Les *Révolutions de Paris* en 1789," ibid., p. 143. Baker takes up and extends Rétat's reading in *Inventing the French Revolution*, pp. 218–20.
108. Michael G. Ketcham, *Transparent Designs: Reading, Performance, and Form in the "Spectator" Papers* (Athens, Ga., 1985), pp. 97–98.
109. Popkin, *News and Politics*, pp. 132–33.

correspondence, as the royal administration itself understood it to be in a 1756 regulation, which stated that "a gazette is nothing but a letter multiplied with the help of printing." Since letter carrying was a monopoly of the state, so too was the distribution of gazettes.[110] The periodical, moreover, retained certain features of reciprocity that betrayed both its origin in epistolary communication and its need to simulate it.

Letters from readers filled the pages of journals, and letters from paid correspondents filled the gazettes. Popkin writes that the editor of the *Gazette de Leyde* "created a journalistic text whose words were often taken verbatim from the letters and documents his correspondents provided." Indeed, the lengthy reports provided by these foreign correspondents were identified for readers as "letters."[111] Readers did not find in the gazettes a forum for the expression of their own views, however. They were the objects of political journalism, like the "addressees of public authority," who, according to Habermas, were the first public formed by the absolutist state.[112] The gazette gave its readers "the raw material for critical judgments of their rulers," admits Popkin, but it did not offer itself as a venue for the public opinion that must issue from these judgments and thus tacitly reinforced the political order that rested on the old representational public sphere. "In reading the *Gazette de Leyde*," he concludes, "ordinary subscribers were simultaneously admitted to the realm of public affairs and yet reminded of their powerlessness to affect it."[113] Only in the literary journals was the reading public transformed from object to subject.

Unlike the gazettes, the journals encouraged their readers to participate in critical epistolary exchange. Bayle had been the first to edit a periodical that depended upon readers' contributions. By 1728 an English imitator could launch his own *Republick of Letters* with a call for collaborators: "I entreat the assistance of all those who wish well to the progress of learning and beg they will favor me . . . with extracts of curious books with such original pieces and accounts of new inventions and machines and any other improvements . . . as are fit to be communicated to the public."[114] Throughout the eighteenth century, such journals functioned as bureaux généraux for the Republic of Letters. Letters from readers were so integral to the enterprise of literary journalism that a 1763 edict regulating the distribution of periodicals included an article specifying that all letters received from subscribers

110. Quoted in Vaillé, "Poste et la presse," p. 39.
111. Popkin, *News and Politics*, pp. 98 and 106.
112. Habermas, *Structural Transformation*, p. 18.
113. Popkin, *News and Politics*, p. 136.
114. Quoted in Eisenstein, *Print Culture and Enlightenment Thought*, p. 7.

would have to be paid for by publishers unless they advised their readers in a public notice to have them franked at the point of origin.[115]

One reader of the *Mercure de France*, a M. Quotin, clearly viewed his
relationship with this journal as epistolary. In June 1755 he wrote to
Duclos, praising him for his thoughts on gratitude and ingratitude
which had appeared in the February number and declaring that he
must be "the man most capable in all the world of giving advice in a
matter of behavior in regards to services." Quotin then presented a
detailed account (six printed pages) of three matters on which he sought
advice, and he gave Duclos two options for responding: he could
write to him directly, or "if you would like to instruct me by means of a
public channel [*une voie publique*] such as the *Mercure*, which I think
would be best because the utility of your response would be spread
farther and you would have the occasion to write a supplement to your
considerations, please suppress the proper names." He then suggested
that Duclos might insert some judicious extracts from the cases he had
just set out by way of examples. In other words, in asking for a response
to his letter Quotin was really feeding Duclos material for a published
article in the form of a letter that would incorporate his own contribution. To protect his provincial self, he asked Duclos not to use real
names and begged him not to show his letter to anyone and not to try to
"penetrate whatever is enigmatic in it if by chance the occasion should
present itself." Duclos's response is lost, but a nineteenth-century description of it from an auction catalog suggests that he was as surprised
as anybody by the position in which his reader had put him. According
to the catalog description, "Duclos was rather astonished to find himself transformed into a consulting moralist; nevertheless, he made a
pronouncement against the puerile amour propre of the person who
reveals to guests the service he has rendered to the host, the merit of
which he thereby lowers. He had the beginning of the letter inserted in
the *Mercure* and sent to M. Quotin the other part that is attached to the
letter."[116] Duclos split the difference, responding to Quotin both privately in the form of a letter and publicly by means of the *Mercure*, as
Quotin had suggested.

Journals served as the meeting ground for a public seeking a forum
and their model was the *Spectator*. "Through the exchange of letters,"
writes Michael Ketcham, "*The Spectator* is shown to be a meeting ground
of public and private, of 'Publick Benefit' and 'Secret' Pleasures." It was

115. *Délibération de la compagnie des administrateurs des postes réglant les rapports de la poste
et des éditeurs d'ouvrages périodiques* (13 November 1763), art. 10, in Vaillé, "Poste et la
presse," p. 67.

116. Quotin to Duclos, 13 June 1755, and catalog description of response dated 17
June 1755, in *Correspondance de Duclos*.

also the meeting ground of readers who read each other's letters. Letters broadened the discursive range of the journal by introducing topics of interest to the variety of readers and their differing viewpoints, and they established what Ketcham calls "a common body of shared opinion." Through the incorporation of readers' letters, the *Spectator* thus managed to multiply perspectives from which a topic could be viewed and to harmonize them with a unifying editorial voice. The reader is thus brought into the community created by the periodical through incorporation of his or her letters in it. "*The Spectator* acknowledges its readers' contributions, it assimilates the letters into its own vocabulary and its own conventions of description. As a result they, too, conform to and confirm its picture of social cohesion by endorsing the language that makes this picture visible." The unifying language of the editor, moreover, into which individual letters were "translated," created the community of the *Spectator* "club" not only by harmonizing different views but also by making possible communication among readers who might otherwise have been mutually incomprehensible, locked into their own exclusive discourses. There was, of course, illusion practiced here, a sleight of hand which turned the "letter" as an independent expression of its "author" into an integral part of the discourse of the editor. "Letters from different sources are published together to contribute to a speaking community contained, literally, within the borders of *The Spectator*'s sheets of paper," Ketcham explains. But

> the letters, which supposedly represent diverse opinions, originate in *The Spectator*'s own speculations and stand as substitutes for it. They represent an exchange of opinions, yet they are mirrors of *The Spectator* that reflect its ideas and its vocabulary as transposed into other hands. . . . The published *Spectator* may be seen as an actual dialectic of opinions, a medium of communication between readers. Or it may be seen as a fabrication, where all responses to *The Spectator* are *The Spectator*.[117]

Under the control of a strong editor such as Addison or Steele, a journal could be both a forum for the exchange of ideas from and between readers and the expression of an editorial voice that defined their common discursive ground. Under a weaker editor, however, that ground could be significantly less stable. From Nina Gelbart's study of the *Journal des Dames* we learn how an active readership could shape a

117. Ketcham, *Transparent Designs*, pp. 125–32. See also Habermas, *Structural Transformation*, p. 42.

journal from its very first issue, making of it a more open forum than an eighteenth-century editor might imagine.[118]

In 1758 a young man by the name of Thorel de Campigneulles decided to launch himself in the Republic of Letters with a journal aimed at a female audience. His prospectus promised light and frivolous fare suitable for ladies and inoffensive to public authority, but this objective was already under attack when the inaugural issue of the *Journal des Dames* appeared in January 1759. In that very first issue, Campigneulles printed a letter from an anonymous reader who advised him to show more respect for his female readers by being more serious. "Doubtless in response to the admonition," Gelbart writes, "he played down feminine frivolity. He also printed articles, probably by contributors, that were far more controversial than he had wished." In his fourth and last issue, the fledgling editor found himself so entangled in the web made of his expectations of his female readers and theirs of his journal that he "was forced to print a story from an elderly nobleman's sexually frustrated young wife, who had finally contrived to install her lover in the château as a domestic. 'You must print this,' she teased, 'for you have promised it suffices to be female to appear in your pages.'" The lesson that young Campigneulles learned too late was that a journal was not the property of its editor but a forum for its readers. "He did not want an exchange with his audience," Gelbart explains, "had no intention of diagnosing its social situation, and shunned the notion of becoming its spokesman. In just four months, however, he had discovered that simply inviting the participation of women in his paper opened a dialogue that threatened to challenge dominant presuppositions and evoke unorthodox responses." And the lesson was not lost on Campigneulles's successor at the *Journal des Dames*, who had a high level of reader participation because he presented his journal as an open dialogue. Yet he too was to see his journal get away from him, as his readers "misconstrued his chivalrous efforts in their behalf [and] transform[ed] his innocent paper into a forum for transgressive, socially disruptive reflections."[119]

Why did eighteenth-century readers take such a proprietary interest in the journals they read? What was it that allowed them to view a journal not simply as an instrument to inform and amuse them but as a forum for intellectual exchange with editors, writers, and other readers? The epistolary origins of the periodical press provide one sort of answer to this question, especially when we see how close to the formal surface of journals these origins remained in the eighteenth century.

---

118. Gelbart, *Feminine and Opposition Journalism.*
119. Ibid., pp. 53, 59, 66, 85–86.

Another answer can be found in the new practice of subscription, by
which periodical readerships were formed and which was used in many
other creative and far-reaching ways. The ways in which subscription
was used in the Enlightenment Republic of Letters help us to understand how reading could be the basis of community and thus how a
reading public could become a political force.

Public Subscription

"Subscribers to periodicals were responding to a fairly new medium," writes Nina Gelbart, "almost as if they were joining a club."[120]
The periodical and the practice of subscription developed at the same
time. Although the periodicity of periodicals has been studied, the
practice and mechanics of subscription have not been fully appreciated. Historians have generally viewed the public subscription as an
intermediate stage in the capitalist development of literary and artistic
production. "The patron's place is taken by the publisher," writes Ar-
nold Hauser, and "public subscription, which has very aptly been called
collective patronage, is the bridge between the two." Subscription,
Hauser continues, retains some of the personal relationship between
author and public that characterized aristocratic patronage. Only with
"the publication of books for a general public, completely unknown to
the author," does publication fully "correspond to the structure of a
middle-class society based on the anonymous circulation of goods."[121]

Public subscription, like so many other aspects of the French Enlightenment, was an English import. The development of the term *subscribe*
sheds light on the evolution of literary subscription in the first century
of its use. The French term, like the English one, originated in the
practice of signing one's name to a document to signify acceptance of
its provisions: to underwrite by writing one's name at the bottom. Soon,
a figurative meaning developed: to subscribe meant to agree with or
adhere to a set of beliefs. By the sixteenth century, when merchant
capitalism required the commitment of funds, subscription acquired a
material base. It was no longer enough merely to espouse ideas to

120. Ibid., p. 34.

121. Quoted in Habermas, *Structural Transformation*, p. 258 n. 24. Subscription continues to be examined primarily as a matter of material production rather than ideological
commitment; see, e.g., Denis Hollier, ed., *A New History of French Literature* (Cambridge,
Mass., 1989), where it figures in the article "Intricacies of Literary Production," by
English Showalter, Jr. Showalter views subscription in the same light as manuscript circulation: as an alternative to "normal publication methods" necessitated by piracy on the
one hand and government censorship on the other (pp. 433–34).

subscribe to them; one had to put one's money where one's mouth was. In the seventeenth century, this sort of subscription was for the first time employed for publishing ventures. Izaak Walton's polyglot Bible, published in 1657, was the first literary work sold by public subscription.[122] The practice spread, and Alexander Pope, for one, sold an edition of Homer by public subscription early in the eighteenth century.

In France the public subscription was first employed by a consortium of Parisian booksellers to support the publication of *Antiquité expliquée et représentée en figures* by the Benedictine dom Bernard de Montfaucon in 1716. With the death of Louis XIV, the state lost interest in supporting works of religious erudition; at the same time, the regent's infectious Anglomania suggested the use of public subscription as a solution to the bookseller's problem of raising capital to launch large and expensive projects, just two months after the introduction of John Law's bank. Although the bank failed, the practice of subscription thrived, especially after 1750, when the philosophes dominated the Republic of Letters. Public subscription may have begun as a way to fill the gap left by the withdrawal of royal patronage, but in the hands of the philosophes it became a positive choice as a means of engaging the public in their many projects, not just the publication of books.

The *Encyclopédie* represented the movement toward the public through subscription as it led the movement away from royal patronage in academies. And as the *Encyclopédie* transformed rather than simply translated an English reference work, the French transformed the English practice of subscription. Whereas English subscribers liked to play the part of patron by having their names displayed in subscription lists, the French rarely did so. It may be, as Wallace Kirsop suggests, that, like their German contemporaries, the French saw this practice as vulgar and provincial.[123] It seems more plausible, however, that the reluctance of the French to have their names displayed in the works to which they subscribed was rooted in the need to keep private (that is, secret) one's ideological commitment.

To focus on the material base of subscription while ignoring the ideological commitment it implied is to miss half the import of the practice. Certainly there were noncontroversial subscription projects, such as *Le Monde primitif*, whose subscribers committed themselves only out of friendship to the author and at no risk to themselves.[124] But in

122. Diderot, "Souscription," in *Encyclopédie* 15:416–17; Wallace Kirsop, "Mécanismes éditoriaux," in Martin and Chartier, *Histoire de l'édition française* 2:31.

123. Kirsop, "Mécanismes éditoriaux," p. 32.

124. Wallace Kirsop, "Cultural Networks in Pre-revolutionary France: Some Reflexions on the Case of Antoine Court de Gébelin," *Australian Journal of French Studies* 18 (September–December 1981): 231–47.

the hands of the philosophes, the practice of public subscription, like the concept of the Republic of Letters, took on its fullest resonance. To make a commitment publicly was often no light matter in an age and a place in which commitment to the integrity of private conscience had clearly been withdrawn by the monarchy with the Revocation of the Edict of Nantes and then with the Refusal of Sacraments controversy. To subscribe publicly was to let one's neighbors, one's priest, one's king know where one stood.[125]

Yet to purchase a book or periodical through subscription was not the solitary practice represented by Luther's profession of faith before the Diet of Worms. To subscribe also meant to join a community of subscribers—Gelbart's club. It was one means of becoming part of a public. When Diderot was arrested and the *Encyclopédie* was thus in danger of falling through, the pressure on the monarchy to release him came not only from particular influential subscribers but from the very number of subscribers and the public they had become. Public subscription allowed the French reading public to voice ideological commitment publicly, while protecting their privacy as individuals. As an expression of public opinion, the subscription was both collective and anonymous.

Subscription to periodicals or membership in a reading club that subscribed to them performed an essential function for the Republic of Letters by keeping its citizens connected with one another and engaged in the intellectual activity that united them. Subscriptions to periodicals made members out of readers, citizens out of subscribers. If today we join organizations such as Common Cause or the American Historical Association and, as members, receive at regular intervals the organization's publication, this is a reversal of the experience of the eighteenth century. The right of freedom of association was not won in France until 1901. In the eighteenth century individuals found association through subscription, rather than the other way around.

Reading, subscription, and membership came together in various ways. One possibility was the "Project for a Society for all the Literary Papers," proposed in Lyon in 1759, but whose author thought it could be profitably imitated throughout the provinces. The idea was for fifteen people to pay a certain sum each to subscribe jointly to about a dozen periodicals. By a round-robin system, all the members would be able to read all the papers and journals. "The advantages of these societies are based on two maxims," the author wrote: "1) I give so that you may give to me, *Do ut des* . . . 2) In leaving the first hand, pass along to the next, *Da sequenti*."[126]

125. On the Refusal of Sacraments controversy, which lasted from 1749 to 1756, see Van Kley, *Jansenists and the Expulsion of the Jesuits* and *Damiens Affair*.

126. Quoted and discussed in Labrosse, "Fonctions culturelles," in Labrosse and Rétat, *Instrument périodique*, p. 47. See also Gelbart, *Feminine and Opposition Journalism*, p. 44.

Whether or not the Lyon scheme ever got off the ground, its functions were increasingly fulfilled by *cabinets littéraires* or *chambres de lecture*, reading rooms where, for a fee, one had access to a wide array of periodicals. According to Popkin, there were probably more than a thousand such reading rooms in Europe by 1789.[127] Of two sorts of chambres de lecture in eighteenth-century France, the most widespread by the 1770s were run by booksellers who sought to augment their business by renting books and provided reading rooms for their rental customers. In Metz, for example, a bookseller opened a *cabinet littéraire* as part of his bookshop in 1770. By 1775 he could boast of having 200 readers; two years later the number had risen to 379.[128] Each of these readers was a member who paid an annual fee.

Another sort of reading room was established at the initiative of readers themselves, the direct institutional descendant of schemes such as that of the Lyon reader. In the same year in which he proposed the round-robin reading group, a chambre de lecture was established in Nantes. According to its regulations, the 125 members would pay a set amount and would also elect a board of commissioners. The commissioners' responsibility was to arrange for subscriptions to "all the gazettes and all the periodical works most useful to the society," as well as "to buy in Nantes or order from Paris carefully chosen good books, preferably in folio and quarto, concerning business, shipping, history, the arts, and literature, as well as some new and interesting pamphlets."[129] Arthur Young described this chambre de lecture after he visited it in 1788: "An institution common in the great commercial towns of France, but particularly flourishing in Nantes, is a *chambre de lecture*, or what we should call a book-club, that does not divide its books, but forms a library. There are three rooms, one for reading, another for conversation, and the third is the library; good fires in winter are provided, and wax candles."[130]

Subscribing, like reading itself in the eighteenth century, was no solitary pursuit.[131] Nor was it isolated from other activities. The reading of the written word was integrated into the governing discourse of the age, conversation. The chambre de lecture in Nantes was more than a reading room; it was a locus of discussion centered on and stimulated by reading. "To read alone," wrote Galiani to Diderot during the first year of his "exile" in Naples, "with no one to talk to, no one to argue with or to dazzle, or to listen to, or to make listen to me, this is

127. Popkin, *News and Politics*, p. 130.
128. Chartier, *Cultural Uses of Print*, pp. 209–10.
129. Quoted ibid., pp. 211–12.
130. Young, *Travels in France*, pp. 133–34.
131. See Chartier, *Cultural Uses of Print*, chaps. 6 and 7.

impossible. Europe is dead for me."[132] Like the salon for which Galiani yearned, the provincial reading room was a social institution in which a community was created through discourse, both oral and written. Just as writers at their most idealistic moments saw themselves as engaged in a collective project of Enlightenment, so did readers at times read and subscribe collectively and thus engage actively with the philosophes, joining through their subscriptions and reading clubs the Republic of Letters, whose center in the distant Parisian salons they imitated in their own collective practices of reading.[133]

In the eighteenth century, subscription implied much more than mere passive consumption of periodical works. Readers were expected and encouraged to participate in the journalistic enterprises they endorsed by contributing to them. Three years after Bayle's English imitator launched the *Present State of the Republick of Letters* with an appeal to his readers, Samuel Johnson of Connecticut answered it, and thereby achieved the distinction of making the first American contribution to a European literary journal.[134] Closer to home, Genlis recalled in her memoirs her pleasure in reading in the *Mercure de France* a poem addressed to her by her husband.[135] Periodicals, which reached a much broader public than did private newsletters, and which could turn personal correspondence into public writing, opened up the Parisian salon world, making it the center of a Republic of Letters that stretched from Edinburgh to Naples, and from St. Petersburg to Philadelphia. As readers became contributors, they established themselves as active citizens of the republic.

Public subscription was used to support all sorts of projects. Voltaire, whose *Henriade* had been sold by public subscription in London in 1728, offered the public a new edition of Corneille's works in 1764 in order to raise money for the playwright's impoverished daughter.[136] A year later he was behind a project to raise money for the Calas family through the sale by subscription of engravings of their plight. According to Grimm, the group that devised this project took its lead directly from the English: "In the distress that is feared for these unfortunates, we have learned that in England a subscription has been opened in their favor, and we would like to imitate from afar this generous example." The idea, as Grimm explained it to his subscribers, was for the

132. Galiani to Diderot, 5 September 1772.
133. Habermas draws many of the same conclusions in his discussion of German reading societies in *Structural Transformation*, pp. 72–73.
134. Fiering, "Transatlantic Republic of Letters," p. 656.
135. Genlis, *Mémoires* 1:249.
136. Kirsop, "Mécanismes éditoriaux," in Martin and Chartier, *Histoire de l'édition française* 2:32.

"small number of friends," whose idea this was, to pay for the engraving and present the original to Mme Calas. "But we are counting on opening a subscription for the print for the profit of this family so worthy of the interest of the whole of Europe," he continued. "Everyone will be able to take part in it according to his abilities, and I would very much like to have the pleasure of being charged with lots of orders and commissions for this subscription; nothing in the world would satisfy me more than to have this advantage over my rivals." Having thus opened the subscription in describing it as news to his readers, Grimm went on to make it fully public by means of an eleven-page prospectus that bore the title "Project of subscription for a tragic and moral print."[137]

In fitting tribute to his lifelong efforts to stir the public and engage them in the combat against *l'infâme*, Voltaire's fellow citizens in the Republic of Letters commissioned a statue of him in 1770 and opened it to public subscription. If kings could commission statues of themselves to represent the majesty of the monarchy, then the citizens of the Republic of Letters, in the name of the public, could commission one of Voltaire to represent their polity in republican fashion.[138]

The networks of intellectual exchange were crucial for the success of subscription projects. The public found out about such projects and the opportunity to subscribe to them in the salons themselves and through letters, newsletters, and published journals and gazettes, as well as the pamphlet prospectus. As Kirsop observes, "The success of the formula [of public subscription] . . . is attested by the prospectuses and above all by the announcements in the journals. This is how one discovers that subscriptions played a leading role in Parisian fine printing."[139] The networks through which such calls for support traveled were so efficient that the organizers of the Voltaire statue project had met their goal in three months, even before the project was announced in the published journals and even though they tried to limit each subscription to a modest amount (two livres) in order to ensure that the project was truly public and not dominated by a few large patrons.[140]

Through subscription, the eighteenth-century public was given the opportunity to support (financially and ideologically) and participate in a wide variety of projects that attest to the creativity with which this novel practice was approached. The great balloon experiments of the

137. *Correspondance Littéraire*, 15 April 1765.
138. Goodman, "Pigalle's *Voltaire Nu.*"
139. Kirsop, "Mécanismes éditoriaux," in Martin and Chartier, *Histoire de l'édition française* 2:32.
140. Goodman, "Pigalle's *Voltaire Nu,*" pp. 87–88 and 97.

1780s were sponsored in part through public subscriptions.[141] Those who filled the Champ de Mars in July 1783 to watch the first balloon rise in Paris were no mere spectators: they were part of the experiment they had publicly endorsed. When Benjamin Franklin came to Paris with his lightning rod, he gave public demonstrations that were supported by those who chose to subscribe. If the subscribers to the *Encyclopédie* were taking the place of the royal patron of the French Academy, then those who subscribed to scientific experiments and demonstrations were challenging the Academy of Sciences. Neither was it simply a matter of shifting patronage from the monarchy to the public. Rather, subscription gave the public a voice in its endorsement of projects in which it believed, a voice that formed an important part of the public opinion that took shape in France in the eighteenth century.

In a study of the functions of the periodical in the eighteenth century, Claude Labrosse argues that the journal structured reading and thus was instrumental in shaping the reading public. "The periodical," he asserts, "is an instrument suited to governing the reading of texts."[142] Like salon conversation, the periodical formed a context in which texts were read, and the editor played the governing role of the salonnière. And yet, as Emile Benveniste and his successors have taught us, there is a significant gulf between *la parole* and *le mot* which can never be satisfactorily bridged. Unlike the salonnière, the eighteenth-century journal editor could not control his or her discursive field. If, for example, "their grids make it impossible for a reading to be plural or infinite," the multiple grids superimposed by a reading public that subscribed to several different journals could break through this limitation in one way, while readers' responses in the form of letters to editors and open letters could do so in another. "The periodical," writes Labrosse, "decides and proposes what is readable, that is, what one should and can read, what it is desirable to read, and goes as far as [to decide] the way in which a group of readers should read. . . . A reading is the choice of a path, that is, a direction to take." The periodical, he concludes, created a reading "that is thus no longer simply the decision of a subject."[143] It did not, however, create a reading that was fully determined, and its readers were not so anonymous as Labrosse would have us believe.[144] In fact, while periodicals structured reading, they also

141. See Charles Coulston Gillispie, *The Montgolfier Brothers and the Invention of Aviation* (Princeton, 1983).

142. Labrosse, "Fonctions culturelles," in Labrosse and Rétat, *Instrument périodique*, p. 34.

143. Ibid., pp. 52–53.

144. Ibid., pp. 66–67.

created the space for criticism. Indeed, they asked their readers to respond to them, making readers' contributions an important part of their publications and acknowledging their own responsiveness to reader demand.

Thus, the great paradox of the Enlightenment Republic of Letters is instantiated in the journal as both the space of editorial control of reading and, at the same time, the ground on which writers and readers met for an exchange of ideas and information—news in the broadest sense. The journal aimed to shape readers, certainly, but to shape them into a critical reading public that, by this definition, could not be controlled. The community of readers was a community of individuals because each was given the opportunity, and even encouraged, to become a contributor, an active citizen of the Republic of Letters in the pages of the journal to which he or she subscribed. If we look at eighteenth-century periodicals as the epistolary works they are, we can see them as the locus of a community bound together in the uneasy fashion of the Republic of Letters.

The creation of a critical reading public was the project to which the men of letters who gathered in Parisian salons dedicated themselves, a way to realize Diderot's goal of "changing the common way of thinking." This goal, however, eluded them, for the more the philosophes reached out to shape the reading public in their own image, the more its reading empowered that public to assert its newfound independence by challenging the claims of the men of letters. To their dismay, the philosophes discovered that the very practice of publication tore the Republic of Letters apart as surely as it expanded it.

CHAPTER 5

Into Print: Discord in the Republic of Letters

S'il faut détester les cabales, il faut respecter l'union des véritables gens de Lettres, c'est l'unique moien de leur donner la considération qui leur est nécessaire.

—VOLTAIRE TO MARMONTEL

Non in solo pane vivit homo. Pour moi, je ne vis que d'amitié.

—GALIANI TO MORELLET

Over the course of the 1760s, the philosophes had created for themselves a true community. As a response to enemies ranging from Rousseau and Elie-Cathérine Fréron to the Sorbonne and the Parlement, they developed a collective sense of identity, values, and purpose which found its institutional base in the Parisian salons and its medium of enlightenment in the epistolary form. If external threats helped to bring them together, however, internal strife soon began to tear them apart. As the philosophes became increasingly engaged with public matters and with the public itself through the medium of print, they pushed the limits of comity that were established in the well-governed precincts of the salons. Although the philosophes continued to meet and to correspond, they were unable to maintain the unity that came from adversity and the comity made possible by polite conversation.

The year 1770 was marked by public tension and calls for unity and friendship, but the decade that it ushered in was to be fraught with bitter *querelles*, starting with the debates on the grain trade and ending miserably with the musical war between the Gluckistes and the Piccinistes.[1] These battles, unlike their predecessors of the seventeenth century, produced much embarrassment, for they were fought out in public among writers unable to develop a critical discourse that would transcend the ugliness of insult. Seventeenth-century writers had embraced the paradigm of warfare, issuing parodies and burlesques such as the *Nouvelle allégorique, ou Histoire des derniers troubles arrivés au royaume d'éloquence* and the *Histoire poëtique de la guerre nouvellement déclarée entre les anciens et les modernes*.[2] Underlying these *querelles* was a belief in hierarchy, for the most able writer would be the one left standing over his vanquished opponent, ready to take on the next contender. The satire was his sword.

In the eighteenth century, this model of scholarly combat was challenged by a collectivist paradigm that asked not who was the best but what contribution the writer made. In the pages of the *Nouveau Mercure*, a M. de Villemont asked if it was right to scorn Corneille, for example, because he was inferior to Racine, or Lucan because he was inferior to Virgil, Juvenal, and Horace. A writer should not be subjected to ridicule merely because his work is not perfect. Instead of sneering at those who provided the public with translations from the Latin or Greek as mere compilers or faulting a "judicious and methodical Author" who has taken great pains to compose a dictionary, one ought to appreciate them for putting their talents to good use. Villemont, however, was not hopeful that the Republic of Letters could be reformed, "since the majority of Authors seem to have agreed among themselves forever to tear each other apart." "It is easy to conclude," he wrote, "that in this type of war equity always enters in less than jealousy or passion."[3] Augustin Simon Irailh, the author of *Querelles littéraires, ou Mémoires pour servir à l'histoire des révolutions de la République des Lettres depuis Homère à nos jours* (1761), agreed. "In all ages, in all nations where

1. The grain debates are the focus of this chapter. The music war was the *querelle* whose ugliness caused Meister to mourn the double loss of Lespinasse and Geoffrin in 1777. It is documented by François Lesure, ed., in *Querelle des Gluckistes et des Piccinnistes*, 2 vols. (Geneva, 1984), and discussed in Robert Isherwood, "The Third War of the Musical Enlightenment," *Studies on Voltaire and the Eighteenth Century* 4 (1975): 223–45; and James H. Johnson, "Musical Experience and the Formation of a French Musical Public," *Journal of Modern History* 64 (June 1992): 191–226.

2. Antoine Furetière, *Nouvelle allégorique, ou Histoire des derniers troubles arrivés au royaume d'éloquence* (1658), ed. Eva van Ginneken (Geneva, 1967); and François de Callières, *Histoire poëtique de la guerre nouvellement déclarée entre les anciens et les modernes* (Amsterdam, 1688). I am indebted to Susan Hiner and Barbara Ching for these references. Van Ginneken lists several other titles in this genre in her introduction to the *Nouvelle allégorique*, p. xvii.

3. Villemont, "Réflexions sur la guerre perpétuelle qui règne entre les Auteurs modernes," *Mercure de France* 39 (December 1740; rpt. Geneva, 1969): 2562–79. This article was reprinted from the *Nouveau Mercure*, May 1720, pp. 3–15.

the sciences and the arts have flourished," he wrote, "the spirit of jealousy and division has always accompanied them. . . . What a shame for humanity that this sort of malady reigns principally during the centuries when great talents shine, and that ours, which is said to be that of philosophy, should not even be exempt."[4]

The philosophes of the eighteenth century denied over and over again that they were engaged in *querelles* or that they meant to show anything less than respect for those with whom they disagreed. In theory, at least, they embraced the new assumptions that valued each person's contribution to the enterprise of Enlightenment. But while they noisily claimed to be beating their intellectual swords into plow-shares, presenting themselves as productive citizens whose sole aim was to contribute to the good of society, they found it impossible to throw off either the reputation of intellectual duelers or the reality of person-al combat. With publicity itself seen as a positive value, traditional notions of honor and reputation were constantly threatened. The po-lite discourse of Enlightenment could not be sustained in the public world of print, where the royal policing of the book trade was a poor substitute for the republican governance of salonnières. Despite the honest efforts of the philosophes to free the search for truth from the divisive personal relations of the age and to embrace the practice of public debate, the movement from controlled salon discourse to the public world of print destroyed their dreams of harmony and unity every time. The Republic of Letters was falling into anarchy and dis-cord as surely as would the monarchy itself in 1789.

On 6 January 1770 the new year and the new decade were ushered in at the rue Royale home of the baron d'Holbach with the coronation of Diderot as the *roi des fèves*. The Fête des Rois was the first celebration of the year on the liturgical calendar. Each year family groups throughout France gathered on that day for a feast whose high point was the cutting of a cake that hid within it a fava bean or *fève*. Whoever was dealt the piece with the bean would be the *roi des fèves*. The Fête des Rois opened the carnival season, and like Mardi Gras, with which the season would culminate, it was an occasion for social and political inver-sion. Throughout France, lucky subjects were king for a day, and even at the king's table, Louis XV was obliged to cede his throne to someone chosen by fortune rather than blood.[5]

The philosophes who gathered at d'Holbach's were not in the least

4. Augustin Simon Irailh, *Querelles littéraires, ou Mémoires pour servir à l'histoire des révolutions de la République des Lettres, depuis Homère jusqu'à nos jours* (Paris, 1761; rpt. Geneva, 1967), pp. viii–ix, 8.

5. Emile Magne, *Les Plaisirs et les fêtes au XVIIᵉ siècle* (Paris, 1930), p. 205; Roger Vaultier, *Les Fêtes populaires à Paris* (Paris, 1946), pp. 29–33.

constrained by their citizenship in a secular Republic of Letters from celebrating this most Catholic and royal of festivals. When the crown fell to Diderot in 1770, he rose to the occasion by proclaiming "Le Code Denis." Issued spontaneously in verse, it asserted the values of the Republic of Letters, in contrast to those of monarchy:

> In his states, to all who breathe
> A sovereign claims to give the law;
>   It's the opposite in my empire:
>   The subject reigns over the king.
> Divide and conquer, the maxim is old.
> It was that of a tyrant, it is thus not mine.
> To unite you is my desire; I love liberty;
>   And if I have any will,
>   It is that each should follow his own.
> Friends, who compose my court,
> To the god of wine render homage;
> Render homage to the god of love.[6]

King Denis sought not to divide his subjects in order to have more power over them but to unite them in order that they might all be free and happy. Moreover, unity was to be achieved not by the imposition of a royal will from above but by the exercise of freedom. Friendship was the bond that would hold free citizens together, the model for his ideal polity, and it was friendship that Diderot was to defend in the year to come. He was not alone. By October, the patriarch Voltaire was sending out the same message: "My children, love one another, for who the devil will love you?"[7]

Friendship was strained by the publication of works that generated significant public debate. The most important of these was Galiani's *Dialogues sur le commerce des blés*, which emerged from the presses in December 1769. Since Galiani had left Paris before he could complete the manuscript, he was dependent on the post to keep him in touch with developments in France after his book came out: economic developments that would bear out his bleak predictions about the results of new legislation loosening regulations on the grain trade and political developments in the Republic of Letters as the reviews and responses to

6. In Denis Diderot, *Correspondance*, ed. Georges Roth, 16 vols. (Paris, 1955–1970), 10:15–16.

7. Voltaire to Grimm, 10 October 1770, D16693. The letter was included in the *Correspondance Littéraire* for 15 November 1770; Epinay excerpted it for Galiani in her letter of 29 October (in Galiani, *Correspondance*). On the importance of friendship in Diderot's thought and intellectual practice, see Blandine L. McLaughlin, *Diderot et l'amitié, Studies on Voltaire and the Eighteenth Century* 100 (1973).

his book came in. Galiani's voluminous correspondence, primarily with Epinay, was his lifeline as he tried to reconcile himself to his new status as a corresponding member of the Republic of Letters. It is also a detailed personal record of the struggles that took place in the republic in 1770 and of Galiani's important role in them.[8]

Galiani's "Dialogues sur le Commerce des Blés"

The *Dialogues sur le commerce des blés* fell upon Paris like a bombshell (to use Galiani's own expression)[9] for two equally significant, and not unrelated, reasons: first, it challenged French public policy and the physiocratic economic principles on which it was based, and second, it confronted the physiocrats' intellectual style head on and presented itself as a better way to do *philosophie*. At issue in the debate on the grain trade once Galiani entered it was not only the economic system of France but the constitution of the Enlightenment Republic of Letters.

Galiani challenged the physiocrats' attempt to identify *philosophie* entirely with themselves by championing the salon values of politeness, harmony, and government (*police*). Attacks on Galiani—especially Morellet's *Réfutation de l'ouvrage qui a pour titre "Dialogues sur le commerce des blés"*—attacked these values. In its turn, Diderot's *Apologie de l'abbé Galiani* was above all a defense of Galiani's dialogic method and an attack on the impoliteness of Morellet and on his betrayal of friendship.

The pamphlet wars that were to result in legislation liberalizing the French grain trade began with the *Essai sur la police générale des grains*, written by Claude-Jacques Herbert in 1753.[10] When the royal physician François Quesnay entered the fray in the late 1750s, this liberal economic theory was transformed into "physiocratic science."[11] By 1759 when Henri-Léonard-Jean-Baptiste Bertin was named controller general, the physiocrats (generally referred to at the time simply as *écon-*

---

8. The post had its disadvantages as well. Galiani's demission was precipitated by a letter in which he had commented to a friend about the Family Compact, the treaty system that allied France with Naples. The letter was intercepted by the French postal service and turned over to Choiseul, who was looking for an excuse to send Galiani home. See Wilson, *Diderot*, p. 553; and Perey and Maugras, "Galiani, ses amis et son temps," in Galiani, *Correspondance* 1:xxxviii–xliv.

9. Galiani to Epinay, 18 November 1769.

10. Steven L. Kaplan, *Bread, Politics, and Political Economy in the Reign of Louis XV*, 2 vols. (The Hague, 1976), 1:105. Kaplan's exhaustive and intelligent study is the primary basis for my understanding of the debates on the grain trade.

11. Kaplan argues that physiocracy was a science, "to the extent that it elaborated a universally valid method, combining rational analysis, empirical diagnostics, and model-making in the pursuit of immutable laws which explain social and economic relations and make political decision-making intelligible": ibid., 1:114–15.

omistes) could unleash a flood of pamphlets to try to sway the new administrator to their position.[12] By 1763 they had succeeded, and Bertin issued a law that "opened commerce to all comers . . . , guaranteed unimpeded circulation in the interior, prohibited the police from interfering with the trade in any way, and dispensed buyers or sellers from paying road, river, or bridge tolls on their grain."[13] Bertin's successor took up where he had left off, extending liberalization of the grain trade to exportation in an edict issued in July 1764.

By the fall of 1768 France was in the throes of a severe subsistence crisis. In November bread prices peaked in Paris and riots were reported throughout the provinces. The controller general called an assembly of general police, whose deliberations marked the beginning of physiocracy's fall from grace in official circles. Against this backdrop and stimulated by it, Galiani began writing a set of dialogues that challenged physiocratic theory and the administrative practice based on it, especially the exportation edict of July 1764.

Galiani's *Dialogues*, begun in the fall of 1768, were published in late December 1769, coinciding with the announcement of the appointment of a new controller general, Joseph-Marie Terray.[14] In the interim, however, the author had been recalled from his post as secretary to the Neapolitan embassy and forced to return to Naples after ten years in Paris. When he left in the summer of 1769, he entrusted his hastily finished manuscript to Epinay, who, along with Diderot, did the final editing and saw to the publication of the *Dialogues* that fall.[15]

The *Dialogues* feature three characters: the chevalier Zanobi, who speaks for the author; the Marquis de Roquemaure, modeled after the Marquis de Croismare, who had already figured as the softhearted object of the pleas of Diderot's fictional nun Suzanne in *La Religieuse*; and, starting with dialogue five, the Président, modeled on Armand-Henri Baudoin de Guémadeuc, a royal official and another of Galiani's Parisian friends.[16] Over the course of four weeks between 24 November and 14 December 1768, eight dialogues take place before and after a dinner whose hostess we hear about but never meet.[17]

---

12. Ibid., 1:132.

13. Ibid., 1:138.

14. *Correspondance Littéraire*, 1 January 1770; *Mémoires Secrets*, 9 February 1770.

15. The autograph manuscript is in the Houghton Library at Harvard University. It has been edited by Philip Koch and published as *Dialogues entre M. le marquis de Roquemaure et M. le chevalier Zanobi*, no. 21 in the series Analecta Romanica (Frankfurt am Main, 1968). All references here are to the 1770 edition, published as *Dialogues sur le commerce des blés* (Paris, 1984), and will be noted in the text parenthetically. Where the published version diverges significantly from the manuscript, I have noted the change.

16. Galiani to Epinay, 28 April 1770.

17. In the published version, the fifth dialogue ends with a gambling party, but Galiani's original manuscript ends it with a dinner. This is the only editorial change the

Galiani's dialogues developed out of salon conversations,[18] but they are also Platonic: the Chevalier plays the role of Socratic teacher and the Marquis his Alcibiades.[19] The Président is introduced because the Marquis is too foolish, too easily manipulated to demonstrate the validity of the Chevalier's arguments. The new interlocutor is the model of the modern, enlightened man.[20] It is significant that Galiani's interlocutors carry modern names and titles: his symposium is modern because the problems with which it deals are contemporary. Galiani's dialogues thus define a middle ground between the symposium and the salon: an ideal space in which modern men converse reasonably and wittily about matters of public concern, but without interference from either passion or ego; a space in which the intellectual leadership of the man of letters is accepted but not followed blindly, by men of varied intelligence but universal goodwill who honestly seek to improve themselves and their society. In addition, Galiani's dialogues idealize the salon by making it self-governing: there is no hint of the clash of male egos or of the need for female governance.

The Platonic cast of the dialogues allowed Galiani to be more authorial, more directing, than he would have been in a salon conversation. The Chevalier and the author behind him substitute for the salonnière as the reader's guide through the complexities of the topic. Because the roles of salonnière and philosophe are collapsed, the dialogues are somewhat less open-ended and balanced than one would imagine salon conversation to be.

---

author protested. On 3 February 1770 he wrote to Epinay: "If sales produce a second edition, I beg you to pay great attention to these corrections and, beyond that, I ask you for heaven's sake to get rid of . . . this gambling party and put the *dinner* back in. I don't know what madness has come over you that you would have me pass for a *gambler*, rather than a *gourmand*. I am a *gourmand*, and not by any means a *gambler*. What's wrong with speaking of dinner, when one speaks only of grain?"

18. Diderot to Sophie Volland, [12 and 22 November 1768].

19. Grimm read the characters this way in *Correspondance Littéraire*, as did Fréron in the *Année Littéraire*. Both articles are reprinted in Galiani, *Correspondance* 1:512–13.

20. Galiani, *Dialogues*, p. 91. Here is how Diderot explained the two interlocutors: "Society is divided into two classes of men: those who understand badly and talk about everything; this is the majority, and the Marquis the representative; the others are ignorant and seek to instruct themselves; this is the minority, figured in the *Dialogues* by the Président": Diderot, *Apologie*, in *Oeuvres politiques*, p. 80. Galiani was to learn that Baudoin, the model for the Président, was a scoundrel. First he lost his post as *maître des requêtes* and was exiled to the provinces when it was discovered that he had pocketed some silver from a dinner party given by Hue de Miroménil, the *garde des sceaux*. When the parlements were disbanded in 1771 by the new chancellor, Maupeou, Baudoin was one of the first to sign up as a member of the new Maupeou parlements. "This caused the doors of many houses to be shut on him," wrote Epinay to Galiani, "and notably that of his aunt, your good friend." See Galiani, *Correspondance*, p. 100 n. 2; and Epinay to Galiani, 18 February 1771, in *La signora d'Epinay e l'abate Galiani: Lettere inedite (1769–1772)*, ed. Fausto Nicolini (Bari, 1929). All letters written by Epinay are from this edition unless otherwise noted.

If the structure of the dialogues is thus not strictly that of salon conversation, the discursive values that it expresses are. Throughout the dialogues, the Chevalier speaks for a kind of politeness that enables rather than stifles contestation, while he argues against the pedantic, enthusiastic, and disputatious spirit of the physiocrats. The very form of the dialogue was meant by Galiani and understood by readers such as Voltaire to represent the practice and the spirit of the Enlightenment Republic of Letters.[21]

Galiani's dialogic method both activates and spotlights the discussion of reasons and reasoning, and operates by means of practical examples and particular cases. The solution to the problem of famine—and indeed, to all social, political, and economic problems—will thus lie in the dialogic method, since, as the Chevalier asserts, "the reason poorly discussed, the experience badly applied, the example taken from a dissimilar case, are the causes of all our errors" (13).

The Chevalier also establishes the value of independent thinking when he advises his interlocutor: "Let us imitate the great Colbert, and not follow him. . . . Let us do what a good head like that of the great Colbert would have done today" (22). Galiani's aim is to break out of the oppositions established by the physiocrats by applying critical reason to concrete cases. In doing so, he also tries to break the chain of assertion and refutation that characterizes the disputatious discourse of traditional scholarly practice. Breaking the model, however, means leading the reader into uncharted and uncertain terrain. The Marquis expresses the implied reader's fears when he worries that his ideas may not conform to those of the Chevalier, and that he may thus be proven wrong. The Chevalier, however, redefines the concern as a matter not of right and wrong, but of politeness. "It is only your politeness that can make you regard as a humiliation not being of the same opinion as I," he tells the Marquis (22–23).

Disagreement is neither a matter of right and wrong nor impolite. The Chevalier allays the Marquis's fears in the end by asking to be treated simply as one more book to be read (23–24).[22] Galiani has

---

21. Galiani to Epinay, 27 March 1770, dated in *Lettres de l'abbé Galiani à Madame d'Epinay*, ed. Eugène Asse, 2 vols. (Paris, 1882). Galiani's dialogues display all the formal characteristics of Enlightenment dialogues which I identified in my study of Diderot's *Supplément au voyage de Bougainville*: first, having no psychological depth, they are non-mimetic and thus create critical distance; second, they instantiate both the universality of thought and the particularity of action; and third, as models for reading, they effect an implied pedagogy through the identification of the reader with the interlocutor. See Goodman, *Criticism in Action*, pp. 172–74.

22. The reader outside the text here merges with the Marquis, as they (and we) settle down to "read" together the Chevalier's contribution to the debate on the grain trade. Diderot was to use this same device in the *Supplément*. See Goodman, *Criticism in Action*, pp. 174–75.

inscribed the print debate between himself and the physiocrats within a polite conversation between the Chevalier and the Marquis in which disagreement and politeness both become possible, and right and wrong are displaced by the process of reasoned conversation itself. This was Enlightenment politeness, since its function was to enable critical discussion.

The relationship of politeness between interlocutors was extended to the author's relationship with his (implied) readers.[23] The Chevalier criticizes the physiocrat Nicolas Baudeau for insulting his readership by affecting a popular style, while he treats even the foolish Marquis with marked courtesy and delicacy. Even as the Marquis's foolishness is exposed time after time, he is never insulted and always treated as worthy of being instructed, of participating in the dialogue. The distinctive feature of Galiani's *Dialogues* is the way in which the Chevalier criticizes opposing arguments without humiliating or insulting those who present and defend them. Throughout, it is the Marquis who fears he will offend his guest, and the Chevalier who reassures him (e.g., 55–57). And when the Marquis suggests that the Chevalier is trying to make a fool of him, the Chevalier protests: "I am not laughing; I pity you and it's not only you that I pity. I pity entire nations that have been fooled by the zeal of a few well-intentioned men who have wanted to be useful and have fooled themselves" (61).

The important opposition here is not between the Chevalier and the Marquis, but between the philosophe Galiani and the physiocrats: between philosophes and zealots. And Galiani makes his case not by refuting the physiocrats but by having his Chevalier enlighten his Marquis by teaching him how to read the physiocrats' work critically. The intended end, moreover, is not the destruction of the physiocrats but the public good, which both Galiani and the physiocrats saw as the responsibility of the man of letters (79–81). Galiani, however, did not see it as his job to prescribe a cure-all for the ills of the body politic; rather, the philosophe was to monitor the changes that body had undergone over time and to assist nature in adapting to them (86–87). The philosophe's task was to criticize, but only to the end of improving what existed, and only on the basis of reasoned argument and proof (89).

Just as the *Dialogues* provide a model of polite discussion to counter

23. On the idea of the implied reader, see Wolfgang Iser, *The Implied Reader: Patterns of Communication in Prose Fiction from Bunyan to Beckett* (Baltimore, 1974); and Goodman, *Criticism in Action*, pp. 174–85. In the fifth dialogue the Chevalier again displays his politeness when he apologizes for committing one of the sins of polite conversation: interrupting. "Pardon me if I interrupt you," he says to the Président. "This impoliteness is perhaps not so great as that of not responding to you if I had let you finish, and that's my excuse" (99).

disputatious argumentation, they also demonstrate the philosophe method of sound reasoning and an appreciation of the reasoning process, rather than "correct" answers. Whereas the Marquis tends to see debate solely as a matter of winning and losing (and thus always loses), the Président is able to appreciate the Chevalier's reasoning. "I admire . . . how the Chevalier advances in his reasoning," he says, "little by little, step by step; how he connects his ideas, how he closes in and imperceptibly approaches conclusions" (149). The dialogue form allowed Galiani the indulgence of a cheering section, but it also made the important point that "a truth that pure chance gives birth to like a mushroom in a meadow is good for nothing" (148; see also 192).

The first dialogue establishes polite conversation as the discourse of political and economic debate. Later ones expose forms of false reasoning into which the Marquis unwittingly falls: generalizing from a particular; reasoning by analogy; and omitting relevant factors such as chance and human nature (94, 146–53, 174–75). It was not enough to assert one belief or deny the validity of another, Galiani was telling his readers; nor was it sufficient to refute opposing arguments syllogistically. Critical practice required the application of reason to particular historical and geographical circumstances and an understanding of probabilities derived from chance and human nature.[24] The dialogues are both a model of enlightened discussion and a pedagogy for sound reasoning.

Galiani also opposed philosophe practice to that of the physiocrats by confronting the issue of "seriousness." The philosophes always had to defend themselves against the charge of being insufficiently serious. Recent commentators, echoing the physiocratic suspicion of wit and gaiety, have tried to explain the success of the *Dialogues* by separating "style" from "substance" and minimizing the originality of the latter.[25] Substance and style, however, are not so easily separated. The issue at stake went beyond grain policy to the policing of words. In the *Dialogues*, Galiani made a case for the Enlightenment "style" against that of

24. Montesquieu is generally credited with having introduced geography and climate into discussions of political theory with *De l'esprit des lois*, and Rousseau made chance central to his understanding of history in his *Discours sur l'inégalité*. On Rousseau, see Goodman, *Criticism in Action*, chap. 4; on the importance of probability in social science in the eighteenth century, see Baker, *Condorcet*, chap. 3. In Naples, Galiani had attended lectures by Giambattista Vico, whose "new science" gave a central role to historical particularity. See Perey and Maugras, "Galiani, ses amis et son temps," in Galiani, *Correspondance* 1:xiv; and Fausto Nicolini, *Giambattista Vico e Ferdinando Galiani* (Turin, 1918).

25. Kaplan, *Bread, Politics* 2:593–94; Huguette Cohen, "Diderot's Machiavellian Harlequin: Ferdinando Galiani," *Studies on Voltaire and the Eighteenth Century* 256 (1988): 148; Franco Venturi, *Europe des Lumières: Recherches sur le 18ᵉ siècle* (The Hague, 1971), pp. 176 and 182–83.

the physiocrats, which he later called the "genre ennuyeux."[26] He referred to "these economists who become enraged, not because I have
not adopted their principles, but because I do not adopt their style."[27]
Within the text, the Marquis accuses the Chevalier of not talking seriously enough about matters of such grave importance. In dialogue 6,
for example, he complains to the Chevalier: "You talk about very great,
very serious things and in truth you speak of them too lightly." The
Chevalier defends his gaiety: "One must dwell on minor things in order
to set them off and give them an importance that they wouldn't have.
Grave matters must be lightened, otherwise they would become un-
bearably heavy" (121).

Unlike the pamphlets and treatises of the physiocrats, Galiani's work
aims to please its readers by being aggressively pleasant, aggressively
sociable. It does not, however, aim *merely* to please. The end is never out
of sight: one pleases in order to enlighten. A useful work is one that is
not only true, but read. Pleasing the reader does not mean confirming
his or her prejudices, telling the reader what he or she wants to hear.
Rather, the representation of polite conversation becomes the medium
of a form of discourse that is at once rational, responsible, useful,
pleasant, and polite.

Throughout the *Dialogues* Galiani contrasts the doctrinaire spirit of
the physiocrats to his own critical spirit, his gaiety to their ponderous-
ness. In the seventh dialogue he turns the tables on the physiocrats by
calling their pamphlets ornaments of an indulgent monarchy which
grace the fertile fields of a well-ordered state like spring flowers (176;
see also 212). He defines the decorative not by its style, but by its lack of
utility. Galiani's *Dialogues* is an amusing book, but it is also useful, precisely because it attracts and engages readers. Utility (and thus value) is
identified with the rhetorical project of shaping an enlightened reading public; unreadable and unread books are merely decorative.

Polite conversation is thus opposed to a kind of discourse that asserts
itself as serious but is really only boring. Traditional pedantry, combined with the new scientistic language of the physiocrats, was a killing
combination. But polite conversation was also opposed to enthusiasm
or zealotry. The eighth and final dialogue explores most directly the
contrast between Enlightenment reason as articulated in conversation
and physiocrat enthusiasm. When the Chevalier jokes that the main
value of discourse is its ability to aid digestion, the Président responds:

> You want to cheer things up as usual; but your gaiety itself is a great
> philosophy; it throws a calm over meditation, it extinguishes enthusiasm,

26. Galiani to Sartine, 27 April 1770.
27. Galiani to Morellet, 26 May 1770.

the great enemy of reason. It makes one perceive all things in the light of their natural grandeur. The illusion of perspective disappears; I have felt this effect in me since I have had the pleasure of listening to you, and I have experienced that it is much less the things you have told us than the way of looking at them that has made me a philosophe.(203–4)

Cool, calm, reason is here opposed to the warmth of enthusiasm. Galiani's gaiety is not a distraction, a relief from the coldness of reason, but is instrumental in attaining the critical temperature.[28] It is in the Enlightenment tradition of Montesquieu's *Lettres persanes*: a means of alienating the reader from the familiar in order to attain critical distance.[29] The physiocrats, by contrast, are cast with the enemies of Enlightenment: religious fanatics whose enthusiasm blinds their reason.

In Enlightenment discourse, *enthusiasm* was a code word for religious fanaticism.[30] To call the physiocrats "enthusiasts" was to associate them with the worst excesses of religion, to damn them as a sect whose philosophy was metaphysical rather than empirical and dogmatic rather than critical, to claim that their appeal was made through enthusiastic preaching rather than reasoned discussion. It was to argue that physiocracy was a sectarian religion rather than commonsense *philosophie*. Galiani was hardly alone in characterizing the physiocrats as a sect,[31] but in the *Dialogues* he explored the implications of enthusiasm for enlightenment.

28. The pun here on *critical*—critical temperature and critical distance—is embedded in the etymology of the related words *crisis* and *criticism*. See Koselleck, *Critique and Crisis*, pp. 103–4 n. 15.

29. See Goodman, *Criticism in Action*, 19–52.

30. Voltaire, "Enthousiasme," in *Dictionnaire philosophique*, ed. René Pomeau (Paris, 1964), p. 176; *Encyclopédie*, s.v. "Enthousiasme," "Enthousiaste," "Enthousiastes," 5:719–22.

31. See, e.g., *Mémoires Secrets*, 18 April 1770: "The sect of economists has had for several years its own journal, *Les Ephémérides du citoyen*. . . . It is run by one of their apostles, and each one deposes there the elements and the results of the common doctrine." (See also the entry for 29 May 1770.) Grimm wrote in the *Correspondance Littéraire* for 15 February 1768: "The aged Quesnay has all the qualities of the leader of a sect. He has made his doctrine a mixture of common truths and obscure visions. He writes little himself, and if he writes, it is not to be understood. The little that he has shown to us himself of his ideas is an unintelligible apocalypse." As late as 1783, Mercier placed the chapter "Economistes" directly after "Enthousiasme" in his *Tableau de Paris*, showing the connection between the two in his own mind, and noting that the term "enthusiast has become an insult": Louis-Sébastien Mercier, *Tableau de Paris*, 12 vols. (Amsterdam, 1783–1788), 6:194–202. When Turgot attempted to implement physiocrat policy, he attracted the same abuse: "It is inconceivable to what excess of delirium philosophic enthusiasm can carry certain once-exalted heads," wrote the *Mémoires Secrets* on 29 October 1776; "this is how the Economists are regarded who, more than ever, are a corps, compose a sect, and have imagined ceremonies and formulas of initiation. It is now M. Turgot who presides over the assemblies. . . . The ex-minister, moreover, seems to have for his part a strong dose of enthusiasm."

The Chevalier explains the problem of enthusiasm and the powerful rhetoric it can stimulate in the following way:

> Virtue, the desire to do good, is a passion in us like all others. It is rare to find; but when it is found, it is too violent. Indeed, it is more violent than any other; because when the needle of good stimulates us, no bridle of remorse stops us. This violence and this ardor produce enthusiasm. One persuades oneself of what one desires without discussion, and others are persuaded by the warmth of the discourse, and because one is a virtuous man. One does not give good reasons, but one has the frankness of the truth, the courage of virtue, the fire of one's own persuasion, and one pulls along others who see no reason for mistrust. Believe me; have no fear of rogues or the wicked, sooner or later they will be unmasked. Fear the upstanding man who is deceived. (206)

The great man, the Chevalier goes on, must couple his passion for the good with the coolness of the wicked. "He must desire ardently and, however, discuss calmly, wait patiently" (206–7).

If the enthusiast captures the reader by seducing him with the innocence of his passion, building trust in his honest heart, the philosophe does just the opposite: through dialogue and various forms of wit and irony he forces the reader to mistrust him, to challenge, to doubt. He cools passions and sharpens minds. Galiani damned the physiocrats not as evil but as well intentioned. The danger they posed was the seductive power of passionate error, against which the only effective weapon was a critical wit. Indeed, amusement might be the only way to retain an audience without seducing it. What the Chevalier argued and Galiani demonstrated was that gaiety was the rhetoric of Enlightenment because it forced readers to keep their wits about them, while it amused them and thus kept their interest. If enthusiasm was the enemy that *philosophie* aimed to combat, then gaiety was essential to the job.

Enthusiasm was seductive because it lulled the reader into trusting someone whose good intentions would lead him down the garden path. The enthusiast was a Pied Piper who succeeded because the reader, unless he or she had learned to read and think critically, was as trusting as a child. The *Dialogues* are a pedagogy in the Enlightenment project of turning children into responsible adults. As Kant was to write in 1784, "Enlightenment is man's emergence from his self-imposed immaturity."[32]

Galiani inscribed polite conversation as a discourse of moderation and reason between the poles of pedantry and religious enthusiasm. The critical use of reason practiced by the philosophes challenged the

32. Kant, "What Is Enlightenment?" in *Perpetual Peace*, p. 41.

doctrinaire spirit of both pedants and religious enthusiasts. Or as d'Alembert put it in the *Discours préliminaire* to the *Encyclopédie*: "It is inspired men who enlighten the people and enthusiasts who lead them astray. The bridle that we are obliged to impose upon the license of the latter should in no way harm that liberty which is so necessary to true philosophy and from which religion can draw the greatest advantages."[33]

Galiani ended the *Dialogues* the way he began, with reflections on the value of conversation. "Details ought never to be a subject of conversation," the Chevalier tells the Président; "one must have one's hands on the work and just do it" (256). Later, he elaborates on the difference between conversation and administration (*police*): "*Police* is a business of details; it always looks at particular cases. If it becomes universal, it becomes an annoyance. In particular circumstances, it produces good order." He then uses a comparison to make his point and the point is doubly made. If, he says, "you put guards at every street corner, you will destroy the natural liberty of those who pass by; but if you only place them at the entrance of the theater, you do them a great service" (272). On the one hand, the Chevalier is saying that police are used appropriately when they respond to specific circumstances; on the other, he is making a general point about the *theory* of police, rather than himself specifying where and when it is necessary. He thus distinguishes between the general level of the discussion and the specificity of administration, the subject of that discussion. The solution to the political and economic problems set out in the text must be specific, but the discussion of them must be general. The general ought not, however, to be confused with the universal, which, in theory or practice, is always inadequate. General rules developed through reasoned discussion can be applied to specific circumstances, but universal principles, being absolute, can only be imposed upon them. The issue is not whether liberty or police ought to reign but in what circumstances each is applicable and why.

The book ends not with such a pronouncement by the Chevalier, but with the conclusions of his interlocutors. Not surprisingly, the Marquis declares himself fully satisfied with all the Chevalier's ideas. The Président, on the other hand, closes the text with the response the author would have his readers share: "As for me, Monsieur le Chevalier," he

---

33. D'Alembert, *Preliminary Discourse*, p. 72. On similar developments in England, see Brian Vickers, "The Royal Society and English Prose Style: A Reassessment," in *Rhetoric and the Pursuit of Truth*, 45–63; and J. G. A. Pocock, "Edmund Burke and the Redefinition of Enthusiasm: the Context as Counter-Revolution," in *The French Revolution and the Creation of Modern Political Culture 3: The Transformation of Political Culture (1789–1848)*, ed. François Furet and Mona Ozouf (Oxford, 1989), pp. 19–36.

says, "I will always be indebted to you for having taught me more than ever that all political questions deserve a serious discussion, and that nothing should be taken to excess" (273).

Galiani thus leaves the reader with the central issues in the debate on the grain trade as he sees them. First, subsistence policy is a *political* and not simply an economic or technical matter. Second, since it is political, and therefore of public concern, it needs to be the subject of debate or discussion. Third, this discussion is serious as it is represented in the *Dialogues*—amusingly. Finally, the value of moderation is reasserted. The major lesson of the *Dialogues* is not a verdict on the utility or moral rightness of particular laws but the model of serious discussion through which that verdict is reached and the spirit of moderation which guides it and defines that discussion as polite. The "answer" to the question whether or not the edict that liberalized the grain trade was a good law should emerge from a discussion based on these principles.

In Naples, Galiani waited impatiently for responses to his book. Although he was a well-known figure in the salons of Paris, much admired for his brilliance, his outrageous sense of humor, and his storytelling ability, he had published little.[34] He was accustomed to acting discursively within the controlled precincts of the salon and would now learn firsthand what happened when one sent one's words beyond them through the mechanism of print.

The Physiocrats Fight Back

By all contemporary accounts, Galiani's book was a devastating success. The *Mémoires Secrets* was lavish in its praise: "The author discusses with a finesse, a marvelous sagacity the most abstract questions of political economy. He casts on these matters luminous and profound views that he is able to reconcile with all the lively and brilliant gaiety of the most frivolous man of the world."[35]

The *Mémoires* went on to report that the physiocrats were contemplating a counteroffensive but that prospects of success were dim. Steven Kaplan confirms the rumor: "So alarmed were the *économistes* by the

34. Prior to the *Dialogues* Galiani had published *De la moneta* (1749), which was highly acclaimed both in Italy and abroad, and *Della perfetta conservazione del grano* (1754). Both were published anonymously, although the author became well known as a result of the first and was plagiarized as a result of the more perfect anonymity of the second. His only other major work was a funeral oration for Pope Benedict XIV (1758). "After that," Galiani wrote in a letter to Epinay (13 December 1770), "I became a politician and, in France, I produced only children and books that have not seen the light of day."

35. *Mémoires Secrets*, 9 February 1770.

positive impression they feared the *Dialogues* made on the public," he writes, "that they sent forth three of their leading spokesmen to refute them."[36] Abbé Pierre-Joseph-André Roubaud's *Récréations économiques, ou Lettres . . . à M. le chevalier Zanobi* was typical, simply restating physiocrat doctrine and attacking Galiani as a reactionary mercantilist and an apostate of *philosophie* who "deserved to be banished from philosophical circles for seeking only to 'deepen prejudices and increase fears.'"[37] Lemercier de La Rivière was no less hostile. He called Galiani "dishonest, naive and wishy-washy," intellectually inferior to the physiocrats, "a man of levity rather than of science, utterly ignorant of the 'first truths' and 'immutable principles of the social order.'"[38] At the same time, however, Lemercier gave lip service to Galiani's critique of enthusiasm and personal attack, thereby distancing himself from such practices, even as he employed them. "It is to be wished," he wrote,

> that all sarcasm, all bitterness be banished absolutely; that one never allow either a personal insult [*inculpation*] or any of these *traits de chaleur* that seem always to announce that one defends the cause of one's own amour propre rather than that of the truth; that one believes oneself to have the right to give one's own opinion as a general law and to substitute despotically one's personal authority for that of evidence and reason.[39]

Clearly, the physiocrats understood that Galiani's book was as much about the definition of *philosophie* as it was about the grain trade. Indeed, in echoing Galiani's critique of physiocracy's warmth as a substitute for truth and of the elevation of their passionately held beliefs to the level of natural law, Lemercier acknowledged that he knew what was at stake in Galiani's critique. He acknowledged that at issue also were the definition and attribution of words such as *chaleur*, *vérité*, *opinion*, and *raison*.

The physiocrats believed themselves to be the true bearers of *philosophie* because their fundamental principles, scientific method, and the

---

36. Kaplan, *Bread, Politics* 2:603–4.

37. Ibid., 2:604. The two other physiocrat responses were by the abbé Nicolas Baudeau, author of two works that Galiani had specifically criticized in the *Dialogues*; and Pierre-Paul François Joachim Henri Lemercier de La Rivière, whose *L'Intérêt général de l'état, ou La Liberté du commerce des blés . . . avec la réfutation d'un nouveau système publié en forme de "Dialogues sur le commerce des blés"* (Amsterdam, 1770) was the basis of Galiani's *La Bagarre*.

38. Kaplan, *Bread, Politics* 2:605.

39. Quoted by Galiani in *La Bagarre: Galiani's "Lost" Parody*, ed. Steven Laurence Kaplan (The Hague, 1979), pp. 68–69. Galiani called attention to the demurral in his parody: "It is to be wished that all sarcasm, all bitterness be banished absolutely, and that one never follow the example and the model of Monsieur l'Abbé Roubeau in his economic recreations" (ibid.).

understanding of the social field based on them were, in their view, identical with it. The debate on the grain trade was a debate on *philosophie* because the physiocrats, in Kaplan's words, "made the grain issue into the litmus of enlightenment; those who adhered to the cause of liberty constituted the forces of light, of science and progress; those who opposed it represented darkness, superstition, and backwardness."[40]

The physiocrats, in other words, identified their set of beliefs with the Enlightenment. Galiani—along with Voltaire, Diderot, Grimm, and others—understood *philosophie* as a set of intellectual values and practices that challenged dogmatic systems of belief. For them, physiocracy brought together precisely those values that *philosophie* opposed: *esprit de système* and *esprit de parti*.[41] Historians since Carl Becker have liked to think of the Enlightenment as simply another religion, the inverse of the Catholicism the philosophes criticized, but Galiani's *Dialogues* run directly against this interpretation.[42] While Galiani was identifying the danger of physiocratic *economic* principles for the French state, he also made clear the danger of physiocratic *intellectual* principles for the Republic of Letters. As he wrote in a letter to his friend Antoine-Raymond-Gabriel Sartine, head of the Paris police and the man in charge of the book trade:

> I have thought to procure some good to France, and above all to ward off, in important matters that are not metaphysical questions of theology, this spirit of enthusiasm and of system that spoils everything. I will not procure any change in the administration of the grain trade; but, at the least, I have succeeded in revealing that people whom I esteemed for the purity of their economic intentions, and who seem to be philosophes, are a veritable small occult sect, with all the faults of sects, jargon, system, taste for persecution, hatred against outsiders, clamoring, viciousness, and pettiness. They are the true Jansenists of Saint-Médard of politics.[43]

40. Kaplan, Introduction to Galiani, *La Bagarre*, p. 20.

41. Besides Galiani's *Dialogues*, the most often cited philosophe critique of the physiocrats as a sect is Voltaire's *L'Homme aux quarante écus* (1768).

42. Carl L. Becker, *The Heavenly City of the Eighteenth-Century Philosophers* (New Haven, 1932).

43. Galiani to Sartine, 27 April 1770. Despite the bold colors with which the opposition between physiocracy and *philosophie* was painted in the eighteenth century, historians have blurred the distinction between them. See esp. Elizabeth Fox-Genovese, *The Origins of Physiocracy: Economic Revolution and Social Order in Eighteenth-Century France* (Ithaca, 1976), pp. 43–46. Peter Gay, whose term "the science of freedom" Fox-Genovese adopts to describe physiocracy, is more ambivalent about the relationship between *philosophie* and physiocracy. See Gay, *Enlightenment* 2:496 and *The Party of Humanity: Essays in the French Enlightenment* (New York, 1971), p. 275. Perhaps this ambivalence reflects his critique of Becker's argument that the Enlightenment was just a new form of religion. Gay's Enlight-

Having written the *Dialogues* to discredit the physiocrats as a sect of fanatics and thus to undermine their attempts to define *philosophie* as physiocracy, Galiani's next problem was how to resist his natural impulse to defend himself against his critics and thus perpetuate the dynamic of assertion and refutation fueled by insult. In February he asked Epinay if she thought him "so little philosophical" as not to send him "the responses, the replies, the attacks (*injures*) that are vomited against the poor chevalier Zanobi." Heroically, he went on: "You would give me the greatest pleasure by mailing them to me. I am ready for anything."[44] But when the physiocrat responses came in, their viciousness clearly pained him. His fortitude and determination were tested to the limit.

"Certainly, I will respond to no one," Galiani wrote to a friend on 24 March; "I have not written a work for the foolish pleasure of disputation. I thought to write a useful book. . . . Men of a calm spirit will find that there is something good and true in these dialogues. Fanatics are never good for anything, and one must not waste one's time either in combating or in persuading them."[45] On 7 April he assured Epinay that he was "quite resolved not to respond in any way to anyone"; three weeks later he made the same assurance to Sartine.[46] On 2 June he took some of his own medicine: he turned his pain into laughter by making a joke of the attacks on him. "Do you know that I really am charmed by the way in which I am treated," he told Epinay. "I have the distinction of coarse insults. This honor had been accorded only to Voltaire by the dogs of Saint-Médard."[47]

Epinay had replied to Galiani's earlier request to be sent the critiques of his *Dialogues* by assuring him that they were not worth sending since, being unreadable, they were not being read.[48] Now, having asserted the honor of being publicly reviled, Galiani told her: "What you have communicated to me about the satires against me determines me not to

---

enment was scientific, and science is the *opposite* of religion. See "Carl Becker's Heavenly City," in *Party of Humanity*, pp. 188–210. But if physiocracy is understood to be the purest form of *philosophie* because it is the most *scientific*, then *philosophie* itself becomes subject to the kind of criticism that Becker launched and Gay contested: science, as Fox-Genovese argues, is simply a new ideology, a new religion.

44. Galiani to Epinay, 24 February 1770.

45. Galiani to M. Pellerin, 24 March 1770.

46. Galiani to Sartine, 27 April 1770.

47. Galiani again compared the physiocrats to the Jansenists in letters to Epinay of 20 and 24 November 1770. On 28 April he called them "a true sect of *Illuminés*," complete with prophecies and visions; on 5 May he referred to Pierre Du Pont de Nemours, one of the major physiocrats, as "Dupont Nostradamus." See also Galiani to Sartine, 27 April 1770.

48. Epinay to Galiani, 18 March 1770.

respond. I want to make these gentlemen suffer the greatest of tor-
ments; that of not knowing if I have read them. I will enjoy the privileges of the dead."

By the end of July, however, Galiani was finding it impossible to play
dead. Having read Roubaud's *Récreations économiques*, he was furious.
"Note that the author stamps his book with authenticity, and signs it, in
promising to respond in it to me and to the public," he wrote Epinay.
What outraged him was the personal calumny that Roubaud threw in
under the cover of a public response to his arguments. To *publish* an
insulting story against the *person* of the author was a violation of the
"rules of decency" which the censorship apparatus of the state was
empowered to enforce. "I have always believed that, sooner or later, the
ministry would recognize the service that I have rendered it by sacrificing myself before a troupe of the most impudent and rude [*malhonnête*]
fanatics, in order to unmask them, and to expose their foolish ambition
and their seditious views," he wrote to Epinay. "But what I never would
have believed is that M. de Sartine, our good friend Sartine, our incom-
parable Sartine, would allow someone to print against me such atro-
cious vulgarities and such revolting details."[49]

Was Galiani simply being overly sensitive? Was he hypocritical in
calling for censorship? Were the physiocrats right in calling him an
enemy of liberty and philosophy if he would not acknowledge their
freedom to print what they liked? I think not. Galiani's position was
enlightened in eighteenth-century terms. It was the same position
taken by Geoffrin when she appealed to Choiseul to have the gazettes
print retractions of Guasco's insults against her. It was the same position taken by the enlightened lawyer Servan, who saw it as the
monarchy's responsibility to maintain "civil peace and the *douceurs* of
society" by encouraging the production of political criticism while controlling the circulation of personal insult.

Galiani saw Roubaud's attack on him as a threat to the order of
society as well as to his personal honor: "I think that the economists
should be happy to have caused the French to be without bread, without aiming also to make them lose their *moeurs* and decency," he wrote
to Epinay.[50] Two weeks later he expressed his frustration again, calling
upon the French nation to do its duty by him:

Must the most polite and the most *policé* nation in the world consent to
watch being treated in this way a foreigner, who has stolen nothing, taken
nothing, asked nothing of a nation where he was a little representative of
the truth, but in the end chargé d'affaires of a great prince, friend and

49. Galiani to Epinay, 27 July 1770.
50. Ibid.

issue of Bourbon blood. M. de Sartine, . . . doesn't he feel a little guilty of *lèse-amitié*, and of having not done what public decency demanded, even in a nation in which liberty of the press should be encouraged? I do not ask to be avenged. I ask for an honor and it is due me.[51]

Philosophes from Voltaire to Duclos had declared France the most polite of nations and saw the French Republic of Letters as participating in that politeness. Galiani was a champion of *police* as the key to politeness, to a civil society, as the basis of order in matters of grain and of language. Sartine, to whom he was asking Epinay to appeal, was, after all, both his friend and the lieutenant general of police. If we understand *police* as Galiani and many of his enlightened contemporaries did, as the basis of an "orderly liberty" and the necessary defense against anarchy and chaos, then it is easy to see his reaction here, as well as his approach to the problems of the grain trade, as entirely consistent with the values and practices of the salon-based Republic of Letters. As he had learned the value of governance in the economy of salon conversation and advocated it in the economy of subsistence, he now called upon it in the territory of print. As in the salon and the grain trade, liberty and license were two quite different things, and *police* was what kept the first from degenerating into the second by keeping it orderly.[52] "You will tell me that I ought to scorn all this," Galiani conceded in closing his letter to Epinay. "I don't know anything about that. I do know that a nation sustains itself only by the observance of rules, and I know, myself, that without the virtues of tolerance, of pardoning insults, and other *moineries*, the Romans founded the greatest of empires. I know that with different maxims, the moderns have everywhere remained pygmies and pigs."

Epinay did speak to Sartine, and his decision confirmed both her own assessment of the situation and Galiani's prediction—that it was not worth getting upset about. "The abbé is right," she quoted Sartine as saying, "but I can't read everything. All I can do is refer it to the

51. Galiani to Epinay, 11 August 1770. In the very next paragraph Galiani remarked that he had once wanted to be named an honorary member of the French Academy of Inscriptions, but "the idea of finding myself right next to M. the abbé Guasco disgusted me." Guasco's name was synonymous with the kind of behavior he associated with the physiocrats. He too had committed *lèse-amitié*, first by using his friendship with Montesquieu to enter the home of Geoffrin for treacherous reasons, and then by publishing Montesquieu's letters without permission.

52. This is precisely how Kaplan understands Galiani's position on the grain trade. Introduction to Galiani, *La Bagarre*, pp. 44–45. It is also consistent with Nicolas Delamare, *Traité de la police* (1705), discussed in Gordon, "Idea of Sociability," pp. 42–44. Chartier, too, sees *police* as the central term in understanding both the grain trade and the book trade: *Cultural Origins*, pp. 44–46.

censor. I have given him a dressing down. If this scrap by the abbé Roubaud had been read and had made the slightest sensation, I would have raged. But it is as if it never existed; I would have caused people to read it by suppressing it."[53] Together, Epinay and Sartine, in their roles as friends and as maintainers of order, managed to contain the situation until Galiani himself calmed down.

By the time Galiani received the letter informing him of Sartine's decision, he had already come up with a more amusing solution. He released his frustration and hostility in *La Bagarre*, a parody of Lemercier's refutation of the *Dialogues*. He sent it to Epinay in installments to be read by her, Diderot, Grimm, d'Holbach, and other close friends and left it up to her to decide if it should go beyond that small circle of friends. For himself, he felt (regretfully) that it probably ought not.[54] She agreed, and it remained unpublished until the twentieth century.[55] By November, Epinay could reassure him that the physiocrats

> had lost one hundred percent since your book [came out] and especially since people began dying of hunger. Their writings are mocked everywhere . . . . You triumph. The public does you justice. Listen! In the last month business has taken me, by the way, into different societies very far from our own, among people of diverses classes: there is only one voice, and it is for you.[56]

Thus, although Galiani was hurt and enraged by the response of the physiocrats, he did manage—with the help of his friends—to refrain from entering the vicious circle of public response and counterinsult his book had tried to break. Of much greater concern to him than the rudeness of the physiocrats, however, was the reaction of Morellet. Morellet, as we have seen, was a stalwart of the Enlightenment salons. He was also Galiani's oldest friend in Paris.[57] He was no less a friend

53. Epinay to Galiani, 24 August 1770.
54. Galiani to Epinay, 25 August 1770 (dated by Asse in *Lettres de l'abbé Galiani*).
55. In his introduction to *La Bagarre*, Kaplan argues that Galiani wanted to publish all along, but the "committee" headed by Epinay refused to give him the go-ahead (pp. 25–38). This may well have been the case. This "committee" was functioning in the same way as that headed by d'Alembert and Lespinasse in regard to Hume's response to Rousseau in 1766. Like the committee of actors who decided whether or not a script would be staged at the Comédie-Française, these committees decided whether or not to go public.
56. Epinay to Galiani, 3–10 November 1770.
57. Galiani to Morellet, 26 May 1770: "Remember that you were my first acquaintance in Paris. You are for me (I cannot think about it without shedding tears) *primogenitus mortuorum*, the oldest of those I have lost. It is to you that I owe my introduction to Mme Geoffrin, to d'Alembert, and to so many others." Perhaps Galiani does exaggerate a bit here, but I think he is burying his tongue in his cheek in order to express real pain: the loss of friendship and the Parisian world based on it.

because he embraced the physiocrats' economic ideas. Galiani was convinced that Morellet would at least understand how friendly, polite, reasonable—that is, enlightened—debate was carried on, even if he continued to disagree about the best grain policy. But Morellet missed the message of politeness entirely. His *Réfutation de l'ouvrage qui a pour titre "Dialogues sur le commerce des blés"* was a disputatious attack whose main purpose was to annihilate and humiliate his adversary.

Morellet's "Réfutation"

When Galiani first heard that Morellet was criticizing his work in the salons and planning to write a response, he was neither surprised nor concerned. "He's a man with his heart in his head and his head in his heart," he wrote to Epinay.

> He reasons with passion and acts on principle. This is what I love about him with all my heart, even though he reasons differently; and he loves me to madness also, even though he thinks of me as *Machiavellino*. For the rest, I believe that his heart, which is the most virtuous and the best in the world, will bring his head along, and that he will end up by not responding and by loving me even more.[58]

The assurance with which Galiani wrote of Morellet's imminent return to reason was based on the assumption that he would come to understand the "secret" of the *Dialogues*: that they were a model discussion of the complex problems of grain legislation which displayed the kind of reasoning on which policy ought to be based; they were not a doctrinaire solution to those problems. Galiani expected him to understand because, although Morellet's *ideas* were physiocratic, his *experience* was philosophic. "Panurge has dined with us for ten whole years, and at least as long as he didn't cover his head with oilcloth, some drop of common sense and of philosophy must have penetrated it in the course of ten years."[59] When it became clear that Morellet was not getting the point, Galiani wrote him a letter in which he "revealed the secret" by telling him, "Instead of refuting me, explain to me." Discouraged by this time, Galiani told Epinay: "He won't have understood me, but others will understand me, and I have no doubt at all that in the end they will figure out my meaning."[60]

58. Galiani to Epinay, 27 [January] 1770.
59. Galiani to Epinay, 26 May 1770.
60. Galiani to Epinay, 12 May 1770. At least one reader already had understood: see the review of the *Dialogues* in *Mémoires Secrets*, 9 February 1770.

Undeterred, Morellet wrote his refutation. In his preface he acknowledged his friendship with Galiani and swore that it was never his intention "to wound the Author," since he distinguished between "the person and his book."[61] Having gotten the niceties out of the way, Morellet launched his attack. He called Galiani "a man with a glib tongue, in love with paradox," who gave "new form to old prejudices" and dressed up "in seductive colors obvious falsehoods" (2). He portrayed himself, by contrast, as the tireless defender of liberty, zealous to protect it from a "dangerous enemy" whose strategy was to dress up a lie in order to "seduce many people, who seek in books amusement more than truth" (2–3). By adhering to true principles and resisting the "dominating spirit" of the *Dialogues*, Morellet explained, he was able to resist this seduction.

Morellet's indictment of the *Dialogues* as a seductress possessed of a "dominating spirit" gendered the combat between physiocrat and philosophe as masculine and feminine. It recalls the perennial charge that association with salonnières feminized the philosophes and undermined their seriousness. Morellet, not surprisingly, charged Galiani with the same crime. "As to the dominating spirit," he wrote,

I believe I see in the Dialogues little attachment to what the Author himself regards as the truth; indifference, lightness concerning a matter that is serious and of interest; an affected respect for all received opinions; constant flattery for the authority of all times and all places; a very marked taste for despotism; a dogma of infallibility concerning those who govern. (3–4)

Morellet's style of refutation was personal: it was hand-to-hand combat; it was the war of the sexes. Morellet relished the fight, and he could not understand why Galiani did not share his pleasure in it. In letters exchanged that spring, Morellet and Galiani had staked out their ground. "You are quite decided against liberty," wrote Morellet; "I offer combat: we will understand each other very well." Galiani, however, refused the proffered glove. He was for liberty, too, he explained; the real difference between himself and the physiocrats was that he was for liberty without fanaticism, "because fanaticism, or enthusiasm, has never seemed to be good for anything except making revolts."[62] The dialogue form allowed Galiani to engage in a model discussion of the problems of the grain trade without directly refuting the physiocrats'

---

61. André Morellet, *Réfutation de l'ouvrage qui a pour titre "Dialogues sur le commerce des blés"* (London, 1770), pp. 3–4, hereafter cited in the text.
62. Galiani to Morellet, 26 May 1770.

solution to them. He staged the dialogues precisely as an alternative to disputatious combat. Had Morellet understood what was at issue in Galiani's critique of the physiocrats, he could not have refuted the *Dialogues* as an argument about economic theory and policy.

Because Morellet understood debate only as disputation, he could not make the distinction between the author and the argument, and he could not understand Galiani's refusal to engage him in combat. He took Galiani's criticism as a personal insult, and indeed, he was able to read the *Dialogues* only as a personal insult and a refutation of the physiocrats which, in turn, needed to be refuted. He explained his entry into the field of combat as a matter of both "personal interest" and impartial defense. His interest was personal because, like the physiocrats, he was what Galiani had called a "modern Writer" and thus needed to defend himself against the charge that he too was "useless and dangerous." He felt compelled to defend the physiocrats, who were being directly insulted, because he identified with them, but even as a disinterested party, Morellet would have felt called upon to defend a group of admirable men who were being "disparaged as a corps of visionaries, as blind enthusiasts, and worst of all, as inciting revolt and sedition" (14–15). Knowing that such a defensive action would be offensive as well, Morellet could only "ask [Galiani's] pardon in advance" for the personal attacks his refutation would necessarily entail (15).

Morellet concluded his introduction with some thoughts on the form of Galiani's text, which, he maintained, fell short of proper disputation. The Chevalier's interlocutors, he pointed out, did little but praise or agree with him.

> Because with their extreme indulgence and their blind faith, without ideas of their own, without any knowledge of the reasons that one could oppose to the Chevalier's assertions, they would be as disposed to shower me with praise as him. But I thought that I would not gain any solid glory from having myself praised by hirelings who could do nothing but repeat what they have been told, and I have limited my ambition to having my readers say that "I am clear" and that "I am right," two very short and dry *éloges*, but which will satisfy my modesty. (28–29)

The interlocutors were not legitimate because they were not qualified to argue the physiocrat position and therefore served no purpose except to stroke the egos of the Chevalier and his creator. From Morellet's point of view, they were simply stooges, the equivalent of paid lackeys, since they were created by the author and thus served only his interest and not that of the truth.

Finally, Morellet confronted Galiani on the issue of readability. He did not flatter himself, he said, that he could give his work as agreeable a form as that of the *Dialogues*, but he saw no reason to try. "Provided that I am not boring," he asserted, "I will console myself for not being entertaining." If Galiani's dialogues were said to resemble those of Plato, he went on, that did not in any way validate them or their form, since "Plato does not resemble the truth, and the issue here is the truth" (19).

Morellet then laid out the four "articles" of Galiani's "argument" he intended to refute, thereby recasting the *Dialogues* into a refutable form. For the next three hundred pages or so he proceeded to "refute the doctrine of the Author" (46, 84, 177) and to expose "manifest contradiction[s]" (52, 63, 183) as well as "paralogism[s]" (73, 145) in his "argument." He accused Galiani of using "the usual artifice of those who wish to obscure the clearest truths" (63–64); of wishing to "mask" injustice and "stifle" remorse (106); of "believing that he can clothe in seductive colors" (149) one of the many "paradoxes" of which he is enamored (149, 171). Twice he called Galiani's arguments "laughable" (171, 206), and three times he suggested that imagination had gotten the better of him (137, 206, 227). In contrast to his own "clear and precise definitions," Morellet found Galiani's work "vague" and "incoherent" and his reasoning "subtle" (177, 183). In the end, he concluded that although he could not claim, even in such a large tome, to have "resolved all the Author's objections," he did believe that the principles he had laid out "would suffice to destroy those to which [he] had not expressly responded" (356).[63]

Deep within the refutation of Galiani's "argument," Morellet buried a critique of his method. He contested Galiani's claim that his book was "certainly the book of a philosophe, and [that] it alone is capable of forming a philosophe and a policy maker [*homme d'état*]."[64] He refused to accept the premise that a *demonstration* of the process of working through a problem is of more value in educating the public than the *presentation* of any solution to that problem might be.

> After one has reflected on a given subject, [and] one has taken a side, I do not see how a Writer can serve his readers in affecting a skepticism that he himself no longer has. In the search for truth, the mind strays down a thousand obscure paths before recognizing the main route, but once [the writer] knows it, he ought to put his readers onto it right away and spare them his own errors. (236)

63. Morellet made a similar claim in his *Mémoires* thirty years later: "I believe that I can say that I did not leave standing a single one of the sophisms that the Italian made use of in order to attack the liberty of [the grain] trade" (p. 173).

64. Galiani to Epinay, 27 March 1770 (dated by Asse in *Lettres de l'abbé Galiani*).

The writer's responsibility to the public was to reveal the truth as he knew it. If Galiani did not know the truth, then he had nothing to reveal; if he did know it, then he was deceitful in affecting a skepticism that he did not hold. Moreover, he was self-indulgent. By focusing on means rather than end, Galiani gave "too much importance to the most fugitive ideas and even to errors." His readers, far from thanking him for leading them down multiple garden paths, ought not to pardon him for amusing himself by watching them seek a truth that he had already found (236–37).

Because Morellet saw truth as an object that, once found, was to be offered to the public by means of an argument, he represented Galiani's emphasis on the method of seeking answers as a ruse and a bit of sophistry. In the end, Morellet condemned the game Galiani was playing because he believed it was designed not to reach the truth but to embarrass those "against whom one disputes." It displayed the "subtlety of a sophist much more than the sagacity of a philosopher" (237). In other words, in the stylized combat of disputation, Galiani was rewriting the rules in order to play dirty. Morellet minimized Galiani's critique of the dogmatism of the physiocrats by characterizing Galiani as simply "irritated" by it. Of considerably greater importance, in his view, was the skepticism the *Dialogues* produced. "Skepticism and the desperation to know the truth result from the reading of his Work; and Readers content with an agreeable but frivolous dispute, in which the points have only been run through lightly, remain disgusted for a more serious investigation" (238).

Galiani was amazed when he read Morellet's response. How could a philosophe, no matter what his views on matters economic, ally himself with fanatics and defend dogmatism over skepticism? How could a philosophe defend boring pedants by attacking a philosophic work as less than serious? How could one friend make such accusations against another? No wonder Galiani suggested, with a certain playful irony (which Morellet apparently did not appreciate), that the unsigned letter in which he received Morellet's response was written by some "pseudo-Morellet." "Neither the tone, nor the style, nor the thoughts, nothing in the end, resembles you. Who then has written this letter? And you, what has become of you? Do you exist? Are you dead? Have you changed?"[65]

Underlying Galiani's expression of amazement was a more serious suspicion that this was in fact not the real Morellet, because the attack he penned was not his own but that of those who paid him. Galiani knew by the beginning of February that Morellet was writing a re-

65. Galiani to Morellet, 26 May 1770.

sponse to the *Dialogues*, but not until late March did his Parisian contacts inform him that Morellet had "received orders from the Government to respond to the *Dialogues*. He has thus declared [himself] to be
the guard and the constabulary of the economists." A week later Galiani sent Morellet a letter via d'Holbach.[66]

D'Holbach passed the letter on to Morellet without showing it to
anyone, as Galiani had requested. Galiani wanted to keep the debate
with his oldest Parisian friend within the bounds of friendship and
trusted d'Holbach not to betray that confidence. Beyond fulfilling his
commission as trustworthy intermediary, d'Holbach tried to persuade
Morellet to keep his reply within the bounds of that same friendship. In
the letter to Galiani in which he reported having fulfilled his charge he
went on to say:

> The abbé must have responded to you at great length. I did all I could
> with him to moderate his "economic" bile; but I don't know if my reasons
> convinced him, just as I am unaware of the purpose for which he has
> taken up the cause of the [physiocrat] authors so warmly. . . . His *Réfuta-
> tion* has not appeared yet. I hope that he will have made it in a way so as
> not to hurt you, in view of the fact that, otherwise, it would not be able to
> avoid displeasing those persons capable of appreciating the process, and
> above all, your friends, among whom I very much wish you to count me.
> However, you know the bad-tempered spirit that theology breeds, and I
> well fear that this spirit has not disappeared in the abbé.[67]

Morellet's response, delivered to Galiani by means of the diplomatic
pouch of the French ministry, was not in Morellet's hand and it was
unsigned. When Galiani described his receipt of this missive in his
response to Morellet, he made clear that while it could be called "some
kind of letter," it violated the norms of epistolary exchange in the
Republic of Letters. He suspected that these "eight mortal pages" were
not written by the abbé Morellet whose company he had kept in Paris
for ten happy years.

Later in the same letter, Galiani replied to a rumor Morellet had
been circulating around Paris that his own confidence had been violated: he was claiming that Epinay had obtained a copy of his as-yet-
unpublished refutation from Sartine and had sent it to Galiani.[68] Gal-

66. Galiani to Epinay, 3 and 31 March 1770; Galiani to d'Holbach, 7 April 1770. This
is the exchange that I used in chap. 4 to illustrate how letters circulated through the
salons.

67. D'Holbach to Galiani, 3 June 1770, in "Lettres inédites du baron et de la baronne
d'Holbach à l'abbé Galiani," ed. Fausto Nicolini, *Etudes Italiennes*, n.s. 1 (January–March
1931): 30–31.

68. Epinay had reported the rumor to Galiani in her letter of 5–7 May 1770.

iani denied that he had seen Morellet's manuscript and gave his own explanation of why he had written to him back in April:

> It was M. de Sorba [minister plenipotentiary of Genoa in Paris] who first wrote to me that you had received orders from the Government to refute me. Then the chevalier de Magallon announced to me a combat to death against you in a closed field. M. Schutz, secretary of the Danish embassy, M. Nicolaï, our former undersecretary, M. de Militerni, M. Giambone, M. de Courtanvaux and many others wrote me the same thing. No one sent me any details about your book, and if madame d'Epinay has seen it, she certainly would not have admitted it to me.[69]

Galiani's sources were reliable. It was indeed at the instigation of the government that Morellet wrote his *Réfutation*. In his *Mémoires*, however, Morellet defended himself against the charge of *lèse-amitié* and of treason against the Republic of Letters by someone who had sold out to the monarchy: "The Minister of Finances, who paid me, was entitled to dispose of my time when he had need of it," he explained.

> M. Trudaine de Montigny had the same right in his capacity as intendant of finances and commerce, and above all as my benefactor and my friend. Questions of administration that were constantly being raised entered into the objects of my studies.
>
>   From this it happened that M. d'Invau invited me to write my two first memoirs against the Indies Company; M. de Choiseul and M. Trudaine, the *Réfutation de l'abbé Galiani* . . . ; M. Trudaine, my *Théorie du paradoxe contre Linguet*; M. de Sartine and M. Lenoir, different memoirs on the provisioning of Paris; that M. Turgot, during his ministry, requested various works from me.

Morellet's list of commissioned works continued until 1789 when, much to his regret, his undertakings, like those of so many others, were abruptly terminated.[70]

   Morellet situated his refutation of Galiani within a nonpartisan list of state employers which included both Choiseul, who had been responsi-

---

Though I find no specific basis for Morellet's suspicion, there was a general sense of insecurity in regard to literary property at this time. More to the point, according to Epinay, Morellet was already writing a refutation of Galiani in October 1769, months before the *Dialogues* were published. She suspected that Court de Gébelin, the censor to whom Sartine had assigned the text, was passing it around among his physiocrat friends: Epinay to Galiani, 4 October 1769. Was Morellet revealing his own unethical practices in accusing Galiani and Epinay of engaging in them?

69. Galiani to Morellet, 26 May 1770.
70. Morellet, *Mémoires*, p. 169.

ble for Galiani's dismissal from Paris, and Sartine, Galiani's friend, who had helped get the *Dialogues* through the system. In addition, he minimized his personal investment in the *Réfutation* by characterizing it as one of many "involuntary distractions" from his own work. Moreover, the job he was asked to do was simply "to second the reasonable views of the ministry, and in particular of M. le duc de Choiseul, in favor of the liberty of commerce."[71] To exculpate himself further, Morellet went on to accuse Galiani of being antiphilosophic and to say that the *Dialogues* did not in fact represent Galiani's principles at all, since he had none!

> These were much less the development of the principles of the abbé, who scarcely had any, than malice against M. de Choiseul, protector of the liberty of the grain trade, against the economists, and even, in various ways, against the philosophes; but this malice was pleasant, delicate, ingenious, and it was no small undertaking to repel it, since it is difficult to use pleasantry defensively, and since, when one responds with serious arguments, it happens that he who has managed to make people laugh easily keeps the laughers and yes-men on his side.[72]

Finally, Morellet quoted at length from two of Turgot's letters—one written to him and the other to Lespinasse—which were both highly critical of the *Dialogues* and noted the futility of trying to respond to them because of their form and tone. In addition, Turgot had expressed his regrets that Morellet was too busy to write a response. It was not, however, either Turgot's flattery or his own confessed "taste for polemic" that Morellet said decided him upon his course. Instead, "the very success of the *Dialogues* was a prod for me, and I dreamed [*ambitionnais*] of the glory of vanquishing all the difficulties in making a good response."[73] Avoiding all mention of the tone of his own piece, Morellet cast himself as the brave knight who, against the greatest odds, had set out to win glory for himself and his king (Choiseul, Turgot) by

71. Ibid., p. 170.
72. Ibid.
73. Ibid., pp. 170–72. He dates the two letters he quotes as follows: Turgot to Morellet, 19 January 1770; Turgot to Lespinasse, 26 January 1770. On 18 March, Epinay quoted to Galiani a rather different version of Turgot's views: "Here . . . is a terrible book. Those who would wish to respond will fail and will not be read. It will have the fate of *L'Esprit des lois*." Clearly she was censoring the criticism in the hopes of avoiding a storm, and she was (in this case, at least) successful. On 7 April Galiani responded: "I am thrilled with the judgment of M. de Turgot; I had a premonition of it in my heart. I had the highest esteem for his excellent judgment, and I would always have betted that he would have liked the *Dialogues*." Even though Galiani knew that Turgot was a firm believer in the liberalization of the grain trade, his own belief was that Turgot, like Morellet, would appreciate the *Dialogues* as an expression of *philosophie*.

single-handedly slaying the antiphilosophic, antiliberal (but basically silly and harmless) dragon that was Galiani.

A satisfactory explanation of Morellet's motivation can take seriously his combative spirit and desire for victory and glory.[74] But it must also acknowledge that Morellet's claim to personal heroism drew upon a political model far different from that articulated by Thomas three years earlier in his *discours de réception*. If Morellet's civic role as a man of letters was to slay dragons for the state, then the autonomy of the Republic of Letters was seriously in question. The interchange between Morellet and Galiani was compromised not only because Morellet's position as an employee of the state undermined his claims to represent the truth but also because loyalty to his employers undermined his friendship with Galiani, and friendship was at the heart of the Republic of Letters. As Galiani himself suggested in a letter to d'Holbach: "He forgets that he is my friend, in order to think only of the friendship of M. the former controller general."[75]

It is at least as significant that the terms by which the debate on the grain trade could be made public were in the hands of the state. Diderot and Epinay had begun negotiating on Galiani's behalf with Sartine and the censors as early as July 1769, as part of the process of getting the *Dialogues* to press and on the market.[76] Not until 11 December, however, could Epinay write the worried author to say that his book was printed; another two weeks and more negotiations were necessary before it was actually announced for sale—that is, truly published by being made available to the public.[77] Before then, however, Galiani, feeling panicky and helpless, wrote to Epinay: "Is it possible that the best of men, the most worthy magistrate, the man who loves me most in all the world, and whom I love and esteem the most, in short, M. de Sartine, would wish out of sheer amusement [*gaîté de coeur*] to ruin me and an honest bookseller?"[78]

It was not, however, simply Sartine's goodwill toward his friend that got Galiani's book through the system. Of crucial importance was a change at the top. On 21 December the controller general, Etienne Maynon d'Invau, whose son-in-law was Morellet's physiocratic employer, Jean-Charles-Philibert Trudaine de Montigny, and whose patron was Galiani's enemy Choiseul, was replaced by Terray, who was opposed to liberalization. "I observe," wrote Galiani in January, "that it

---

74. Diderot, however, did not take it seriously. See *Apologie*, in *Oeuvres politiques*, pp. 72–73 and n. 1.
75. Galiani to d'Holbach, 21 July 1770.
76. Epinay to Galiani, 26 July 1769.
77. Epinay to Galiani, 11 and 24 December 1769.
78. Galiani to Epinay, 18 December 1769.

was necessary to fire a controller, cause enormous bankruptcies, pro-
voke the overturning of the State, in order that my small book might
appear."[79]

When Morellet's *Réfutation* came off the presses in June 1770, it was
immediately confiscated by order of either Sartine or Terray or both.[80]
It was released only in 1774, when Turgot was named to the post of
controller general that first Invau, then Terray, had held. Indeed, Turgot sent out hundreds of copies of the *Réfutation* to his intendants.
Thus, according to Steven Kaplan, it became "one of the most widely
distributed tracts of liberal propaganda of the seventies, serving not
only as a belated rejoinder to Galiani but as an apology for Turgot's
own liberalization program."[81]

Recentering the Republic of Letters in the Parisian salons was a significant move away from state sponsorship of learning in the academies, but the work of the citizenry continued to be compromised, or at
least to give the appearance of being compromised, in situations such
as Galiani's debate with Morellet concerning grain policy. The problem
was, first, that government officials were in the business of hiring pens
to promote their interests, and such a synecdochic conception of the
writer forced him to give up (or at least suspend) his citizenship in the
Republic of Letters. Second, publication, which alone could make public such debates as the one Galiani was trying to initiate, was controlled
by the state. Moreover, such publication as was permitted brought the
wrong response.

Galiani's attempt to introduce a new form of political writing and
political debate in the *Dialogues sur le commerce des blés*, a form that
represented the principles and practices of the Republic of Letters
rather than the monarchy or the church, was resisted by a fellow philosophe who served two masters. At the same time, it was subverted by
state officials who viewed publication in relation to their own interests
rather than as a free institution of the Republic of Letters. And even
Galiani showed himself not to be above the conflict of particular interests and enlightened practices when he praised Terray for stopping the
distribution of Morellet's work because "it [was] no longer the time to
dissertate, it [was] time for you to think about bread, and about the
cruel famine that menaces you, by retracting a bad law that you have
made."[82]

79. Galiani to Epinay, 20 January 1770.
80. Galiani first credited Sartine in a letter to Epinay, 7 July 1770, but a week later he
wrote to J. B. A. Suard that it was the controller general who had opposed publication:
Galiani to Suard, 14 July 1770 (dated by Asse in *Lettres de l'abbé Galiani*).
81. Kaplan, *Bread, Politics* 2:607–8.
82. Galiani to J. B. A. Suard, 14 July 1770.

When Kant wrote his answer to the question "What is Enlightenment?" in 1784, he should have remembered the debates on the grain
trade, especially since they continued right through the 1770s. Had he
done so, he might not have maintained that it is possible to restrict the
use of a person's reason in a civic post or office without thereby compromising the free use of that same person's reason in the public
sphere of the literate world.[83] The two worlds were hard to separate in
the lived experience of those who inhabited both. Thomas's eloquent
solution to the acknowledged conflict experienced by the subject of the
French monarchy who was also a citizen of the Republic of Letters,
which had resounded triumphantly in the French Academy only three
years earlier, fell apart as philosophes tried to serve the truth, the
republic, and the monarchy. Internal strains in the Republic of Letters
reflected the unresolved difficulties of trying to live and work in two
polities whose values, practices, and institutions set them at odds.
Moreover, such tensions only reinforced the sensitivity to insult and the
personal combativeness among men of letters, and these could not be
effectively transformed into collective energy. Pushing and pulling between the monarchy and the republic intensified the pressure on individuals, who found it even more difficult to govern themselves under
the spotlight of publicity. Because the Parisian police were servants of
the state, they could not govern the Republic of Letters according to the
norms and values of the republic; because salonnières had no authority
outside the closed circles of their salons, they were unable to govern the
discourse beyond their walls in the public world of print. The project of
Enlightenment could not withstand the stresses of publication.

The strains in the Republic of Letters which the debate on the grain
trade brought to the surface were threats to friendship and to the
political relations the republic modeled on it. Galiani had represented
his conflict with Morellet this way several times, but he was not the only
one to believe that the republic itself was threatened when friendship
was betrayed. Diderot was even more outraged by Morellet's *Réfutation*.
More than anyone else, he understood that the *Dialogues* demonstrated
how to change the common way of thinking by inviting the reading
public to participate in forms of discourse developed in the Enlightenment Republic of Letters. Morellet had violated both the norms of
friendship and the rules of enlightened discourse. Diderot's *Apologie de
l'abbé Galiani* was therefore an act of friendship and in defense of
friendship. Its main concern, as Ellen Marie Strenski has said, was not
the grain trade but philosophical method.[84]

83. Kant, "What Is Enlightenment?" in *Perpetual Peace*, p. 42.
84. Ellen Marie Strenski, "Diderot: For and against the Physiocrats," *Studies on Voltaire and the Eighteenth Century* 57 (1967): 1452.

Diderot's "Apologie"

Diderot, who had rung in the new year with a poem to unity and friendship, first read Morellet's *Réfutation* in March 1770, when Sartine asked him to be one of the official censors for it. Such a choice was only fair, since Sartine had named someone close to the physiocrats as censor for Galiani's *Dialogues*.[85]

In a letter to Sartine, Diderot made his case against the *Réfutation*. First, it did not stand up against the *Dialogues* and thus was not an effective refutation. Second, there was no point in publishing it since it would sit on the shelf unread with all the failed physiocrat attempts to refute Galiani. Third, it was unnecessarily hostile and personal, since Morellet was not himself a physiocrat and therefore had no justification for treating Galiani as an enemy. Fourth, publication would only hurt Morellet because, caring little about the ethics of what he was doing, he would damage his reputation in the eyes of both the public and his friends. Finally, Diderot made it clear that if he did publish the *Réfutation*, Morellet would hurt a friend who had repeatedly demonstrated his own goodwill.[86]

Diderot's critique was thorough, but it was not the report of a censor for the French monarchy. Indeed, Diderot cast himself as a citizen-reviewer for the Republic of Letters. Rather than consider the implications of publication for the state, Diderot evaluated the soundness of Morellet's argument, its persuasiveness, whether or not it added anything new to the debate, and how well it accorded with the ethical standards of the Republic of Letters. Diderot's recommendation, moreover, was not really for Sartine but for the author: Morellet would be wiser to put his criticism in the form of a letter to Galiani instead of publishing it. "The only way that the critic could take advantage of his work, would be to make out of it a long letter that he would send to the one whom he called, in Paris, his friend," advised Diderot. "There would be in this sacrifice less to lose than to gain."[87] Diderot saw no purpose in taking up the sword against a friend in defense of the physiocrats. Since Morellet did not claim to have been personally injured by the *Dialogues*, he was making an enemy out of a friend for no reason: he could not persuade the public to his side, and he had no personal interest in making a debate into a dispute.

85. Epinay to Galiani, 4 October and 4 November 1769.
86. Diderot to Sartine, [10 March 1770].
87. Diderot made this point directly to Morellet a few months later in regard to a letter Morellet had received full of "notes and reflections" on his *Dictionnaire de commerce*. Morellet wanted to know if Diderot knew who had sent it; Diderot's answer was simple: "It is one of your friends, since he has not had his observations printed and he sends them to you." Reported by Epinay to Galiani, 15 August 1770.

"I see with sorrow that men of letters care less about their moral character than their literary talent," Diderot reflected. "This refutation will do a lot of harm to M. l'abbé Morellet, who must not expect either the indulgence of the public or that of his friends; and that is what I would make it my duty to tell him if I could explain myself without betraying the confidence with which you have honored me." He would also, he said, show Morellet those letters in which Galiani expressed his continued friendship for Morellet and his confidence that that friendship would not be betrayed despite their different views on economic matters. To make his point, Diderot then quoted a few of those passages to Sartine. "From which you will conclude," he wrote, "that the little Italian machiavellist understands the procedures a bit better than the French philosophe does."

Like so many letters written in the eighteenth century, this one was meant to be passed along to a third party. Clearly, there was no need for Diderot to convince Sartine of Galiani's character and expressions of friendship; it was Morellet who needed to be reminded. Because Diderot had been given Morellet's manuscript in confidence, he could not himself advise the author not to publish it without betraying that confidence. And since, "as a censor," he found "nothing that could prevent its publication," his aim was to persuade Sartine to talk Morellet into withdrawing it, and to help Sartine in doing so.[88]

Whether or not Sartine did pass Diderot's letter on to Morellet is not known; what is known is that Epinay, to whom Diderot had shown it, got his permission to send a copy to Galiani. Thus Diderot's first defense of his friend was redirected to function in the traditional manner as both an expression and bond of friendship.[89] With his letter to Sartine, Diderot demonstrated his commitment to his friends, both Galiani and Morellet, and to the principle of freedom of the press. Meanwhile, he fulfilled his obligation to Sartine, while refusing to act as censor for the state. He was also, and not incidentally, looking out for what he considered to be the best interests of men of letters and their republic. In serving the monarchy as a "censor," Diderot had acted in the interest of the Republic of Letters and of friendship.

---

88. Epinay wrote to Galiani (18 March 1770) that when Sartine had read the report he commented to Diderot, "This is a very strong and harsh letter." Diderot replied, "It is so that you can show it to the author, sir, that I have written it. I have signed it so that he may see it and know that it is by me."

89. On friendship and the epistolary bond, see Goodman, *Criticism in Action*, pp. 54–55. When Vernière writes that "the indiscreet Mme d'Epinay sent a copy of the letter to Galiani on 18 March," he seriously misrepresents her action, her character, and her role as intermediary between Galiani and the Parisian philosophes, especially Diderot and Grimm: Introduction to Diderot, *Apologie*, in *Oeuvres politiques*, p. 64.

It is worth noting that Diderot was not afraid to recommend suppression of a work when he found such action to be warranted. Like Geoffrin, like Galiani, he drew the line at personal insult. When Sartine consulted him in June concerning an anonymous play, *Satyrique, ou L'Homme dangereux*, Diderot suggested that Sartine should block its performance for reasons that showed the interests of the monarchy and the republic to be one: "It is not for me, monsieur, to give you advice," he wrote;

> but if you can manage in such a way that it would not be said that twice, with your permission, those of your fellow citizens who are honored in all parts of Europe, have been publicly insulted; whose works are devoured near and far; whom foreigners revere, summon, and recompense; who will be cited, and who will conspire to the glory of the French name when you no longer exist, nor they either; whom travelers make it a duty to visit now while they are here, and whom they will make it an honor to have known when they return to their country, I think, sir, that you will act wisely. . . .
>
> The philosophes are nothing today, but they will have their turn. They will be spoken of; the history of the persecutions that they have endured will be told; of the flat and unworthy manner in which they have been treated in the public theaters; and if you are named in this history, as one cannot doubt, it ought to be with praise. This is my advice, sir, and here it is with all the frankness that you expect from me. I fear that these rhymesters are no less the enemies of the philosophes than they are yours.[90]

The play was closed by order of the police before it opened. That same month, however, Sartine also blocked distribution of Morellet's *Réfutation*. Epinay could not even get a copy to send to Galiani.[91]

If Diderot chose to act rather as a peer reviewer than as a censor in regard to Morellet's *Réfutation*, his action had no apparent effect. On the one hand, Morellet continued to seek publication of his manuscript; on the other, Sartine and Terray decided to block distribution of it in order to further a public policy to which Morellet's work was opposed. And Diderot himself would not let the matter rest. He contin-

90. Diderot to Sartine, [June 1770]. The first instance to which Diderot refers is Pallisot's play *Les Philosophes*, which had been performed in Paris in 1760. Although Diderot did not know who the author of the *Satyrique* was, he suspected that it was again Palissot, and he was right. See the notes to the letter.

91. Epinay to Galiani, 12 June 1770. When she wrote to him again on 28 June, she showed sympathy for Morellet, whose "little joke" was costing him a lot of money (1,500 livres) because, instead of prohibiting the publication of Morellet's manuscript, the police seized all the copies after it was printed.

ued to think about the problems of the grain trade. Three times—in August, October, and January—he relayed specific questions and arguments to Galiani via Epinay. With her mediation, he thus carried on an epistolary discussion with Galiani that constituted the continuation of the *Dialogues*.[92]

In November, Diderot wrote to two friends, Sophie Volland and Grimm, that he had run into Morellet, and amazingly, Morellet had given him his only printed copy of the *Réfutation* and asked him for his comments.[93] A week later, Diderot wrote to Grimm that he would send him a copy of the letter he had written to Morellet.[94] But Diderot never sent the letter, either to Morellet or to Grimm. Perhaps he decided that Morellet would not appreciate his frank comments. Perhaps he decided for once to fight fire with fire, for it was presumably that letter which formed the basis of the *Apologie de l'abbé Galiani*, which Diderot finished in January—at about the same time he wrote his last letter to Galiani about the *Dialogues*.[95] In other words, Diderot was simultaneously conducting an epistolary discussion with Galiani and writing what scholars tend to call the "refutation of the refutation."[96] It is significant, however, that what Diderot first titled "Notes sur un ouvrage intitulé *Réfutation* . . ." became in later versions not a "refutation" but an "apology." Even though the text remains in its last form a series of notes that respond, page by page, to Morellet's arguments, it reads more like a heated debate than a disputatious refutation.[97]

Since the first publication of the *Apologie* in 1954, scholars have found it an embarrassment. Anthony Strugnell, after identifying it as a key text in the development of Diderot's political thought, admits that it is not a "great work; it is clumsy, untidy, and repetitive."[98] Paul Vernière calls it a "choleric work . . . in its confidences and indiscretions"; the "violence of the tone," he maintains, prohibited its publication.[99]

---

92. Epinay to Galiani, 9 August and 29 October 1770, 20 January 1771. During this period Galiani also corresponded directly with J. B. A. Suard concerning the grain trade: Galiani to Suard, 8 September 1770. Suard's letters to Galiani, one written 6 August 1770 and the other 14 October 1770, are published in "Lettere inedite di G. B. Suard all'abate Galiani," ed. Fausto Nicolini, in *Mélanges de philologie, d'histoire, et de littérature offerts à Henri Hauvette* (Paris, 1934), pp. 461–69.

93. Diderot to Volland, 2 November 1770; Diderot to Grimm, 2 November 1770.

94. Diderot to [Grimm, 10 November 1770].

95. Vernière, Introduction to Diderot, *Apologie*, in *Oeuvres politiques*, pp. 64–65.

96. Ibid., p. 65; Kaplan, *Bread, Politics* 2:608; Cohen, "Diderot's Machiavellian Harlequin," p. 147.

97. Vernière reproduces the first page of each of the four manuscripts found in the fonds Vandeul, Bibliothèque Nationale, as plates in Diderot, *Oeuvres politiques*.

98. Anthony Strugnell, *Diderot's Politics: A Study of the Evolution of Diderot's Political Thought after the "Encyclopédie"* (The Hague, 1973), p. 128.

99. Vernière, Introduction to Diderot, *Apologie*, in *Oeuvres politiques*, pp. 65 and 67.

Kaplan calls Diderot's tone "pitilessly cruel and ironical."[100] Those who have studied the four extant manuscripts of the *Apologie*, however, note the development of the text from a refutation that is highly *personnel*, to a fairer critical work: the number of citations from Morellet that are directly refuted declines, and the tone becomes less spontaneous, personal, and aggressive. From a personal attack on Morellet, it was moving in the direction of a defense of Galiani and a polemic against physiocracy.[101] What began as an angry response to Morellet's betrayal of Galiani's friendship was being transformed into a defense of *philoso-phie* against physiocracy, a reassertion of the practice and message of Galiani's *Dialogues*. This did not mean, as Franco Venturi points out, that Diderot simply defended all of Galiani's *ideas* against Morellet's refutation of them.[102] His ongoing epistolary discussion with Galiani was inscribed in the *Apologie* as an affirmation of the practice it instanti-ated.[103] Diderot's point was not that Galiani was "right" and Morellet "wrong": rather, he was championing both his friend and the dialogic method for advancing the encyclopedic project of changing the com-mon way of thinking.

From the opening sentence, the *Apologie* is cast in terms of friend-ship: "The first reflection that comes to mind is about the author of this work. One asks oneself what kind of man is this abbé Morellet, who is the friend of the abbé Galiani and who writes against the abbé Galiani, who is the enemy of the Economists and who writes in favor of the Economists.[104] Diderot's answer to this question was twofold: first, Mo-rellet was someone who betrayed a friend in order to "pay his court" to the man who paid him; second, he was "the most *personnel* man that I know; a violent and thoughtless man, who runs after everything and lacks everything. This is a man who loves himself" (71). Diderot went on to say that Morellet had no ideas of his own and was unreadable. He compared Morellet to Galiani: Morellet was a man of sense, but Galiani was a man of genius; thus anyone could have written the *Réfutation*, while only Galiani could have written the *Dialogues*. Most important, "Galiani thinks and makes us think; the other makes himself heard

100. Kaplan, *Bread, Politics* 2:608.
101. Herbert Dieckmann, *Inventaire du fonds Vandeul et inédits de Diderot* (Geneva, 1951), p. 86; Venturi, *Europe des Lumières*, pp. 188–89.
102. Venturi, *Europe des Lumières*, p. 189.
103. Vernière notes several arguments in the *Apologie* based on arguments relayed to Galiani by Epinay or repeating them wholesale: Introduction to Diderot, *Apologie*, in *Oeuvres politiques*, pp. 85 (9 August 1770 and 20 January 1771), 91 (20 January 1771), 102 (29 October 1770). Vernière assumes that Epinay did nothing more than transcribe the philosophe's thoughts. I would suggest that they were discussed under her guidance and that conveying the arguments was an extension of her salonnière function.
104. Diderot, *Apologie*, in *Oeuvres politiques*, p. 69, hereafter cited in the text.

because he is right, but he does not make you think because he does not think and because he tires you and bores you" (72).

Diderot responded to Morellet's charge that Galiani was adept at seducing those who sought amusement rather than truth. The truth, he argued, was so rarely found and so hard to recognize when it was, "that if one is not amused, all is lost. What would I have left of the abbé Galiani if he had not amused me? What will be left of your *Réfutation*, if you have not instructed me?" (73). Thus, while Morellet may have been right to call Galiani often subtle and frivolous, at least he had "gaiety of style and genius." Morellet, by contrast, was "hard, dry, boring"; he had achieved nothing since he had not in any way clarified the issues at hand (97). Diderot accused Morellet of being intentionally dull (96).

By defining the text simply as a repository of truth, Morellet had limited its value, for no one could be sure that he had indeed found the truth. He had also exposed his own hypocrisy. To his claim that Galiani showed little regard for the truth, Diderot replied: "My dear abbé, Galiani loves the truth more and money less than you do" (74). Whereas Morellet had opposed truth to amusement, Diderot suggested that the real opposition was between truth and venality, an opposition by which Morellet's claims were compromised.[105] Further, Morellet had mistaken the "impartiality" of Galiani's use of dialogue for "indifference" to the truth. And why? Because Morellet was dogmatic and Galiani was inquisitive; because Morellet loved disputation and Galiani loved conversation. "It is because you are always on a school bench and the abbé is always on a sofa" (74).

Diderot was contrasting scholastic disputation to the polite conversation of the salon. He reasserted this point later when he called Morellet "the master [*licencié*] . . . with his hundred thousand syllogisms" (89). He also reminded Morellet ("who has deafened us for ten years in *bonne compagnie* and after dinner") that it was disingenuous to suggest that Galiani's representation of *la bonne compagnie* discussing liberty of commerce after dinner was unrealistic (122).[106] The point was not simply that Morellet was arguing against the practices of the Enlightenment Republic of Letters but that he had himself participated in and profited from them for years and now was *publicly* turning against them. He was thus either a traitor or a hypocrite or both.[107]

In the *Apologie*, Diderot elaborated on the point he had made in his letter to Sartine concerning the propriety of Morellet's doing battle for the physiocrats.

105. Diderot makes this point repeatedly. See ibid., pp. 75, 78, 107, 113, 122.
106. Galiani had made the same complaint to Epinay in his letter of 26 May 1770.
107. It is tempting to see Morellet as another Rousseau, but the difference between them is important. Rousseau developed an entire oeuvre, if not a philosophy, that re-

> If you are an Economist and you attack the abbé as he attacked the Economists, everything would be according to the rules; but if you are in no way an Economist, and the abbé Galiani is your friend, you discuss [*agitez*] the question with your friend strongly, discuss scrupulously his reasons, but do not go beyond that; no matter how lightly you graze his person, you are indecent and uncivil and you will be told that: why do you get yourself mixed up in this? Why not leave to those who believe themselves insulted the care of repelling the injury? (81)

The simple answer, of course, was that Morellet got involved because someone paid him to do so. But this passage also makes clear that Diderot believed very strongly in the rules of polite conversation and in the role of propriety in keeping discourse civil. And the rules were necessary precisely because of people such as Morellet. Diderot was angry because Morellet was willing to sell out his friends and the Republic of Letters with them, but he also recognized that Morellet's personality was part of the problem: "It is only the rage to contradict which makes [you] imagine so extravagantly" (88).

Finally, Diderot responded to Morellet's attack on the form of Galiani's work. "You do not like abbé Galiani's skeptical way of proceeding," he wrote. "Too bad for you, because it is very fine, very pleasant, very delicate, very amusing, but it demands genius. Nothing conforms more to the search for and the persuasion to the truth; to the search, because in doubting one becomes certain of everything; to persuasion, because one throws passion off the trail" (112).

Carol Sherman calls the *Apologie* a "poetic" of the dialogue form.[108] It was clearly from Galiani that Diderot learned the value and the possibilities of the dialogue as a (if not *the*) genre of enlightenment, and the *Apologie* was a defense of that form as Galiani had reinvented it. Vernière tells us that for years Diderot had been investigating the biological and medical questions that would form the subject matter of the *Rêve de d'Alembert*. Not until the summer of 1769, however, when he was editing Galiani's *Dialogues*, did he get the idea to give them dialogue form. By the first week of September, the *Rêve* was finished.[109] On 11 September, Diderot wrote a long letter to Volland in which he men-

---

jected the premise of sociability. Morellet, however, not only continued to frequent the salons and other social spaces of the Republic of Letters but went on to write the essays on contradiction and conversation in an effort to legitimate his disputatious practice within the framework of Enlightenment sociability.

108. Carol Sherman, *Diderot and the Art of Dialogue* (Geneva, 1976), p. 43.

109. Paul Vernière, Introduction to Diderot, *Le Rêve de d'Alembert*, in *Oeuvres philosophiques*, ed. Vernière (Paris, 1964), pp. 250–52.

tioned that he was in the midst of correcting the proofs of Galiani's *Dialogues* and later reminded her that he had written his own dialogue between himself and d'Alembert. "In rereading it," he wrote, "I got the wild idea of writing a second one, and it has been done. . . . It is titled d'Alembert's Dream. It is not possible to be more profound and more crazy."

By the end of September, Diderot had finished his work on the proofs of Galiani's *Dialogues*, but he had also learned a lesson about writing his own. Through J. B. A. Suard, Lespinasse had learned that she was an interlocutor in Diderot's text, and she protested. As her friend, d'Alembert demanded that the work be burned in his presence. Diderot destroyed it in his own way: he tried to rewrite it by changing the names of the interlocutors. "There is nothing here but a broken statue," he wrote in his letter of apology, "but so broken that it was almost impossible for the artist to repair it. There have remained around him a number of fragments whose true place he has been unable to recover." With regret he noted that others had found the first version to have "originality, force, verve, gaiety, naturalness, and even to be of some consequence. The majority of these qualities so essential to the dialogue have vanished from these." He sacrificed all of this, he told d'Alembert, to friendship.[110] A year later he condemned Morellet for sacrificing friendship to the production of a text. "If this is the way you treat your friends," he wrote in the *Apologie*, "I don't want to be one of them" (113).

Diderot had learned from Galiani the attributes of dialogue; he learned from d'Alembert and Lespinasse that friendship could be a legitimate constraint on it. For one of the major lessons taught by Galiani was that contemporary problems needed to be treated in a contemporary context: modern *philosophie* required *dialogues des vivants*, not *dialogues des morts*. How could one account for changes over time and place and present modern views if one's interlocutors were locked in some ancient past? "Had I wished to sacrifice the richness of the material to the nobility of the tone," Diderot wrote to Volland, "Democritus, Hippocrates, and Leucippus would have been my characters; but verisimilitude would have enclosed me within the narrow limits of ancient philosophy, and I would have lost too much."[111] Diderot was a novice at the art of dialogue, but over the course of the next ten years he would continue to perfect it, such that today he has effaced Galiani as its modern master.[112] "The dialogue," Diderot wrote in the

110. Diderot to d'Alembert, [end of September, 1769].
111. Diderot to Volland, [31 August 1769].
112. Sherman, *Diderot and the Art of Dialogue*, pp. 30–53; Wilson, *Diderot*, pp. 551 and 554; Jean Fabre, "Galiani et la société française à l'époque de Louis XV," in Enrico Cerulli

Apologie, "allows for repose and digressions. The dialogue is the true means of instruction; for, what do the master and the disciple do? They dialogue endlessly" (112).

Unlike the other works of Diderot's maturity, the *Apologie* did not even circulate in the *Correspondance Littéraire*. Vernière, who thinks that "the violence of the tone" would have prohibited publication, does not explain why Diderot chose not to circulate it. He suggests further that the fall of Choiseul in December 1770 made publication "politically useless" anyway, since with Choiseul went any discussion of liberalization of the grain trade.[113] That discussion was reopened, however, with the appointment of Turgot as controller general in 1774 and his release of Morellet's *Réfutation*.

During the vitriolic *guerre de farines* that followed Turgot's freeing of the grain trade, the controller general's friend Condorcet publicly attacked not Galiani but Jacques Necker, who had published his own essay *Sur la législation et le commerce des grains* in 1775. For three months in 1775, Keith Baker tells us, Condorcet "remained in Picardy stalking his literary prey with a hostility so venomous that his friends feared for his title as *le bon Condorcet*." Lespinasse pleaded with him to "put moderation in your tone and vigor in your substance. It is the cause of reason and humanity you are defending. Beware of utilizing so common and so feeble a means of rebuttal as to answer with insults."[114]

In a series of published works, Condorcet blamed Necker for the market riots that had erupted throughout France. Amélie Suard later wrote that there had been an unresolved conflict between Condorcet's head and his heart:

> This hatred, so unjust, that he had for M. Necker and that afflicted me so, this hatred, he had only for his principles of political economy. . . . He was going to govern by his principles, and from that moment M. de Condorcet declared against him a war to the death. . . . There was, I am saying, between the malice of his spirit and the goodness of his heart, a contrast that has always distinctively struck me. His intolerance in regard to political opinions was incredible.[115]

---

et al., eds., *Convegno italo-francese sul tema: Ferdinando Galiani* (Rome, 1975), p. 165. I have been guilty of ignoring Galiani's influence in my own treatment of Diderot's use of dialogue in *Criticism in Action*.

113. Vernière, Introduction to Diderot, *Apologie*, in *Oeuvres politiques*, p. 65; see also Strugnell, *Diderot's Politics*, p. 123 n. 18.

114. Baker, *Condorcet*, pp. 61–62.

115. Amélie Suard, commentary on letter from Condorcet to her, [November 1774], in *Correspondance inédite de Condorcet et Madame Suard*, pp. 150–51.

Soon after Condorcet's *Lettre d'un laboureur de Picardie* was published, Suard wrote to him about a conversation she had had with one of his readers, a man she had met as she traveled to Ferney to pay homage to Voltaire: "He spoke to me of M. Turgot, of the *économistes* and of the work that has annoyed you so much. He made much of it. He blames you for having responded with insults. 'He is, however, a virtuous man,' he said. I spoke of your virtues with all the tenderness that they inspire in me, but you cannot imagine how sad it made me to hear you reproached for an injustice I could not justify."[116] A few days later Condorcet wrote a letter to Suard's husband that was more reminiscent of the chevalier de Rohan, who had punished the young poet Voltaire for his insolence, than of the patriarch of the Republic of Letters, whom he admired as much as anyone did: "One must punish the insolence of these parvenus," he wrote of the Neckers; "one must teach them that one remains what one is, no matter how rich one becomes, and it is only venal souls who accord consideration to opulence. The reign of finance is over, it must learn to be modest. This man and his *caillette* of a wife can say what they want, and that won't make him any less of a speculator (or paper merchant) who has written a bad book."[117]

Suard, to whom Condorcet expressed his hostility toward the "foreigner enriched at the expense of [his] country"—a slur reminiscent of one of Morellet's attacks on Galiani—was put in the bind of friendship and patronage, for Condorcet was his friend and Necker was his patron. "You have written me, my good friend, four lines that have hurt me a great deal. Why do you choose me for the confidant of outrageous insults that you spread against a man whom I esteem, whom I love, whom I ought to love?" Suard went on to explain the seriousness of insulting Necker publicly: "All my tastes and my feelings draw me to you and attach me to you; but the more I love you, the more your public wrongs afflict me; I am honored by your virtue, and I am vain of your reputation."[118]

Condorcet, passionately involved in the substance of the argument, was deaf both to the Suards' pleas to think of his reputation and to Lespinasse's concerns for the forms that made comity and discourse possible in the Republic of Letters. In the end, Lespinasse's friendship for Condorcet took the form that Epinay's had for Galiani: she helped him get his manuscript through the press. In a letter to Condorcet she

116. Amélie Suard to Condorcet, [9 or 10 May 1775], ibid.
117. Condorcet to J. B. A. Suard, 14 May 1775. Condorcet also replied to Amélie Suard's letter sometime that month and wished her well on her pilgrimage to "the old man of Ferney who laughs at all this." Both ibid.
118. J. B. A. Suard to Condorcet, 18 May [1775], ibid.

echoed Epinay's letters to Galiani: "And when M. Necker and the abbé Galiani are forgotten, your book will remain with the force that truth gives it, supported by instruction. You will have enlightened the ignorant and you will have confounded the evil."[119] For Lespinasse, the main attraction of the Republic of Letters was friendship, and even the republic's peace was therefore sacrificed at the altar of her personal friendship with Condorcet.

When the *guerre des farines* raged in 1775, Morellet's *Réfutation* was already dated, part of an earlier battle, and Diderot did not make any attempt to revive that old conflict by trying to publish the *Apologie*. I doubt he ever really intended to publish it, since the recurrent theme in his dealings with Morellet and Galiani was that personal attacks ought not to be published: public writing must rise above the personal. What he did instead of defending Galiani with a personal attack on Morellet was to imitate Galiani by writing dialogues. He did not put them into print, but he circulated them, made them public in the limited sense that he adopted after the completion of the *Encyclopédie*.

If Diderot identified with the Republic of Letters and the project of Enlightenment more than others, it was because he had dedicated himself to the republic and defined its project during the twenty years in which he labored on the *Encyclopédie*. Once he had completed his work there and after failing to win the public's approval in the theater with his plays, Diderot retreated from the public. In November 1765, a month before the last volumes of the *Encyclopédie* were to come from the press, he wrote to Volland: "I learned at the same time that my ego did not need popular support [*rétribution*], that I did not even much care whether I was more or less appreciated by those whom I usually frequent, and that I could be satisfied if there was one man in the world whom I esteemed and who well knew what I was worth."[120]

Diderot was not made for the public eye, and he became increasingly removed from the public sphere that was emerging as the stage of the Republic of Letters. On that stage, as on the boards of the Comédie-Française, Voltaire was the star, the media whiz of the 1760s and 1770s. While Diderot retreated to the small circles of friendship and the circulation of manuscripts, Voltaire took the spotlight. As Diderot's work on the *Encyclopédie* wound down, Voltaire's campaign to *écraser l'infâme* heated up. When Diderot was venting his anger in the *Apologie* in the fall of 1770, Voltaire was calling for unity and friendship among the disarrayed citizenry of the Republic of Letters. And he had the stature

---

119. Lespinasse to Condorcet, 1 June [1775], in Lespinasse, *Lettres inédites*. Cf. Epinay to Galiani, 29 October and 3–10 November 1770.
120. Diderot to Volland, [10 November 1765].

to do so, for by 1770 Voltaire had become the acknowledged (if self-proclaimed) "patriarch" of the Republic of Letters. In the eyes of his contemporaries, he was, at the age of seventy-six, the living embodiment of the republic, so universally acclaimed that its leading citizens decided to erect a statue of him as a representation of the republic. The project to erect a full-length statue of Voltaire (the first time in modern history that any living person other than a reigning monarch was so represented) and to pay for it by public subscription was arguably the most extraordinary event of the year 1770.[121]

The official organizers of the Voltaire statue project were seventeen men and women who gathered one afternoon in April 1770 at the salon of Suzanne Necker. Diderot was there and so was Morellet. Grimm made a full report of the dinner table deliberations of this "house of peers of literature" to the subscribers of the *Correspondance Littéraire*. After naming all those present and remarking that by chance, but in contrast to standard parliamentary practice, all the clerics had been seated at the foot of the table, he drew attention to one of these in particular: Morellet, he explained, had been "strongly indicted by the most moderate judges for having played the year before an equivocal role in the affair of the Indies Company, for wearing under the mantle of *philosophie* the livery of M. Boutin, a distinction incompatible with the prerogatives of the peerage."[122] In Grimm's view, Morellet's presence was a testimony to the generosity of the Neckers, since Jacques Necker had been the director of the company Morellet had argued should be shut down, and which had just in fact collapsed, unable to pay its debts. Epinay had just written to Galiani that "the public places monsieur Necker in the same class as abbé M[orellet], and goes so far as to say that they only pretended to disagree, but that they are nothing but two rogues who, at bottom, understand each other."[123] Diderot had reported the whole miserable episode in a letter to Volland the year before:

> Well then, the Indies Company destroyed and abbé Morellet almost dishonored. He wrote a memoir against the Company. He has been shown to be a mercenary villain who sells his pen to the government against his fellow citizens. Mr Necker has responded with a gravity, a haughtiness, and a disdain that ought to desolate him. The abbé proposes to respond; that is to say that after having stabbed a man with his sword, he wishes to have the pleasure of trampling the corpse underfoot. The abbé sees things

---

121. The following discussion expands on my "Pigalle's *Voltaire Nu*."
122. *Correspondance Littéraire*, 1 May 1770.
123. Epinay to Galiani, 13 April 1770.

better than all of us. A year from now, nobody will remember the dishon-
orable deed, and he will enjoy the pension he has been promised.[124]

Well, Diderot had remembered, and so had Grimm. But there was
Morellet anyway, at the Neckers' table, seated with the other "peers" of
the Republic of Letters, just as Diderot had predicted. And while Diderot and Grimm had a point in suggesting that the traitor ought
perhaps to be exiled from the social territory of the Republic of Letters,
Suzanne Necker may in fact have been truer to its principles in continuing to maintain a neutral space where even someone who had contested her own husband in print should be welcome. The salon was,
after all, a place in which it was supposed to be possible to have precisely these kinds of disagreements about public policy. The complications
came because money and honor were involved.

Viewed in the light of Morellet's tenuous position in the Republic of
Letters in the spring of 1770, his account of the Voltaire statue project
in his memoirs is quite striking: "Around 1772, I find, in the literary
history of my century, the erection of a statue to Voltaire by his contemporaries, the men [gens] of letters, monument to their union and to the
justice rendered to a great man during his life."[125] Morellet must have
felt pretty uncomfortable, sitting there as a peer among those whose
republic he had betrayed, participating in the project whose aim was to
represent a united Republic of Letters to the world. Perhaps that is why
he failed to remember that it happened precisely at the time he was
trying to get his Réfutation through the press, just five weeks after
Diderot had sent his reader's report to Sartine. Morellet remembered
that the statue of Voltaire was meant to a be monument to unity; he
conveniently forgot that he was one of the sources of disunity.

Galiani heard about the project from Epinay, in the same letter,
written on 13 April, in which she told him of the collapse of the Indies
Company, four days before the peers met in formal session at Suzanne
Necker's table. She presented it to him as a joint project of three salons
of the Republic of Letters: "The Sundays of the rue Royal [d'Holbach];
the Thursdays of the rue Sainte-Anne [Helvétius] . . . , and the Fridays
of the rue de Cléry [Necker], have formed the project of erecting a
statue to Voltaire." Morellet, she wrote,

was immediately seized by this project, and has made up an economic
code for its execution. The first law is that one must be a man of letters

124. Diderot to Volland, [23 August 1769]. See also d'Holbach to Galiani, 11 August
and 24 September 1769, in "Lettres inédites du baron et de la baronne d'Holbach,"
pp. 25 and 28.
125. Morellet, Mémoires, p. 174.

who has published in order to subscribe. . . . And, to reach the limit of
his despotism, he has made a list on which he has prescribed without
their consent, what each [member] of the society should pay. . . . Thus,
my dear abbé, if you wish to be part of it, you can charge me with your
commissions or write directly to d'Alembert. As for me, you see that I am
excluded.

A week later, in the same letter in which she reassured Galiani that she
did not believe the rumors that Morellet had been hired to refute him,
Epinay was happy to report also that following the dinner in which the
project was officially inaugurated, Morellet was no longer running the
show. We know from Grimm that he was seated at the foot of the table;
from Epinay we learn that his plan was overruled by the rest of the
company and that "all men [gens] of letters or amateurs can subscribe
for the statue erected to Voltaire."[126]

The purpose of holding the formal session at the Neckers' must have
been to wrest the Voltaire statue project from the grasp of Morellet.
The "parliamentary" proceedings were a solution—a creative one for
eighteenth-century French men and women—to the problem of domination by one person. Submitting questions about who could participate to a vote resolved the problem of tyranny by undermining it and
by instituting an alternative to it: both the substance of the decision to
be inclusive rather than exclusive and the way in which it was attained
were contrary to absolutist and aristocratic practice. It was a solution
that derived from the principles and practices of the Enlightenment
Republic of Letters which the statue was meant to represent.

Epinay was happy with the result of the meeting at the Neckers'
because it meant that she was not excluded from the Republic of Letters. She favored the broad definition that made of the republic something greater than a professional corps of published writers: neither
she nor those who voted Morellet down wanted to reduce the idea of
gens de lettres to mere écrivains or auteurs. The republic Voltaire represented was a voluntary association of all those who shared its values and
participated in the variety of its discursive practices, only one of which
was publication. Salonnières, in particular, would have been excluded
from citizenship in the republic if Morellet's narrow definition had
been accepted. The inclusive definition acknowledged them as active
citizens of the Enlightenment Republic of Letters.[127]

126. Epinay to Galiani, 20 April 1770.
127. I am not suggesting that the requirement of publication excluded all women.
Some women did publish. Indeed, in her letter to Galiani of 13 April, Epinay named two
of them: Suzanne Necker, who had published a poem in the Mercure, and Mme Elie de
Beaumont, who was a novelist. Epinay herself eventually published. Women in their

Galiani, generally insensitive to Epinay's occasional but not very subtle protests against sexism in the Republic of Letters, missed this one too.[128] Instead, he responded to the proposed inscription for the statue: "To Voltaire in his lifetime, by the men [gens] of letters, his compatriots." Galiani, feeling the pain of exile, thought that he was now excluded: "The inscription that they want to place on the base of the statue of Voltaire would be sublime if one admitted to the subscription all the men [gens] of letters of Europe," he complained. "It would be beautiful to call compatriots of Voltaire the English, the German, the Italian, and even the emperor of China, who has just written a poem; but if there are only Frenchmen, the inscription is just trite.[129] Galiani was not, in fact, excluded: the inscription referred to Voltaire's compatriots in the Republic of Letters, not France. In addition, Galiani missed the point that publishing was not the definitive criterion of citizenship. One of the problems of being a corresponding member of the salon, as Galiani was, was that it was difficult to rectify misunderstandings, and sometimes not worth it, considering the time delay involved in sending and receiving letters.

At the end of October, Epinay included in a letter to Galiani excerpts from Voltaire's letter to Grimm, the one in which Voltaire had written: "Now is the time to say to the philosophes . . . what Saint John said to the Christians: my children, love one another, for who the devil will love you?"[130] Galiani did not respond to the patriarch's call to friendship and unity as Epinay had expected he would. Instead, he replied:

> Voltaire is wrong to say to the philosophes: love one another, my children. This need only be said to sectarians. One must say that to *économistes*, to Jansenists; they need to love one another. . . . Philosophes are not made to love one another. Eagles do not fly in company; leave that to

---

capacity as salonnières, however, were excluded by Morellet's definition. And since women experienced many impediments—legal, economic, social, and psychological—to publishing in the eighteenth century, the criterion of publication was de facto sexist. See Carla Hesse, "Reading Signatures: Female Authorship and Revolutionary Law in France, 1750–1850," *Eighteenth-Century Studies* 22 (Spring 1989): 469–87; Geneviève Fraisse, *Muse de la raison: La Démocratie exclusive et la différence des sexes* (Aix-en-Provence, 1989); Goodman, "Filial Rebellion," 28–47.

128. The most interesting case is Epinay's letter to him on 14 March 1772, in which she discussed Thomas's new *Essai sur les femmes*. Galiani's response was a "Dialogue sur les femmes," which he enclosed in a letter to her on 11 April. The characters are again the Marquis and the Chevalier. What is interesting is that they clearly are not very concerned about the "woman question." Instead, they end up in a long digression on the differences between men and animals, which leads them to consider whether religion is natural.

129. Galiani to Epinay, 12 May 1770.

130. Epinay to Galiani, 29 October 1770. The reference is to John 4:7, 11, 21; see Voltaire, *Correspondence*, D16693, n. 2.

partridges, to starlings. Voltaire has never loved, and he is not at all loved by anyone. He is feared, he has his talons, and that is enough. Soar above and have talons, that is the fate of great geniuses.[131]

Diderot was retreating from publishing, and Galiani, exiled from the sociable Parisian center, was now denying the value of friendship and community for the work of *philosophie*. Had it not been for friendship and the sociable spaces of Paris, Galiani would not have published the *Dialogues* in the first place. In a 1768 letter to Volland, Diderot had written that he had "prostrated [himself] before him [Galiani] in order that he might publish his ideas"—the ideas that he had discussed for hours and hours in the salons of Paris.[132] Perhaps it was the misery that publication had caused him, as well as the bitterness of exile, which now drove Galiani to call on the ideal of the solitary genius, despite his experience of ten years of happy and fruitful sociability. Perhaps he no longer believed that it was possible to write freely and critically and still remain within the bounds of civility.

There were external pressures as well, which Galiani knew about from his Parisian correspondents and even the gazettes. On 6 September 1770, according to the *Correspondance Littéraire*, Thomas had made a rather lengthy defense of the "prerogatives of the profession of the man of letters" in a speech at a public session of the Academy. Unfortunately, Thomas's speech coincided with the publication of an indictment of impious, blasphemous, and seditious books. Its author, the *avocat général* of the Parlement of Paris, was himself one of the forty immortals and was present at the occasion.[133] An *affaire* ensued, with Avocat Général Antoine-Louis Séguier taking Thomas's words as a personal insult and an affront to the magistracy itself. The clergy saw it as yet another offense by an academician who seemed always to make the most of innocuous occasions to offend church, state, and aristocracy. Séguier called on his friend and protector the new chancellor, Nicolas-Charles-Augustin de Maupeou, to prohibit the publication of Thomas's speech and to proscribe him from speaking at future public sessions of the Academy. The alternative was the Bastille. Thomas tried to defend himself, to prove that he had written his speech before Séguier's indictment had been published and thus that there was no connection between the two. The philosophes believed him, but others viewed his defense as an act of cowardice, of caving in before the power of the state.

In the view of Lucien Brunel, who analyzed the affair in the 1880s,

131. Galiani to Epinay, 24 November 1770.
132. Diderot to Volland, [22 November 1768].
133. Albert-Buisson, *Les Quarante*, p. 52; *Correspondance Littéraire*, 1 October 1770.

the fallout for Thomas was minor, but for the Academy and the Republic of Letters, it was more serious. He argues that the result mirrored the offense itself, for what Séguier had reacted to as a personal affront because he saw himself being criticized in *public*, became the occasion for inaugurating hostile relations between the monarchy and the philosophe-dominated Academy. Séguier knew "for a long time what antipathy the philosophes, his *confrères*, had for him; it had broken out more strongly than ever after the indictment. . . . He took his revenge in such a way that it extended to all those who had organized this affront, and from that day would cease relations, until then easy and pacific, between the Academy and *le pouvoir*."[134]

In his lengthy report on the Thomas affair, Grimm wrote that Séguier did Thomas a favor in prohibiting the publication of his speech, even if this was a threat to the integrity of the Academy as a corps directly under the protection of the king. Grimm reasoned that Thomas was feeding into the already heightened fear that men of letters were joined in some sort of league or conspiracy:

> Those who wish and seek to render the philosophes odious suppose they have a concerted and coherent plan, accuse them of an association that executes their views, their plans, their projects; and as these accusations multiply day by day, the men of letters will end up by being themselves the dupes; they will think themselves obliged to conspire among themselves, they will give themselves the air of a sect and a clique.

And that could only do them harm. Like Galiani and unlike Voltaire, Grimm feared even the appearance of sectarianism, with its charismatic leaders and its calls to unity through calls to arms. He was concerned about the threat to the Academy, but he was more concerned that zealous philosophes and their champions might reduce the Republic of Letters to either a sect or a corps.

> I swear that the pretensions that I have heard established for some time and of which I am assured the speech of M. Thomas is full, seem to me as little philosophic as they are ill founded. I believe in the communion of the faithful, that is to say, the union of this elite of excellent minds and elevated, delicate, and sensitive souls, dispersed here and there upon the surface of the globe, recognizing one another nevertheless and understanding one another from one end of the universe to the other, in the unity of ideas, impressions, and feelings; but I do not believe in a corps of

134. Lucien Brunel, *Les Philosophes et l'Académie française au dix-huitième siècle* (Paris, 1884; rpt. Geneva, 1967), pp. 193–200.

men of letters, neither in the respect that it demands, nor in the suprem-
acy that it wishes to usurp, nor in any of its pretensions.[135]

Like Diderot and Galiani, Grimm was wary of Voltaire and his desire
to rally the troops of the enlightened to *écraser l'infâme*. The military
posturing overlaid on the language and in the service of friendship was
alien to this generation of philosophes, who had rejected the bellicosity
of seventeenth-century discourse and the sects, leagues, and corps that
underlay it. They tried to reconstruct the Republic of Letters on the
basis of a critical dialogue in which people could disagree without
ridiculing one another. They tried to teach Morellet this lesson, but he
could never learn it.

Morellet had his model in Voltaire himself, for throughout his life
Voltaire relished a good fight. He was the master of biting satire,
of anonymous letters and pamphlets that counterattacked antiphilo-
sophes. Galiani was right to see in him yet another leader looking for
followers, rather than an equal among equals. Voltaire liked being the
patriarch, leading his people in the good fight against *l'infâme*, in the
crusade for *philosophie*. Philosophes such as Diderot, Galiani, and
Grimm, however, had worked toward a different sort of unity based on
a kind of harmony that could emerge only out of the well-governed
exchange of ideas. What they learned over the course of the year 1770,
was that their myth of harmony could not be maintained in the face of
the reality of publication.[136]

135. *Correspondance Littéraire*, 1 October 1770.
136. For a more profound treatment of the myth of harmony, see Pierre Saint-
Amand, *Les Lois de l'hostilité: La Politique à l'âge des lumières* (Paris, 1992).

CHAPTER 6

Masculine Self-Governance and the End of Salon Culture

Il faut convenir qu'on ne pouvait guère imaginer
d'établissement plus contraire aux intérêts de la société, et surtout de la société des femmes. . . . Il y
aurait sûrement à craindre que le goût des clubs
n'amenât insensiblement une révolution très-
marquée et dans l'esprit et dans les moeurs de la
nation.

— *CORRESPONDANCE LITTÉRAIRE*,
MAY 1786

If the limits of salon governance became apparent in the print debates that quickly turned disputatious in the 1770s, the limits of salon sociability had always been clear. Although the salon circle could be expanded through publicity, publication, and epistolarity, sociability itself remained limited to those who gained entrée to the salons themselves, whose numbers were necessarily small. We should therefore not be surprised to learn that the decade of the 1780s saw the formation of institutions of intellectual sociability that proclaimed a new democratic spirit, where a letter of introduction was not required for admission, where the aristocratic rules of polite conversation did not obtain, and where women no longer held either the keys of access or the powers of governance. These new institutions of intellectual sociability challenged the salon as the center of the Republic of Letters.

Often called *musées*, the new institutions that spread throughout France in the 1780s figure in the history of education and are often compared to academies. They are usually seen as a development of Freemasonry and as the precursors of the clubs that would form in 1789, when intellectual sociability would be transformed into political sociability.[1] As voluntary associations, they may well be the key to the transformation of what Habermas calls the literary public sphere into the political public sphere, a transformation that entailed the exclusion of women.[2] In the history of the Republic of Letters, the musées took the place of Enlightenment salons, continuing the quest for an autonomous social base articulated in the *Encyclopédie* and extending the project of Enlightenment to be carried out through it. These new institutions were certainly more fully public than the salons they replaced, but whether or not they were more democratic remains to be seen.

Political autonomy was once again an issue because the fuller publicity of these new centers of sociability brought them under the gaze of a watchful state. Moreover, efforts to attain economic viability raised questions of patronage, intellectual integrity, and the role of the public in new ways. Finally, although the men who established the musées eventually invited women to enter their doors, they did so only to marginalize them as the objects of male learning, the observers of masculine intellectual performance, and the decoration of what was now a masculine cultural space.

The establishment of the musée in the Republic of Letters mirrored another crucial development of the 1780s: the apotheosis of public opinion as an objective tribunal in the political realm. Both developments can be understood as attempts to actualize a fantasy of masculine self-governance whose obvious correlate was the myth of female despotism and whose greatest manifestation was the French Revolution.[3]

1. Hervé Guénot, "Musées et lycées parisiens (1780–1830)," *Dix-huitième Siècle* 18 (1986): 249–50; Johel Coutura, "Le Musée de Bordeaux," *Dix-huitième Siècle* 19 (1987): 162; Louis Amiable, "Les Origines maçonniques du Musée de Paris et du Lycée," *Révolution Française* 30 (January–June 1896): 484–500; Roche, *Siècle des lumières en province* 1:66; Patrice Gueniffey and Ran Halévi, "Clubs and Popular Societies," in *A Critical Dictionary of the French Revolution*, ed. François Furet and Mona Ozouf, trans. Arthur Goldhammer (Cambridge, Mass., 1989), p. 460.

2. Habermas, *Structural Transformation*, pp. 51–56.

3. This fantasy may be found in at least two other discursive fields in the 1780s: in philosophy in the work of Kant, who elaborated a theory of (masculine) reason as self-governing, and in sentimental French fiction. On Kant, see O'Neill, *Constructions of Reason*, esp. chaps. 1 and 2; Laursen, "Scepticism and Intellectual Freedom," pp. 439–55; and Lloyd, *Man of Reason*, pp. 64–70. On sentimental fiction, see Josephine Grieder, "Kingdoms of Women in French Fiction of the 1780s," *Eighteenth-Century Studies* 25 (Winter 1989–1990): 140–56. In *The Family Romance of the French Revolution* (Berkeley, 1992), Lynn Hunt points to the absence of fathers from French novels of this period. "Families without fathers are presented as at once compelling and tragic," she notes (p. 31). The fraternal republic and the regicide as patricide of the 1790s which Hunt sees as following from this crisis of patriarchal authority can be interpreted as the revolutionary attempt to enact the fantasy of masculine self-governance. Its corollary, as she argues, is the demonization of Marie-Antoinette as the "bad mother" (chaps. 3 and 4).

The legacy of the fantasy, the myth, and the Revolution itself has been the exclusion of women from the public sphere created by the Revolution.[4] It has also dominated the historical understanding of the Enlightenment.

The Apotheosis of Public Opinion

Thanks primarily to the work of Keith Baker and Mona Ozouf, the significance of the idea of public opinion as an objective tribunal in the public sphere is now generally recognized.[5] Using a variety of texts, Baker shows that in the 1780s public opinion was represented as a political force that was peaceful, universal, objective, and rational. Jacques Peuchet, for example, saw in the rise of public opinion a new basis of social order, and both Peuchet and Jacques Necker contrasted public opinion to the extremes it happily replaced. Necker wrote of the remarkable effects of public opinion when it reigned "in the midst of a sensitive people, which is neither distracted by political interests nor enfeebled by despotism nor dominated by too seething passions." Peuchet insisted that public opinion "differs from both the spirit of obedience that must reign in a despotic state and the popular opinions that prevail in republican deliberations."[6]

Public opinion was to do for France what the salonnières were supposed to do for the Republic of Letters: it would be the basis of both *police* and *moeurs*, establishing an order that was legitimate because it was not despotic and did not require blind obedience. Despite the anarchy then reigning in the print world of the Republic of Letters, enlightened men of the 1780s chose to believe that the kind of governance represented by salonnières was not necessary in France because men could govern themselves and their discourse by appeal to the tribunal of public opinion. In an age of Enlightenment embodied in public opinion, the policing function of the salonnière seemed unnecessary and thus despotic.

Public opinion itself had undergone a transformation to arrive at this

---

4. Landes, *Women and the Public Sphere*; Fraisse, *Muse de la raison*. While I have serious disagreements with Landes's reasoning, I agree with her conclusion that the French Revolution did exclude women from the public political sphere. I lay out my critique in "Public Sphere and Private Life," pp. 71–77.

5. Baker, *Inventing the French Revolution*, chap. 8; Ozouf, "'Public Opinion' at the End of the Old Regime." See also Sarah Maza, "Le Tribunal de la nation: Les Mémoires judiciaires et l'opinion publique à la fin de l'Ancien Régime," *Annales E.S.C.* 42 (January–February 1987): 73–90; Gordon, "'Public Opinion' and the Civilizing Process"; Goodman, "Hume-Rousseau Affair"; Johnson, "Musical Experience."

6. Both quoted in Baker, *Inventing the French Revolution*, pp. 194 and 196.

point. In 1751 when Duclos wrote his *Considérations sur les moeurs*, "public opinion" signified the policing force that reigned in the area of *les moeurs* and *le monde*: the sphere of moral behavior, beyond the legitimate and practical scope of the law, which set a higher moral standard for those who were both polite and enlightened. Baker calls this the "general social meaning of 'public opinion' as collective judgment in matters of morality, reputation, and taste."[7] As Duclos explained,

> Men having become polite and enlightened, those whose souls were the most *honnête* have supplemented the laws with morality in establishing, by a tacit convention, procedures to which usage has given the force of law among *honnêtes gens*, and which are the supplement of positive laws . . . ; public opinion, which exercises justice in this regard, metes it out in exact proportions, and makes very fine distinctions.

Public opinion, he went on, "being itself the punishment of the actions of which it is the judge, cannot fail to be severe concerning those things which it condemns. There are such actions of which suspicion is the proof, and publicity the chastisement."[8]

Although Duclos did not say so, the tribunal of public opinion which operated in *le monde* was necessarily more concerned with the behavior of women than of men because in addition to a higher standard of behavior for *honnêtes gens*, there was a double standard for men and women. The realm of virtue was not the same for women as it was for men, and the concern with female virtue was greater than the concern for male virtue, as attitudes towards adultery, for example, demonstrate. So much was already clear in the discussion of fidelity and virtue in Montesquieu's *Lettres persanes*.[9]

Like women, men of letters, for whom reputation was the only measure of their worth during their lifetimes, were more concerned about their reputations than other men, for their customary activities and roles were subject to judgment rather than law, and judgment was in the hands of public opinion. Of course, men of letters, like other "great men," could appeal to the higher tribunal of posterity, as Diderot made clear in his letters to the sculptor Etienne Falconet, in which he distinguished between the vanity of women and the genius's desire for immortality.[10] By 1785 Thomas could proclaim to Suzanne Necker that

7. Ibid., p. 187.
8. Duclos, *Considérations sur les moeurs*, pp. 44–45.
9. See Goodman, *Criticism in Action*, pp. 55–63; Dorinda Outram, *"Le Langage Mâle de la Vertu*: Women and the Discourse of the French Revolution," in *The Social History of Language*, ed. Peter Burke and Roy Porter (Cambridge, 1987), pp. 122–32.
10. Diderot to Falconet, 15 February 1766.

because of the spread of enlightenment and the activity of public opinion, "all glory is contemporary for those who have merited it."[11] Men of letters had redefined public opinion to take the place of posterity as a living tribunal. The rationality and universality they claimed for it both legitimated it and made women, the monarchy, and other "irrational" and "subjective" beings into nonparticipating objects of its judgment.

Jacques Necker's understanding of public opinion was similar to Duclos's, but he carried its genealogy one step farther. Like Duclos, he saw the origins of public opinion in the pacification of France following the religious wars and the Fronde. He identified it with "the spirit of society, the love of respect and of praise, [which] have raised in France a tribunal where all men who attract respect to themselves are obliged to be compared: there, public opinion, as from a high throne, awards prizes and crowns, makes and unmakes reputations." But public opinion remained weak under Louis XIV, who vied with it by trying to monopolize encouragements, rewards, and glory. During his regency, the duc d'Orléans did nothing to strengthen public opinion, Necker continued, but since that time, its power had continued to grow, "and today it would be difficult to destroy: it reigns over all minds, and princes themselves respect it." Public opinion was now stronger in France than anywhere else.[12]

The history of public opinion, as it was understood by Duclos and Necker, was bound up with the history of the sociability of le monde, which was both opposed to the court and the basis of modern French cultural identity. Thus Necker called public opinion "this spirit of society, this constant communication among men," recalling the salons while effacing the salonnières from them.[13] In the 1830s the duchesse d'Abrantès located public opinion somewhat differently in relation to salons and salonnières in her Histoire des salons de Paris. Although she was too young to have had direct experience of the prerevolutionary salons, she had learned about them from her mother, who did.[14] Abrantès credited Suzanne Necker, not her husband, as the person who recognized the importance of public opinion. "Mme Necker thought, with reason, that in France public opinion is a power without parallel. This power is no longer today what it once was, and even our children do not understand it." In Jacques Necker's own words (but

11. Thomas to Necker, 26 March 1785, in Antoine-Léonard Thomas, Oeuvres complètes, 6 vols. (Paris, 1825), vol. 6.

12. Jacques Necker, De l'administration des finances de la France (1784), in Oeuvres complètes, ed. Auguste Louis de Staël-Holstein, 15 vols. (Paris, 1820–1821; rpt. Darmstadt, 1970), 4:47–49.

13. Ibid., 4:51.

14. [Laure Junot], la duchesse d'Abrantès, Histoire des salons de Paris: Tableaux et portraits du grand monde, 6 vols. (Paris, 1837–1838), 1:274.

without attribution), Abrantès continued to identify public opinion with women, especially Suzanne Necker:

> In the era of Mme Necker, *the spirit of society*, the need for meeting, for respect and reciprocal praise, had been raised to a tribunal where all the men of society were obliged to compare. There *public opinion*, as from the height of a throne, pronounced its decrees and gave its crowns. . . . The empire of opinion, finally, was immense, and this empire was governed by a woman. It was the mistress of a salon who presided over the judgments that were rendered in her home; it was with her mind, her good taste, that they were edited, and her heart, always at the side of her mind, prevented it from taking a false route.[15]

If Abrantès differed with the men of the 1780s in identifying public opinion with salonnières, she agreed with them about its political power. "In France, in particular," she wrote, "it is the great ascendancy of public opinion that often poses an obstacle to the abuse of authority." She went on to say, however, that in her own day, during the July Monarchy, public opinion had again been weakened, not because the monarchy was strong but because "private societies are destroyed and . . . society in general is dispersed and without ties."[16] The decline of salons meant the decline of public opinion.

Considering how the history of public opinion was embedded in the history of salon sociability, it is no wonder that Rousseau saw vanity and the concern for what others think as the tie that bound philosophes and salonnières together. The concern for public opinion, which men of letters learned from women was the cause of his scathing condemnation of both. Rousseau's conception of public opinion as, in Baker's words, "a challenge to the legislator's art rather than an expression of political will" put him at odds with those who over the course of the 1770s and 1780s came to see it as a rational political concept.[17] It also allowed him to maintain the legitimacy of public opinion in the domestic sphere in which women were properly contained. Rousseau wanted to liberate true, masculine philosophers from both women and public opinion, while continuing to subject women to public opinion and elevating a new political and moral force: the general will that would issue from the wills of men alone.

Duclos, in his 1767 revision of the *Considérations sur les moeurs*, handled the problem in a different way that put him at the forefront of the transformation of public opinion from a social force composed of men

15. Ibid., 1:53–54.
16. Ibid., 1:54–55.
17. Baker, *Inventing the French Revolution*, pp. 186–87.

and women into a political force shaped and upheld by men of letters. "Of all empires, that of *gens d'esprit*, without being visible, is the most extensive," he wrote. "The powerful command, the *gens d'esprit* govern, because in the long run they form public opinion, which sooner or later subjugates or overthrows every kind of despotism."[18]

Men of letters had gotten out from under public opinion both to free themselves from *les grands*, as d'Alembert had urged them in 1753, and to give themselves a new legitimate authority.[19] By 1782 Condorcet could express pity for those who, because they had lived a hundred years earlier, "could not find in gross reason enough immutable and certain principles, [and] were forced to take as a guide the opinion of their century, and to limit their virtue to forbidding themselves, even in private, those actions that this opinion had placed in the rank of crimes." By contrast, his own contemporaries took pride in such humanitarian reforms as the virtual abolition of torture, brought about by "the public voice, this so imperious voice as long as humanity inspires it and it is directed by reason."[20] By 1783 Mercier could write triumphantly in his *Tableau de Paris*: "It is by the *gens de lettres* that the spirit of the capital has become diametrically opposed to the spirit of the court. . . . Masters of opinion, they have made of it an offensive and defensive weapon. Thus has it declared the liveliest war between the *gens de lettres* and *les grands*; but the latter, sure enough, will lose the battle." The strength of this tribunal, according to Mercier, lay in the extralegal position from which men of letters defended liberty and the laws; their authority lay in reason. "They intimidate by means of a vigilant and exact censure," he explained. "Very often they form a unanimous cry that becomes the expression of universal reason."[21]

Left to bear the increased weight of this much stronger tribunal of public opinion were the women who rose to prominence in the Republic of Letters. The newly won authority of men of letters made it all the more difficult to accept the need for governance from the very people who were traditionally most subject to public opinion. The politicization of public opinion over the course of the 1770s and 1780s by men of letters, and the central role they gave themselves in its creation, left the women with whom they were associated as the primary objects of

18. Duclos, *Considérations sur les moeurs*, pp. 138–39, quoted by Baker (*Inventing the French Revolution*, p. 187), who notes that this paragraph was added in 1767.

19. Recall the discussion of d'Alembert's "Essai sur la société des gens de lettres" in chap. 1 and see Baker's discussion of it in *Condorcet*, pp. 12–16.

20. Marie Jean Antoine Nicolas de Caritat, marquis de Condorcet, "Discours prononcé dans l'Académie française, le jeudi 21 février 1782," in *Oeuvres*, ed. A[rthur] Condorcet O'Connor and F[rançois] Arago, 12 vols. (Paris, 1847–1849; rpt. Stuttgart–Bad Canstatt, 1968), 1:397.

21. Mercier, *Tableau de Paris* 2:105–7.

the moral and political judgments of a public opinion now conceptualized and valorized as rational and universal. When the male lawyers
studied by Sarah Maza increasingly took cases from the private realm
of morality to the courts and then appealed to the higher tribunal of
public opinion in printed judicial memoirs to criticize the parlements
and the legal system, they not only legitimated public opinion as a
tribunal but added to the weight of male authority in the judgment of
female virtue.[22]

Isn't this heavy-handed?

Whereas the salonnière was seen as a legitimate governor within the
narrow limits of the salon because she was outside the discourse she
governed, all women were subject to a public opinion that men of
letters (with the help of men of law) claimed now to shape. Mercier
overtly gendered it male when he titled a chapter in the *Tableau de Paris*
"Monsieur le Public." Nevertheless, he had difficulty defining it. "The
public," he asked, "does it exist? What is the public? Where is it? By
what organ does it manifest its will?"[23]

Mercier had difficulty locating the public because, like the Republic
of Letters at midcentury, it lacked a "meeting place." The abbé
Emmanuel-Joseph Sieyès was to second this view in 1788. In order to
have true public opinion, he wrote, one needed "a common point
around which all forces can array and coordinate themselves."[24] Despite this deficiency, however, Mercier asserted that the public did in
fact exist, and to support his claim, he quoted two *mondaine* women:
Mme de Sévigné, who wrote, "The public is neither crazy nor unjust,"
and "another woman full of intelligence" whom he quoted as saying
that "reason is always right in the end [*raison finit toujours par avoir
raison*]."[25] At heart, public opinion had not changed; it was just that
now men of letters were shaping it and the male public was constituting
it, while women joined the "despotic" monarchy as the major objects of
its judgment. Without the assistance of women, Mercier and other men
of letters would now construct a public opinion whose force would be
unchallengeable and irresistible. All that was needed was a meeting
place, a "point de réunion."

"At the end of 1783, and above all in 1784, the *clubs* were founded,"
wrote the royalist historian Félix Rocquain in 1878. "Throughout Paris,
there were nothing but Clubs, Societies, Lycées, Musées. These circles,
in which hardly anyone but men assembled, dethroned the salons,

22. Sarah Maza, *Private Lives and Public Affairs: The Causes Célèbres of Prerevolutionary
France* (Berkeley, 1993).
23. Mercier, *Tableau de Paris* 6:264–65.
24. Quoted in Mona Ozouf, "Public Spirit," in Furet and Ozouf, *Critical Dictionary*,
pp. 771–72.
25. Mercier, *Tableau de Paris* 6:266.

where until that time, women had reigned."[26] Throughout the 1780s and, indeed, right through the revolutionary decade, musées were being proposed and formed in Paris and the provinces.[27] With their rise, women lost the central place they had held in the French Republic of Letters since the seventeenth century.

In 1784 an anonymous female playwright called upon the ghost of Descartes to lead women against this dangerous trend. "Ah, gentlemen," one of her characters cries, "you separate yourselves from us! you think you can humiliate us with your uncivil club . . . We will teach you . . . You will learn that you must not defy Women . . . M. Descartes will restore order." The appeal to Descartes, as Erica Harth has shown, was an attempt to summon up the thinker whom many women credited with giving them the place they were now losing.[28] The new thinking of the clubs was summed up by the playwright's Comtesse: "In order to be a real philosophe, one must not live with women; this noble character would be weakened with us: our virtues hold too much to nature. . . . To betray with audacity; to be enterprising, bold, in short, to wish to dominate; this is what is called being a man" (3). The resentment of women who had suppressed their own egos and subordinated themselves to men in the common interest of the project of Enlightenment, only to find themselves cast aside as detrimental to *philosophie*, comes out when the Comtesse announces that the women are forming their own club. "Like you Gentlemen, we are going to unite, to be self-sufficient. . . . The desire to please you, Gentlemen, has occupied our time: there will be more now for friendship" (4). The implications for the Republic of Letters are made clear when the Comtesse responds to the Chevalier's assertion of his own politeness by calling the men's club he champions "a singularity that confounds you with Savages" (4). And toward the end of the play, the Marquise declares that "these Gentlemen, with their Clubs, their assemblies, would wish perhaps to send us

[handwritten marginal note: rather melodramatic]

---

26. Félix Rocquain, *L'Esprit révolutionnaire avant la Révolution, 1715–1789* (Paris, 1878), p. 415.

27. Guénot, "Musées et lycées," pp. 249–51. On the provincial musées, see Roche, *Siècle des lumières en province* 1:66–68; Coutura, "Musée de Bordeaux"; le baron de Desazars de Montgaillard, *Histoire de l'Académie des sciences de Toulouse: Le Musée, le Lycée, l'Athénée, 1784–1807* (Toulouse, 1908). On sociability in the provinces, see Maurice Agulhon, *Pénitents et franc-maçons de l'ancien Provence: Essai sur la sociabilité méridionale* (Paris, 1984).

28. *Le Club des dames, ou Le Retour de Descartes* (Paris, 1784), p. 2. This one-act play has been attributed to Genlis and is discussed by Harth in *Cartesian Women*, pp. 114–22. The attribution, as she notes, however, is quite uncertain. There may be a confusion between this play and another one, *Le Club des dames, ou Les Deux partis* (1787), a two-act play that Clarence D. Brenner attributes to Genlis: *A Bibliographical List of Plays in the French Language, 1700–1789* (Berkeley, 1947). Whoever the author of the 1784 play is, she is certainly female, as Harth claims. Further references to this play will be cited in the text.

back to pre-Cartesian times" (24). Knocking women back to the Dark Ages would be the end of civilization itself as the French knew it.

But the men who formed clubs and musées in the 1780s did not seem to know this; in fact, they denied it. They denied the need for women as a civilizing force, adopting Rousseau's position that men of letters would be better off without women. In the history of the Republic of Letters, the musées appear as an attempt to realize without the governance of women the ideals articulated in the *Encyclopédie* and to solve the problems it posed: How could knowledge and the people who produced it be brought together to expand and spread that knowledge? How could the values of the republic be given institutional form? How could the republic maintain its autonomy and thus its integrity in relation to the French state? This final chapter in the history of the Enlightenment Republic of Letters tells how women were marginalized in and even excluded from that republic by young men who competed with one another to advance the project of Enlightenment with new forms of association in Paris in the 1780s.

Pahin de La Blancherie: General Agent
of the Republic of Letters

The need to form a center for the Republic of Letters was articulated as early as 1747 in the project for a bureau général. Through the 1770s, Parisian salons served French men of letters as an institutional base, but the salon, with its female governors and limited capacity— both to accommodate an expanding republic and to govern the realm of print—was never a fully satisfactory solution. By the end of the 1770s, a new generation expressed the need to gather men of letters and the knowledge they produced in projects of association. The first of these new projects was promoted by an energetic young man named Claude-Mammès Pahin de La Blancherie.[29]

La Blancherie is best known as Manon Philipon's first love, the man she did not marry. She is best known as Mme Roland, for after she turned down La Blancherie, she married Jean-Marie Roland. Her account of La Blancherie's courtship of her in the memoirs she wrote in 1793, while imprisoned under the Terror, considerably understates the feelings she expressed to a girlfriend in letters written at the time.[30]

29. For biographical information on La Blancherie, see the entry on him by Hervé Guénot in *Dictionnaire des journalistes*, ed. Jean Sgard, supp. 2 (Grenoble, 1983), pp. 168–76.

30. Béatrice Didier, "Madame Roland et l'autobiographie, ou Une Grande autographe de l'époque révolutionnaire: Madame Roland," in *Les Femmes et la Révolution*

Whether the young Manon was carried away by the pleasure of imagining herself a heroine in the genre of *La Nouvelle Héloïse*, writing of her first love to her confidante, or whether the older woman chose to play down what she later decided was a humiliating episode in which she had been made a dupe does not really matter here except in how one chooses to evaluate the character and motives of an ambitious young entrepreneur in the Republic of Letters. Here is the story as Roland told it in her memoirs.

They met in 1773, when he was twenty-one and she was nineteen, at the weekly concerts of a private music society. He proposed and she put him off because he was penniless. Neither she nor her father was interested in a marriage that would lack a sound material base. Her father was also disturbed by the young suitor's plan to invest his prospective wife's dowry in some kind of office that would start him off on a legal career. Both father and daughter, however, liked La Blancherie and his spirit very much and let him understand that he could continue his suit while he tried to make his fortune in some other way. Shortly thereafter, he disappeared from the scene. When he returned in 1775, he was none the richer in property but full of new ideas for a career in the Republic of Letters. He resumed his visits, only to be dismissed again by the father. At that point, Mme Roland wrote in her memoirs, she realized that "it must be true: La Blancherie interested me and I imagined that I could well love him." Nevertheless, she "wrote a beautiful letter that gave La Blancherie his dismissal, which removed all hopes of his responding to me, but which could not destroy those of having pleased, if that would have flattered him." Unfortunately, she learned soon thereafter that La Blancherie had proposed to a number of rich and intelligent young women, all of whom had turned him down.

Some months later, La Blancherie called on Manon Philipon again, this time not to propose marriage but to invite her to contribute to a new journal he was planning. His idea was to found "a work of criticism and morality in *letters*" modeled on the *Spectator*. She let him know that though she wished him and all other writers well, she had no intention of becoming either his wife or a writer. She had no idea, she continued, whether the other young women to whom he had made similar propositions had responded as frankly, but that was her way of doing things. With that she showed him the door, remarking later in her memoirs: "La Blancherie made his retreat in silence. I have never seen him since: but who has not heard, since that time, of *l'agent général de la correspondance pour les sciences et les arts?*"[31]

française, vol. 1: *Modes d'action et d'expression: Nouveaux droits—nouveaux devoirs* (Mirail, 1989), p. 261.

31. [Marie-Jeanne Manon Philipon Roland], *Mémoires de Madame Roland*, ed. Paul de

The history of the musée begins in 1777 with the launching of La
Blancherie's journal whose title, *Nouvelles de la République des Lettres et
des Arts*, cast it in the tradition of Bayle. The original prospectus gave its
purpose in the now-familiar terms of eighteenth-century literary journalism. "The work that we offer to our Country and to foreign Nations
under a title consecrated long ago in Literature," wrote La Blancherie,
"has as its aim to facilitate the communication of minds, opinions,
talents, and research [*travaux*] in all genres." He proposed to publish
the correspondence he would undertake on all subjects with all those
who, because of "their zeal for Letters and the Arts, have a right to
interest the Public." Like the anonymous author of the 1747 project for
a bureau général, La Blancherie promised to avoid politics and religion, as well as "partisan quarrels that could divide Men of Letters and
Artists." He praised the king and his "enlightened Government, which,
following his intentions, encourages useful enterprises and makes
them triumph over all the obstacles raised up against them."[32]

La Blancherie's project was so typical that he needed to explain how
it differed from the competing journals and gazettes that it resembled.
The *Nouvelles* would have a simple and innovative format. The first
part, given over to news, would be organized like contemporary gazettes with dispatches from the great cities of the Republic of Letters;
the second would provide in-depth coverage of the life and works of
the citizens of the republic and would depend on their epistolary contributions.[33] The aim was to make men of letters and their work known
to the reading public and to make them known to each other, to bring
them together. Men of letters would be both the authors and the subject matter of the *Nouvelles*; as subscribers and contributors they would
also be its patrons, and La Blancherie hoped that as such they would
allow their names to be published in the final number each year.[34]

Like his predecessors, La Blancherie was concerned with maintaining the autonomy and integrity of the Republic of Letters. Although he
acknowledged the goodwill of the king and the government, he wanted
to emphasize that men of letters would be self-sufficient in the production of their periodical. If eighteenth-century men of letters had come
to understand early on that the audience for their writing was the

---

Roux (Paris, 1966), pp. 11–15, 281–82, 287–88, 323–26, 330–33. See also the English
edition based on the French of Roux, but not a strict translation of it: *The Memoirs of
Madame Roland*, trans. and ed. Evelyn Shuckburgh (London, 1989), pp. 185–246.

32. [Claude-Mammès Pahin de La Blancherie], *Prospectus* (1777), in *Nouvelles de la
République des Lettres et des Arts* (1779), pp. 3–4, 6–9.

33. Ibid., pp. 4–5. On the geographical organization of gazettes, see Popkin, *News
and Politics*, pp. 108–10.

34. Pahin de La Blancherie, *Prospectus*, in *Nouvelles*, p. 10.

public and not the prince, by now they were claiming further that they needed no patrons outside their own numbers.

La Blancherie's most important innovation, however, was the extension of his journalistic project into a project of direct association with the offer of his editorial office as a meeting place for his contributors and subscribers and a showroom for their work. Authors who sent in announcements were asked to provide copies of their books so that they could be displayed "in the vast theater of this Capital . . . to the glory of Authors and the advantage of commerce." Out-of-towners were invited to think of the editor as their Paris correspondent whose office would serve as a bureau de correspondance as well as a bureau général.[35] Because Paris was now the capital of the cosmopolitan Republic of Letters, La Blancherie could expect that many of his contributors and subscribers would come for a visit. When they did, they were invited to meet other visitors and the local citizenry at his office on Thursday afternoons, where they would also have the opportunity to see the works on display. At these assemblies La Blancherie would also be able to identify those people who were planning trips outside Paris and to give them letters to deliver to his far-flung correspondents. He might not be able to avoid the French postal system entirely, but he could utilize his own network of subscribers and contributors as an independent service for the Republic of Letters.[36]

Within a few months it was clear that the major attraction of La Blancherie's project was the weekly meeting, known eventually as the "assemblée ordinaire" or the "salon de la correspondance." "On the first of this month I was sent the prospectus of a journal titled: *Nouvelles de la république des lettres* by M. Pahin de La Blancherie," the abbé François-Valentin Mulot wrote in the first entry of his journal for the year 1778. "What I admire most in his plan is the assembly that he announces of scholars of all countries; there can without doubt be nothing more useful than this communication of minds." On 18 January, Mulot noted that he had attended his first assembly the previous Thursday, and he named with satisfaction the various men of letters and artists whom he had met there. The next day he received some of the people he had met at La Blancherie's in the Bibliothèque de Saint-Victor, of which he was the librarian. He attended a second meeting on 29 January, and again found "the best company," including Court de Gébelin, who would, as secretary of the Masonic Loge des Neuf Soeurs

---

35. For an example of how the bureau de correspondance functioned, see letters from La Blancherie to the Swedish scholar Torbern Bergman in *Torbern Bergman's Foreign Correspondence*, ed. Göte Carlid and Johan Nordström, vol. 1: *Letters from Foreigners to Torbern Bergman* (Stockholm, 1965), pp. 289–91.

36. Pahin de La Blancherie, *Prospectus*, in *Nouvelles*, pp. 12–14.

(that is, Lodge of the Muses), start a Société Apollonienne in 1780 which would become the Musée de Paris in 1782.[37]

From Mulot's diary we learn something of what went on at one of La Blancherie's first meetings. Several topics were discussed that day, and as Mulot described them, they all revolved around objects: a pair of engravings with accompanying verses, said to be by a sixteen-year-old girl; a marble engraving said to have been found near the city of Catane; a microscope that had just been approved by the Academy of Sciences; and a translation of a scientific work on "the inflammable air of swamps," which had just appeared. The last two objects provoked interest and admiration, but the first two stimulated critical discussion. Could this work have been done by a self-taught young girl? Was the engraving a genuine antiquity or of more recent vintage? In the first case the discussants came to a decision (she must have copied the pictures, but she could have written the verses, since they were about love); in the second case, they remained divided. Clearly, the pleasure for Mulot and the rest of the attendees lay in the discussion itself: they were not driven to make determinations, to legislate, as much as to converse critically. By taking the objects of discussion out of the pages of the journal and into a sociable space, La Blancherie had enabled his readers to engage in the sort of discussion that characterized the salons, instead of selling them his own judgments, as other journalists did. Mulot, who was to join virtually every literary and scientific society in Paris over the course of the next twenty years, first found intellectual sociability in La Blancherie's assemblies, which were opening salon conversation to the subscribers of his journal.[38]

In May 1778 Meister reported on La Blancherie's establishment to the subscribers of the *Correspondance Littéraire*; by June it had made the *Mémoires Secrets*. Meister opened his article with a paean to the entrepreneurial spirit: "There is nothing that cannot be imagined in Paris for acquiring fortune and fame," he wrote; "there is nothing in which one cannot succeed with a little boldness, a lot of persistence, and

37. "Journal intime de l'abbé Mulot (1777–1782)," ed. Maurice Tourneux, *Mémoires de la Société de l'Histoire de Paris et de l'Ile-de-France* 29 (1902): 38–40, 46–47; Amiable, "Origines maçonniques," pp. 485–89.

38. Mulot, "Journal intime," p. 30. Mulot's only criticism of La Blancherie in the beginning was his weakness in controlling certain types of impolite speech, such as droning on and speaking of subjects that might offend particular guests (pp. 47–50). When, after a four-year hiatus, Mulot took up his journal again, he was a member of the Musée de Paris, which he called an "assembly of *gens de lettres* without [letters] patent" (pp. 57–58). His descriptions of the meetings of the musée show how different this establishment was from La Blancherie's. Whereas La Blancherie's was modeled on the salon, the musée was modeled on the academy: rather than critical conversation, it was organized around readings of papers (pp. 77–79, 87–89, 95–96, 115).

stubborn energy." With minimal resources and a lot of hard work, La Blancherie had formed "a quite interesting establishment for distinguished foreigners, scholars, men of letters, and artists." Meister went on to describe the distinctive activities of the weekly meetings. There were neither formal readings nor general conversation, he explained. Visitors were free to read whatever they wanted and to talk with whomever they wanted to meet. Writers and artists gathered just as La Blancherie hoped they would; new books and works of art were indeed on display for people to view. And so many people were turning out that the small apartment where the meetings were held was no longer adequate. Even though Meister found the first volume of the *Nouvelles* mediocre, he saw the weekly meetings as "promising very great advantages to letters, the arts, and to those who cultivate them."[39]

Soon La Blancherie issued a new prospectus that elevated the weekly meeting to an "ordinary assembly of scholars, artists, etc." and made the *Nouvelles* secondary to it.[40] The prospectus of 1779 marked a definitive shift in the focus of the project from a periodical to an association; it transformed journal subscription into club membership, and at a stroke La Blancherie became the founder of the first musée. "It was a complete revolution, a sort of scientific, literary, and artistic '89 that Pahin de La Blancherie . . . had conceived as early as 1775, at the age of 23 years," one admiring biographer has written.[41]

Further testimony as to the success and popularity of La Blancherie's establishment came in a letter from a Richard Derb..., dated 8 May 1779, and published in the London-based francophone *Courrier de l'Europe*. On a recent visit to Paris, Mr. Derb... had visited La Blancherie and had found him extremely helpful. He had then attended the Thursday meeting, where he found walls hung with ancient and modern art; sculptures, mechanical objects, and manufactured goods; books from far and wide and on all subjects; natural history exhibits; and most exciting of all, "a crowd of interesting and famous men whom, successively, M. de La Blancherie was receiving, close to whom he conducted us (for several of us were foreigners), and to whom he presented us in making us known by our tastes." The visitor was thrilled. "In an hour and a half," he wrote, "we saw pass before our eyes a portion of the most scholarly men of this city. I would note to you Dr. Franklin himself, whom I was charmed to see outside his own home. I thought I was seeing again the Portico, the Lyceum! I saw, in fact,

39. *Correspondance Littéraire*, May 1778.

40. [Claude-Mammès] Pahin de La Blancherie, *Correspondance générale sur les sciences et les arts* (1779), p. 8.

41. F[élix] Rabbe, "Pahin de La Blancherie et le salon de la correspondance (1)," *Bulletin de la Société Historique du VIe Arrondissement de Paris* 2 (1899): 30.

more: satisfaction and liberty reigning among this multitude of men who succeeded one another over the course of four hours." One group was watching demonstrations of new machines, while others,

> seated in different circles, conversed upon some subject in the sciences or the arts, several making observations on the price and the merit of the paintings; some, grouped apart, read individually or out loud passages from books; here a conversation in German, there one in English, and everywhere great nobles mixed with scholars and artists: a geometer, a lockmaker, a painter, a musician, etc.

Like the salonnières, whom he clearly emulated, La Blancherie never rested for a moment. He was everywhere, "responding to each one's questions, being polite [*faisant politesses*] to everyone."[42]

The English visitor closed his letter with the information that this magnificent establishment was not without its troubles, beset as it was on all sides by those, motivated by envy and jealousy, who were trying to close it down. Indeed, even the newspapers were engaged in a conspiracy of silence which was making it difficult for La Blancherie to attract the subscribers he needed to get on a sound financial footing. Mr. Derb... had taken a few packages from La Blancherie for London delivery and, more important, had promised to publicize the venture in England. "I promised," he wrote the editor of the *Courrier* in closing, "to consign to your impartial pages this testimony of the recognition that I owe him, and to which I invite all my compatriots in congratulating them for having a correspondent so amiable that I am perhaps the first to announce to them."[43]

The virtues of a general agent for the Republic of Letters were those of the salonnière more than the philosophe. But Meister praised La Blancherie's meetings for their lack of formality and suggested that the general support of the project was based on the novelty of its publicity as well as the nobility of its aims. "Any free, independent association that can serve to render the communication of enlightenment faster and easier deserves encouragement," he wrote, "and it is undoubtedly from this point of view that the institution of M. de La Blancherie has obtained the consent of the police, the vote of the Academy of Sciences and that of various other literary societies."[44] Here Meister revealed not only his own support of an institution that seemed to respond to

---

42. Richard Derb... to the Editor of the *Courrier de l'Europe*, 8 May 1779, in Rabbe, "Pahin de La Blancherie," pp. 40–43.

43. Ibid., pp. 42–43.

44. *Correspondance Littéraire*, May 1778.

the desire for a free and open space for discussion as the basis of enlightenment but also the effective constraints on the establishment of such a space. Salons did not need the consent of the police to open their doors, nor did they need a vote of confidence from royal academies. In what sense, then, can public establishments such as La Blancherie's and those that would be modeled on it in the 1780s be said to have been "free" associations?

Both the *Correspondance Littéraire* and the *Mémoires Secrets* reported La Blancherie's project to their readers because the Academy of Sciences had approved it. La Blancherie's establishment was investigated by a commission from the Academy six years before Anton Mesmer's was. Franklin and Condorcet, who were later to serve on the commission that would declare Mesmer a charlatan, gave La Blancherie their official seal of approval.[45] The commission's report, written by the astronomer Joseph-Jérôme Lefrançois de Lalande, read in part: "We have attended the weekly meetings; we have seen there scholars, artists, and amateurs from almost every part of Europe; we have seen in its registers the proofs of a correspondence that cannot have been formed without considerable efforts, and we have been witness to an energy and a zeal that are very rare, and that can only be useful to the progress of the sciences and the arts." The report concluded that La Blancherie's project deserved to be encouraged because correspondences could not be favored enough, since they "are one of the great means of accelerating the progress of human knowledge."[46] The verdict, which La Blancherie had the privilege of printing in his many advertisements, had been rendered on 20 May 1778. Meister's report in the *Correspondance Littéraire* appeared the same month. The *Mémoires Secrets* first reported on La Blancherie's project the following month.[47]

The Academy's endorsement was not merely good public relations; it was virtually a requirement. There was no freedom of association in the Old Regime: all associations that were not officially authorized were illicit. Since the fourteenth century, the monarchy had consistently issued prohibitions against any assembly not approved by the state. As recently as 1737 the ordinance of the Paris police which had outlawed the Freemasons had been written as a ban on all assemblies; in 1778 the Parlement of Paris upheld action by the police of Lyon that made it "unlawful for all persons regardless of standing and rank to assemble or band together in the town, outskirts, or suburbs without being au-

45. On Mesmer, see Robert Darnton, *Mesmerism and the End of the Enlightenment in France* (Cambridge, Mass., 1968), pp. 62–64.
46. "Extrait des registres de l'Académie royale des sciences de Paris du 20 mai 1778," in Pahin de La Blancherie, *Correspondance générale*, pp. 28–30.
47. *Mémoires Secrets*, 19 June 1778.

thorized."[48] As privileged bodies, moreover, royal academies had the
right to determine whether or not any new institution was encroaching
on their privileged competency. The approval of the Academy of Sciences both legitimated La Blancherie's establishment in the eyes of the
public and the police and guaranteed that the Academy would not
interfere with its operation. When the Academy investigated La
Blancherie's activities, it acted both in its own interest as a privileged
corps and in the monarchy's interest as a royal academy with letters
patent from the king.

Official approval did not, however, solve La Blancherie's financial
problems. Despite the idealistic identification of men of letters as his
true patrons in his original prospectus, the economic precariousness of
the project required more substantial financing. In November 1779 the
Mémoires Secrets reported that the entrepreneur was being forced to
subsidize the *Nouvelles* out of his own pocket and had therefore put out
a call for more substantial subscriptions. "He invites scholars to subscribe and to imitate the King and the Queen, Monsieur, Monseigneur
the Comte d'Artois, and Madame the King's sister, who have taken
several." Even so, La Blancherie's enterprise went under within six
months.[49]

In 1781, however, La Blancherie was back with "forty subscribers of
the highest quality" who had made the deposit on a *hôtel* for the use of
his assemblies. He now had an elaborate financing plan based on three
levels of patronage. To stimulate subscriptions at all levels, he also
proposed a lottery—"to bait the cupidity of the subscribers," the *Mémoires Secrets* explained. "Beyond the advantage of entering freely into
the sanctuary, closed henceforth to the profane," the article continued,
"they will have the hope of possessing by the luck of the draw some of
the precious pieces exposed during the year, which will be acquired
with the excess of the funds coming from various subscriptions, after
expenses have been met."[50]

By referring to the "profane," the *Mémoires Secrets* was implicitly comparing La Blancherie's assembly to the Masonic lodges that had become
increasingly popular over the course of the eighteenth century.[51] Gone

48. Gordon, "Idea of Sociability," pp. 14–15; Jean Morange, *La Liberté d'association en
droit public français* (Paris, 1977), pp. 29–30; William H. Sewell, Jr., *Work and Revolution in
France: The Language of Labor from the Old Regime to 1848* (Cambridge, 1980), p. 41;
Maurice Agulhon, "Vers une histoire des associations," *Esprit*, June 1978, pp. 13–14.

49. *Mémoires Secrets*, 26 November 1779 and 8 May 1780.

50. Ibid., 28 June and 1 July 1781. For contemporary lottery schemes, see John
Goodman, "'Altar against Altar': The Colisée, Vauxhall Utopianism and Symbolic Politics
in Paris (1769–77)," *Art History* 15 (December 1992): 446–48; and Desazars de Montgaillard, *Histoire de l'Académie des sciences*, p. 20.

51. Margaret C. Jacob, *Living the Enlightenment: Freemasonry and Politics in Eighteenth-
Century Europe* (New York, 1991).

were the free and open meetings of men of letters, artists, and amateurs, of Frenchmen and foreigners, equally citizens of a cosmopolitan
Republic of Letters. With the loss of self-patronage, the public space
for free discussion, for the exchange and spreading of enlightenment,
had become a closed club, entry into which was based on money. Now
there were new distinctions: between the "ins" and the "outs" and
among the various classes of subscriber-patrons.

La Blancherie's new scheme for putting his enterprise on a sound
economic footing also followed the pattern of academy formation. Defining its membership and dividing it into categories mimicked the
hierarchical organization of the Academy of Sciences just as much as it
did the Masonic grades.[52] Just as the official organization of the Academy of Sciences in the seventeenth century had caused "the open community of scientists" to disappear,[53] so too did the reorganization of La
Blancherie's assembly close the open community of discourse his project had originally meant to serve.

Publicity had drawn the attention of the academy and the police, and
new regulations put additional limitations on membership. Like the
academies but unlike the salons, La Blancherie's institution was deemed
public and thus needed a set of regulations approved by the police.[54]
These were published in the new prospectus in 1779, which also
included the academy's report and the new system of patronage-
subscription. It was in this same prospectus that La Blancherie refor-
mulated his statement of purpose, making the weekly meeting the
main focus.

Access to meetings, however, was now limited by the new regulations.
Whereas La Blancherie had originally invited all subscribers and visiting scholars to gather at his office, he now established rules of entry.
"The purpose of the assembly adequately indicates who the persons are
that ought to frequent it," he wrote. Lest there be room for doubt,
however, he specified

> all those men known by their rank, their dignities, and by the public
> profession of the sciences, letters, and the arts. No other will be received,

52. Roger Hahn, *The Anatomy of a Scientific Institution: The Paris Academy of Sciences,
1666–1803* (Berkeley, 1971), pp. 129–34. The Academy of Inscriptions was similarly
hierarchical. Twenty of the thirty-two provincial academies followed the hierarchical
model rather than the unitary one of the French Academy. See Roche, *Siècle des lumières
en province* 1:105–6.

53. David S. Lux, *Patronage and Royal Science in Seventeenth-Century France: The Académie de Physique in Caen* (Ithaca, 1989), p. 52. For a comparison between the salon and the
academy in the seventeenth century, see Harth, *Cartesian Women*, chap. 1.

54. Jean-Louis Harouel, *Histoire des institutions de l'époque franque à la Révolution*
(Paris, 1987), pp. 465–66.

> unless he is presented by the persons designated above, or announced by
> a letter in their hand, of which he shall be the carrier.
>
> Foreigners and travelers will be admitted only inasmuch as they are
> invested with a public character, or presented, or announced in the man-
> ner that has just been designated.[55]

La Blancherie also specified who would not be admitted: women.
"Since women will not be admitted at all to the rendez-vous," he explained, "they will be received between noon and three o'clock: they
will have the time that has been requested by ladies of the highest order
to satisfy their curiosity, in regard to the objects on display."[56]

The police had never used their authority to limit access to printed
materials on the basis of either status or gender, but the transformation
of subscription into membership had raised new issues. Readership,
even by subscription, was gender-neutral, even if certain genres or
periodicals, such as the *Journal des Dames*, for example, were aimed at a
single-gender audience and even if subscription rates could be used to
limit potential subscribers by their capacity to pay. Nothing prohibited
men and women equally from reading the *Journal des Dames* or, for that
matter, the *Encyclopédie*; and nothing prohibited the sharing of printed
works by members of reading clubs to spread out the costs, or the
rental of such material, or the printing of cheap editions. Indeed, once
the French stopped writing in Latin, they implicitly opened up readership to literate women as well as men. The character of French writing
in the eighteenth century reflects the appreciation of this new audience. By the eighteenth century, the iconography of reading was exclusively female, whereas before it had been overwhelmingly male.[57]

With a publication project La Blancherie could appeal to a readership undifferentiated by rank or gender; with a project of association,
these criteria were put into play. Under the eyes of the police, La
Blancherie restricted access to his weekly meetings in much the same
way that the academicians did. When the French Academy began holding *séances publiques* in 1673, only men were permitted to watch the
academicians perform; women were not allowed to attend until 1702.
Their exclusion from membership in the academy continued, however,
even though it was de facto and not de jure: nowhere in the regulations
of the French Academy were women mentioned at all.[58]

The history of Freemasonry, too, was gendered male, and since Masonic sociability is increasingly being represented by historians of the

55. Pahin de La Blancherie, *Correspondance générale*, pp. 9–10.
56. Ibid., p. 12.
57. Chartier, "Practical Impact of Writing," in *History of Private Life* 3:147.
58. *Les Femmes et l'Académie française* (Paris, 1981), pp. 9–11.

Old Regime and Enlightenment as the model of enlightened sociability, it is worth examining in some detail.[59] Certainly Freemasonry did become increasingly popular over the course of the eighteenth century, but so did all forms of sociability. It is within the context of sociability, therefore, especially intellectual sociability, that the Masonic phenomenon can best be understood.

Masonic Sociability

The constitutions upon which Freemasonry was based explicitly excluded women.[60] Through a study of Masonic poetry, Jacques Brengues has identified three arguments for this exclusion: first, that women are indiscreet and thus would violate the ideal of secrecy; second, that women cause disorder among men and thus would violate the ideal of harmony; and third, that the inclusion of women would violate the space based on friendship between men with the introduction of love between men and women.[61]

Despite the misogynist basis of Freemasonry—or perhaps because of it—a debate ensued within France around the question of gender.[62] Women protested their exclusion and playwrights mocked it. Suspicions were voiced about what men might be doing without respectable women in their company. Eventually, many men seemed to become bored with their own company, as well as convinced of the need to defend their honor. Louis Guillemain de Saint-Victor expressed the position of the "repentant misogynists" in an "Epître aux dames" drawn from the discourse of mixed-gender sociability which defined French culture. Acknowledging that women were excluded because it was assumed that "pleasures founded on the virtues alone" were beyond them, he explained men's change of heart: "Enlightened and too much

59. Ran Halévi, *Les Loges maçonniques dans la France d'Ancien Régime: Aux origines de la sociabilité démocratique* (Paris, 1984); and Jacob, *Living the Enlightenment*. Halévi is inspired by Augustin Cochin, who saw the lodges as the secret network of the philosophe conspiracy behind the French Revolution—although he cleanses Cochin's model of conspiracy theory. See Cochin, *La Révolution et la libre pensée* (Paris, 1924), pp. xxviii–xxix. Koselleck also focuses on the lodges in his study of the Enlightenment, *Critique and Crisis*, and Michael L. Kennedy looks back to them for origins in *The Jacobin Clubs in the French Revolution: The First Years* (Princeton, 1982).

60. René Le Forestier, *Maçonnerie féminine et loges académiques*, ed. Antoine Faivre (Milan, 1979), p. 37; Margaret C. Jacob, "Freemasonry, Women, and the Paradox of the Enlightenment," in *Women and the Enlightenment*, ed. Margaret Hunt et al. (New York, 1984), p. 69; Jacques Brengues, "La Guerre des sexes et l'amour-maçon dans la poésie," *Dix-huitième Siècle* 19 (1987): 105.

61. Brengues, "Guerre des sexes," pp. 106–10.

62. Le Forestier, *Maçonnerie féminine*, chap. 2.

punished by the isolation and boredom that your absence has made us feel, we are convinced that the purpose of our existence is to live with you, and that we ought to be your friends and your dear companions; that we cannot separate ourselves from you without becoming stupid or unhappy." He concluded his apology with the admission that the exclusion of women was simply an application of the law of the stronger, "a law that we acknowledge to be criminal when it is used in relation to us."[63]

As a result of pressure from women and capitulation by a significant portion of the brothers, "lodges of adoption" began to be formed for female associates around 1760, despite continuing opposition from misogynist Masons. In 1774 lodges of adoption were officially authorized by French Masonry's governing body, the Grand Orient.[64] The character of this new breed of Freemasonry was expressed in a poem sung at the initiation of two women into a French lodge and then published in the *Courrier de l'Europe* in 1777. As Colette Bertrand notes, it reflects "the spirit of gallantry" that the admission of women brought to Freemasonry:

> Welcome to two charming sisters
> Who are being associated into our mysteries;
> By our songs let us celebrate my brothers,
> The end of their vain fears;
> Far from any of us challenging
> The price of their docility,
> If one dared, in truth,
> One would teach them all the rest.
>
> But one must advance by degrees
> To things that must be surprising,
> A secret that one is made to wait for
> Is more ardently desired:

63. Quoted ibid., pp. 25–26.

64. Ibid., pp. 26, 39, 57–58; Colette Bertrand, "Comment la franc-maçonnerie vient aux femmes," *Dix-huitième Siècle* 19 (1987): 208. Janet Burke suggests that the first lodges of adoption were formed between 1737 and 1747. Jacob identifies the first one as a "lodge" composed of Dutch aristocrats and French actresses formed in The Hague in 1751, but Le Forestier thinks it was a spoof and its social composition suggests that it was what he calls a "non-Masonic androgynous society," like the Ordre des Mopses (established throughout Europe in the 1730s and 1740s), which parodied Masonic lodges precisely by admitting both sexes to its membership on an equal footing. See Janet M. Burke, "Freemasonry, Friendship, and Noblewomen: The Role of the Secret Society in Bringing Enlightenment Thought to Pre-Revolutionary Women Elites," *History of European Ideas* 10 (1989): 283 and 290 n. 2; Jacob, "Freemasonry, Women," in Hunt, *Women and the Enlightenment*, pp. 69–91; Le Forestier, *Maçonnerie féminine*, chap. 1.

> Kind sisters, I swear to you
> That a pleasure is being arranged for you,
> You must let go the desire
> To know one day all the rest.[65]

It has been argued that the admission of women extended to them the egalitarian ideal that made the Masonic lodge an institution of the Enlightenment.[66] But even if the practices of Masonic sociability did foster a certain degree of equality and autonomy, as well as a critical spirit, among male Masons, the "sisters" they "adopted" were excluded from these practices. Adoption was the adaptation of Freemasonry to a new foundation in male dominance to replace the old strategy of female exclusion.

Not only did the sisters lack all autonomy within the lodge, but the lodges of adoption were themselves, as the name suggests, dependents of masculine lodges. In approving them, the Grand Orient had stipulated that they had to depend upon a "regular" lodge and that each session to which women were admitted had to be presided over by the (male) "venerable" of the lodge. When the duchesse de Bourbon was named grand mistress of the lodges of adoption in 1775, she received a meaningless title, since neither she nor any other woman was ever mistress of an autonomous female lodge.[67] "The sisters did not found lodges that were independent and their own," writes René Le Forestier; "they were guests in assemblies for which a special rite had been created." Their meetings took place after the secret rite of the men, "and the Sisters had to wait until the end of it before being able to enter the hall."[68]

The sessions devoted to women consisted almost entirely of initiation rituals and grade elevations, with a decidedly moral thrust. The speeches with which the brothers performed these rites were, according to Francesca Vigni, "verbose, emphatic, indeed hyperbolic sermons, in which, behind a rhetorical and precious style, the proclaimed

65. Quoted in Bertrand, "Comment la franc-maçonnerie vient aux femmes," p. 208.
66. Jacob, "Freemasonry, Women," in Hunt, *Women and the Enlightenment*; Janet M. Burke, "Through Friendship to Feminism: The Growth in Self-Awareness among Eighteenth-Century Women Freemasons," *Proceedings of the Western Society for French History* 14 (1987): 187–96; Burke, "Freemasonry, Friendship, and Noblewomen"; Bertrand, "Comment la franc-maçonnerie vient aux femmes," pp. 208–9. The case for Freemasonry as an institution of egalitarian or democratic sociability is made by Halévi in *Loges maçonniques*, and by Jacob in *Living the Enlightenment*. In *Cultural Origins*, Chartier emphasizes the "deliberate exclusion from masonic society of those who had neither education nor wealth" and argues that despite its egalitarian language, Freemasonry replicated the exclusivity of Old Regime society (p. 165).
67. Le Forestier, *Maçonnerie féminine*, p. 58.
68. Ibid., p. 38.

equality of woman is only fictive, since the sisters remained always the eternal minors of the institution."[69] The virtue preached to Masonic sisters was, Le Forestier remarks, "inactive, verbal, and whimpering." In the initiation ritual for the highest female grade, for example, the candidate's answer to the question "What does Freemasonry mean?" began: "I understand [it to be] a virtuous amusement, by means of which we retrace a part of the mysteries of our religion."[70]

But Masonic secrets, not Catholic mysteries, were fundamental to the self-definition of Freemasonry, and women, in the name of virtue, were forbidden to share them, even though these "secrets" were well known to the literate, if profane, public by the 1770s and were formal rather than substantive.[71] Indeed, secrecy was definitive of Freemasonry only because of the insistence on it, and thus the continued formal exclusion of women from the Masonic secrets made all the difference. Instead of being initiated into these secrets, the sisters were tested to see if they had the "virtue" to resist trying to learn them.

In one lodge the initiate was given a password that signified "Academy of Virtue"; in others she received a pair of gloves with the motto "Silence, Virtue" embroidered on them. In a ritual for the lowest grade, the initiate was conducted into the "Garden of Eden" and told that she must eat an apple to be admitted. Doing so, she was told, would be a sign of obedience without which the mysteries would never be revealed to her. If she fell for this line, she was reproached for her moral weakness in allowing herself to be seduced by the "serpent" who corrupted her innocence, blamed for the troubles she had caused, and

69. Francesca Vigni, "Les Aspirations féministes dans les loges d'adoption en France," *Dix-huitième Siècle* 19 (1987): 213–14.

70. Le Forestier, *Maçonnerie féminine*, p. 64.

71. Ibid., p. 32. Mercier included a chapter on Freemasons in the *Tableau de Paris*, where he noted that the police left them alone but that the more rigorous Masons were upset at the looseness of Parisian Freemasonry, signified by the lodges of adoption (*Tableau de Paris* 7:194–96). In the *Almanach du voyageur à Paris* (Paris, 1783 and 1786), L. V. Thierry listed addresses and meeting times of lodges as well as musées. In his unfinished manuscript memoirs, Lieutenant of Police Lenoir wrote: "There appeared before and since the Revolution many printed works for and against the Freemasons." Although Masonry had been prohibited in France until the reign of Louis XV, at that point it was tolerated and the police were well informed as to what happened in the lodges. "Many police officers, who were admitted there under the title of freemason made reports to me, and their reports, true or not, usually contained nothing but the details of Reception, stories of mystifications, and most often gallant intrigues." Nothing went on in them that was contrary to religion, he maintained, and among the names found on lists of pre-revolutionary Freemasons was his own boss, the comte de Maurepas. "Doubtless what has been published in favor of Freemasonry is not very exact," he concluded, "but in what has been published against it, is there not also a lot of exaggeration?": "Mémoires de J.-P. Lenoir," Bibliothèque Municipale d'Orléans, MS 1423, p. 241. I am grateful to Alan Williams for making a copy of this manuscript available to me.

then pardoned out of extreme indulgence. After she promised never to reveal any secrets, the venerable passed his golden trowel over her mouth with the words: "It is the seal of discretion that I apply to you."[72]

When she reached a higher grade, the initiate might be covered in a veil as a "symbol of modesty." The ritual for the highest grade reenacted the temptation of Eve (and Pandora). Here an inverted vase containing a live bird and covered with a plate filled with sand was placed before the candidate, who was told: "This vase that you see contains the final secret of Masonry; it is a sacred trust that the Masons confide to you. As I leave it to you as trustee, permit me to inform you that the least appearance of curiosity that you may show at this moment would deprive you of all the means of arriving at the august grade to which you aspire." She was then left alone for a little while, and afterward the vase was examined to see if it had been disturbed. If it had been, she was assessed a fine and her intiation was suspended; if not, then her wrists were chained together and she was further examined on her "Masonic knowledge." If her answers were correct, "her chains were broken" because she had proved herself virtuous by resisting her natural and sinful curiosity and thus had earned a liberty that was defined as Christian virtue—freedom from the passions. "The sister obeyed," Le Forestier concludes, "and the bird was set free."[73] Having passed all the tests, the grand mistress was, according to the words of the ritual, no more than the "honorable companion of the grand master." If necessary, she could be replaced on her throne by a wax figure, sufficient to fulfill her functions.[74]

The test for the grade of grand mistress, like those that came before it, was moral rather than arduous, in contrast to the men's initiation rites. Care was taken to make sure that the women's "nerves" could handle the pressure, and they were assured that their modesty would not be offended, since they would be asked to do nothing contrary to morals or religion. Since the vast majority of the women initiated were either wife, sister, or daughter of one of the members of the lodge, this is hardly surprising. Only such respectable women figure in the surviving lists of adopted sisters.[75]

In the 1730s French Freemasonry had excluded women in order to create an alternative to the perceived libertinage of dominant forms of sociability of the day, for which women were held responsible. By the

---

72. Le Forestier, *Maçonnerie féminine*, pp. 44–47.
73. Ibid., pp. 47–51, 59; Burke, "Through Friendship to Feminism," pp. 190–91. Burke sees this last ritual as an authentic initiation into an Enlightenment experience of liberty.
74. Le Forestier, *Maçonnerie féminine*, p. 60.
75. Ibid., pp. 35, 43, 60, 61.

1770s Masonic brothers had found a way to include women while maintaining moral and political authority over them. The brothers became
the moral judges of their new sisters, those who initiated them into
secret rites based on male-determined judgments of virtue, merit, and
beauty. Having proved his virtue through membership and advancement in the fraternity, the male Mason was neither threatened by the
seductive power of women nor subject to their authority. He was qualified and entitled to judge them because he was imbued with the Masonic values of fraternity, fidelity, and discretion. He defined and defended the moral order.[76]

The introduction of the Scottish Rite of single-sex sociability into
France constituted, in the words of Jacques Brengues, "a breach in the
salon system of the century instituted, even institutionalized, by wom-
en."[77] It displaced women from the position they had established at the
center of polite sociability in the seventeenth century. With the introduction of lodges of adoption, Freemasonry went further, inverting
the moral order of the salon, according to which men were civilized and
ennobled through their interaction with women. Masonic history and
poetry document men's defense of their new order, while the founding
of Enlightenment salons constituted attempts by women to maintain
their position in society.

When the lodges of adoption were created in the 1770s, they did not
assimilate either the personnel or the values of the Enlightenment
salons. They turned, rather, to the women constructed by the discourse
of heterosexual love: of gallantry, seduction, and sex. At the heart of
Masonic language are the old discourse of gallantry and the new one of
conjugal love, wifely submission, and domestic harmony which would
be adopted by the fraternal republic of 1792.[78]

The exception to the rule was the Loge des Neuf Soeurs, founded in
1775 by the astronomer and academician Lalande. It was an offshoot of
the salon of Anne-Catherine Helvétius and was the lodge from which
the Musée de Paris was to derive. Its history is a tale of woe because it
constantly broke the rules, primarily those regarding the place of wom-
en and the enforcement of secrecy. The brothers did not seem to un-

76. Brengues, "Guerre des sexes," pp. 112–13. Despite male control of Masonic
discourse and institutions, the rare woman could use the discourse of Freemasonry to
challenge the male construction of her, as did one Soeur Daix of the Dijon lodge in a
speech quoted in Vigni, "Aspirations féministes," pp. 217–19. Similar speeches were
made by some members of Jacobin women's clubs not many years later. See Suzanne
Desan, "Constitutional Amazons: Jacobin Women's Clubs in the French Revolution," in
Recreating Authority in Revolutionary France, ed. Bryant T. Ragan and Elizabeth A. Williams
(New Brunswick, 1992), pp. 11–35.
77. Brengues, "Guerre des sexes," p. 116.
78. Hunt, *Family Romance*.

derstand either that women were profane or that publicity (announcements of *fêtes* in the *Mémoires Secrets*, for example) was anti-Masonic. It was not long before the Grand Orient expelled them from the brotherhood.[79]

In the mixed-gender sociability of Freemasonry, which was increasingly popular in the same decade that saw the rise of the *musées*, women were not moral, political, or intellectual equals with their Masonic brothers, nor did they enjoy the central, ordering, harmonizing role of the salonnière. Rather, in the 1780s women's major role in institutions of intellectual and Masonic sociability was to be the displaced objects of male desire and learning and the submissive subjects of male-defined morality.

The Musée de Monsieur

The 1779 regulations of Pahin de La Blancherie's *assemblée ordinaire* excluded women as explicitly as the Masonic constitutions had done fifty years earlier. Only by protesting their exclusion did women earn the observer status already granted by the French Academy in that same distant era. They were allowed to look at the objects on display but not to interact with men. Certain men—those who could demonstrate "public credit"—were granted active citizenship in this configuration of the Republic of Letters, whereas all women were restricted to the role of passive citizens. Although La Blancherie's establishment had room to accommodate more men than either a salon or an academy, admittance was nevertheless restricted according to criteria that were familiar to the eighteenth-century public. Like the salons, it was the space of a social elite; like the academies, it was a masculine space. The significant criterion that did not come into play here was intellectual merit. In the wake of a decade that, thanks to the press, turned the *querelles* of the seventeenth century into public spectacles and scandals, the refusal to judge taste, style, or even literary, artistic, or scientific value was a welcome solution to one of the fundamental problems of the Enlightenment Republic of Letters.

The restriction on female participation in La Blancherie's establishment was not lifted until Jean François Pilâtre de Rozier received permission to admit women to his new Musée de Monsieur in 1781. The *Mémoires Secrets* covered the story on 2 December:

A *Prospectus* is circulating announcing a new establishment that makes M. de la Blancherie . . . shudder, in that it seems the Author must follow in his tracks and soon crush him by a rivalry infinitely more advantageous.

79. Le Forestier, *Maçonnerie féminine*, chaps. 7–10.

It concerns a *Musée*, authorized by the Government, under the protection of MONSIEUR and of MADAME . . . dedicated specifically to favor the progress of various sciences relative to the arts and to commerce.

In contrast to salonnières, who supported one another (by and large) and shared their guests, making sure to hold their gatherings on different days of the week so as not to compete, the men who established musées followed the lead of journalists, engaging in cutthroat competition for the subscribers upon whom their economic survival depended. If Pilâtre had simply offered laboratories and classes, he would not have challenged La Blancherie. Knowing the value of La Blancherie's weekly meetings, however, he made them the foundation of his new venture. To attract subscribers, he gained permission to allow women to join his new association, which put him at a distinct advantage over La Blancherie, for he could offer a meeting place for the Republic of Letters which included women and mimicked the salon.

Pilâtre de Rozier was the apothecary who would soon gain fame in balloon experiments and subsequently lose his life attempting a Channel crossing during one.[80] For a few months in 1780 he had been a professor of chemistry at an institution in Reims whose Parisian counterpart, the Société Libre d'Emulation, had been founded by the physiocrat Baudeau between 1773 and 1776 and survived (intermittently) until at least 1782.[81] Little is known about the Rheims society, but the history of the Parisian Société Libre can be traced.

The Société Libre was a physiocratic initiative inspired by the London Society for the Advancement of the Arts, Manufactures, and Commerce. It was in the tradition of organizations conceived and established since the time of Colbert to develop industry by supporting technological invention.[82] Although the Société Libre was not conceived as an institution of the Republic of Letters, its founding was

80. On Pilâtre and the Musée de Monsieur in its various incarnations, see René Taton, "Condorcet et Sylvestre-François Lacroix (1)," *Revue d'Histoire des Sciences et de Leurs Applications* 12 (April–June 1959): 130–38; Charles Dejob, "De l'établissement connu sous le nom de Lycée et d'Athénée et de quelques établissements analogues," *Revue Internationale de l'Enseignement* 18 (1889): 4–38; William A. Smeaton, "The Early Years of the Lycée and the Lycée des Arts: A Chapter in the Lives of A. L. Lavoisier and A. F. de Fourcroy," *Annals of Science* 11 (1955): 257–67. As these references should make clear, this musée has always been viewed within the history of science, and particularly as an institution for the popularization of science.

81. Arthur Birembaut, "Sur les lettres du physicien Magellan conservées aux Archives nationales," *Revue d'Histoire des Sciences et de Leurs Applications* 9 (1956): 150–51 n. 3, 160.

82. Arthur Birembaut, "Quelques réflexions sur les problèmes posés par la conservation et la consultation des Archives techniques françaises," *Archives Internationales d'Histoire des Sciences* 19 (1966): 79–81; and Birembaut, "Sur les lettres," p. 160 n. 2.

critical in encouraging the establishment of all sorts of "assemblies," according to Lenoir, the head of the Paris police from 1774 to 1785.[83]

The *Mémoires Secrets* first mentions the Société Libre on 15 May 1777, noting that a year after its founding it was "beginning to take form, and perhaps . . . acquire some stability." Already there were many members and ambitious plans: five prizes for the encouragement of the arts and the funds to support them. Two weeks later the *Mémoires* reported that the society was "still founded only on a Letter from the Minister, which permits it to assemble in the convent of the Prémontrés" and which had been obtained only over the opposition of the police. The police were concerned not only about the planned assemblies but also about any publications that might be generated by this new society, over which they wished to exercise censorship. The power to censor its publications would deprive the society "of the ordinary privilege of all the Academies and public societies," noted the *Mémoires*.[84]

The Academy of Sciences also created obstacles. According to the *Mémoires*, the academy was "jealous of the new Société Libre d'Emulation, which is walking in its footsteps and is tending unconsciously to render it useless." Its protests were in vain, however, since "it was not possible to oppose the zeal of Citizens who wished to dedicate funds to the encouragement of the Arts."[85] Four days later, the *Mémoires* reported that women were now getting into the act, "intriguing for the patriotic honor of being [part of] the new establishment of which we have spoken. Several are found among the list of Subscribers."[86]

In the end, however, the academy asserted its privilege as arbiter in scientific matters and proscribed the new society from making any scientific or theoretical judgments. As a group of "amateurs," it would have to limit itself to its stated aim of "utility."[87] By December 1777, "still on the move," according to the *Mémoires*, it had held its "general assembly" and distributed two "encouragements" to inventors of combination locks.[88] A longer report on the "séance publique" a few days later makes clear that the purpose of the society was indeed limited to the encouragement of the practical arts, primarily by the awarding of prizes for "useful inventions," and that its "patriotic" dimension lay in the boost it would give to French manufacturing and agriculture, especially in competition with the English.[89]

83. "Mémoires de J.-P. Lenoir," p. 235. On Lenoir, see Williams, *Police of Paris*, p. 302; and Robert Darnton, "The Memoirs of Lenoir, Lieutenant de Police of Paris, 1774–1785," *English Historical Review*, no. 336 (July 1970): 532–59.

84. *Mémoires Secrets*, 28 May 1777.

85. Ibid., 2 June 1777.

86. Ibid., 6 June 1777.

87. Hahn, *Anatomy*, p. 111.

88. *Mémoires Secrets*, 21 December 1777.

89. Ibid., 24 December 1777.

In his discussion of "the origins of numerous assemblies established in Paris under the name of Clubs, Salons, Societies, etc.," Lenoir wrote that "these sorts of assemblies, imitated from the English, were not authorized in France when in 1779 M. de Maurepas gave to the lawyers MM. Target and Elie de Beaumont the permission that the police had refused them, to form an association of persons of all ranks and conditions, under the title of *Société Libre d'Emulation*."[90] Guy Jean-Baptiste Target and Elie de Beaumont were best friends and the two most prominent and enlightened lawyers in France. In the 1770s and early 1780s they had among their clients two of the king's brothers, his nephew, and the University of Paris. In 1785 Target became the first lawyer in more than a century to be named to the French Academy.[91] A third lawyer who was centrally involved with the Société Libre was the Savoyard Louis-Henri Duchesne, who joined in 1776 and inherited the archives in 1789 when "the megalomania of the abbé Baudeau became patent." At the time he joined the society Duchesne was secretary to the comtesse de Provence and to the physiocratic former finance minister Trudaine de Montigny, who was Morellet's employer as well. At the death of Trudaine in 1777, Duchesne was given naturalization papers, which allowed him to become an *avocat au parlement* the following year.[92]

Target and Elie de Beaumont were not the founders of the Société Libre d'Emulation, but Lenoir remembered them because they had the clout to go over his head to his boss, the king's principal minister, to get permission to operate. According to Lenoir, Maurepas was willing to tolerate an association that seemed to him harmless because, requiring an entrance fee, it could not last long. "In fact," Lenoir added, "the Société Libre d'Emulation did not last long, but after that other assemblies arose under various other names. The Police could not stop them, and although they were illicit according to the laws, the Parlements . . . contributed to establishing them even more than the Tolerance of the government had."[93]

90. "Mémoires de J.-P. Lenoir," p. 235. Either Lenoir got the date wrong and was thinking of 1776 or there was an attempt to revive the société in 1779 by Target and Elie de Beaumont. I favor the former explanation, but the question could perhaps be cleared up by consultation of the archives of the Société Libre, which are in the Archives Nationales (ser. T), according to Birembaut, "Quelques réflexions," p. 81.

91. See Sarah Maza, "The Rose-Girl of Salency: Representations of Virtue in Prerevolutionary France," *Eighteenth-Century Studies* 22 (Spring 1989): 403–5; Michael P. Fitzsimmons, *The Parisian Order of Barristers and the French Revolution* (Cambridge, 1987), pp. 20–28; Durand Echeverria, *The Maupeou Revolution: A Study in the History of Libertarianism, France, 1770–1774* (Baton Rouge, 1985), pp. 40–41; Joseph Hudault, "Guy Jean-Baptiste Target et sa contribution à la préparation de l'édit de novembre 1787 sur l'état civil des protestants" (mémoire pour le diplôme d'études supérieures d'histoire du droit, Université de Paris, 1966), pp. 47–75.

92. Birembaut, "Sur les lettres," p. 151 n. 3.

93. "Mémoires de J.-P. Lenoir," p. 235.

Both La Blancherie and Pilâtre de Rozier drew upon the experience of the Société Libre d'Emulation. It may well have given them both the idea of an assembly of private persons in a public space whose purpose was utility. But the Société Libre was a narrower sort of project than either of the later ones. Its emphasis on prizes also shows it to have been both more directly modeled on and in competition with the Academy of Sciences, as well as more philanthropic than associative in purpose. The subscribers, in effect, were contributing to a fund that would support innovation in agriculture and the arts; they were not brought together to exchange their own ideas. The Société Libre was thus important as an early association of private persons who held public meetings, but unlike the musées and La Blancherie's establishment, it was more philanthropic, in the tradition of patronage, than it was associative, in the tradition of the Republic of Letters.[94]

When Pilâtre de Rozier first proposed his musée in the fall of 1781, he did not call it a "free society." Having learned a lesson from the troubles of La Blancherie, he sought not just member-subscribers but patrons and protectors, and he named his establishment for the most powerful of them, the king's brother, known simply as "Monsieur." Already ensconced in his entourage and employed in the service of Madame his wife (like Duchesne of the Société Libre), Pilâtre lined up a group of blue-ribbon backers.[95] In December the *Mémoires Secrets* could report that the prospectus was circulating and that the musée, authorized by the government and under the protection of Monsieur and Madame, threatened to drive La Blancherie out of business. By January the Academy of Sciences had given Pilâtre its encouragement, and other royal academies had signed on as well: the French Academy, the royal observatory, the royal medical society, and the royal veterinary college had all given their endorsements.[96]

94. At one point, La Blancherie attempted to take over the failed Société Libre, but its true heir was the Société Philanthropique. On 4 July 1783 the *Mémoires Secrets* reported on the establishment of this new institution: "It is composed of citizens of all orders of the state; but since one must be very rich to join, it numbers a lot of financiers among its members. Having no fixed space to assemble, it meets in one of the rooms of the *Musée de Paris*. For its first act of public beneficence, it proposes to accord an annual *secours* to twelve octogenarian workers from this capital. The aspirants are subjected to certain conditions that it prescribes. To the degree that the fund grows, this society will extend its assistance to a greater number of unfortunates of the same sort, and it hopes to be able one day to found its own establishment in which to receive them. But, after the dissolution of the Société libre d'émulation, which had an entirely different basis, what fund is to be made for such establishments in a nation as frivolous [*légère*] as ours." The Société philanthropique did, in fact, survive. See Mercier, *Tableau de Paris* 11:113–14.

95. Amiable, "Origines maçonniques," p. 492.

96. *Mémoires Secrets*, 2 December 1781, 3 January 1782; Charles Cabanes, "Histoire du premier musée autorisé par le gouvernement," *La Nature* (1937): 577–78.

What appealed to the *Mémoires Secrets* was the pedagogical mission of Pilâtre's musée. It had two professed aims: to provide laboratories and scientific equipment for amateurs and professionals, and to instruct beginners in the use of the equipment and to demonstrate its practical applications. Not only would expensive equipment be thus made available to those who could not afford to buy it, but courses would be offered in a variety of useful subjects.[97] By contrast, the *Mémoires* found La Blancherie's establishment "so cold, so vague, so monotonous, so deprived of movement, interest, and instruction" that it was doomed to fail. Pilâtre's musée was so much more "useful" that it would soon replace and absorb it. Telling in this judgment was the author's overt disgust for the entrepreneurial spirit for which Meister had praised La Blancherie. "The motives of cupidity, the mercantile ideas that have been mixed up with this project," he declared, "must necessarily turn off people who are experimental [i.e., 'scientific'] and know the maneuvers of all these literary intriguers."[98] A former officer of the musée later pointed to the modest price of subscriptions as evidence that its goal was solely the "propagation of enlightenment."[99]

In fact, Pilâtre was simply a better entrepreneur than La Blancherie, as his immediate and tremendous success, as well as those who have studied his finances, attests. Not only did he use his position at court to gain government authorization and the endorsements of the official corps of the Republic of Letters; he also took advantage of his competitors in the private sector. When a group was expelled from the Musée de Paris, he welcomed them to join him, offering to transfer memberships at no cost; he also offered membership privileges to all the members of the Société Patriotique de Bretagne. By the time of Pilâtre's death in 1785 the Academy of Sciences itself had taken out a group subscription, with the name of its perpetual secretary, Condorcet, heading the list.[100]

Pilâtre's second prospectus, probably written in 1783, was followed by the government-approved regulations. It advertised the Musée de Monsieur as a place where those who could not get into all the various establishments that made Paris the capital of the Republic of Letters could learn everything they needed to know: "The Capital possesses many interesting establishments whose details are as unknown to the nationals as to foreigners," the reader was informed, and "the pro-

97. *Mémoires Secrets*, 3 December 1781.

98. Ibid., 10 December 1781.

99. M[édéric] L[ouis] E[lie] Moreau de Saint-Méry, *Discours sur l'utilité du musée établi à Paris prononcé dans la séance publique du 1re décembre 1784* (Parma, 1805), n.p.

100. Cabanes, "Histoire du premier musée"; Taton, "Condorcet et Lacroix", pp. 131–32; Dejob, "De l'établissement," p. 10.

fessors of the Musée who have gained entrée into most of these establishments, will explain here all that would escape the curiosity of travelers."[101] Why go anywhere else? Pilâtre's establishment was the musée of all musées.

M. L. E. Moreau de Saint-Méry's *Discours sur l'utilité du musée* reveals not only the purposes and structure of this establishment but also the very specific role that women were asked to play in it. In 1784 Moreau was elected secretary of the musée when Pilâtre democratized the association, partly to attract more subscribers and partly to allow himself to withdraw from administrative work to concentrate on his balloon projects.[102] The subscribers were asked to elect an administrative board and a perpetual secretary, and the latter position fell to Moreau.[103] In 1805 Moreau had printed in Parma a deluxe edition of the speech he had delivered as the newly inaugurated secretary of this society, full of hope and promise, whose purpose was not *limited* to utility, as that of the Société Libre had been—but *dedicated* to it. "What more certain proof of the utility of this establishment," he asked,

> than the eagerness with which people come from all over to [join] it; than the very objects with which the spaces are decorated and that speak of this utility? In fact, in whatever direction you look around, everything here announces the cult that is rendered to the sciences, everything says how admirable are the secrets of nature, to the research into which this temple is consecrated. (1–2)

Moreau elaborated at some length on the services the musée offered to the public which would justify its claim to utility. These services can be grouped in four categories: association, instruction, exhibition, and decoration.

The associative function should by now be familiar: it was the one proper to the Enlightenment Republic of Letters. For the brotherhood of scholars, wrote Moreau, the world is a single *patrie*, and they dedicate their lives to study for the sake of humanity itself. "This is really the charm of science," he explained, "that it conducts man to consider himself worthless if he is not useful" (4–5). If the Academy of Sciences had managed to separate real science from utility in its turf battle with

101. Quoted in Cabanes, "Histoire du premier musée," p. 579.
102. Taton, "Condorcet et Lacroix," p. 133.
103. Moreau de Saint-Méry, *Discours*, n.p., hereafter cited in the text. Although the title "perpetual secretary" comes from the academic tradition, the elected administrative committee may have had its roots in the Anglophile *sociétés littéraires*. See M. Kay Flavell, "The Enlightened Reader and the New Industrial Towns: A Study of the Liverpool Library, 1758–1790," *British Journal for Eighteenth-Century Studies* 8 (1985): 20.

the Société Libre, Moreau would return to the discourse of the *Encyclopédie* to argue that the two were inseparable. If the Société Libre had to limit itself to questions of utility, the musée would place *émulation* itself —competition—in the service of the highest good that was utility.[104]

And yet Moreau had to admit that such grand ideas of intellectual association were hardly new. Indeed, the eighteenth century honored the sciences more than any previous era, and the Republic of Letters was already full of establishments ·whose goal was the same as the musée's (7–8). The novelty of the Musée de Monsieur as Moreau promoted it was that "the beacons of light" generated by the association of scholars and men of letters gathered there would attract novices and thus contribute to the expansion of the Republic of Letters through its project of enlightenment.

Through the use of modern technologies of publicity, the *Encyclopédie* had tried to improve upon the ancient library of Alexandria, in which all knowledge was gathered, only to be lost in a blaze of fire. The model of the musée was the museum attached to that library, in which the scholars employed by the emperor Ptolemy lived and worked, cataloging and commenting on the books that represented his imperial power. As the library had been made public through print thirty years earlier, so too would the musée that was its human dimension become a public association.[105]

It was just one step from the Parisian musée as a beacon of Enlightenment, to a national "encyclopedic and popular academy," conceived in 1785 by Barthélémy-Pélagé Georgelin Du Cosquer, secretary of the Société Patriotique de Bretagne. Georgelin proposed to establish "a common center of *lumières* at the *Musée de Paris*, which would correspond with all the provincial Academies." This plan would respond to "the unanimous wish of Scholars, who would like all the Academies to be united *into a single one*, in order that the *written Encyclopedia* might be transformed into a *living Encyclopedia* of all persons proper to perfecting the *ensemble* of human knowledge." Geogelin believed that such a

104. In "'Altar against Altar,'" John Goodman identifies emulation as "a key concept in the discourse of French academic culture" (p. 440). The English fails to capture the full meaning of the French term, which includes both "rivalry" or "competition" and "imitation."

105. *Encyclopédie* 5:637, 10:893. On the library and museum at Alexandria, see Mostafa el-Abbadi, *The Life and Fate of the Ancient Library of Alexandria* (Paris, 1990), pp. 84–90; Luciano Canfora, *The Vanished Library*, trans. Martin Ryle (London, 1989); and Diana Delia, "From Romance to Rhetoric: The Alexandrian Library in Classical and Islamic Traditions," *American Historical Review* 97 (December 1992): 1449–67. The author of a prospectus for a musée in Toulouse specifically named Alexandria as his model. See "Lettre au rédacteur des *Affiches*," 7 July 1784, in Desazars de Montgaillard, *Histoire de l'Académie des sciences*, p. 34.

society would represent the best answer to the question recently posed by the Academy of Rouen: "What is the means of carrying the Encyclopedia to the highest degree of perfection?"[106]

Georgelin also noted that his aim was to "second the charitable desire" of the royal minister Vergennes, "to increase the taste for knowledge in each Province." Such a desire had first been expressed to the ministry by Condorcet in a private memorandum to Maurepas in 1774. As the new perpetual secretary of the Academy of Sciences, Condorcet had proposed that the provincial academies be associated under the leadership of Paris in order to promote enthusiasm for the sciences throughout the realm and to render France "similar in some way to Bacon's Atlantis."[107] He failed in this endeavor because of resistance from the provincial academies, whose members were not interested for the most part in being satellites of Paris, fearing, as one objector put it, that "every kind of association involves obligation and bondage, especially of a provincial academy with that in the capital. The one neces-

---

106. [Barthélémy-Pélagé Georgelin du Cosquer], *Vues patriotiques sur l'établissement en Bretagne et dans toute la France d'une académie encyclopédique et populaire* (n.p., 1785), pp. 6–7 and 22. On attempts by the provincial academies to unite by means of correspondence and journals—the traditional means of the Republic of Letters—in the 1760s and 1770s, see Keith M. Baker, "Les Débuts de Condorcet au secrétariat de l'Académie royale des sciences (1773–1776)," *Revue d'Histoire des Sciences et de Leurs Applications* 20 (1967): 259–67. As late as 1784 the *Nouveau Supplément à la France Littéraire* published a "Lettre adressé au rédacteur . . . sur un projet d'association entre les académies" (vol. 4, pt. 2, pp. xi–xiv). The Société Patriotique de Bretagne was centered in Rennes but had established "in different Cities Committees of Correspondence that considerably extend its utility": [Georgelin du Cosquer], *Vues patriotiques*, p. 15. On the Société Patriotique, see Augustin Cochin, *Les Sociétés de pensée et la Révolution en Bretagne (1788–1789)*, 2 vols. (Paris, 1925), esp. 1:25–31; and Jean Quéniart, *Culture et sociétés urbaines dans la France de l'ouest au XVIIIe siècle* (Paris, 1978), pp. 434–35. Ferdinand Dubois de Fosseux, elected secretary of the Academy of Arras in 1785, initiated a bureau de correspondance the following year, with a similar aim. See Léon-Noël Berthe, *Dubois de Fosseux, secrétaire de l'Académie d'Arras, 1785–1792, et son bureau de correspondance* (Arras, 1969), p. 152. The idea for committees of correspondence may have come not only from the bureaux de correspondance that connected people in the provinces with Paris but also from the American Revolution, in which such committees were overtly political. See Edward D. Collins, "Committees of Correspondence of the American Revolution," *Annual Report of the American Historical Association for the Year 1901*, 2 vols. (1902), 1:245–71; and Richard D. Brown, *Revolutionary Politics in Massachusetts: The Boston Committee of Correspondence and the Towns, 1772–1774* (Cambridge, Mass., 1970). Surprisingly, no connection has been made between the Société Patriotique de Bretagne and the Breton Club formed by Breton representatives of the third estate to the Estates General in Versailles in the spring of 1789, and out of which the Jacobin Club would be formed that fall. Michael Kennedy, for example, considers *chambres littéraires* as "the most direct precursors" of the Jacobin clubs, but goes on to clinch his argument that the clubs were "essentially new entities" by noting that "the title *Société patriotique et littéraire*, which they frequently adopted, underlined their widened interests": *Jacobin Clubs*, pp. 8–10.

107. Baker, "Débuts de Condorcet," p. 256; Baker, *Condorcet*, pp. 47–52.

sarily becomes dependent on the other." In addition, as several objec-
tors pointed out, the provincial academies were generally not narrowly
limited to the sciences and did not always stratify their membership as
the Parisian academy did.[108]

Condorcet misjudged the politics of the situation, but he also failed
because, unlike La Blancherie, Pilâtre, Moreau, and Georgelin, he tried
to subsume the Republic of Letters under the narrow compass provided by a royal academy, and one dedicated only to the sciences. He
withdrew his proposal in 1775, but the following year he submitted an
even more radically absolutist plan to another royal official, Chrétien
Guillaume de Lamoignon de Malesherbes, in which, according to Keith
Baker, he proposed "to liberate scientific organization from the social
slavery of the Ancien Régime" by reorganizing all the provincial academies and the new agricultural societies to conform to a uniform model, and then subjecting them to central direction from Paris.[109] What
Malesherbes did with this extraordinary proposal is not known, but had
it been implemented, it would have been the Maupeou coup of academic culture!

By the time Moreau de Saint-Méry gave his speech in 1784, the
benefits of association among men of letters were so well known and
well appreciated that he could sum them up in a paragraph:

> Finding themselves united by the same spirit, they enlighten one another
> reciprocally by communicating their views, their ideas, each one taking
> from this type of society his portion of knowledge augmented. And what
> commerce is more attractive than that in which loss is unknown, in which
> one can enrich others without divesting oneself, and in which exchange
> adds more to that which one already possesses? An effect, almost miracu-
> lous, of the association of educated men in which gain is always found
> without costing anybody anything! (10–11)

This was old ground, but the very venerability of it by 1784, its trite-
ness, speaks for the embeddedness of the musée in the world created
by the philosophes and their *Encyclopédie*. La Blancherie had translated
journal subscription into membership with a weekly meeting; Pilâtre
transformed the *Encyclopédie* itself into a direct pedagogy.

The body of Moreau's speech was dedicated to a description of the
various subjects to be taught at the musée and, of course, their utility.
He began with the natural and physical sciences but certainly did not

---

108. Baker, *Condorcet*, p. 52; Roche, *Siècle des lumières en province*, pp. 71–74. Roche
also documents a 1774 proposal for unification of academies made by a member of the
Academy of Rouen to his colleagues (pp. 70–71).

109. Baker, "Débuts de Condorcet," pp. 273–76.

end there. All the talk of the cult of science should not mislead the modern reader into thinking that the eighteenth-century man of letters considered only the "hard" sciences useful. No, everything fell into the cult of science, beginning with modern languages, which would enhance the associative function among men fundamental to advances in the understanding of nature, while adding one more pleasure to be experienced by those who would be visiting the capital: the charm of being understood (20).

In addition to foreign languages, the musée would also give instruction in French, the language of "reason and urbanity" (21–22). It would even offer a course in "literary history," but not in the new, more scientific study of grammar, which would be taken up by the revolutionaries in the new curricula of the 1790s.[110] Courses in history proper and the fine arts would round out the curriculum (23–26).

The pedagogical aim of the musée was to make available to Parisians of modest means the broad sweep of Enlightenment knowledge. As La Blancherie had translated journal subscription into membership with a weekly meeting, Pilâtre had transformed the subscription project of the *Encyclopédie* itself into a direct pedagogy with courses of instruction drawn from the *topoi* of the magnum opus of the Enlightenment. The musée's library, as one historian of science has pointed out, included the natural scientist Buffon and the *Mémoires* of the Academy of Sciences, but also La Fontaine's *Fables* and the works of Corneille and Rousseau. "Certainly there is nothing to disdain in all this," he writes disdainfully, "but the whole could not be said to constitute a systematically collected documentation for a scientific institute."[111]

The third service offered by the musée was exhibition. Like La Blancherie's meeting space, the musée would serve as a venue of public display for the works of artists, artisans, and inventors. Unlike La Blancherie, who simply wanted to help creative people sell their products, Moreau saw exhibition as a means of attracting the critical atten-

110. Françoise Douay, "La Langue de la Raison et de la Liberté: The Crisis of Rhetoric in the Age of Oratory, 1789–1809," *Proceedings of the Consortium on Revolutionary Europe, 1750–1850, 1991* ([Tallahassee], 1992): 185–93. During the revolutionary decade, when the musée continued to operate under various names (Lycée, Lycée Républicain, Athénée), it was most associated with its course in literary history given by La Harpe (and for a year or so during the Terror by Mercier, when La Harpe was in prison). Historians of science, however, continue to represent the musée as a *scientific* institution. See, e.g., Dejob, "De l'établissement," p. 7; and Smeaton, "Early Years of the Lycée," pp. 257–67.

111. Cabanes, "Histoire du premier musée," p. 581. The 1788 catalog of the library has been reprinted by Wallace Kirsop in "Some Documents on the History of the French Book Trade in the Eighteenth Century," *Australian Journal of French Studies* 24 (1987): 265–88. It includes the titles of 128 books, of which many are sets, and 28 are periodicals. The range is indeed broad, and all titles are in French.

tion needed by young artists to develop their talents (27–29). "In exposing their works," he explained, artists and inventors "will have the public as judge and will themselves be such in regard to others. Their rivalry [*émulation*], thus excited, will produce new masterpieces and they will no longer need to beg for advice and public approval. Here their talents will serve both as titles and as protectors" (27–29). The utility of exhibition lay in exposing work to peer review by an enlightened public conceived as equals in matters of judgment and thus as contributors to the cultivation of talent. The practice of critical discourse which La Blancherie had brought out of the pages of his journal and into his meetings was thus formalized in the musée.

Decoration, the final service the musée offered the public, was something else altogether. It was the function women were to fulfill. Moreau offered women to the (male) public as an added incentive to join the Musée de Monsieur rather than its rivals. "I will be reproached perhaps for having waited so long before speaking of an advantage that this Musée does not share with any other establishment relative to the sciences," he said, in closing his speech. Members of the musée would have the pleasure of seeing among them

> that adored sex which seems to come here to dispute with the sciences for their admirers. Seduced by superficial men who . . . have persuaded them that scholars were somber and unsociable beings, women have for a long time taken pleasure in their frivolity; but they know at last, by their own experience, that the love of the sciences takes nothing away from the social virtues: they even have the talent to make this love serve to render even more dangerous the seductive art of pleasing. Charming sex, how much your presence adds to the pure pleasures that are tasted in this asylum! Embellish it often, and the sciences will have there an even more assiduous cult. (29)

La Blancherie and the *Mémoires Secrets* had read the strategy right when they saw the admission of women to Pilâtre's musée as an attempt to draw in more male subscribers.[112] The seductive role given women in the musée was most clearly marked in the differential subscription rates: women subscribed at half price.[113]

How different this mixed-gender society was from the salon! There

112. *Mémoires Secrets*, 3 January 1782.

113. Moreau de Saint-Méry, *Discours*, n.p. Pilâtre's biographers play the seduction theme in a different key: they apologize for his "weakness" in decking science out in ribbons and bows, since they agree with him that, to attract women to serious study, he had to seduce them in ways that would be inappropriate to the masculine search for truth: [Antoine Tournon], *La Vie et les mémoires de Pilâtre de Rozier* (Paris, 1786), pp. 47–49; and Dejob, "De l'établissement," p. 8.

the salonnière had been at the very center of conversation, controlling and guiding it, keeping it within the bounds of politeness. And if over the years some men had written petulantly of their dissatisfaction with having to be judged by women in the salons, with having to work with and through them to attain their goals of literary fame and fortune, such men had now found a solution to their problems: men would advise and judge one another, and women would embellish the public space in which they did so.

Pilâtre succeeded in attracting women to the musée,[114] but he did not address their intellectual aspirations. By 1787, there was a perceived need for a Musée des Dames, which was established the following year by the baronne Duplessy under the protection of the royal minister Loménie de Brienne. Like the earlier Masonic lodges of adoption and the later Jacobin women's clubs, however, this separate institution was far from equivalent to the male-centered musées. As the founder herself wrote: "Enlightenment, useful or agreeable knowledge, far from distracting women from caring for the household, gives them on the contrary more facility, more ardor, to fulfill the duties of mother and wife." Thus, she continued, "society as a whole can only gain in all respects by the instruction of women; . . . nothing can contribute to it as effectively as an Academic Assembly, a Musée solely dedicated to this purpose."[115]

Pilâtre and Moreau were not interested in spreading enlightenment to women; they simply wanted to make enlightened men more attractive to women, and women more attractive to enlightened men. Only for this reason were women invited to take the courses offered by the musée and to mingle with the real (male) scholars, students, and men of letters in this "salon" without a salonnière.

The founders of musées saw no need for women to act as salonnières, but they did recognize a need to offer to the enlightened and enlightenable male public the kind of social space that women had been shaping in their Parisian homes for the better part of two centuries. The 1783 regulations of the Musée de Monsieur described the establishment in salonlike terms as "forming a free society, which has as its basis that precious equality that mixes ranks without confusing them."[116] A third and final prospectus, published in 1785, presented a more salonlike musée than ever. It would still be a meeting place for men of letters where young people could find instruction, encouragement,

Her only explanation is a kind of vague revenge motif

114. Cabanes, "Histoire du premier musée," pp. 578–79.

115. La baronne Duplessy, "Avant-propos," _Repertoire des lectures faites au musée des dames_ (Paris, 1788), vol. 1, pt. 1, pp. 8–11.

116. Quoted in Cabanes, "Histoire du premier musée," p. 580.

and advice, but this prospectus pointed out the agreeableness of the company, especially for foreign visitors, who, "enjoying the same advantages as the nationals, will also have an infinitely more precious one, that of finding themselves all of a sudden at the center of the arts and of *la bonne compagnie*." At the musée they would be able "to enjoy the pleasures of conversation in a room dedicated to that use."[117]

The kind of social space described by the English visitor to La Blancherie's Thursday meeting in 1779 would now be found in the Musée de Monsieur: the social space at the center of the Republic of Letters which was also the center of *la bonne compagnie*. There was no need to join any rival establishment. Unlike La Blancherie, Pilâtre emphasized that the presence—not, however, the activity—of women was key to the success of such a social and intellectual space. "Women," he wrote, "who, by the care they take to cultivate their minds, and by their success in more than one field, prove to us every day the progress of our century, will inspire, by their presence alone at the Musée, that urbanity that makes the charm of all society, and which could not exist without them."[118]

Mercier made the same connection between the sociability of the Republic of Letters and that of the salons in the first volume of his *Tableau de Paris*. Under the heading "Patrie du vrai philosophe," he reminisced about his youth, when he was infatuated by Rousseau's seductive picture of man alone in the woods, contemplating nature and getting away from it all. By his late twenties, however, when he had read more and knew more about life and about people, he came to realize that the great cities were the true home of the philosophe, "or at least there is no middle ground, and one must either be entirely a man wandering in the woods, or one must live in Paris in *la bonne compagnie*."[119]

In the *Tableau de Paris*, Mercier was particularly concerned with two related problems that bear on the meaning of the new musées: the need for a meeting place for the Republic of Letters and for the public and the difficulties faced by travelers visiting the city in search of its true riches: enlightenment and sociability.[120] The musées established by La Blancherie and Pilâtre were attempts to resolve these problems, but neither, in Mercier's view, could have complete success, for a variety of reasons that are worth examining.

---

117. [François Pilâtre de Rozier], *Musée de Monsieur et de Mgr. le comte d'Artois* (prospectus) (Paris, 1785), p. 3.

118. Ibid.

119. Mercier, *Tableau de Paris* 1:24–26.

120. Visitors' problems are discussed in the chapters "Etrangers" and "Des étrangers," in ibid., 2:318–22 and 11:44. Further references will be made in the text.

Mercier saw the Academy of Sciences as one model of unity and reciprocal exchange, but like the founders of musées, he had a vision of knowledge that was encyclopedic rather than narrowly scientific, and so the scientific academy could not provide a full solution to the problems he saw. In addition, Mercier recognized the limitations imposed by the dependence of the academy on the monarchy. Other societies, he suggested, should steep themselves in the "truly philosophical spirit, which animates and directs the observations, the works, and the pronouncements of the academy of sciences" (5:138–39, 140–41).

In consecutive chapters, "On Different Observers" and "Intellectual Differences," Mercier established how the encyclopedic goal of bringing together all fields of knowledge was related to the need to gather all those who cultivated them. "Thus," he wrote in the first piece, "while scholars are regarded among themselves with a sort of disdain, while the mechanic has no conception of the celebrity of the poet, and the latter in return scarcely regards [the former] at all, the impartial observer sees the arts and sciences head on, being perfected by taking seemingly opposed routes, and which must come together at the same point" (2:136–37). If it was easy to see how the arts and sciences must come together, it was more difficult to establish communication among those people dedicated to them. "The musician, the geometer, the poet, the painter, the moralist, the sculptor, the chemist, the man of politics, [all] equally men of genius, can scarcely communicate," wrote Mercier in "Différences des esprits" (2:141).

Volumes later, however, Mercier was praising the Paris of the salons and polite conversation precisely for making possible the kind of communication that was lacking elsewhere in the capital and which made Parisian men of letters the models for all Europeans. Nowhere else, he proclaimed, could the man of letters understand or be understood. Elsewhere, people thought that words alone made up a conversation, but in Paris there was a sort of "electricity" that made conversation true communication and more than the sum of its verbal parts:

The greatest detractors of the capital, struck by this prompt communication of ideas, this swift electricity of minds, these natural graces of style, have retained a profound memory of the conversation that reigns in Paris among the educated, the sudden bursts of light [clartés] to which it gives birth, the happy urbanity that colors the most obvious contradiction; and the Englishman, the Italian, the German who have been witnesses of this interesting struggle of minds, will render homage to the expression of the Parisian philosophe. He is made to give lessons in this genre to all the other peoples of the earth. (7:262–64)

In other words, the ideal of the Republic of Letters, and of Paris as its capital, was still located in the conversations that took place in the salons, where women were naturally and necessarily present. The "posterity of the true philosophes" (as this chapter was titled) was to be found only in the increasingly rare salon conversation.

"One scarcely sees today these societies that were noted some time ago," Mercier wrote in "Bureaux d'esprit." "They have been dissolved, because the taste for letters has spread everywhere" (6:261–62). In Mercier's view, the decline of the stature of academicians had transformed salons into mere "bureaux d'esprit," in which women had become "directors of literature," making judgments, trying to be mediators in matters of literary substance and style. The new salonnière opens her door to writers without talent and then "presides over her little tribunal, where in judging she is the first one judged." Lacking the skill of her predecessors, she is unable to maintain harmony in her salon, and "division comes into the flock." "Distinguished women," according to Mercier, have thus renounced the role of salonnière and left it to the "little wives of academicians, who need to enhance [plâtrer] the reputation of their husbands, and who are also curious to judge for themselves the talent of young authors" (6:262–64). This was Rousseau's critique of salonnières all over again, but now separated from criticism of men of letters. Rousseau had attacked the philosophes through the women who "feminized" them; Mercier now ridiculed the women who aspired to emulate the great salonnières, while in no way associating them with the heirs of the philosophes—such as himself.

It is not by chance, I think, that the chapter "Bureaux d'esprit" is sandwiched between "Musées" and "Monsieur le public."[121] The contrast between the musées and the salons is thus made clear, but so is the uneasy connection between them. Mercier defined the musées as "new establishments that some individuals are trying to naturalize among us." He discussed La Blancherie's venture and mentioned Pilâtre's prospectus, which had just appeared. "They will have considerable trouble succeeding," he wrote, "because there is too little liberty in our government for each one to give a sure development to his own views, and because the capital has tastes and fantasies, rather than a true and

---

121. H. Temple Patterson's description of the *Tableau* as "utterly chaotic" is typical of Mercier criticism but not, I think, fair: *Poetic Genesis: Sebastien Mercier into Victor Hugo, Studies on Voltaire and the Eighteenth Century* 11 (1960): 42. I am not claiming that there is an overarching order to Mercier's text, but I do find meaning in the juxtaposition of certain chapters. In addition to the ones mentioned here, recall "Economistes" and "Enthousiasme." Réal Ouellet and Hélène Vachon make a similar case for the significance of juxtaposition in the *Lettres persanes*: "*Lettres persanes*" *de Montesquieu* (Paris, 1976), p. 79.

constant love for the sciences and the arts." He doubted that Pilâtre would have any more success than the "indefatigable" La Blancherie, whose musée

> has opened, closed, fallen, risen up; it has wandered around all the neighborhoods, and has never been able to receive a fixed and solid position because men will never assemble to mingle their ideas, their views, their enterprises, anywhere but in a republic. We will always lack a meeting point for eloquence, for belles lettres, for philosophy; those who cultivate these arts must work isolated. (6:259–60)

To Mercier, the need for a meeting place for the Republic of Letters was painfully obvious. The Academy of Sciences was inadequate because it was too narrow in its focus and, like all royal academies, was dependent on the monarchy. The salons were not satisfactory either, because they were too constricted in size and because they were ruled by women, who, in asserting their ability and authority to judge merit and taste, created discord rather than harmonizing egos. And the musées would fail too because the Parisian public was too fickle and because "all public assembly is too contrary to the spirit of the French government" (6:261). The Republic of Letters could never find a true center except in a republic, and the basis for that new republic lay in "Monsieur le public."

When the men of the 1780s designed and marketed new institutions of intellectual sociability for the male citizens of an expanding Republic of Letters, they continued to evoke the salon society that their new establishments were meant to displace. But women were not to be the active centers of these new institutions. In both La Blancherie's establishment and the Musée de Monsieur, they were marginalized, as was their value to the assembly. Women could do no more than examine objects of male creation in La Blancherie's establishment; in Pilâtre's they were allowed to associate with the creative males who made those objects, but only to attract more of them to the association and to overcome their own prejudices about the unattractiveness of men and their science.

Unlike the philosophes who wrote *éloges* of the great salonnières of the 1770s, the men who founded musées in the 1780s saw no necessary role for women in shaping and governing the social and intellectual space of the Republic of Letters. Women were an attraction and a desired object, but they were no longer an active, ordering force. In defining these new institutions and delimiting the role that women were allowed to play in them, men took their lead not from the salons but from the Masonic lodges. The memberships in musées and lodges overlapped significantly, and despite the important differences between them, we can see the similarity in how they regulated and circumscribed women's role.

Increased Competition and the Struggle for Survival

In January 1782, a month after the *Mémoires Secrets* announced the new Musée de Monsieur, La Blancherie fought back, seeking and gaining permission to allow women into his meetings. However, the *Mémoires* commented, "since his rival has the same ability, [he] cannot flatter himself that he will draw in the crowd that has turned away from him to run to the other, who, in turn, has given him the final blow by also receiving amateurs free of charge."[122] Not only had Pilâtre received the privilege of admitting women to his association, but he was also allowed to do exactly what La Blancherie had been restrained from doing when his informal meetings were formalized through the official regulations: hold open house. With his powerful patrons and connections, Pilâtre had managed to establish an institution that had all the attractions La Blancherie had been denied, and the loss of which had turned his free and open space for the Republic of Letters into a closed club of men of consequence.

In April the *Mémoires* reported that La Blancherie was now using publicity to fight back. He had sent a letter to the editor of the *Journal de Paris* advertising his *Correspondance générale et gratuite pour les sciences et les arts*, and the *Mémoires* was reporting on the contents of the published letter.[123] In it La Blancherie reminded the public that those who could benefit from joining his association included not only scholars and men of letters but also "all those people to whom their communication can be useful and agreeable. *This is its goal.*" He emphasized that he offered a "*free [gratuit]* capital for correspondence concerning details relative to the sciences and the arts." This "capital" served two functions, coordinating "the correspondence by letters and by people." The *Mémoires* went on to recall the history of La Blancherie's financial difficulties and to report that the restructuring of the previous year had been so successful that the enterprising La Blancherie was now resolved to use his surplus to reimburse needy artists. The following day, the *Mémoires* reported that La Blancherie intended to take over the defunct Société Libre d'Emulation. To administer the new association

122. *Mémoires Secrets*, 3 January 1782.
123. Ibid., 22 April 1782.

he had formed a committee that reflected what were now two categories of patrons: "the protectors" and "the associates or protégés." This division, observed the *Mémoires*, "must not greatly please everyone."[124] Inexorably, financial constraints were shaping the social and political structure of the association, despite La Blancherie's efforts to make it free and open.

By 28 October the *Mémoires* was expressing amazement at the success of "the indefatigable M. de La Blancherie," who was continuing his publicity campaign and raking in patrons, ordinary subscribers, and cash. Before the year was out it reported in utter dismay that "one is inundated more and more with advertisements from founders of Musées that have been teeming for the last two months: M. de La Blancherie, the first of all these literary charlatans, is being extolled without letup in all the foreign and national gazettes."[125] Pilâtre de Rozier put out a new prospectus for his Musée, parading the names of his illustrious patrons and vaunting the salonlike atmosphere he offered. And a new competitor, the abbé Edmond Cordier de St. Firmin, had entered the lists with a Musée Littéraire, which, it was feared, would draw the public away from the more scientific establishments with its attractions of "several pretty women, enchanting music, likable poets, [and] eloquent orators."[126] At the other extreme was the Museum or Club Politique, which had been established in April by the foreign correspondent Pascal Boyer. He promoted and received authorization from the ministry for his establishment as an alternative to the unruly free discussions that took place daily in the gardens of the Palais Royal—but on condition that it would concern itself with neither "the government nor religion, and that women would not be admitted." The *Mémoires Secrets* added: "One certainly suspects that there will necessarily be some emissary, acknowledged or not, of the police who will watch over these assemblies."[127]

124. Ibid., 23 April 1782.
125. Ibid., 17 November 1782.
126. Ibid. Cordier de Saint-Firmin's musée had broken off from Court de Gébelin's Musée de Paris. Another group of "dissidents" rented space from Pilâtre toward the end of 1783. See Amiable, "Origines maçonniques," for the complicated history of divisions and rivalries within the Musée de Paris.
127. *Mémoires Secrets*, 1 and 4 April 1782. On Boyer, see Popkin, *News and Politics*, pp. 72–74. An English visitor to Paris in the summer of 1776 described the scene in the Palais Royal: "These gardens furnish a charming and a very rational amusement. They consist of long walks separated by rows of trees, and those over some of the walks are bent into an arch. These walks are often extremely full of well-dressed people, and there are common chairs under the trees on each side of the walk. Where any of the company are disposed to sit, a party draw their chairs into a circle and enter into lively, gallant, or philosophic conversations as they are disposed; and they all seem very sociable and happy. Everything here seems to lead to sociability and the pleasure of conversation as

Not only had La Blancherie's enterprise survived, but it had inspired the founding of others like it. With increased competition, however, La Blancherie was employing ever more creative means to keep his establishment afloat. In August 1783 it was reported that he had raised funds by using his meeting rooms as a concert hall and ballroom the previous winter and then had decided to use them as an art gallery, kicking things off with a Vernet show. This last idea, however, had cost him, for it brought him into a continuing struggle between the Academy of Painting and its rivals which had begun in 1776, when the academy forced the dissolution of the Academy of Saint-Luc, an artisanal corporation of nonroyal painters.[128] In 1777 the comte d'Angiviller, who oversaw artistic matters for the monarchy, had forced the Colysée, a general pleasure space, to close down because it had dared to mount exhibitions of paintings and even to issue catalogs of them. At the time, the *Mémoires Secrets* had noted its surprise, for it saw the Colysée, in its diverse activities, as much more than a rival to the official salons of painting.[129]

Now in 1783 the academy again complained that its privileges were being violated, despite the fact that it had endorsed La Blancherie's original prospectus five years earlier.[130] Even more annoying, La Blancherie had given his establishment the new name of Salon de la Correspondance, which the academy must have seen as a reference to their salons. For d'Angiviller, this was the last straw, and in November he ordered La Blancherie to close down.[131] With the support of his patrons, La Blancherie again fought back. He refused to recognize the authority of d'Angiviller and went before the Conseil des Dépêches to ask that the harassment cease and that he be issued the letters patent that would give his establishment proper legal standing. While he awaited a decision, he was granted permission to operate. In January, however, La Blancherie conceded defeat and announced the final meeting of his general assembly.[132]

---

the *chief end of Man*" (Thomas Bentley, *Journal of a Visit to Paris, 1776*, ed. Peter France [Brighton, 1977], p. 31).

128. Jules Guiffrey, "Histoire de l'Académie de Saint-Luc," *Archives de l'Art Français*, n.s. 9 (Paris, 1925).

129. See *Mémoires Secrets*, 2 August 1777. The whole affair is chronicled in the entries of 18 August and 6 September 1776; 31 July, 11 September, 29 September, and 5 October 1777. See John Goodman, "'Altar against Altar,'" for an excellent history of the various arts establishments of the 1770s and their struggles with d'Angiviller.

130. Mulot, "Journal intime," p. 38. Clearly it was the mounting of exhibitions and possibly the issuing of catalogs that the academy and its protector found threatening. The idea of a meeting space for artists and amateurs, a public salon modeled on Geoffrin's Mondays, was seen as a useful idea.

131. *Mémoires Secrets*, 20 August, 24 November 1783.

132. Ibid., 24 November 1783, 17 January 1784.

With La Blancherie (temporarily) out of the picture (his establishment would rise one more time), competitors old and new sought to profit from his defeat. Pilâtre increased his subscribers and his revenues substantially over the course of the next year. In December 1784 the *Mémoires Secrets* reported that he had 40,000 livres in subscriptions at La Blancherie's expense. In April it had announced the opening of a Lycée de Paris "on the ruins" of La Blancherie's "musée."[133]

When the police tried to shut down the musées in 1786 on the grounds that seditious remarks had been made in them, they failed, "experiencing in regard to this subject a resistance to which [they] felt obliged to give way."[134] The failed attempt suggests the desperation of the monarchy in the closing weeks of the year that would end in the calling of the Assembly of Notables.

In the flurry of those final weeks of 1786, the *Mémoires Secrets* noted its surprise at *not* learning of the reopening of La Blancherie's Salon de la Correspondance, which had previously been "announced each year with so much emphasis." The *Mémoires* had never thought much of La Blancherie, but now that his struggle was finally over (and this time it really was), it gave him credit for his achievement (while reporting on his 40,000 livres of debt) and pointed to his eight-year struggle with economic and political adversity as a lesson for those who would emulate him: "This fate of the first founder of all the lycées, musées, clubs, and other establishments of this sort, is the same that threatens those who, seeking to give themselves, at the public's expense, a rather precarious stability, have in the same way no more resources to sustain it."[135]

La Blancherie did fail in the end, but not without leaving behind a legacy in the form of a new sort of institution of intellectual sociability. He was a model for other young men who would launch projects of association for a Republic of Letters shaped by the project of enlightenment but too big, too public, and too self-assured for the feminine space of the salon. The musées situated the Republic of Letters square-

---

133. Ibid., 18 December, 28 April 1784. The printed prospectus bore the title *Lycée de Paris: Club littéraire qu'on va former dans les bâtimens nouveaux du Palais Royal, sous la protection immédiate de S. A. A. Monseigneur le duc de Chartres, & sous la direction de M. Bassi* (Paris, 1784). It refers back to Addison and Steele and the English club tradition while rehearsing many of the themes from La Blancherie and Pilâtre.

134. "Mémoires de J.-P. Lenoir," p. 235. The "seditious remarks" were probably a speech given by Condorcet in what had been the Musée de Monsieur but was now, after the tragic death of its founder in June 1785, refinanced, placed under the direct administrative control of the comte de Provence, reorganized along more pedagogical lines, and renamed the Lycée. The scandal it caused was reported in the *Mémoires Secrets*, 20–26 November 1786. On the Lycée, see Taton, "Condorcet et Lacroix," pp. 130–53.

135. *Mémoires Secrets*, 21 November 1786.

ly in a masculine public sphere that both displaced women from its center and directly challenged the monarchy.

The revolution that transformed the Republic of Letters began not in 1789 but in 1778, when men began to meet without the supervision of women in an assembly organized by Pahin de La Blancherie, the self-styled general agent of the Republic of Letters. When the literary public sphere was transformed into the political public sphere in 1789, it had already become masculine; the "democratic" republic of 1792 would reflect the limitations and exclusions of the Republic of Letters of the 1780s.

good to locate the moment but the question 'why' is still unanswerd.

correspondance

polite conversation

Salon

La Blancherie 1780s

Musée

correspondance association

Brissot's career shows this transition

1790s

Political Public S.

Cercle social Amis de la vérité

Bouche de fer

Political for Public at Large

Popular society

Jacobin Club

CONCLUSION

The Enlightenment Republic of Letters and the French Revolution

C'est de la République des Lettres que nous atten-
dons le triomphe du patriotisme et de la Vérité.

— *Le Tribun du Peuple*

Qui pourrait résister à la confédération des écrivains généreux qui vont former le directoire du
Cercle social, et fonder une correspondance active
dans la République des Lettres?

— *La Bouche de Fer*

The person who most closely followed La Blancherie in trying to establish a center for the Republic of Letters was not a rival but a disciple, Jacques-Pierre Brissot de Warville, who would go on to play an important role in the French Revolution. Brissot and his various activities in the 1780s provide a key to understanding how the Enlightenment Republic of Letters was transformed into a revolutionary Republic of Letters, which continued the quest for a Parisian center through the discursive practices of correspondence and association but without the governance of women.

Brissot's Lycée de Londres

On 17 January 1784, in the same entry in which d'Angiviller's victory over La Blancherie was announced, the *Mémoires Secrets* also informed its readers of a new venture inspired by him: "While M. *Brissot de Varville* establishes in *London* a *Lycée*, or Assembly and Correspondence for the meeting and communication of Men [*Gens*] of Letters of all countries," it reported, "the establishment of M. de *la Blancherie*, which has served as a model for it, collapses and falls."[1] Brissot later explained that he had decided to establish his lycée in London partly because he was concerned about the lack of communication between English and French scholars, writers, and readers and also because he did not believe it was possible to establish a free association within France, where government interference was constant.[2] Anyone who had observed the trials and tribulations of La Blancherie and the machinations of Pilâtre to drum up influential patrons and academic credentials would have come to the same conclusion. Indeed, Mercier made the point explicitly in his chapter "Musées" in the *Tableau de Paris*: "Every public assembly is too contrary to the spirit of the French government," he concluded,

> and every society that does not make its own laws and that receives them, cannot either maintain itself, or cherish its work. These sorts of establishments seem to me impractical because in Paris relationships are only superficial, and because the prohibitions are so easy, so compounded, that nothing is required but the foolish report of a subaltern, or the bad mood of a bureaucrat, to dissolve the assembly of the men who are the most enlightened and the most animated by the public good.[3]

Brissot's Lycée de Londres was to consist of three parts: a regular assembly of scholars; a correspondence into which Brissot would enter with all the members and whose center he would be; and a periodical publication whose purpose was to make works in English known to French readers.[4] Like La Blancherie, Brissot was concerned to explain that he was not merely proposing a new journal. He adopted the form of a journal, he explained in his prospectus of 1783, simply to attract the public. "A volume would scare the majority of readers," he wrote, whereas a pamphlet "tempts them, it is read, and the good is done."[5] As to the title, *Correspondance Universelle* . . . , he chose it over *Annales, Journaux,* and *Mémoires* because he saw the correspondence as the "means by which all useful memoirs are collected and published" (4).

1. The prospectus for the Lycée de Paris, also printed in 1784, mentioned that "London itself has recently come to accommodate the project of a Frenchman who has announced the *Lycée de Londres*": Bassi, *Lycée de Paris*, p. 6.

2. [Jacques-Pierre Brissot de Warville], *Mémoires de Brissot . . . sur ses contemporains, et la Révolution Française*, ed. F. de Montrol, 4 vols. (Paris, 1830), 2:218.

3. Mercier, *Tableau de Paris* 6:261.

4. Brissot, *Mémoires* 2:218–19.

5. [Jacques-Pierre Brissot de Warville], *Correspondance universelle sur ce qui intéresse le bonheur de l'homme et de la société* (Neuchâtel, 1783), no. 1, p. 3, hereafter cited in the text.

Brissot's innovation was to focus on what he called "observers." In the spirit of the Enlightenment Republic of Letters, he congratulated his own age for having finally freed itself from the "systematic spirit" of Descartes to arrive at last at observation.[6] The problem now was how to develop and coordinate observers and observations; the solution was communication. Like Diderot and d'Alembert before him, Brissot asked how enlightenment could proceed with "strokes of light still scattered around."

> If good observations are made, they are circumscribed in a narrow circle, and the good that they achieve is local. The memoirs of observers, after having occupied several meetings in an academy, are soon forgotten, and good ideas evaporate while the bad ones continue to subsist. Moreover, writers get tired of fighting, of seeing themselves fighting uselessly. To some energy is lacking, to others a circumstance proper to develop it, to all a center of reunion to render their efforts useful.
>
> The correspondence that we are announcing will bring an end to these obstacles; it will form this center where all the ideas, the observations, the facts, the projects relative to the happiness of the individual and society will come together; from there enlightenment will spread and circulate throughout Europe. (10–11)

Whereas La Blancherie had cautiously noted those areas of inquiry and criticism which his correspondence would avoid so as not to threaten the monarchy, Brissot surveyed the vast intellectual and political landscape he would tackle, ranging forthrightly through human rights, criminal law, police, morality, education, and *éloges* of statesmen and men of letters. "To say what is, what may be useful or harmful to social man, this is our object," he proclaimed boldly (12).

The range of knowledge and issues to be handled was matched in Brissot's plan only by the range of people he invited to enter the subscription list as observers. In the tradition of Bacon and the *Encyclopédie*, he recognized the need for a "crowd" of observers to achieve a task so enormous that no single Cartesian man could tackle it. His mission was to establish "a center where all the relations reach their end, where they are put in order, where they are published." Observers would be

6. He seems here to be confusing Voltaire's distinction between the philosophic *esprit systématique* and the Cartesian *esprit de système*. Mercier had written similarly in a chapter of the *Tableau de Paris* titled "De différens observateurs": "In a capital one must have a great number of men who work at the edifice of the sciences. Reduced to a small number, they would do less: what eludes one, rewards the vigil of the other. What chance, that sovereign of the human sciences, furnishes, would pass before inattentive and distracted eyes; but they are open today, and they watch nature incessantly" (2:137). Like Suzanne Necker, the observers imagined by Mercier and Brissot are paying attention.

drawn from "all countries, all governments, all classes, and even both sexes" (21).

In tune with his decade, Brissot invited the full range of "observers" both because he was advertising for paying subscribers and because he saw in each group a particular perspective that would help to complete the empirical work he envisioned. That is, he did not simply seek a large, undifferentiated mass of individual observer-subscribers but identified specific groups whose observations only they could make; the role of each observer was circumscribed by the class he or she represented. Women, for example, were endowed by nature "with a sagacity that renders them especially proper to observe," and thus they would "instruct us concerning early education, the passions that move the human heart, whose labyrinth perhaps they alone can illuminate" (21–22). Brissot's project was encyclopedic in regard to persons and to knowledge; both fell into fields and classes in need of organization for their full utility to be realized.

Brissot's boldness, however, was tempered in accordance with the principles of the Republic of Letters. Proclaiming utility and truth to be his sole guides, he claimed that his would be the first work "unsullied either by partisan spirit or by indecent critiques." It would thus serve as the "honorable repository for new discoveries, for projects born of the love of humanity" (23). He had no intention to "write the satire of any government, to seek to weaken the ties that unite sovereign to subjects, to wish to shake any throne: a reproach so many times made against the philosophes." True philosophes, he asserted, were in no way seditious (23–24). As Thomas had described the man of letters almost twenty years earlier, Brissot now presented himself to the subscribing public and the policing state: as a model citizen. In the language of the 1780s, he could also add that among those whom fortune had placed near the throne were men who "respect public opinion, and the writers who direct it; without doubt, these ministers will welcome this project" (24). Kings, ministers, and subjects would all have to support such a useful project, and Brissot called on men of letters inside and outside academies whose primary attachment was to the search for moral and political truths to join him. "In uniting our efforts, we could render men both better and happier!" (25).

Like Pilâtre and the other founders of musées after La Blancherie, Brissot envisaged an association from the very beginning, but like La Blancherie, he retained epistolary periodical publication as an integral part of his plan. Between December 1782 and November 1783 Brissot managed to publish twelve numbers of the *Correspondance Universelle*; in January 1784 he inaugurated the *Journal du Licée de Londres*.[7] The lycée,

7. *J. P. Brissot: Correspondance et papiers*, ed. Cl. Perroud (Paris, 1912), pp. xxv, xxvii;

however, never opened. Even in England, it seems, the obstacles to forming a free association were too great for a French citizen of the Republic of Letters to overcome. Brissot never really got on his feet economically, but the blow that wiped him out was political: in July 1784 he found himself in the Bastille, "implicated," as his biographer puts it, "in the production of certain libels."[8] That was the end of his London venture.

When Brissot wrote his memoirs in the 1790s, he infused the account of his London project with a revolutionary spirit that rings falsely anachronistic. Only now, he claimed, could he make explicit the revolutionary intentions behind his plan to open a center for the Republic of Letters:

> In order to demolish despotism, I formed a project that seemed to me infallible. It was necessary, in order to prepare a general insurrection against the absolute governments, to enlighten minds ceaselessly, not by means of well-reasoned and weighty works, since the people do not read them; but by means of small writings, such as those spread by Voltaire to destroy religious superstition; by way of a journal that would spread the light in all directions.[9]

In retrospect, Brissot could represent the lycée as the work of a revolutionary. As its founder, he was the link between Voltaire and the Revolution. "I had remarked that if philosophical books were the best vehicle of political revolutions, great obstacles were opposed to their efficacy," he continued, making explicit the connection between *philosophie* and revolution. "Full of this idea," he explained, "I imagined that the project of spreading the great political principles in France would be easily effected if the intrepid and enlightened friends of liberty could unite, communicate their ideas and compose their works in a place where they could be printed and circulate throughout the earth."[10] The only place where that was possible was Voltaire's land of liberty, England.

At this point in his narrative, Brissot went beyond representing the

---

[Brissot], *Journal du Licée de Londres, ou Tableau de l'état présent des sciences et des arts en Angleterre* (Paris, 1784).

8. Eloise Ellery, *Brissot de Warville: A Study in the History of the French Revolution* (Boston, 1915), p. 27. Whether or not Brissot in fact was guilty and whether or not he subsequently became a police spy have been the subjects of heated contemporary and historical debate, as well as vehement denials by Brissot. For the latest rounds, see Darnton, *Literary Underground*, chap. 2; the challenge to it by Frederick A. de Luna, "The Dean Street Style of Revolution: J.-P. Brissot," *French Historical Studies* 17 (Spring 1991): 159–90; and Darnton's response to the challenge, "Brissot Dossier."

9. Brissot, *Mémoires* 2:60–61.

10. Ibid., 2:61.

project of Enlightenment as the Revolution, and the philosophe (himself) as the revolutionary: he claimed that the lycée had been a "cover" meant to hide his revolutionary aims. "To announce such a project openly, would be to sink it," he wrote; "it was necessary to give it a cover to fool the cabinet of Versailles, and this cover was quite natural."

> I imagined executing in London a part of the establishment for the sciences and the arts created by Lablancherie in Paris. I would form there a lycée, a museum, where, on certain days of the week, scholars, philosophes from the whole universe, would meet, and where all the productions of the arts would be brought together; I dreamed also of a journal consecrated to the propagation of the results of these scientific meetings, and which would serve as a passport for the philosophical and political truths with which it was necessary to inoculate all French minds.[11]

But the same Old Regime economic and political constraints that had plagued all men of letters who had tried to form similar institutions in the 1780s operated against Brissot's lycée. In his memoirs he transformed economic failure into political fiction so as to construct a self-justificatory narrative. In so doing Brissot created the veil that conspiracy theorists from Augustin Barruel to Augustin Cochin have since said lay over the "real intentions" of the philosophes. Brissot created it in order to legitimate himself as a revolutionary *avant la lettre* before the tribunal of the Terror. His retrospective fiction should not color our understanding of the young Brissot's quite typical experience as an enterprising young citizen of the Republic of Letters of his day, inspired by its general agent, Pahin de La Blancherie.

Robert Darnton has given us a very different picture of Brissot as the consummate outsider, the failure whose *ressentiment* drove him to tear down the literary establishment of the Republic of Letters and the rest of the Old Regime with it.[12] He argues that Brissot's failure in London and his subsequent incarceration in the Bastille marked his failure *as a philosophe*, turning him first into a police spy, then into a Grub Street hack, and finally into a liar and a revolutionary—a fallen man. "The story of his spying deserves emphasis," Darnton asserts,

> not in order to pass judgment on Brissot, but in order to understand him. His *embastillement* did not prove the purity of his patriotism, as he argued later. It corrupted him, and in the corrupting it confirmed his hatred of the Old Regime. . . . No wonder that his rage broke out during the Revolution in declamations against the debauchery of Lenoir and the

11. Ibid., 2:62.
12. Darnton, *Literary Underground*, pp. 41–70; Darnton, "Brissot Dossier."

other men at the top of the Ancien Régime: they had deflowered the earnest young bourgeois who had left Chartres to pursue the dream of becoming a philosophe.[13]

Brissot maintained that he was always both a philosophe and a revolutionary; Darnton assumes that this was impossible because the two were radically opposed. "Once the Revolution came, the opposition between the high- and low-life of literature had to be resolved. Grub Street rose, overthrew *le monde*, and requisitioned the positions of power and prestige. It was a cultural revolution." Within Brissot himself a moral transformation had to occur, a corruption of the philosophe through the need for money, to turn him into the "typical" revolutionary whose opposite we have already met: Suard, the "typical" late Enlightenment philosophe.[14]

Whereas Suard worked successfully within the system of salon and court patronage, Darnton says, Brissot failed, and along with his fellow failures, who seethed with resentment not only against Lenoir and the police but against the Suards of the salons (presumably both husband and wife), he rode the Revolution when 1789 came around. While Suard lay low and, coward that he was, betrayed his friend Condorcet —the only real philosophe left—Brissot, the failure in the Republic of Letters, became prominent and prosperous.[15] Of course, Brissot also became a victim of the Jacobin Terror, and although he expressed Rousseauean ideas during the Revolution and even identified with Rousseau when the Terror could turn anyone into a paranoiac, he was also the Brissot of the Brissotins and the Cercle Social—a friend, colleague, and collaborator of Mercier, Roland, and Condorcet.

The issue here, as Darnton himself emphasizes, is not just the character and career of one man but the relationship between the Enlightenment Republic of Letters and the French Revolution. Brissot figured that relationship as a hidden continuity by claiming in his memoirs that his actions as a citizen of the Enlightenment Republic of Letters masked and were motivated by his aims as a revolutionary. Darnton unmasks Brissot by arguing that he was never pure, either politically or philosophically, because he sold out to support his family after failing to make it in a Republic of Letters that was a "lie."[16] The poverty induced by this failure changed Brissot's life by making him vulnerable to the corruption entailed in writing for pay and spying for the police. His seething resentment against those who corrupted him turned him

13. Darnton, *Literary Underground*, pp. 43 and 68.
14. Ibid., pp. 37, 3, 69; Darnton, "Brissot Dossier," p. 192.
15. Darnton, *Literary Underground*, pp. 20–21, 69.
16. Ibid., p. 23.

into a revolutionary. As a revolutionary, however, Brissot was forced to become a liar, to fashion himself as pure and thus to deny the very process that had transformed him from a philosophe into a revolutionary. In unmasking Brissot as a liar and a spy, Darnton seeks to reveal the process by which revolutionaries—and by them the Revolution—were formed.

There is a continuity between the Enlightenment Republic of Letters and the French Revolution to be found in Brissot's life. It lies not, however, in the deep-seatedness of his revolutionary aims but in his continuation of the practices of the Republic of Letters. These practices are most evident in Brissot's project for the Lycée de Londres and his membership in the revolutionary Cercle Social; they are articulated in a speech on the "utility of patriotic and popular societies," which he gave at the Jacobin Club on 28 September 1791. Through Brissot we can see how the Enlightenment Republic of Letters was transformed into a revolutionary Republic of Letters.

The Cercle Social and the Jacobin Club

Brissot was the most important political leader in the Cercle Social, and the Cercle Social was at the heart of the revolutionary Republic of Letters from 1790 to 1793.[17] The Cercle Social actually began in the fall of 1789 with a group of fifteen men associated with the radical priest Claude Fauchet. As they represented themselves, this group was "composed of old friends, united by principles and by feelings since long before the birth of the National Assembly."[18] Brissot was one of them. On 21 February 1790 the following announcement appeared in the *Moniteur*:

> Under the name of Cercle social, a new establishment has just been formed which deserves to be distinguished from that crowd of associations that print newssheets. A *bouche de fer*, placed in front of a shop, rue du Théâtre-de-la-Nation, receives all the opinions [*avis*], letters, memoirs or complaints that are thrown in. By this means, those who wish to unmask abuses while remaining anonymous are assured of doing so. The box is opened once a day in the presence of the Cercle social, and the most salient and useful pieces are printed under the title of *Bouche de fer*.
>
> This sort of public censure [*censure*], quite different from royal censor-

17. Gary Kates, *The "Cercle Social," the Girondins, and the French Revolution* (Princeton, 1985), p. 76; Marcel Dorigny, "Le Cercle social, ou Les Ecrivains au cirque," in *La Carmagnole des muses: L'Homme de lettres et l'artiste dans la Révolution*, ed. Jean-Claude Bonnet (Paris, 1988), pp. 49–50. I depend on both of these fine studies for my understanding of the Cercle Social.

18. Quoted in Kates, "*Cercle Social*," pp. 55–56.

ship [*censure*], is one of the surest guarantees of liberty, since it offers to each individual the means to make known the abuses that he discovers, his projects for improvement, and in general, public opinion, against which it would be vain to rise up.[19]

The "iron mouth" had its origins in the civic space of Renaissance politics, where it had been used for denunciations of spies and heretics; in Augustan England, it had become an institution of the Republic of Letters when Addison adopted it as the letter box for the *Guardian*, successor to the *Tatler* and the *Spectator*. He placed it conveniently at the door of a coffeehouse.[20] The Cercle Social drew upon the entire tradition in instituting the *bouche de fer* as the means by which public opinion, in its new and broadest sense, could be collected by a group of men of letters whose role it was to articulate and represent it. The men of letters who formed the Cercle Social cast this same activity in a Rousseauean mold when they fused the notion of public opinion with that of the general will, making the *bouche de fer* the direct repository of the will of the people. They collapsed the opposition between Rousseau and the philosophes by collecting, editing, and publishing anonymous letters.[21]

The Cercle Social did maintain the distinction between men of letters and the public, however. Its members limited association to themselves and invited other men of letters to join them in editing the letters they received. They connected with the public via a mediated system of communication that was epistolary and printed. They gave their name to the journal in which they represented public opinion and the general will to the reading public, but the Cercle Social and the *Cercle Social* remained distinct entities. As men of letters had before them, this group, whose very basis was the friendship that characterized relations in the Republic of Letters, acted, Gary Kates explains, "as a kind of enlightened window." Now, however, it was "the desire of the people [which] could be more clearly seen" through it. The mediating and representative function of the Republic of Letters was in this way adapted to the revolutionary moment.[22]

19. Quoted in Dorigny, "Cercle social," p. 49.

20. Kates, "*Cercle Social,*" p. 56 n. 54.

21. Ibid., pp. 56–57; Dorigny, "Cercle social," p. 54; Baker, *Inventing the French Revolution*, p. 25. It is significant that letters could be anonymous. In the eighteenth century there were no mailboxes, and letters were paid for by the receiver, rather than stamped by the sender, to guard against anonymous letters. The decision of the Cercle Social to accept, indeed encourage, anonymous letters is a further indication of the merging of the closed traditions of Venetian and Rousseauean notions of censure with the open exchange of the Republic of Letters and the conception of public opinion derived from it. See Goodman, "Epistolary Property," in Brewer and Staves, *Conceptions of Property*.

22. Kates, "*Cercle Social,*" pp. 56–57.

In October 1790 the friends who formed the Cercle Social expanded
the limits of their association beyond the salon model of friendship to
the musée model of membership, just as Pahin de La Blancherie had
done a decade before. They broke open the Cercle Social, replacing the
journal that had carried that name with a new one whose title, *Bouche de
Fer*, emphasized the openness of the mailbox rather than the closure of
the circle. In it they announced a new association, the Confédération
Universelle des Amis de la Vérité, which would open their *cercle* and
extend the friendship of the Republic of Letters to the subscribing
public. For the first two weeks, entry to the meetings of the new association was free, and five to eight thousand people showed up. Then,
predictably, the founders of the Cercle Social formed themselves into a
"directory," established a set of regulations (now called a "constitution"), and decided to tie membership in the association to subscription
to the journal. They also offered reciprocal privileges (free membership) to members of competing associations, such as the Jacobins, as
well as to deputies to the National Assembly, just as Pilâtre de Rozier
had done in marketing the Musée de Monsieur. They admitted women
separately from men, and they prohibited them from speaking.[23]

Subscription was not cheap, but the Amis de la Vérité became probably the largest club in France, with a membership that fluctuated between three and six thousand.[24] The scale of this association was thus
radically different from that of the musées, but the Confédération des
Amis de la Vérité otherwise resembled them. Journal subscription remained the basis of association membership, and both meetings and
publication were based on the model pioneered by La Blancherie.

"A magnificent idea brings us together," Claude Fauchet proclaimed
in his opening address to the confederation in October 1790. "It concerns the beginning of the confederation of men, the coming together
of useful truths; tying them into a universal system, getting them accepted into national government; and working in general harmony
with the human spirit to compose world happiness." The directory of
the Cercle Social tried to carve out a special niche for the confederation

23. Ibid., pp. 68–83; Dorigny, "Cercle social," pp. 52–53. Eventually the confederation became the first club to admit women as regular members. Etta Palm d'Aelders gave
a speech there on 30 December 1790: Kates, *"Cercle Social,"* p. 122. This later admission
of women follows the pattern of the musées, although somewhat speeded up, as was
generally true of revolutionary developments. It is certainly significant that women
spoke in the confederation, but it is also worth considering the establishment of a separate Confédération des Amies de la Vérité by Palm in March 1791 (and of Jacobin
women's clubs) as following the pattern of Masonic rather than salon sociability. On the
Amies, see Kates, pp. 124–26; on the Jacobin women's clubs, see Desan, "Constitutional
Amazons," in Ragan and Williams, *Recreating Authority.*

24. Kates, *"Cercle Social,"* p. 83.

by explaining that their aim was neither to found a political club like the Jacobins or the Cordeliers nor to compete with the National Assembly by proposing legislation but to raise and debate the broader political and philosophical questions that would contribute to the formation of public opinion and the general will. The subject matter had already been laid out by Brissot in his prospectus for the Lycée de Londres. As the *Courrier de Lyon* reported in November 1790: "They will discuss all questions relative to politics, religion, legislation, virtue, sociability, and everything which constitutes the rights and happiness of men."[25] "This was the ambition of the Cercle social," writes Marcel Dorigny: "to be the site of a vast public debate, until that time confined to literary circles and to the salons, in order to be projected in the full light of day before public opinion."[26]

As in the musées, each meeting of the Amis de la Vérité began with a speech, followed by a general discussion in which all (men) were free to participate. Secretaries were on hand to record the views expressed. Further speeches were given, and texts were read by authors who were present. Letters and memoirs that had been mailed in or deposited in the *bouche de fer* were also read to the assembly and then published in the *Bouche de Fer*, expanding the epistolary circle through the medium of print. By means of the post, letters came in to the editors from provincial capitals stretching from Strasbourg and Besançon in the east to Brest and Bordeaux in the west. Memoirs and pamphlets were published by the Cercle Social's own press.[27]

In forming the Confédération des Amis de la Vérité, the Cercle Social contributed to the institutional changes that transformed the Enlightenment Republic of Letters into a revolutionary Republic of Letters. "The Cercle social is not a club," the *Bouche de Fer* explained in February 1791. "It is an association of citizens spread all over the globe." The confederation was "a weekly rendezvous of all clubs, societies, and committees."[28] The mission of the Cercle Social was, in Dorigny's words, "the regeneration of the human race begun in America and pursued in France since 1789, an ambition founded on a collective conception of the regenerative role of men of letters."[29] Men of letters had been developing new ways to spread enlightenment for more than half a century; now the Cercle Social had the unprecedented oppor-

25. Quoted ibid., p. 80.
26. Dorigny, "Cercle social," p. 53.
27. Ibid., pp. 53, 55; Kates, "*Cercle Social,*" pp. 82–83. Both Kates and Dorigny devote significant portions of their studies to the Imprimerie du Cercle Social, whose work lies beyond the bounds of my book.
28. Kates, "*Cercle Social,*" p. 93.
29. Dorigny, "Cercle social," p. 57.

tunity to use those practices—unprecedented because the Revolution had not only destroyed despotism but prepared the people to receive the enlightenment that they were in a unique position to give.

In tune with this new imperative, the Cercle Social was ready to change its form again when the political upheaval following the royal family's flight to Varennes erupted on 21 June 1791. Two days later the *Bouche de Fer* announced: "It is time to address ourselves to the most numerous class of citizens."[30] Membership in the confederation was separated from subscription to the *Bouche de Fer*, and the association was opened again to anyone who wanted to attend. The issues discussed at the meetings became more practically political: Rousseau's political theory gave way to discussions of the right to petition. The *bouche de fer* became the repository of political news, as did its journalistic namesake, now a daily account of events rather than a thrice-weekly forum for discussion.[31]

The transformation of the confederation into a popular society was also the culmination of a power struggle between the Cercle Social and the Jacobin Club which had begun the previous fall, when both groups had tried to establish themselves as the center of an epistolary network of individuals and associations.[32] The Cercle Social envisioned a universal federation centered in Paris. Correspondents would send news to the *Bouche de Fer* from the provincial cities of France and Europe and would report on the progress of the "cercle social" itself. Secondary centers would serve as mediating channels, but "the points of correspondence will go out from each of these individual centers in order to arrive at the general center: thus the federative system will be universal and, however, reduced to a unity, the necessary form of perfection."[33]

The centralizing drive was also a response to needs expressed by provincial club members. As with the provincial academies, however, centralization was, in the end, resisted. As early as December 1789, a club in Dijon had begun to establish epistolary contacts with other towns in Burgundy; other clubs soon did the same, and the volume of correspondence increased rapidly. As citizens of the Republic of Letters had done before them, the new patriots discovered the high cost in time and especially money which an extensive correspondence entailed. One club petitioned the postal administration for special fixed rates for club correspondence; another advised affiliates to take advan-

30. Kates, "*Cercle Social*," pp. 156–57.

31. Ibid., pp. 159–60.

32. Ibid., pp. 93–96.

33. Dorigny, "Cercle social," pp. 58–59. Kates notes that the letters section of the *Bouche de Fer* was sometimes so long that club news had to be issued in a supplement: "*Cercle Social*," p. 188.

tage of their deputy's franking privileges; the boldest demanded free postal service.[34]

In November 1790, a month after the *Bouche de Fer* began publication, two other solutions were proposed to coordinate correspondence through print: the first was a *Mode de Correspondance pour les Corps Sociétaires de France*, printed as a circular (letter) by the Jacobin Club of Riom; the second was the *Journal des Amis de la Constitution*, whose prospectus emanated from the Paris Jacobin Club.[35] At that time the Paris Jacobins had sent out a circular accusing the Cercle Social of attempting to divide France into "sects." They prohibited their clubs from affiliating with any other club in Paris. Some provincial clubs responded by banning the reading of Cercle Social publications at their meetings. Despite attempts by the Cercle Social to establish itself as the center of a network of correspondence and association through appeals in the *Bouche de Fer*, it could not overcome either the more authoritarian tactics or the disinformation campaign of its Parisian rival.[36]

When the prospectus for the Jacobins' *Journal des Amis de la Constitution* appeared shortly after the circular from Riom that November, many clubs apparently believed that the *Journal* was the *Mode de Correspondance* that the Riom club had asked Paris to establish. The first issue did in fact devote about half its space to summaries of letters received. Its editor, Choderlos de Laclos, the author of *Les Liaisons dangereuses*, the pinnacle of the French epistolary novel, was, of course, an old hand at epistolary editing. The clubs, however, wanted unedited correspondence, not an epistolary text; requests were made to print all the correspondence unedited and thus to have the *Journal* serve as a perfect substitute for the post. But the *Journal*, like the *Cercle Social*, the *Bouche de Fer*, and eighteenth-century journals from the *Spectator* to the *Mercure*, retained its mediative editorial role. By February the Beaune club, which had decided in December to depend on the *Journal* for its mail, announced that it could not do so. Other clubs were also dissatisfied with the *Journal* as a substitute for correspondence, and on 19 February the Riom club, protesting that the *Journal* did not fulfill the "need for an organ of general correspondence," went back to proposing a new method of reducing postal costs.

Laclos responded to the criticism and to the appearance of a new daily called the *Mercure Universel*, which proclaimed itself a "central point of correspondence," by offering to print an epistolary supplement to the *Journal* if one hundred clubs agreed to subscribe at addi-

34. Kates, "*Cercle Social*," p. 94; Kennedy, *Jacobin Clubs*, pp. 11–12, 15–16, 19–20, 36.
35. Kennedy, *Jacobin Clubs*, pp. 67–70.
36. Ibid., p. 60. See also Gueniffey and Halévi, "Clubs and Popular Societies," in Furet and Ozouf, *Critical Dictionary*, pp. 458–72.

tional and prohibitive cost. In the end, the *Journal* failed as a correspondence, and the clubs went back to direct epistolary exchange, but they retained their associational affiliation with the Jacobins.[37] By the spring the Cercle Social had pretty much lost the battle to the Jacobins over the associational form of the club network and who would be the center of the Revolution and the revolutionary Republic of Letters.

In the new political climate after the flight to Varennes in June 1791, the Paris Jacobins split between republicans and Orléanists. The Cercle Social went republican. On 17 July, while five thousand Parisians gathered at the Champ de Mars to petition the National Assembly to rescind its decision to reinstate the king, Nicolas Bonneville, the editor of the *Bouche de Fer*, composed a letter to the Jacobins in which he proposed the expulsion of the Orléanists and the merging of the two clubs. Such a union would resolve the conflict between the two rival centers and strengthen the revolutionary cause by establishing a single confederation and a single network of correspondence and association. "A society where there will be such enlightenment, energy, and effective power, can save liberty by a universal correspondence, at the center of which will be only truth, common to all," he wrote.[38]

On the Champ de Mars, martial law was declared, and National Guard troops fired on the demonstrators, killing a dozen of them. Four days later, Bonneville announced that the Confédération des Amis de la Vérité would cease to meet; a week later the directory of the Cercle Social announced that the *Bouche de Fer* would cease publication. Neither ever appeared again, and the name of the Cercle Social was thereafter given over exclusively to the publishing business.[39] In the end, the competition between the Cercle Social and the Jacobins to be the center of an epistolary network of revolutionary association contributed to the collapse of the confederation and the merger of its leadership into the Jacobin Club in the fall of 1791. The Cercle Social printing house soon became the unofficial press of a Jacobin club led by Brissot and his friends from the Cercle Social; the Jacobin Club, in turn, became the social and political base of the political party that was known by contemporaries as the Brissotins.[40]

On 28 September 1791 Brissot, now the president of the Jacobin Club, gave a speech to the assembled members on "the utility of patri-

37. Kennedy, *Jacobin Clubs*, pp. 68–72. Eventually the *Journal* itself went under, as virtually all journals and newspapers did, for reasons that were economic and political as well as editorial and epistolary. On the periodical press, see Jeremy D. Popkin, *Revolutionary News: The Press in France, 1789–1799* (Durham, 1990).

38. Kates, "*Cercle Social*," pp. 169–70.

39. Ibid., pp. 170–71.

40. Ibid., p. 172 and pt. 3.

otic and popular societies."[41] The speech was a defense against the attempt by the Constituent Assembly to close the clubs because of the danger they allegedly posed as centers of sedition. "Wishing to deliberate," the indictment read, "they usurp political power, they impede the administration in its work, [so] that it is necessary to deny them the faculty of deliberation and to reduce them to the status of those societies in which pleasure and curiosity bring individuals together" (1–2).

Mere pleasure and curiosity had never been the basis of association for either Brissot or the Republic of Letters: utility was. Now, in the revolutionary Republic of Letters, Brissot pushed the principle of utility further, extending it to the necessity of forming associations with the single purpose of political discussion. "It must be proved," Brissot argued, "that patriotic societies have the right to discuss political matters, and must not cease doing so; that the revolution can be consolidated only in multiplying societies in every class of the citizenry; that the spirit of equality can be preserved only by the perpetual mixing of Functionaries and the Citizens in these societies" (2). The right of the people to assemble peaceably, to communicate their ideas, to "shed light" on the conduct of public servants, and to discuss the laws they made was inalienable, Brissot maintained, and no one who had witnessed "the tremendous progress of the public spirit" could deny it. How could these rights be exercised, he asked, except through public assembly? (3–4). Only public discussion could "prepare" good laws because only such discussion could communicate the general will and "general opinion" to the lawmakers (5).

Like philosophes before him, Brissot continued to believe in the primary value of the communication of ideas, of discussion, even as the goal of that exchange shifted from happiness based on knowledge to revolution based on law and law based on the general will and public opinion. The Revolution gave the Republic of Letters a narrower, more political focus and also a broader appeal, but it did not change its basic discursive structures and values. Rather, the Revolution offered these structures and values to the new Republic of France that Brissot and men of letters like him were actively working to form.

Brissot also continued to believe in law itself as the basis of liberty. "The free man wishes the law, obeys the law," he asserted, "but he can believe that the law is worthless" (6). Should he then disobey bad laws? No: "Free men know and get used to obeying a bad law until it is revoked; but in obeying it, these free men occupy themselves with

41. Ibid., p. 199. J[acques]-P[ierre] Brissot [de Warville], *Discours sur l'utilité des sociétés patriotiques et populaires, sur la nécessité de les maintenir et de les multiplier partout* (Montauban, n.d.), hereafter cited in the text.

seeking the means to achieve this revocation. Now, how can that be achieved, if one does not have the liberty to discuss the motives behind the law, the consequences it can entail?" he asked (6–7). Brissot's words echoed those of Diderot, written twenty years earlier in his as-yet-unpublished *Supplément au voyage de Bougainville*: "We will speak out against senseless laws until they are reformed," Diderot had written, "and in waiting, we will submit ourselves to them."[42] Diderot's dialogic *Supplément*, like Galiani's *Dialogues sur les blés*, which had inspired it, was the very model of critical discussion Brissot now advocated. He did not need to have read the *Supplément* to hold Diderot's view: he had himself participated in the movement to reform the French legal system which had begun when Voltaire championed Calas and Morellet published his translation of Beccaria's *On Crimes and Punishments* in the 1760s, and had continued right up to 1789 in hundreds of works written by French men of law and letters.[43] Brissot's own contributions were a *Théorie sur les lois criminelles* (1781), which he dedicated to Voltaire, and a ten-volume *Bibliothèque criminelle du législateur et du philosophe* (1782).

In his speech to the Jacobin Club, Brissot expressed the urgent need to apply the discursive values and practices of the Enlightenment Republic of Letters to the political possibilities opened up by the Revolution. These included the transformation of the public into a free people. "Observe that a people that has once recovered its liberty regresses only with difficulty," he noted; "that the right to reason and to discuss becomes for it a daily need; that if one denies it the faculty to satisfy [that need], it abandons itself to grumbling, to discontent, to insurrection" (11). And reasoning and discussing were properly done in public assemblies, not in closed, private, English-style clubs, which represented partisan spirit, or in cafés and taverns, to which "free men born to assemble [would be] reduced only to satisfy together their animal needs" (16–18). Brissot advocated the increased publicity that followed the path already laid out by the practices of sociability over the course of the eighteenth century.

"The societies are so far from being the antechamber of troubles," Brissot proclaimed, that they are in fact "the surest means of preventing them: because they are the means of perfecting human reason, of spreading it in all classes, of distributing a greater dose to each individual; and individual reason is the true preventative of troubles" (12). The press, too, was necessary for instructing the citizenry and generating debate, but print cost money, whereas popular assembly could be free. "The tribune can supply the dearth of the press," explained Bris-

42. Diderot, *Supplément*, in *Oeuvres philosophiques*, p. 515.
43. See Maza, *Private Lives*, chap. 5.

sot. "A single man can in a single instant at once enlighten a crowd of individuals" (13). "Let us not doubt, Sirs," he continued, "that the final degree of perfection of human reason and public instruction will be in the universal institution, right up to the smallest villages, of these popular clubs, these fraternal societies" (14).[44]

The utility of the clubs lay not simply in the scale of enlightenment that could be achieved in them. Like other men of letters who chafed under the discipline of polite conversation, Brissot found in the Revolution the possibility of that discursive freedom associated with the masculine open-air assemblies of the Germanic barons, the Roman forum, the Athenian lyceum. In the tradition of the *Encyclopédie* and the musées, he targeted royal academies as the institutions opposed to a new discursive liberty. "Liberty forms its friends, its great men quite otherwise, and at much less expense!" he exclaimed. "Disdaining the ostentatious apparatus of scientific chairs that fatten laziness in order to mislead ignorance, it is outdoors, it is without patents, it is in free tribunes, it is in the places open to all men, it is in the midst of a free, animated, large [*nombreuse*] discussion, that it forms its students" (15). In these new forums men would learn to know themselves and their true value; here a truly enlightened discourse would develop, free of insult and contempt, because men would learn not to judge rashly but to reason critically (16). Brissot took the fantasy of masculine self-governance that had shaped the Republic of Letters in the 1780s to new heights, finding in the pure discursive liberty of fraternal popular societies the very basis of both Enlightenment and Revolution.

However, just as the public had become the people in the Cercle Social's formulations, and the general will and public opinion had become indistinguishable, Brissot's notion of enlightenment was now collapsing the distinction between criticism and dogma, reason and enthusiasm, which had been articulated with such insistence by philosophes such as Diderot and Galiani over the course of the eighteenth century. Enlightenment was collapsing into propaganda.

In August 1792 the work of the Cercle Social was subsidized by the Brissotin ministry to the tune of 100,000 livres, used to form a Bureau de l'Esprit Public, a new sort of bureau de correspondance. The epistolary form was now blatantly serving ends that were less critical than dogmatic: the circular letters sent out by the bureau were more like pastoral letters than *lettres persanes*. As its chief, Roland was soon able to report to the Legislative Assembly that he had "multiplied the circular

44. There were, however, arguments on both sides about the relative value and drawbacks of speech and print for revolutionary as well as prerevolutionary enlightenment. As Kates notes, Brissot himself wrote in August 1791 that "the great tribune of humanity has been found: it is the press." See Kates, *"Cercle Social,"* pp. 177–80.

letters," favoring "the distribution of writings that seemed to [him] the most appropriate for enlightening citizens on the state of things and on their true interests."[45] The printing house of the Cercle Social became the press of the government Bureau de l'Esprit Public, publishing newspapers and pamphlets that furthered the embattled cause of the Brissotin ministry.[46]

Athough the Brissotin ministry failed to integrate the practices of the Republic of Letters into the mechanisms of the state, Brissot's ideal of a popular and patriotic society was at its heart the Enlightenment ideal of "constant communication" based on the idea that all men had the right "to communicate their ideas." "Intrigue and corruption," he exclaimed, are "the friends of shadows" (17, 20). Not even the English had attained this ideal, for their closed clubs supported a partisan spirit that French men of letters had always seen as a threat to Enlightenment. Enlightenment, however, now had a directly political meaning and application. "Do you wish to be instructed?" Brissot asked the legislators among his listeners and readers. "Come into this society; you will receive here enlightenment, you will communicate it, and from this fraternal mixture will burst forth the public good. Remember that Cato, leaving the Senate, abandoning his great ideas, learned to be a man by conversing with the people in the public place" (21). Now the people, led by men of letters such as Brissot, would enlighten the legislators through the communicative practice of the Enlightenment Republic of Letters. The salons and musées in which this practice had developed would give way to popular societies, where men, with no one to govern them but themselves, would meet openly, publicly, to discuss among themselves and to communicate with their representatives the results of their discussions. Good legislation would emerge from this practice, not mysteriously but because of its basis in reason and its publicity. "Political operations" need not and ought not to be shrouded in mystery, Brissot argued. "These operations must be founded on reason, and reason has nothing to fear from publicity. It is publicity that must be the force of free legislation; because this force is not in the ideas of a single man, it is in the general will, in public opinion" (21–22).

Diderot and Rousseau would no doubt have been horrified to see how Brissot had resolved the irreconcilable conflict between them by collapsing the distinction between public opinion, with its discursive practices, and the general will whose basis was a radically different epistemology that denied not only representation but discussion itself.

45. Ibid., pp. 235–36.
46. Ibid., pp. 248–50.

"Public deliberation will be one thing," Rousseau had written, "the general will another."[47] For Brissot, the general will and public opinion were the same thing. This new force was more popular and democratic than the public opinion invoked by the men of letters of the Old Regime, but it was articulated through the social and discursive practices of the Republic of Letters. Less Rousseauean than Diderotian or Galianian or Neckerian, it was the revolutionary political ideal of a citizen of the Republic of Letters.

This is not the way Brissot's speech has always been interpreted. Ran Halévi and Patrice Gueniffey have seen in the Jacobin Club under Brissot an "autonomous body" intent on dominating, even tyrannizing over the legally elected Legislative Assembly. "No longer a mere 'thinking society,'" they write, adopting Cochin's pejorative term, "it had become an instrument of power." Rather than see Brissot's defense of the popular societies as a defense of a free and open discursive practice, they interpret it as an assertion of extralegal and extrarepresentational authority.[48] By emphasizing denunciation, discipline, and censure, Halévi and Gueniffey support their argument, based on Furet and Cochin, that all forms of free association—from the "sociétés de pensée" of the Old Regime (whose basis and model were secret Masonic societies) to the clubs of the Revolution—sought not to open public discussion but to close it by imposing their particular will on those they gathered and on the state, first the monarchy, then the elected assemblies. They endorse the position of Deputy Isaac René Guy Le Chapelier, who, four months after his law that denied workers the right to associate passed the Constituent Assembly, and the day after Brissot gave his speech in the Jacobin Club, proclaimed that the Revolution was over and that henceforth any discussion of political matters outside the Assembly could serve no good purpose.[49] "Like all spontaneous institutions formed according to the purest motive—but soon deviating from their goal as a result of considerable change in circumstance and of various other causes," Le Chapelier said in his report to the Assembly,

these popular societies have taken on a kind of political existence they ought not to have.

As long as the Revolution lasted, this state of affairs was almost always more useful than harmful. . . .

But when the Revolution is ended and the constitution of the state is

47. Quoted in Baker, *Inventing the French Revolution*, p. 250. See also Gordon, "Idea of Sociability," pp. 30–31.
48. Gueniffey and Halévi, "Clubs and Popular Societies," in Furet and Ozouf, *Critical Dictionary*, pp. 467–68.
49. Ibid., pp. 468–69.

fixed, when all public powers have been delegated and all the authorities brought into existence by that constitution, then its proper functioning requires that everything be restored to the most perfect order. Nothing must hinder the action of the constituted authorities, deliberation and power must be located where the constitution has placed them.[50]

The day before, the king had announced that the Revolution was over; Le Chapelier, invoking the new constitution, echoed the king. More important, he asserted that with the end of the Revolution must come the end of political discussion outside the legally constituted confines of the Assembly. The Republic of Letters would have to be depoliticized, reduced again to the "literary" role it had played in the seventeenth century. The debate on the fate of the clubs was just the latest site of the contest between the Republic of Letters and the French state, a contest that was fought within each man of letters who was at the same time a citizen of the republic and a subject of the state. As the monarchy turned into a republic, French men of letters found that dual citizenship remained difficult to sustain.

For a moment, Brissot had found himself the leader of the Jacobin Club and the center of a Brissotin ministry; for a moment he seemed in his person and his practices to have merged the Republic of Letters and the French state, just as in his thinking he merged the people with the public and the general will with public opinion. But the moment was an illusion. For it turned out to be impossible (at least for Brissot) to inscribe the principles and practices of the revolutionary Republic of Letters into the revolutionary French state. Indeed, the Jacobin Club itself quickly became an instrument of state propaganda rather than a free discursive institution of the Republic of Letters. The Enlightenment aim of reforming the monarchy on the model of the Republic of Letters remained beyond the abilities of Brissot, despite his unique position as a leading citizen of both polities at the revolutionary moment when it seemed possible at last to bring them together.

A Reevaluation of Tocqueville

At least since Alexis de Tocqueville published *L'Ancien Régime et la Révolution* in 1856, it has been a commonplace of scholarship on the French Revolution that the Enlightenment produced no true political

---

50. "National Assembly Debate on Clubs," trans. Keith Michael Baker, in *University of Chicago Readings in Western Civilization*, vol. 7: *The Old Regime and the French Revolution* (Chicago, 1987), ed. Baker, p. 279.

discourse: the philosophes, we have been taught, were starry-eyed (if rationalist) dreamers who engaged in no more than a "kind of abstract, literary politics," excluded as they were from the domain of "real" practical politics.[51] Indeed, both the "failure" of the Enlightenment and the "utopian" nature of the revolution that followed (from) it have been ascribed precisely to the philosophes' alienation and exclusion from real politics. This is one point on which Tocqueville and Marx agreed. The recent turn away from Marx and toward Tocqueville as the basis of a "revisionist" interpretation of the French Revolution has not, therefore, recuperated the Enlightenment as central to or even specifically significant in what is now referred to as the "political culture" of the Old Regime.

The work of historians such as Keith Baker and Dale Van Kley has shown that the healthy pamphlet literature that developed in France during the second half of the eighteenth century engaged the monarchy in public political debate with *parlementaires* and other citizens. Sarah Maza's work on the *mémoires judiciaires* traces the further development of this public discourse about matters of public concern into a judicial arena in which the voices of king and parlement were relegated to the sidelines and lawyers took center stage in the name of their clients. All this research has served to define a vibrant political culture that grew stronger and reached deeper into French society in the years that led up to the Revolution.

The question of the relationship of the Enlightenment to this new political culture, however, remains unanswered. Just because they now acknowledge a real political culture and a true political discourse during what they call the Age of Enlightenment, historians have not concluded that the philosophes shaped or even participated in it. Indeed, Robert Darnton has argued most strongly that the Revolution drew upon a culture that developed in opposition to that of the Enlightenment; Dale Van Kley has been at pains to identify *parlementaire* discourse with Jansenism and not with the Enlightenment; and Jeremy Popkin and others find journalists rather than philosophes central to the creation of French political culture.[52] In the major collective volume on the subject, *The Political Culture of the Old Regime*, the first volume of *The French Revolution and the Creation of Modern Political Culture*, the philosophes play a marginal role at best.[53]

51. Alexis de Tocqueville, *The Old Régime and the French Revolution*, trans. Stuart Gilbert (Garden City, N.Y., 1955), p. 139.

52. Van Kley, *Jansenists and the Expulsion of the Jesuits*; Popkin, "Pamphlet Journalism"; Censer and Popkin, *Press and Politics*; Gelbart, *Feminine and Opposition Journalism*.

53. See review essays by Sarah Maza, "Politics, Culture, and the Origins of the French Revolution," *Journal of Modern History* 61 (December 1989): 704–23; and Jack Censer,

Keith Baker's *Inventing the French Revolution: Essays on French Political Culture in the Eighteenth Century* is the central text in this new historiography that seeks to establish and characterize the political culture of the Old Regime. Baker confronts Tocqueville head on, but not by arguing that Enlightenment discourse was constitutive of a real political culture. Rather, he explores the broader discursive context within which the philosophes functioned. "The philosophes need to be considered within the spectrum of political language existing in their own day," he writes, "not artificially insulated from it."[54] The philosophes thus play a role in Baker's representation of the political culture of the Old Regime, but only as one of the groups that participated in politics, "the activity through which individuals and groups in any society articulate, negotiate, implement, and enforce the competing claims they make upon one another and upon the whole."[55] The philosophes contributed to political culture to the extent that they helped to voice or shape the vocabulary to voice these political claims.

On the way to making this argument, Baker confronts another aspect of Tocqueville's condemnation of the philosophes. "Their very way of living led these writers to indulge in abstract theories and generalizations regarding the nature of government, and to place a blind confidence in these," wrote Tocqueville. "For living as they did, quite out of touch with practical politics, they lacked the experience which might have tempered their enthusiasms."[56] The inexperience of the philosophes was, moreover, shared by their readers, who were thus easily swayed to follow them. The French nation and its leading intellectuals were the victims of the destruction of ancient political freedom in France. Out of the debris of ancient freedom remained only "one form of it," in Tocqueville's vision: "We could indulge, almost without restriction, in learned discussions on the origins of society, the nature of government, and the essential rights of man." These discussions, however, were no more than "literary excursions into politics."[57] The result of the leadership of literary men, Tocqueville concluded, "was nothing short of disastrous; for what is a merit in the writer may well be a vice in the statesman and the very qualities which go to make great literature can lead to catastrophic revolutions."[58]

In response to Tocqueville, Baker argues that much of Enlighten-

---

"The Coming of a New Interpretation of the French Revolution?" *Journal of Social History* 21 (Winter 1987): 295–309.

54. Baker, *Inventing the French Revolution*, p. 23.
55. Ibid., p. 4.
56. Tocqueville, *Old Regime*, p. 140.
57. Ibid., pp. 141–42.
58. Ibid., p. 147.

ment thinking was directly engaged with contemporary political issues, and many Enlightenment thinkers, from Montesquieu to Turgot, were as engaged in the practical politics of the Old Regime as anyone. Their readers, moreover, were no babes in the political wood, but members of a ruling elite. The provincial academies, which were their "principal institutional expression," did not remove the local elites from the political arena to the realm of merely literary pursuits and abstract discussion. Rather, they enhanced their solidarity and power.[59]

It seems to me that there is another way to approach Tocqueville's verdict on the Enlightenment. Baker has made a compelling case for the existence of a real political culture, not just an *abstract* politics, in which the philosophes participated. I hope that my own work has challenged Tocqueville's claim that the politics of the Enlightenment was not simply abstract but also (merely) *literary*. I have tried to challenge the assumption that the way in which the philosophes lived their lives, organized around salon discussion, was, on the level of social and intellectual practice, antithetical to political culture and political practice. Tocqueville conceived of the literary as the opposite of the real, and salon discussion as the antithesis of political practice. Because the politics of the philosophes was literary as well as abstract, its effects were pernicious, and they remained pernicious because of the social practices in which the philosophes indulged. In this view both Marx and Cochin were to agree with him. Baker, following Daniel Roche, has argued for the political character of the principal social and intellectual institution of the philosophes' readers, the provincial academies; I am making just such a claim for the philosophes' own central institution: the Parisian salon.

I thus call into question—collapse, even—both of Tocqueville's operative distinctions: between the literary and the political and between salon discussion and political practice. The political culture of the Old Regime was shaped in part by the social and discursive practices of philosophes and salonnières, whose central institution was the Parisian salon and whose discursive mode was epistolary and conversational. If the Enlightenment did not single-handedly produce the political culture of the Old Regime, it at least gave it literary form and endowed it with a set of values and practices that were republican at least as much as they were literary, because they were the values and practices of the Republic of Letters.

My purpose has been to understand the Enlightenment Republic of Letters as a set of social and discursive practices and in particular to articulate the specific roles played by men and women in it. Looking at

59. Baker, *Inventing the French Revolution*, p. 20.

the French Enlightenment in this way establishes it as part of cultural history. It no longer appears as the emanation of disembodied male reason, a moment in the history of ideas. Rather, the Enlightenment comes alive as a social and discursive activity in which men and women participated in ways that reflected the broadly cultural values of the Republic of Letters and the new imperatives that they themselves constructed as the project of Enlightenment.

Biographical Sketches

The well-known men of letters of the eighteenth century—
Voltaire, Diderot, Rousseau, d'Alembert, Condorcet—need no
introduction. But as the story of the Enlightenment Republic
of Letters includes so many more people than these few, I offer the
following biographical sketches to help my readers and satisfy their
curiosity.

ABBÉ JACQUES DELILLE (1738–1813)   Born near Clermont in the
Auvergne, Delille was descended from the Renaissance jurist Michel
de l'Hôpital on his mother's side. At the death of his father he received a small income, with which his mother sent him to study at the
Collège de Lisieux in Paris. He taught at the Collège de Beauvais and
then at the Jesuits' collège in Amiens after their expulsion from
France in 1762. He eventually returned to Paris, where he taught at
the Collège de la Marche and the Collège de France. He was a poet
but was best known for his translations of poetry, especially of Virgil's
Georgics (1769). His most important original poems were *Les Jardins*
(1780), *L'Imagination* (1806), and *La Conversation* (1812). In 1772 he
was elected to the French Academy along with Suard, but the king
used his veto, and they had to be reelected in 1774. He was asked to
write some occasional poetry for the Revolution but declined, and in
1794 he left Paris for the quiet of the provinces. The following year
he left France for Switzerland, and then Germany and England,
where he translated *Paradise Lost*. He returned to Paris in 1801 and
was named to the French Institute, which replaced the royal academies of the Old Regime.

CHARLES PINOT DUCLOS (1704–1772)   Duclos was born in Dinant in Brittany, the son of a hatter. He was educated in Paris and elected to the Academy of Inscriptions in 1739. In the 1740s he published some rather popular novels and then the *Histoire de Louis XI* (1745). His most important work was *Considérations sur les moeurs de ce siècle* (1750). He was elected to the French Academy in 1747 and served as its perpetual secretary from 1755 until his death. He was named royal historiographer at the departure of Voltaire for Prussia in 1750. The citizens of Dinant appointed him mayor in 1744, and he served as a representative of the Third Estate to the Estates of Brittany. He was ennobled by Louis XV at the request of that body.

LOUISE-FLORENCE-PÉTRONILLE TARDIEU D'ESCLAVELLES, MARQUISE DE LALIVE D'EPINAY (1726–1783)   When she was orphaned young and penniless, Louise Tardieu d'Esclavelles was taken in by rich relatives. She married one of the sons of this household in a love match that soon proved disastrous. Her husband spent his fortune on gambling and mistresses. She found love and companionship elsewhere, eventually with Grimm, who was her lover from 1753 until her death thirty years later. She was not a salonnière, but her house was a second home to Grimm, Diderot, Galiani, and others who were her close friends. For a time Rousseau was her guest as well. As a writer she won the first *Prix d'Utilité* from the French Academy in 1774 for her *Conversations d'Emilie*. She was a major contributor to the *Correspondance Littéraire* and took charge of it for periods of up to eighteen months when Grimm was away on diplomatic business. Her other major work is an unfinished roman à clef, *Histoire de Madame de Montbrillant*, published after her death.

ABBÉ FERDINANDO GALIANI (1728–1787)   Galiani was born in Chieti in the Abruzze in Italy. He was raised in Naples by his uncle, who was royal chaplain and later archbishop there. He was educated first by his older brother, then by the Celestine brothers, and then by attending lectures at the University of Naples. He was a brilliant scholar in many fields, with particular interests in economics and archaeology. He made his first mark in the Italian Republic of Letters with a treatise *Della moneta* (1750), contributed to lavish volumes on the excavations at Herculaneum, and was recognized by and welcomed into various Italian academies.

In 1750 Galiani took minor orders in order to claim an ecclesiastical stipend. His political career began in 1759, when he was named secretary of state and, later that year, secretary to the Neapolitan ambassador to France. He arrived in Paris in 1760 and fulfilled his duties there until recalled to Naples at the insistence of Choiseul in

1769. During his years in France he published nothing, but he wrote the *Dialogues sur le commerce des blés* hastily before his departure. Upon his return to Naples, Galiani took positions in the Council of Commerce, the Council of Finances, and the Superintendancy of the Royal Purse. He maintained an extensive correspondence (notably with Epinay) and published two works: *Le Socrate imaginaire* (1778), a comic opera, and *Del dialetto napoletano* (1779). A new edition of his correspondence is currently being undertaken in France.

MARIE-THÉRÈSE RODET GEOFFRIN (1699–1777) Born in Paris and orphaned young, she was married off at fourteen with a substantial dowry to the wealthy director of the royal glassworks at Saint-Gobain. Although she had been pious in her childhood and youth, she became less so in her twenties, when her intellectual curiosity developed. She began to frequent the salon of her neighbor Mme de Tencin, where she became a regular until the death of her mentor (and of her own husband) in 1749. Before that time she had already begun her own salons: one on Mondays for artists and *amateurs* of art, the other on Wednesdays for men of letters. She was an important patron of artists and men of letters, known for her generosity to both. She was not a writer and published nothing. Her correspondence with Stanislas Poniatowski, king of Poland, whom she considered her adopted son, has been published.

FRIEDRICH-MELCHIOR GRIMM (1723–1807) Grimm was born in Ratisbon in Bavaria. His parents were poor, but they provided for his future with an education. He arrived in Paris in 1749 as the tutor for the children of the German comte de Schomberg. He later took a position as reader for the duke of Saxe-Gotha, and then as secretary to the duc d'Orléans. In 1776 he was named ambassador to France and made a baron by the duke of Saxe-Gotha. Throughout the 1770s and 1780s he traveled on diplomatic missions to central and eastern Europe. Grimm published very little, but he contributed significantly to the Republic of Letters as editor of the manuscript *Correspondance Littéraire* from 1753 until 1776 (with help when he traveled from Epinay, Diderot, and Meister). Under his leadership, the subscription list grew from three to fifteen, and it provided him with a substantial income. He was Diderot's best friend and Epinay's lover. When the Revolution came, Grimm left Paris with the rest of the diplomatic corps and retired to Gotha. In 1795 Catherine the Great named him plenipotentiary minister to Lower Saxony.

JEAN-FRANÇOIS DE LA HARPE (1739–1803) La Harpe's parentage is uncertain but was probably impoverished nobility. He grew up in Paris, where he was a scholarship student at the Collège d'Harcourt.

At school he excelled especially in rhetoric, but he went on to distinguish himself as a poet. His first poem was published in 1759, and he eventually wrote and published in all the poetic and theatrical genres of the period. He won many prizes for his work and was elected to the French Academy in 1776. Ten years later he was invited to be professor of literature at the new Lycée in Paris. His lectures were very popular and were later published as *Cours de littérature*. Despite his republican sympathies, he was imprisoned toward the end of the Terror in 1794. In prison he underwent a religious conversion, and for the rest of his life he wrote and taught about literature and against the philosophes.

JULIE-JEANNE-ELÉANORE DE LESPINASSE (1732–1776) Lespinasse was the daughter of the comtesse d'Albon, who raised her to the age of sixteen. When her mother died, Lespinasse was taken in by her sister as a governess, but this could only be a temporary situation. Because she was the child of an adulterous liaison and lacked a dowry, her status in the household and the Old Regime was uncertain. In 1754, on the verge of entering a convent, she was rescued from taking the veil without a vocation by Mme Du Deffand, the sister of Lespinasse's brother-in-law, who invited her to join her in Paris as a companion.

With Lespinasse at her side, Du Deffand launched an important salon. After ten years, however, the two women had a falling out, and in 1764 Lespinasse, with the support of Geoffrin, left to live on her own and to start her own salon. From 1765 until her death in 1776, she was at home every evening, from about five until eight o'clock. She published nothing in her lifetime, but was known for two chapters she wrote in the manner of Lawrence Sterne's *Sentimental Journey*. Since her death she has been known primarily for her very intense love letters to the comte de Guibert, published in the nineteenth century.

JEAN-FRANÇOIS MARMONTEL (1723–1799) Marmontel was born in the small town of Bort in the Limousin. His family was poor, but local nuns taught him to read, and the local priest taught him Latin. He was further educated at the Jesuit collège in Mauriac and planned to join the order, but when his father died and he became the sole support of his family, he decided against the priesthood. In 1741 he took a post teaching philosophy in a seminary in Toulouse, and while there he won three poetry prizes from the local Académie des Jeux Floraux. At the urging of Voltaire, with whom he was now corresponding, he went to Paris in 1745 to make his fortune in the Republic of Letters. In 1746 and again the following year he won the poetry prize from the French Academy. He supported himself with tutoring and saw his first play, *Denys le Tyran*, performed to great acclaim in 1748. He contributed articles on literary topics to the *Encyclopédie* and in 1761 published the very popular *Contes moraux*. *Bélisaire* (1767), a political novel, was perhaps his most important work. He was employed as a secretary in the Department of Royal Buildings in the 1750s but gave up the post for the editorship of the *Mercure de France* in 1758. He was elected to the Academy in 1763 and succeeded d'Alembert as its perpetual secretary in 1783. In 1771 he succeeded Duclos as royal historiographer. When the Lycée opened in 1786, he was given the chair of history. Marmontel married Morellet's niece in 1777, and during the Revolution he and his family moved out of Paris to the country, where they lived modestly. In 1797 he was elected to the Conseil des Anciens. His *Mémoires* were published posthumously in 1804.

LOUIS-SÉBASTIEN MERCIER (1740–1814)   Mercier was born in Paris, the son of a swordmaker, and educated at the Parisian Collège Mazarine. After the Jesuits were expelled in 1762, he was hired to teach rhetoric at their collège in Bordeaux. He later returned to Paris, where in 1771 he published the futuristic utopian novel *L'An 2440, rêve s'il en fût jamais*. He edited the *Journal des Dames* for a couple of years (1775–1776), and wrote for and on the theater. His most important work was the twelve-volume *Tableau de Paris* (1781–1788).

Mercier played an active role in the Revolution. With Jean-Louis Carra he launched the *Annales Patriotiques* in 1789. He was a member of the Cercle Social and one of the editors of the *Chronique du Mois*. He was elected to the Convention, where he was a moderate and a loyal supporter of Brissot. He voted against the execution of the king and was arrested along with the rest of the Girondins in June 1793. He survived the Terror, however, and was elected to the Council of Five Hundred under the Directory, and to the Institute when it was formed.

ABBÉ ANDRÉ MORELLET (1727–1819)   The son of a paper merchant in Lyon, Morellet studied with the Jesuits there and went to Paris as a student in 1741. He trained for the priesthood and studied theology at the Sorbonne. In the 1750s he contributed articles on religion and philosophy to the *Encyclopédie*, and he defended the philosophes in 1765 with a pamphlet against Pallisot's play *Les Philosophes*. A year later he translated Beccaria's *On Crimes and Punishments* into French. In the 1760s and 1770s he was employed by the Ministry of Finance, which allowed him to pursue his own research for a dictionary of commerce that he never completed while he worked for the ministry's free-trade policies. He received a pension from the state in 1783 and was elected to the French Academy in 1784. He was its director when it was shut down in 1792 and saved its archives. Having lost his income from both church and state with the Revolution, he supported himself at the end of the century with translations from the English. He published four volumes of *Mélanges* in 1818; his *Mémoires* were published posthumously in 1821.

SUZANNE CURCHOD NECKER (1739–1794) Her father was a Calvinist pastor who died when she was young. She moved with her mother to the nearby city of Lausanne. There she was active in a women's literary academy, the Académie de la Poivrière. When her mother died, she took a position as governess with a family that was moving to Paris. She arrived there in 1764, and through her employer she met Jacques Necker, a banker from Geneva who went on to distinguish himself in the administration of the French monarchy and to contribute to the Republic of Letters. They married in 1765. The next year she gave birth to a daughter, Anne-Louise Germaine, and began a salon. The daughter grew up to be the writer Germaine de Staël; the salon met weekly on Friday afternoons and continued until the departure of the Neckers from France for Switzerland in 1790. Suzanne Necker published virtually nothing during her lifetime. After her death her husband published a pamphlet she had been completing against divorce (1794), and five volumes of *Mélanges* (1798) and *Nouveaux mélanges* (1801) culled from the notebooks in which she had been writing down thoughts, essays, *portraits,* and *éloges* for nearly thirty years.

AMÉLIE PANCKOUCKE SUARD (1743–1830) The daughter of a printer in Lille, she went to Paris in 1762 with her brother, who started a printing house there that was to dominate the trade in the 1770s and 1780s. Through him she met Suard, whom she married in 1766. In the 1780s she wrote some pieces that her husband published as editor of the *Journal de Paris.* They were later included in her *Lettres de Madame Suard à son mari sur son voyage à Ferney* (1802), letters that had circulated in the *Correspondance Littéraire* in the 1770s. After the Revolution she published *Madame de Maintenon peinte par elle-même* (1810) anonymously and *Essais de mémoires sur M. Suard* (1820) for private circulation. Her correspondence with Condorcet has recently been published.

JEAN-BAPTISTE-ANTOINE SUARD (1734–1817) Suard was born in Besançon and studied at the local collège. He left there in the wake of a duel and arrived in Paris to make his fortune in the Republic of

Letters in 1751. He soon teamed up with the abbé Arnaud, and
together they edited, at different times, the *Journal Etranger*, the *Gazette de France*, and the *Gazette Littéraire de l'Europe*. He married Amélie
Panckoucke in 1766. In 1772 he was elected to the French Academy
along with Delille, but the king used his veto, and they had to be
reelected in 1774. In the 1780s he edited the *Journal de Paris* and was
employed by the monarchy as a censor. He was also known for his
translations from the English, especially of Robertson's *History of
Charles V*. He did not support the Revolution, but he survived it and
went on to edit another journal, *Le Publiciste*, and to publish his
Mélanges de littérature in 1804.

ANTOINE-LÉONARD THOMAS (1732–1785) Thomas was born in
Clermont-Ferrand and, having lost his father young, was sent to Paris
by his mother to study at the age of ten. He took up the law but soon
abandoned it for the Republic of Letters, supporting himself with a
teaching position at the Collège de Beauvais, part of the University of
Paris. In 1759 he published *Jumonville*, a poem that established him as
a writer, but his true métier turned out to be the *éloge*. Between 1759
and 1765 he won the French Academy's prize for eloquence five
times. He suffered from ill health, but his success as a writer led to an
offer of a position as secretary to the minister of foreign affairs which
relieved him of the burden of teaching. In 1766 he was elected to the
Academy and was eventually named its director.

Works Cited

PRIMARY SOURCES

Manuscript Materials

Geoffrin papers in Etampes family papers. Private collection, Paris.
"Mémoires de J.-P. Lenoir." Bibliothèque Municipale d'Orléans, MS 1423.

Letters, Memoirs, and Correspondences

[Abelard, Peter, and Heloise]. *The Letters of Abelard and Heloise*. Translated by Betty Radice. Harmondsworth: Penguin, 1974.
Angiviller, Charles Claude Flahaut, comte de La Billarderie d'. *Mémoires: Notes sur les "Mémoires" de Marmontel*. Edited by Louis Bobé. Copenhagen: Leven & Munksgaard; Paris: Klincksieck, 1933.
Bentley, Thomas. *Journal of a Visit to Paris, 1776*. Edited by Peter France. Brighton: University of Sussex Library, 1977.
[Bergman, Torbern]. *Torbern Bergman's Foreign Correspondence*. Edited by Göte Carlid and Johan Nordström. Vol. 1, *Letters from Foreigners to Torbern Bergman*. Stockholm: Almqvist & Wiksell, 1965.
[Brissot de Warville, Jacques-Pierre]. *J. P. Brissot: Correspondance et papiers*. Edited by Cl[aude] Perroud. Paris: Picard, 1912.
_____. *Mémoires de Brissot . . . sur ses contemporains, et la Révolution française*. Edited by F[rançois Mongin] de Montrol. 4 vols. Paris: Ladvocat, 1830.
[Condorcet, Marie-Jean-Antoine-Nicolas Caritat, marquis de, and Amélie Panckoucke Suard]. *Correspondance inédite de Condorcet et Madame Suard, 1771–1791*. Edited by Elisabeth Badinter. Paris: Fayard, 1988.
[Condorcet and Anne-Robert-Jacques Turgot]. *Correspondance inédite de Condorcet et de Turgot*. Edited by Charles Henry. Paris: Charavay frères, 1883.
[D'Holbach, Paul Thiry, baron, and Charlotte-Suzanne, baronne]. "Lettres inédites du baron et de la baronne d'Holbach à l'abbé Galiani." Edited by Fausto Nicolini. *Etudes Italiennes*, n.s. 1 (January–March 1931): 20–40.

Diderot, Denis. *Correspondance*. Edited by Georges Roth. 16 vols. Paris: Minuit, 1955–1970.

Duclos, Charles Pinot. *Correspondance de Charles Duclos (1704–1772)*. Edited by Jacques Brengues. Saint-Brieuc: Presses Universitaires de Bretagne, 1970.

[Epinay, Louise-Florence-Pétronille Tardieu d'Esclavelles, marquise de Lalive d', and Ferdinando Galiani]. *La Signora d'Epinay e l'abate Galiani: Lettere inedite (1769–1772)*. Edited by Fausto Nicolini. Bari: Laterza & Figli, 1929.

Galiani, Ferdinando. *Correspondance*. Edited by Lucien Perey and Gaston Maugras. 2 vols. Paris: Calmann-Lévy, 1890.

———. *Lettres de l'abbé Galiani à Madame d'Epinay*. Edited by Eugène Asse. 2 vols. Paris: Charpentier, 1882.

Genlis, [Stéphanie Félicité Ducrest de Saint-Aubin], la comtesse de. *Mémoires inédites . . . sur le dix-huitième siècle et la Révolution française depuis 1756 jusqu'à nos jours*. 10 vols. Paris: Ladvocat, 1825.

Hobbes, Thomas. "The Autobiography of Thomas Hobbes." Translated by Benjamin Farrington. *Rationalist Annual* (1958): 22–31.

[Lespinasse, Jeanne-Julie-Eléanore de]. *Letters of Mlle de Lespinasse*. Translated by Katharine Prescott Wormeley. Boston: Hardy, Pratt, 1903.

———. *Lettres de Mlle de Lespinasse*. Edited by Eugène Asse. Paris, n.d.

———. *Lettres inédites de Mademoiselle de Lespinasse*. Edited by Charles Henry. Paris: E. Dentu, 1887.

Marmontel, Jean-François. *Correspondance*. Edited by John Renwick. 2 vols. Clermont-Ferrand: Institut d'Etudes du Massif Central, 1974.

———. *Mémoires*. Edited by John Renwick. 2 vols. Clermont-Ferrand: G. De Bussac, 1972.

Morellet, André. *Lettres de l'abbé Morellet à Lord Shelburne*. Edited by Edmond Fitzmaurice. Paris: Plon, 1898.

———. *Mémoires sur le dix-huitième siècle et sur la Révolution*. 2 vols. Paris: Ladvocat, 1821.

———. *Mémoires sur le dix-huitième siècle et sur la Révolution*. Paris: Mercure de France, 1988.

Nicolini, Fausto. "Lettere inedite del d'Alembert, del maresciallo di Brissac, e del marchese di Croismare all'ab. Galiani." *Revue de Littérature Comparée* 10 (1930): 747–59.

Nisard, Charles. *Mémoires et correspondances historiques et littéraires inédits—1726 à 1816*. Paris: Michel Lévy Frères, 1858.

[Poniatowski, Stanislas, king of Poland, and Marie-Thérèse Geoffrin]. *Correspondance inédite du roi Stanislas-Auguste Poniatowski et de Madame Geoffrin (1764–1777)*. Edited by Charles de Mouÿ. Paris: Plon, 1875.

[Roland, Marie-Jean Manon Philipon]. *Mémoires de Madame Roland*. Edited by Paul de Roux. Paris: Mercure de France, 1966.

———. *The Memoirs of Madame Roland*. Translated and edited by Evelyn Shuckburgh. London: Barrie & Jenkins, 1989.

Rousseau, Jean-Jacques. *Correspondance complète*. Edited by R. A. Leigh. 50 vols. Geneva: Voltaire Foundation, 1965–1985.

[Suard, Jean-Baptiste-Antoine]. "Lettere inedite di G. B. Suard all'abbate Galiani." Edited by Fausto Nicolini. In *Mélanges de philologie, d'histoire, et de littérature offerts à Henri Hauvette*, pp. 461–69. Paris: Presses Françaises, 1934.

———. "Lettres inédites de Suard à Wilkes." Edited by Gabriel Bonno. *University of California Publications in Modern Philology* 15 (1932): 161–280.

Voltaire, [François Marie Arouet de]. *Correspondence*. In *The Complete Works*. 107 vols. Edited by Theodore Besterman. Geneva: Voltaire Foundation, 1968–1977.

Other Primary Sources

Abrantès, [Laure Junot], la duchesse d'. *Histoire des salons de Paris: Tableaux et portraits du grand monde.* 6 vols. Paris: Ladvocat, 1837–1838.

Almanach de la Poste de Paris par une Société des Gens de Lettres. N.p., 1772, 1774.

Bacon, Francis. *Advancement of Learning.* Edited by Joseph Devey. New York: P. F. Collier, 1902.

Badinter, Elisabeth, ed. *Qu'est-ce qu'une femme?* Paris: POL, 1989.

[Bassi]. *Lycée de Paris: Club littéraire qu'on va former dans les bâtimens nouveaux du Palais Royal, sous la protection immédiate de S. A. A. Monseigneur le duc de Chartres, et sous la direction de M. Bassi.* Paris, 1784.

[Brissot de Warville, Jacques-Pierre]. *Correspondance universelle sur ce qui intéresse le bonheur de l'homme et de la société.* Neuchâtel: Société typographique; London: Cox, 1783.

——. *Discours sur l'utilité des sociétés patriotiques et populaires, sur la nécessité de les maintenir et de les multiplier partout.* Montauban, n.d.

——. *Journal du Licée de Londres, ou Tableau de l'état présent des sciences et des arts en Angleterre.* Paris: Périsse le jeune, 1784.

Callières, François de. *Histoire poëtique de la guerre nouvellement déclarée entre les anciens et les modernes.* Amsterdam, 1688.

Le Club des dames, ou Le Retour de Descartes. Paris, 1784.

Condillac, Etienne Bonnot de. *Essai sur l'origine des connaissances humaines.* Paris: Galiléo, 1973.

Condorcet, Marie Jean Antoine Nicolas de Caritat, marquis de. *Oeuvres.* Edited by A[rthur] Condorcet O'Connor and F[rançois] Arago. 12 vols. Paris: Firmin Didot, 1847–1849; rpt. Stuttgart–Bad Canstatt: Frommann, 1968.

D'Alembert, Jean Le Rond. *Lettre à M. J. J. Rousseau sur l'article "Genève".* . . . Amsterdam, 1759.

——. *Oeuvres complètes.* Paris, 1822.

——. *Preliminary Discourse to the Encyclopedia of Diderot.* Translated by Richard N. Schwab. Indianapolis: Bobbs-Merrill, 1963.

Delille, J[acques]. *La Conversation.* Paris: Michaud, 1812.

Diderot, Denis. *Lettre sur les aveugles.* Edited by Robert Niklaus. Second edition. Geneva: Droz, 1963.

——. *Oeuvres complètes.* Edited by Roger Lewinter. 15 vols. Paris: Club Français du Livre, 1970.

——. *Oeuvres philosophiques.* Edited by Paul Vernière. Paris: Garnier, 1964.

——. *Oeuvres politiques.* Edited by Paul Vernière. Paris: Garnier, 1963.

Diderot, [Denis], and [Jean Le Rond] d'Alembert, eds. *Encyclopédie, ou Dictionnaire raisonné des sciences, des arts, et des métiers.* 17 vols. Paris, 1751–1765.

Duclos, Charles Pinot. *Considérations sur les moeurs de ce siècle.* Edited by F. C. Green. Cambridge: Cambridge University Press, 1939.

Duplessy, la baronne. *Repertoire des lectures faites au musée des dames.* Vol. 1. Paris, 1788.

Epinay, [Louise-Florence-Petronille Tardieu d'Esclavelles, marquise] d'. *Histoire de Madame de Montbrillant.* Edited by Georges Roth. 3 vols. Paris: Gallimard, 1951.

Furetière, Antoine. *Nouvelle allégorique, ou Histoire des derniers troubles arrivés au royaume d'éloquence.* Edited by Eva van Ginneken. Geneva: Droz, 1967.

[Gaillard, Gabriel-Henri]. *La Rhétorique françoise à l'usage des jeunes demoiselles.* Paris, 1787.

Galiani, Ferdinando. *La Bagarre: Galiani's "Lost" Parody.* Edited by Steven Laurence Kaplan. The Hague: Martinus Nijhoff, 1979.

———. *Dialogues entre M. le marquis de Roquemaure et M. le chevalier Zanobi*. Edited by Philip Koch. Analecta Romanica 21. Frankfurt am Main: Klosterman, 1968.

———. *Dialogues sur le commerce des blés*. Paris: Fayard, 1984.

Garat, Dominique-Joseph. *Mémoires historiques sur la vie de M. Suard*. 2 vols. Paris: A. Belin, 1820.

Genlis, [Stéphanie Félicité Ducrest de Saint-Aubin], la comtesse de. *Dictionnaire critique et raisonné des étiquettes de la cour*. 2 vols. Paris: P. Mongi aîné, 1818.

———. *Les Dîners du baron d'Holbach*. Paris: Trouve, 1822.

[Georgelin Du Cosquer, Barthélémy-Pélagé]. *Vues patriotiques sur l'établissement en Bretagne et dans toute la France d'une académie encyclopédique et populaire*. N.p., 1785.

Grimm, Friedrich-Melchior, et al., *Correspondance littéraire, philosophique, et critique*. Edited by Maurice Tourneux. 16 vols. Paris: Garnier, 1877–1882.

[Heathcote, Ralph]. *A Letter to the Honorable Mr. Horace Walpole, concerning the Dispute between Mr. Hume and Mr. Rousseau*. London, 1767.

[Hume, David]. *A Concise and Genuine Account of the Dispute between Mr. Hume and Mr. Rousseau*. London, 1766.

Hume, David. *Essays Moral, Political, and Literary*. Edited by Eugene F. Miller. Indianapolis: Liberty Classics, 1985.

Irailh, Augustin Simon. *Querelles littéraires, ou Mémoires pour servir à l'histoire des révolutions de la République des Lettres, depuis Homère jusqu'à nos jours*. Paris, 1761; rpt. Geneva: Slatkine, 1967.

Kant, Immanuel. *Perpetual Peace and Other Essays*. Translated by Ted Humphrey. Indianapolis: Hackett, 1983.

La Harpe, Jean-François de. *Correspondance littéraire*. 5 vols. Paris: Migneret, 1801–1807.

Lesure, François, ed. *Querelle des Gluckistes et des Piccinnistes*. 2 vols. Geneva: Minkoff, 1984.

"Lettre adressé au rédacteur de ce nouveau supplément, sur un projet d'association entre les académies." *Nouveau Supplément à la France Littéraire* 4, pt. 2 (1784): xi–xiv.

Locke, John. *The Second Treatise of Government*. Indianapolis: Bobbs-Merrill, 1952.

———. *Some Thoughts concerning Education*. Edited by John W. Yolton and Jean S. Yolton. Oxford: Oxford University Press, 1989.

Mémoires secrets pour servir à l'histoire de la République des Lettres en France, depuis MDCCLXII jusqu'à nos jours. 36 vols. London: John Adamson, 1780–1789; rpt. Westmead, Eng.: Gregg International, 1970.

Mercier, Louis-Sébastien. *Le Bonheur des gens de lettres*. London [Paris]: Cailleau, 1766.

———. *Tableau de Paris*. 12 vols. Amsterdam, 1783–1788.

Montaigne, Michel de. *Essais*. Edited by Maurice Rat. 2 vols. Paris: Garnier, 1962.

Montesquieu, Charles-Louis de Secondat, baron de. *Lettres persanes*. Edited by Paul Vernière. Paris: Garnier, 1975.

———. *Oeuvres complètes*. Edited by Daniel Oster. Paris: Intégrale, 1964.

Moreau de Saint-Méry, M[édéric] L[ouis] E[lie]. *Discours sur l'utilité du musée établi à Paris prononcé dans la séance publique du 1re décembre 1784*. Parma: Bodoni, 1805.

Morellet, André. "De l'esprit de contradiction." *Mercure de France*, 15 August 1778, 138–52; 25 August 1778, 258–78. Rpt. Geneva: Slatkine, 1971.

———. "Essai sur la conversation." *Mercure de France*, 5 November 1778, 5–22. Rpt. Geneva: Slatkine, 1971.

———. *Mélanges de littérature et de philosophie du 18ᵉ siècle*. 4 vols. Paris: Lepetit, 1818.

———. *Réfutation de l'ouvrage qui a pour titre Dialogues sur le commerce des blés*. London, 1770.

Morellet, André, [ed.]. *Eloges de Madame Geoffrin, contemporaine de Madame Du Deffand*. Paris: H. Nicolle, 1812.

[Mulot, l'abbé]. "Journal intime de l'abbé Mulot (1777–1782)." Edited by Maurice Tourneux. *Mémoires de la Société de l'Histoire de Paris et de l'Ile-de-France* 29 (1902): 19–124.

Naigeon, Jacques-André. *Mémoires historiques et philosophiques sur la vie et les ouvrages de D. Diderot.* Paris: Brière, 1821.

Necker, Jacques. *Oeuvres complètes.* Edited by Auguste Louis de Staël-Holstein. 15 vols. Paris: Treuttel et Wurtz, 1820–1821; rpt. Darmstadt: Scientia Verlag Aalen, 1970.

Necker, [Suzanne Curchod]. *Mélanges extraits des manuscrits de Mme Necker.* Edited by Jacques Necker. 3 vols. Paris, 1798.

———. *Nouveaux mélanges extraits des manuscrits de Mme Necker.* Edited by Jacques Necker. 2 vols. Paris: C. Pougens, 1801.

Pahin de La Blancherie, [Claude-Mammès]. *Correspondance générale sur les sciences et les arts.* 1779.

———. *Nouvelles de la République des Lettres et des Arts.* 1779–1787.

[Pilâtre de Rozier, François]. *Musée de Monsieur et de Mgr. le comte d'Artois.* (Prospectus.) Paris, 1785.

"Projet pour l'établissement d'un bureau général de la République des Lettres." *Bibliothèque Raisonnée des Ouvrages des Savans de l'Europe* 39 (July–September 1747): 202–21.

Richelieu, [Armand Jean du Plessis, duc de]. *The Political Testament of Cardinal Richelieu.* Translated by Henry Bertram Hill. Madison: University of Wisconsin Press, 1961.

Rousseau, Jean-Jacques. *Oeuvres complètes.* Edited by Bernard Gagnebin and Marcel Raymond. 4 vols. Paris: Gallimard, 1959–1969.

———. *Politics and the Arts: Letter to M. d'Alembert on the Theatre.* Edited and translated by Allan Bloom. Ithaca: Cornell University Press, 1968.

Servan, [Antoine-Joseph] Michel de. *Oeuvres choisies.* Edited by [St-Xavier] de Portets. 5 vols. Paris: Didot l'aîné, 1822.

Staël-Holstein, [Germaine] de. *Oeuvres.* 3 vols. Paris: Lefèvre, 1858.

Suard, [Amélie Panckoucke]. *Essais de mémoires sur M. Suard.* Paris: P. Didot, 1820.

Thierry, L. V. *L'Almanach du voyageur à Paris.* Paris, 1783, 1786.

[Thomas, Antoine-Léonard]. *Discours prononcés dans l'Académie françoise, le jeudi, 22 janvier 1767, la reception de M. Thomas.* Paris, 1767.

———. *Oeuvres complètes.* 6 vols. Paris: Verdière, 1825.

[Tournon, Antoine]. *La Vie et les mémoires de Pilâtre de Rozier.* Paris, 1786.

Villemont, M. de. "Réflexions sur la guerre perpétuelle qui règne entre les auteurs modernes." *Mercure de France* 39 (December 1740): 2562–79. Rpt. Geneva: Slatkine, 1969.

Voltaire, [François Marie Arouet de]. *Dictionnaire philosophique.* Edited by René Pomeau. Paris: Garnier-Flammarion, 1964.

———. *Letters on England.* Edited and translated by Leonard Tancock. Harmondsworth: Penguin, 1980.

———. *Oeuvres complètes.* 52 vols. Paris: Garnier, 1877–1885.

Young, Arthur. *Travels in France during the Years 1787, 1788, 1789.* Edited by M[atilda Barbara] Betham-Edwards. London: G. Bell, 1924.

SECONDARY SOURCES

Abbadi, Mostafa el-. *The Life and Fate of the Ancient Library of Alexandria.* Paris: UNESCO/UNDP, 1990.

Agulhon, Maurice. *Pénitents et franc-maçons de l'ancien Provence: Essai sur la sociabilité méridionale.* Paris: Fayard, 1984.
_____. "Vers une histoire des associations." *Esprit,* June 1978: 13–18.
Albert-Buisson, François. *Les Quarante au temps des Lumières.* Paris: Fayard, 1960.
Altman, Janet Gurkin. *Epistolarity: Approaches to a Form.* Columbus: Ohio State University Press, 1982.
Amiable, Louis. "Les Origines maçonniques du Musée de Paris et du Lycée." *Révolution Française* 30 (January–June 1896): 484–500.
Badinter, Elisabeth. *Emilie, Emilie, ou L'Ambition féminine au XVIIIe siècle.* Paris: Flammarion, 1983.
Baker, Keith Michael. *Condorcet: From Natural Philosophy to Social Mathematics.* Chicago: University of Chicago Press, 1975.
_____. "Les Débuts de Condorcet au secrétariat de l'Académie royale des sciences (1773–1776)." *Revue d'Histoire des Sciences et de Leurs Applications* 20 (1967): 229–80.
_____. *Inventing the French Revolution: Essays on French Political Culture in the Eighteenth Century.* Cambridge: Cambridge University Press, 1990.
Baker, Keith Michael, ed. *The Old Regime and the French Revolution.* University of Chicago Readings in Western Civilization, vol. 7. Chicago: University of Chicago Press, 1987.
_____. *The Political Culture of the Old Regime.* Vol. 1 of *The French Revolution and the Creation of Modern Political Culture.* Oxford: Pergamon, 1987.
Beauvoir, Simone de. *The Second Sex.* Translated by H. M. Parshley. New York: Vintage, 1974.
Becker, Carl L. *The Heavenly City of the Eighteenth-Century Philosophers.* New Haven: Yale University Press, 1932.
Becker, Lawrence C. *Reciprocity.* London: Routledge, 1986.
Benhamou, Paul. "The Periodical Press in the *Encyclopédie.*" *French Review* 59 (February 1986): 410–17.
Berthe, Léon-Noël. *Dubois de Fosseux, secrétaire de l'Académie d'Arras, 1785–1792, et son bureau de correspondance.* Arras: CNRS, 1969.
Bertrand, Colette. "Comment la franc-maçonnerie vient aux femmes." *Dix-huitième Siècle* 19 (1987): 205–9.
Birembaut, Arthur. "Quelques réflexions sur les problèmes posés par la conservation et la consultation des Archives techniques françaises." *Archives Internationales d'Histoire des Sciences* 19 (1966): 21–102.
_____. "Sur les lettres du physicien Magellan conservées aux Archives nationales." *Revue d'Histoire des Sciences et de Leurs Applications* 9 (1956): 150–61.
Blum, Carol. *Rousseau and the Republic of Virtue: The Language of Politics in the French Revolution.* Ithaca: Cornell University Press, 1986.
Bonnat, Jean-Louis, and Mireille Bossis. *Ecrire, Publier, Lire: Les Correspondances (Problématique et économie d'un "genre littéraire").* Nantes: Université de Nantes, Département de Psychologie, 1983.
Bonnet, Jean-Claude, ed. *La Carmagnole des muses: L'Homme de lettres et l'artiste dans la Révolution.* Paris: Armand Colin, 1988.
Bray, Bernard, Jochen Schlobach, and Jean Varloot, eds. *La Correspondance Littéraire de Grimm et de Meister (1754–1813).* Paris: Klincksieck, 1976.
Brengues, Jacques. "La Guerre des sexes et l'amour-maçon dans la poésie." *Dix-huitième Siècle* 19 (1987): 105–18.
Brenner, Clarence D. *A Bibliographical List of Plays in the French Language, 1700–1789.* Berkeley: Associated Students' Store, 1947.
Brewer, John, and Susan Staves, eds. *Conceptions of Property in Early Modern Europe.* London: Routledge, 1994.

Bright, Charles, and Susan Harding, eds. *Statemaking and Social Movements: Essays in History and Theory*. Ann Arbor: University of Michigan Press, 1984.

Brown, Richard D. *Revolutionary Politics in Massachusetts: The Boston Committee of Correspondence and the Towns, 1772–1774*. Cambridge: Harvard University Press, 1970.

Brunel, Lucien. *Les Philosophes et l'Académie française au dix-huitième siècle*. Paris: Hachette, 1884; rpt. Geneva: Slatkine, 1967.

Burke, Janet M. "Freemasonry, Friendship, and Noblewomen: The Role of the Secret Society in Bringing Enlightenment Thought to Pre-Revolutionary Women Elites." *History of European Ideas* 10 (1989): 283–93.

———. "Through Friendship to Feminism: The Growth in Self-Awareness among Eighteenth-Century Women Freemasons." *Proceedings of the Western Society for French History* 14 (1987): 187–96.

Burke, Peter, and Roy Porter, eds. *The Social History of Language*. Cambridge: Cambridge University Press, 1987.

Cabanes, Charles. "Histoire du premier musée autorisé par le gouvernement." *La Nature* (1937): 577–83.

Calhoun, Craig, ed. *Habermas and the Public Sphere* (Cambridge: MIT Press, 1992.

Canfora, Luciano. *The Vanished Library*. Translated by Martin Ryle. London: Hutchinson Radices, 1989.

Cassirer, Ernst. *The Philosophy of the Enlightenment*. Translated by Fritz C. A. Koelln and James P. Pettegrove. Boston: Beacon, 1955.

Censer, Jack. "The Coming of a New Interpretation of the French Revolution?" *Journal of Social History* 21 (Winter 1987): 295–309.

Censer, Jack R., and Jeremy D. Popkin, eds. *Press and Politics in Pre-revolutionary France*. Berkeley: University of California Press, 1987.

Cerulli, Enrico, et al., eds. *Convegno italo-francese sul tema: Ferdinando Galiani*. Problemi attuali di scienza e di cultura, no. 211. Rome: Academia Nazionale dei Lincei, 1975.

Chartier, Roger. *The Cultural Origins of the French Revolution*. Translated by Lydia G. Cochrane. Durham: Duke University Press, 1991.

———. *The Cultural Uses of Print in Early Modern France*. Translated by Lydia G. Cochrane. Princeton: Princeton University Press, 1987.

———. *Lectures et lecteurs dans la France d'Ancien Régime*. Paris: Seuil, 1987.

———. "Text, Symbols, and Frenchness." *Journal of Modern History* 57 (1985): 682–95.

Chartier, Roger, ed. *Passions of the Renaissance*. Translated by Arthur Goldhammer. Vol. 3 of *A History of Private Life*, edited by Philippe Ariès and Georges Duby. Cambridge: Harvard University Press, 1989.

Cochin, Augustin. *La Révolution et la libre pensée*. Paris: Plon, 1924.

———. *Les Sociétés de pensée et la Révolution en Bretagne (1788–1789)*. 2 vols. Paris: Champion, 1925.

Cohen, Huguette. "Diderot's Machiavellian Harlequin: Ferdinando Galiani." *Studies on Voltaire and the Eighteenth Century* 256 (1988): 129–48.

Collins, Edward D. "Committees of Correspondence of the American Revolution." *Annual Report of the American Historical Association for the Year 1901*. 2 vols. (1902), 1: 245–71.

Compère, Marie-Madeleine. *Du collège au lycée (1500–1850): Généalogie de l'enseignement secondaire français*. Paris: Gallimard, 1985.

Coutura, Johel. "Le Musée de Bordeaux." *Dix-huitième Siècle* 19 (1987): 149–64.

Cranston, Maurice. *The Noble Savage: Jean-Jacques Rousseau, 1754–1762*. Chicago: University of Chicago Press, 1991.

Darnton, Robert. "The Brissot Dossier." *French Historical Studies* 17 (Spring 1991): 191–205.

_____. *The Great Cat Massacre and Other Episodes in French Cultural History.* New York: Basic Books, 1984.

_____. "In Search of Enlightenment: Recent Attempts to Create a Social History of Ideas." *Journal of Modern History* 43 (March 1971): 113–32.

_____. *The Literary Underground of the Old Regime.* Cambridge: Harvard University Press, 1982.

_____. "The Memoirs of Lenoir, Lieutenant de Police of Paris, 1774–1785." *English Historical Review*, no. 336 (July 1970): 532–59.

_____. *Mesmerism and the End of the Enlightenment in France.* Cambridge: Harvard University Press, 1968.

Dauphin, Cécile, et al. "Women's Culture and Women's Power: An Attempt at Historiography." Translated by Camille Garnier. *Journal of Women's History* 1 (Spring 1989): 63–88.

Davis, Natalie Zemon. *Society and Culture in Early Modern France.* Stanford: Stanford University Press, 1965.

Dejob, Charles. "De l'établissement connu sous le nom de Lycée et d'Athénée et de quelques établissements analogues." *Revue Internationale de l'Enseignement* 18 (1889): 4–38.

Delia, Diana. "From Romance to Rhetoric: The Alexandrian Library in Classical and Islamic Traditions." *American Historical Review* 97 (December 1992): 1449–67.

Delorme, Suzanne, and René Taton, eds. *L'"Encyclopédie" et le progrès des sciences et des techniques.* Paris: PUF, 1952.

De Luna, Frederick A. "The Dean Street Style of Revolution: J.-P. Brissot." *French Historical Studies* 17 (Spring 1991): 159–90.

Dennis, Michael. *Court and Garden: From the French Hôtel to the City of Modern Architecture.* Cambridge: MIT Press, 1986.

Desazars de Montgaillard, le baron de. *Histoire de l'Académie des sciences de Toulouse: Le Musée, le lycée, l'athénée, 1784–1807.* Toulouse: Douladoure-Privat, 1908.

Dibon, Paul. "Communication in the Respublica Literaria of the 17th Century." *Res Publica Litterarum* 1 (1978): 42–55.

_____. "L'Université de Leyde et la République des Lettres au 17e siècle." *Quaerondo* 5 (1975): 4–38.

Dieckmann, Herbert. *Inventaire du fonds Vandeul et inédits de Diderot.* Geneva: Droz, 1951.

Douay, Françoise. "La Langue de la Raison et de la Liberté: The Crisis of Rhetoric in the Age of Oratory, 1789–1809." *Proceedings of the Consortium on Revolutionary Europe, 1750–1850, 1991*, pp. 185–93. [Tallahassee]: Institute on Napoleon and the French Revolution, Florida State University, 1992.

Duchet, Michèle. *Anthropologie et histoire au Siècle des Lumières: Buffon, Voltaire, Rousseau, Helvétius, Diderot.* Paris: Maspero, 1971.

Durand, Yves, ed. *Hommage à Roland Mousnier: Clientèles et fidélités en Europe à l'époque moderne.* Paris: PUF, 1981.

Durkheim, Emile. *The Evolution of Educational Thought: Lectures on the Formation and Development of Secondary Education in France.* Translated by Peter Collins. London: Routledge & Kegan Paul, 1977.

Echeverria, Durand. *The Maupeou Revolution: A Study in the History of Libertarianism, France, 1770–1774.* Baton Rouge: Louisiana State University Press, 1985.

Eisenstein, Elizabeth L. *Grub Street Abroad: Aspects of the French Cosmopolitan Press from the Age of Louis XIV to the French Revolution.* Lyell Lectures, 1989–90. Oxford: Clarendon, 1992.

_____. *Print Culture and Enlightenment Thought.* The Sixth Hanes Lecture Presented by the Hanes Foundation for the Study of the Origin and Development of the Book. Chapel Hill: University of North Carolina Rare Book Collection/University Library, 1986.

_____. *The Printing Press as an Agent of Change: Communications and Cultural Transformations in Early Modern Europe.* 2 vols. Cambridge: Cambridge University Press, 1979.

Elias, Norbert. *The Court Society.* Translated by Edmund Jephcott. New York: Pantheon, 1983.

_____. *Power and Civility.* Vol. 2 of *The Civilizing Process.* Translated by Edmund Jephcott. New York: Pantheon, 1982.

Ellery, Eloise. *Brissot de Warville: A Study in the History of the French Revolution.* Boston: Houghton Mifflin, 1915.

Epstein, Julia, and Kristina Straub, eds. *Bodyguards: The Cultural Politics of Gender Ambiguity.* New York: Routledge, 1991.

Febvre, Lucien, and Henri-Jean Martin. *The Coming of the Book: The Impact of Printing, 1450–1800.* Edited by Geoffrey Nowell-Smith and David Wooton. Translated by David Gerard. London: Verso, 1984

Les Femmes et l'Académie française. Paris: Opale, 1981.

Les Femmes et la Révolution française. Vol. 1: *Modes d'action et d'expression: Nouveaux Droits—nouveaux devoirs.* Mirail: Presses Universitaires du Mirail, 1989.

Fiering, Norman S. "The Transatlantic Republic of Letters: A Note on the Circulation of Learned Periodicals to Early Eighteenth-Century America." *William and Mary Quarterly* 33 (October 1976): 642–60.

Fitzsimmons, Michael P. *The Parisian Order of Barristers and the French Revolution.* Cambridge: Cambridge University Press, 1987.

Flavell, M. Kay. "The Enlightened Reader and the New Industrial Towns: A Study of the Liverpool Library, 1758–1790." *British Journal for Eighteenth-Century Studies* 8 (1985): 17–35.

[Foucault, Michel]. *The Foucault Reader.* Edited by Paul Rabinow. New York: Pantheon, 1984.

Fox-Genovese, Elizabeth. *The Origins of Physiocracy: Economic Revolution and Social Order in Eighteenth-Century France.* Ithaca: Cornell University Press, 1976.

Fraisse, Geneviève. *Muse de la raison: La Démocratie exclusive et la différence des sexes.* Aix-en-Provence: Alinéa, 1989.

France, Peter. *Politeness and Its Discontents: Problems in French Classical Culture.* Cambridge: Cambridge University Press, 1992.

Fried, Michael. *Absorption and Theatricality: Painting and Beholder in the Age of Diderot.* Chicago: University of Chicago Press, 1980.

Furet, François. *Interpreting the French Revolution.* Translated by Elborg Forster. Cambridge: Cambridge University Press, 1981.

Furet, François, and Jacques Ozouf, eds. *Reading and Writing: Literacy in France from Calvin to Jules Ferry.* Cambridge: Cambridge University Press, 1982.

Furet, François, and Mona Ozouf, eds. *A Critical Dictionary of the French Revolution.* Translated by Arthur Goldhammer. Cambridge: Harvard University Press, 1989.

_____. *The Transformation of Political Culture (1789–1848).* Vol. 3 of *The French Revolution and the Creation of Modern Political Culture.* Oxford: Pergamon, 1989.

Fuss, Diana. *Essentially Speaking: Feminism, Nature, and Difference.* New York: Routledge, 1989.

Garlick, Barbara, Suzanne Dixon, and Pauline Allen, eds. *Stereotypes of Women in Power: Historical Perspectives and Revisionist Views.* New York: Greenwood, 1992.

Gay, Peter. *The Enlightenment: An Interpretation*. 2 vols. New York: Knopf, 1966–69.
_____. *The Party of Humanity: Essays in the French Enlightenment*. New York: Vintage, 1971.
_____. *Voltaire's Politics: The Poet as Realist*. New York: Vintage, 1965.
Gelbart, Nina Rattner. *Feminine and Opposition Journalism in Old Regime France: "Le Journal des Dames."* Berkeley: University of California Press, 1987.
Gérard, Mireille. "Art épistolaire et art de la conversation: Les Vertus de la familiarité." *Revue de l'Histoire Littéraire de la France* 78 (1978): 958–74.
Gillispie, Charles Coulston. *The Montgolfier Brothers and the Invention of Aviation*. Princeton: Princeton University Press, 1983.
Glotz, Marguerite, and Madeleine Maire. *Salons du XVIIIème siècle*. Paris: Nouvelles Editions Latines, 1949.
Goldsmith, Elizabeth C. *Exclusive Conversations: The Art of Interaction in Seventeenth-Century France*. Philadelphia: University of Pennsylvania Press, 1988.
Goncourt, Edmond and Jules de. *La Femme au dix-huitième siècle*. Paris: Flammarion, 1982.
Goodman, Dena. *Criticism in Action: Enlightenment Experiments in Political Writing*. Ithaca: Cornell University Press, 1989.
_____. "Filial Rebellion in the Salon: Madame Geoffrin and Her Daughter." *French Historical Studies* 16 (Spring 1989): 27–47.
_____. "The Hume-Rousseau Affair: From Private *Querelle* to Public *Procès*." *Eighteenth-Century Studies* 25 (Winter 1991–1992): 171–201.
_____. "Pigalle's *Voltaire Nu*: The Republic of Letters Represents Itself to the World." *Representations* 16 (Fall 1986): 86–109.
_____. "Public Sphere and Private Life: Toward a Synthesis of Current Historiographical Approaches to the Old Regime." *History and Theory* 31, no. 1 (1992): 1–20
Goodman, John. "'Altar against Altar': The Colisée, Vauxhall Utopianism, and Symbolic Politics in Paris (1769–77)." *Art History* 15 (December 1992): 434–69.
Gordon, Daniel. "The Art of Conversation, or The Concept of Society in the British Enlightenment." Unpublished paper.
_____. "The Idea of Sociability in Pre-Revolutionary France." Ph.D. dissertation, University of Chicago, 1990.
_____. "'Public Opinion' and the Civilizing Process in France: The Example of Morellet." *Eighteenth-Century Studies* 22 (Spring 1989): 302–28.
Gougy-François, Marie. *Les Grands salons féminins*. Paris: Debresse, 1965.
Grieder, Josephine. "Kingdoms of Women in French Fiction of the 1780s." *Eighteenth-Century Studies* 23 (Winter 1989–90): 140–56.
Grimshaw, Jean. *Philosophy and Feminist Thinking*. Minneapolis: University of Minnesota Press, 1986.
Guénot, Hervé. "Musées et lycées parisiens (1780–1830)." *Dix-huitième Siècle* 18 (1986): 249–67.
Guiffrey, Jules. "Histoire de l'Académie de Saint-Luc." *Archives de l'Art Français*, n.s. 9. Paris: Edouard Champion, 1915.
Habermas, Jürgen. *The Structural Transformation of the Public Sphere: An Inquiry into a Category of Bourgeois Society*. Translated by Thomas Burger with the assistance of Frederick Lawrence. Cambridge: MIT Press, 1989.
Hahn, Roger. *The Anatomy of a Scientific Institution: The Paris Academy of Sciences, 1666–1803*. Berkeley: University of California Press, 1971.
Halévi, Ran. *Les Loges maçonniques dans la France d'Ancien Régime: Aux origines de la sociabilité démocratique*. Paris: Armand Colin, 1984.

Hanley, Sarah. "Engendering the State: Family Formation and State Building in Early Modern France." *French Historical Studies* 16 (Spring 1989): 4–27.

Harouel, Jean-Louis. *Histoire des institutions de l'époque franque à la Révolution.* Paris: PUF, 1987.

Harth, Erica. *Cartesian Women: Versions and Subversions of Rational Discourse in the Old Regime.* Ithaca: Cornell University Press, 1992.

Haussonville, [H. Gabriel Paul Othenin de Cléron], comte d'. *Le Salon de Mme Necker.* 2 vols. Paris: Calmann-Lévy, 1882.

Hekman, Susan J. *Gender and Knowledge: Elements of a Postmodern Feminism.* Boston: Northeastern University Press, 1990.

Hesse, Carla. "Reading Signatures: Female Authorship and Revolutionary Law in France, 1750–1850." *Eighteenth-Century Studies* 22 (Spring 1989): 469–87.

Hollier, Denis, ed. *A New History of French Literature.* Cambridge: Harvard University Press, 1989.

Hudault, Joseph. "Guy Jean-Baptiste Target et sa contribution à la préparation de l'édit de novembre 1787 sur l'état civil des protestants." Mémoire pour le diplôme d'études supérieures d'histoire du droit, Université de Paris, 1966.

Hulme, Peter, and Ludmilla Jordanova, eds. *The Enlightenment and Its Shadows.* London: Routledge, 1990.

Hunt, Lynn. *The Family Romance of the French Revolution.* Berkeley: University of California Press, 1992.

———. "French History in the Last Twenty Years: The Rise and Fall of the *Annales* Paradigm." *Journal of Contemporary History* 21 (1986): 209–24.

———. *Politics, Culture, and Class in the French Revolution.* Berkeley: University of California Press, 1984.

Hunt, Lynn, ed. *Eroticism and the Body Politic.* Baltimore: Johns Hopkins University Press, 1990.

Hunt, Margaret, et al., eds. *Women and the Enlightenment.* New York: Institute for Research in History and Haworth Press, 1984.

Iser, Wolfgang. *The Implied Reader: Patterns of Communication in Prose Fiction from Bunyan to Beckett.* Baltimore: Johns Hopkins University Press, 1974.

Isherwood, Robert. "The Third War of the Musical Enlightenment." *Studies on Voltaire and the Eighteenth Century* 4 (1975): 223–45.

Jacob, Margaret C. "The Enlightenment Redefined: The Formation of Modern Civil Society." *Social Research* 58 (Summer 1991): 475–95.

———. *Living the Enlightenment: Freemasonry and Politics in Eighteenth-Century Europe.* New York: Oxford University Press, 1991.

———. *The Radical Enlightenment: Pantheists, Freemasons, and Republicans.* London: George Allen & Unwin, 1981.

Johnson, James H. "Musical Experience and the Formation of a French Musical Public." *Journal of Modern History* 64 (June 1992): 191–226.

Le Journalisme d'Ancien Régime: Questions et propositions. Lyon: Presses Universitaires de Lyon, 1982.

Kaiser, Thomas E. "This Strange Offspring of *Philosophie*: Recent Historiographical Problems in Relating the Enlightenment to the French Revolution." *French Historical Studies* 15 (Spring 1988): 549–62.

Kany, Charles E. *The Beginnings of the Epistolary Novel in France, Italy, and Spain.* Berkeley: University of California Press, 1937.

Kaplan, Steven L. *Bread, Politics, and Political Economy in the Reign of Louis XV.* 2 vols. The Hague: Martinus Nijhoff, 1976.

———, ed. *Understanding Popular Culture: Europe from the Middle Ages to the Nineteenth Century.* Berlin: Mouton, 1984.

Kates, Gary. *The "Cercle Social," the Girondins, and the French Revolution.* Princeton: Princeton University Press, 1985.

Keener, Frederick M., and Susan E. Lorsch, eds. *Eighteenth-Century Women and the Arts.* New York: Greenwood, 1988.

Keller, Evelyn Fox. "The Gender/Science System, or Is Sex to Gender as Nature Is to Science?" *Hypatia* 2 (Fall 1987): 37–49.

Kennedy, Michael L. *The Jacobin Clubs in the French Revolution: The First Years.* Princeton: Princeton University Press, 1982.

Ketcham, Michael G. *Transparent Designs: Reading, Performance, and Form in the "Spectator" Papers.* Athens: University of Georgia Press, 1985.

Kirsop, Wallace. "Cultural Networks in Pre-revolutionary France: Some Reflexions on the Case of Antoine Court de Gébelin." *Australian Journal of French Studies* 18 (September–December 1981): 231–47.

——. "Some Documents on the History of the French Book Trade in the Eighteenth Century." *Australian Journal of French Studies* 24 (1987): 253–308.

Klein, Lawrence E. "Berkeley, Shaftesbury, and the Meaning of Politeness." *Studies in Eighteenth-Century Culture* 16 (1986): 57–68.

——. "Coffee Clashes: The Politics of Conversation in Seventeenth- and Eighteenth-Century England." Unpublished paper.

——. "The Third Earl of Shaftesbury and the Progress of Politeness." *Eighteenth-Century Studies* 18 (Winter 1984–1985): 186–214.

Kors, Alan Charles. *D'Holbach's Coterie: An Enlightenment in Paris.* Princeton: Princeton University Press, 1976.

Koselleck, Reinhart. *Critique and Crisis: Enlightenment and the Pathogenesis of Modern Society.* Cambridge: MIT Press, 1988.

Labrosse, Claude, and Pierre Rétat. *L'Instrument périodique: La Fonction de la presse au XVIIIᵉ siècle.* Lyon: Presses Universitaires de Lyon, 1985.

LaCapra, Dominick. *History and Criticism.* Ithaca: Cornell University Press, 1985.

Landes, Joan B. *Women and the Public Sphere in the Age of the French Revolution.* Ithaca: Cornell University Press, 1988.

Laqueur, Thomas. *Making Sex: Body and Gender from the Greeks to Freud.* Cambridge: Harvard University Press, 1990.

Laursen, John Christian. "Scepticism and Intellectual Freedom: The Philosophical Foundations of Kant's Politics of Publicity." *History of Political Thought* 10 (Autumn 1989): 439–55.

——. "The Subversive Kant: The Vocabulary of 'Public' and 'Publicity.'" *Political Theory* 14 (November 1986): 584–603.

La Vopa, Anthony J. "Conceiving a Public: Ideas and Society in Eighteenth-Century Europe." *Journal of Modern History* 64 (March 1992): 79–116

Lebrun, François, Marc Venard, and Jean Quéniart, eds. *Histoire générale de l'enseignement et de l'éducation en France.* Vol. 2: *De Gutenberg aux Lumières (1480–1789).* Paris: Nouvelle Librairie de la France, G.-V. Labat, 1981.

Le Forestier, René. *Maçonnerie féminine et loges académiques.* Edited by Antoine Faivre. Milan: Arché, 1979.

Lloyd, Genevieve. *The Man of Reason: "Male" and "Female" in Western Philosophy.* Minneapolis: University of Minnesota Press, 1984.

Lougee, Carolyn C. *"Le Paradis des Femmes": Women, Salons, and Social Stratification in Seventeenth-Century France.* Princeton: Princeton University Press, 1976.

Lough, John. *The Contributors to the "Encyclopédie."* London: Grant & Cutler, 1973.

Lucas, Colin, ed. *Rewriting the French Revolution.* Oxford: Clarendon, 1991.

Lux, David S. *Patronage and Royal Science in Seventeenth-Century France: The Académie de Physique in Caen.* Ithaca: Cornell University Press, 1989.

MacCormack, Carol, and Marilyn Strathern, eds. *Nature, Culture, and Gender*. Cambridge: Cambridge University Press, 1980.

McLaughlin, Blandine L. *Diderot et l'amitié. Studies on Voltaire and the Eighteenth Century* 100 (1973).

Magne, Emile. *Les Plaisirs et les fêtes au XVIIe siècle*. Paris: Martin-Dupuis, 1930.

Martin, Henri-Jean, and Roger Chartier, eds. *Histoire de l'édition française*. Vol. 2: *Le Livre triomphant, 1660–1830*. Paris: Promodis, 1984.

Martin, Kingsley. *French Liberal Thought in the Eighteenth Century: A Study of Political Ideas from Bayle to Condorcet* New York: Harper & Row, 1963.

Maza, Sarah. "Politics, Culture, and the Origins of the French Revolution." *Journal of Modern History* 61 (December 1989): 704–23.

———. *Private Lives and Public Affairs: The Causes Célèbres of Prerevolutionary France* Berkeley: University of California Press, 1993.

———. "The Rose-Girl of Salency: Representations of Virtue in Prerevolutionary France." *Eighteenth-Century Studies* 22 (Spring 1989): 395–412.

———. "Le Tribunal de la nation: Les Mémoires judiciaires et l'opinion publique à la fin de l'Ancien Régime." *Annales E.S.C.* 42 (January–February 1987): 73–90.

Merrick, Jeffrey. "Royal Bees: The Gender Politics of the Beehive in Early Modern Europe." *Studies in Eighteenth-Century Culture* 18 (1988): 7–37.

Morange, Jean. *La Liberté d'association en droit public français*. Paris: PUF, 1977.

Mornet, Daniel. *La Vie parisienne au XVIIIe siècle: Leçons faites à l'Ecole des hautes études sociales*. Paris: F. Alcan, 1914.

Mousnier, Roland. *The Institutions of France under the Absolute Monarchy, 1598–1789: Society and the State*. Translated by Brian Pearce. Chicago: University of Chicago Press, 1974.

Nicolini, Fausto. *Giambattista Vico e Ferdinando Galiani*. Turin: E. Loescher, 1918.

Offen, Karen. "The Woman Question in Modern France." Unpublished manuscript.

Okin, Susan Moller. *Women in Western Political Thought*. Princeton: Princeton University Press, 1979.

Olivier, Louis A. "Bachaumont the Chronicler: A Questionable Renown." *Studies on Voltaire and the Eighteenth Century* 143 (1975): 161–79.

O'Neill, Onora. *Constructions of Reason: Explorations of Kant's Practical Philosophy*. Cambridge: Cambridge University Press, 1989.

Ong, Walter J. *Fighting for Life: Contest, Sexuality, and Consciousness*. Ithaca: Cornell University Press, 1981.

Ouellet, Réal, and Hélène Vachon. *"Lettres persanes" de Montesquieu*. Paris: Hachette, 1976.

Ozouf, Mona. "'Public Opinion' at the End of the Old Regime." *Journal of Modern History* 60 (September 1988): S1–21.

Pardailhé-Galabrun, Annik. *The Birth of Intimacy: Privacy and Domestic Life in Early Modern Paris*. Translated by Jocelyn Phelps. Cambridge: Polity, 1991.

Pateman, Carol. *The Disorder of Women*. Stanford: Stanford University Press, 1989.

Patterson, H. Temple. *Poetic Genesis: Sebastien Mercier into Victor Hugo. Studies on Voltaire and the Eighteenth Century* 11 (1960).

Pedley, Mary Sponberg. "The Subscription List of the *Atlas Universel* (1757): A Study in Cartographic Dissemination." *Imago Mundo* 31 (1979): 66–77.

Picard, Roger. *Les Salons littéraires et la société française, 1610–1789*. New York: Brentano's, 1943.

Popkin, Jeremy D. *News and Politics in the Age of Revolution: Jean Luzac's "Gazette de Leyde."* Ithaca: Cornell University Press, 1989.

——. "Pamphlet Journalism at the End of the Old Regime." *Eighteenth-Century Studies* 22 (Spring 1989): 351–67.

——. *Revolutionary News: The Press in France, 1789–1799.* Durham: Duke University Press, 1990.

Porter, Charles A., ed. *Men/Women of Letters.* Special issue of *Yale French Studies,* no. 71 (1986).

Proust, Jacques. *Diderot et l'Encyclopédie.* Paris: Armand Colin, 1962; rpt. Geneva: Slatkine, 1982.

Quéniart, Jean. *Culture et sociétés urbaines dans la France de l'ouest au XVIIIᵉ siècle.* Paris: Klincksieck, 1978.

Rabbe, F[élix]. "Pahin de La Blancherie et le salon de la correspondance (1)." *Bulletin de la Société Historique du VIᵉ Arrondissement de Paris* 2 (1899): 30–52.

Ragan, Bryant T., and Elizabeth A. Williams, eds. *Recreating Authority in Revolutionary France.* New Brunswick: Rutgers University Press, 1992.

Ranum, Orest. "Courtesy, Absolutism, and the Rise of the French State, 1630–1660." *Journal of Modern History* 52 (September 1980): 426–51.

Rétat, Pierre, ed. *L'Attentat de Damiens: Discours sur l'événement au XVIIIᵉ siècle.* Paris: CNRS; Lyon: Presses Universitaires de Lyon, 1979.

Rhetoric and the Pursuit of Truth: Language Change in the Seventeenth and Eighteenth Centuries. Papers read at a Clark Library Seminar, 8 March 1980. Los Angeles: William Andrews Clark Memorial Library, UCLA, 1985.

Roche, Daniel. *The People of Paris: An Essay in Popular Culture in the Eighteenth Century.* Translated by Mark Evans and Gwynne Lewis. Berkeley: University of California Press, 1987.

——. *Les Républicains des lettres: Gens de culture et Lumières au XVIIIᵉ siècle.* Paris: Fayard, 1988.

——. *Le Siècle des lumières en province: Académies et académiciens provinciaux, 1680–1789.* 2 vols. The Hague: Mouton, 1978.

Rocquain, Félix. *L'Esprit révolutionnaire avant la Révolution, 1715–1789.* Paris: Plon, 1878.

Rothney, John, ed. *The Brittany Affair and the Crisis of the Ancien Régime.* New York: Oxford University Press, 1969.

Saint-Amand, Pierre. *Les Lois de l'hostilité: La Politique à l'âge des lumières.* Paris: Seuil, 1992.

Schiebinger, Londa. *The Mind Has No Sex? Women in the Origins of Modern Science.* Cambridge: Harvard University Press, 1989.

Schlereth, Thomas J. *The Cosmopolitan Ideal in Enlightenment Thought: Its Form and Function in the Ideas of Franklin, Hume, and Voltaire, 1694–1790.* Notre Dame: University of Notre Dame Press, 1977.

Schwartz, Joel. *The Sexual Politics of Jean-Jacques Rousseau.* Chicago: University of Chicago Press, 1984.

Scott, Joan W. "Deconstructing Equality-versus-Difference, or The Uses of Poststructuralist Theory for Feminism." *Feminist Studies* 14 (Spring 1988): 33–50.

Sée, Henri. "La Création d'un bureau de correspondance générale en 1766." *Revue d'Histoire Moderne,* no. 7 (January–February 1927): 51–55.

Ségur, [Pierre Marie Maurice Henri], le marquis de. *Julie de Lespinasse.* Paris: Calmann-Lévy, 1905.

——. *Le Royaume de la rue Saint-Honoré: Madame Geoffrin et sa fille.* Paris: Calmann-Lévy, 1897.

Sennett, Richard. *The Fall of Public Man: On the Social Psychology of Capitalism.* New York: Vintage, 1978.

Serres, Michel. *The Parasite*. Translated by Lawrence R. Schehr. Baltimore: Johns Hopkins University Press, 1982.

Sewell, William H., Jr. *Work and Revolution in France: The Language of Labor from the Old Regime to 1848*. Cambridge: Cambridge University Press, 1980.

Sgard, Jean, ed. *Dictionnaire des journalistes*. Supplement 2. Grenoble: Presses Universitaires de Grenoble, 1983.

Sheriff, Mary D. *Fragonard: Art and Eroticism*. Chicago: University of Chicago Press, 1990.

Sherman, Carol. *Diderot and the Art of Dialogue*. Geneva: Droz, 1976.

Smeaton, William A. "The Early Years of the Lycée and the Lycée des Arts: A Chapter in the Lives of A. L. Lavoisier and A. F. de Fourcroy." *Annals of Science* 11 (1955): 257–67.

Sonnet, Martine. *L'Education des filles au temps des Lumières*. Paris: Cerf, 1987.

Spencer, Samia I., ed. *French Women and the Age of Enlightenment*. Bloomington: Indiana University Press, 1984.

Starobinski, Jean. *The Invention of Liberty, 1700–1789*. Translated by Bernard C. Swift. Geneva: Skira, 1964.

Steegmuller, Francis. *A Woman, a Man, and Two Kingdoms: The Story of Madame d'Epinay and the Abbé Galiani*. New York: Knopf, 1991.

Still, Judith, and Michael Worton, eds. *Textuality and Sexuality: Reading Theories and Practices*. Manchester: Manchester University Press, 1993.

Strenski, Ellen Marie. "Diderot: For and against the Physiocrats." *Studies on Voltaire and the Eighteenth Century* 57 (1967): 1435–55.

Strugnell, Anthony. *Diderot's Politics: A Study of the Evolution of Diderot's Political Thought after the Encyclopédie*. The Hague: Martinus Nijhoff, 1973.

Tate, Robert S., Jr. *Petit de Bachaumont: His Circle and the "Mémoires Secrets."* Studies on Voltaire and the Eighteenth Century 65 (1968).

Taton, René. "Condorcet et Sylvestre-François Lacroix (1)." *Revue d'Histoire des Sciences et de Leurs Applications* 12 (April–June 1959): 127–58.

Thomas, Chantal. *La Reine scélérate: Marie-Antoinette dans les pamphlets*. Paris: Seuil, 1989.

Thorne, Barrie, Cheris Kramarae, and Nancy Henley, eds. *Language, Gender, and Society*. Rowley, Mass.: Newbury House, 1969.

Tocqueville, Alexis de. *The Old Regime and the French Revolution*. Translated by Stuart Gilbert. Garden City, N.Y.: Anchor, 1955.

Tomaselli, Sylvana. "The Enlightenment Debate on Women." *History Workshop Journal* 20 (1985): 101–24.

Ultee, Maarten. "The Republic of Letters: Learned Correspondence, 1680–1720." *Seventeenth Century* 2 (January 1987): 95–112.

Vaillé, Eugène. "Guides et livres de poste sous l'Ancien Régime." *Bulletin d'Informations, de Documentation, et de Statistique*, no. 12 (December 1934): 37–58.

———. *Histoire des postes françaises jusqu'à la Révolution*. Paris: PUF, 1946.

———. "La Poste et la presse sous l'Ancien Régime." *Bulletin d'Informations, de Documentation, et de Statistique*, no. 5 (May 1936): 33–68.

Van Kley, Dale K. *The Damiens Affair and the Unraveling of the Ancien Régime, 1750–1770*. Princeton: Princeton University Press, 1984.

———. *The Jansenists and the Expulsion of the Jesuits from France, 1757–1765*. New Haven: Yale University Press, 1975.

Vaultier, Roger. *Les Fêtes populaires à Paris*. Paris: Myrte, 1946.

Venturi, Franco. *Europe des Lumières: Recherches sur le 18e siècle*. The Hague: Mouton, 1971.

Vigni, Francesca. "Les Aspirations féministes dans les loges d'adoption en France." *Dix-huitième Siècle* 19 (1987): 211–20.

Wagner, Jacques. *Marmontel, journaliste, et le "Mercure de France" (1725–1761)*. Publications de la Faculté des lettres de Clermont-Ferrand, no. 34. Grenoble: Presses Universitaires de Grenoble, 1975.

Walmsley, Peter, "Civil Conversation in Locke's *Essay*." *Studies on Voltaire and the Eighteenth Century* 303 (1992): 411–17.

Waquet, Françoise. "Qu'est-ce que la République des Lettres? Essai de sémantique historique." *Bibliothèque de l'Ecole des Chartes* 1 (1989): 473–502.

Wiedemann, Conrad, and Sebastian Neumeister, eds. *Res Publica Litteraria: Die Institutionen der Gelehrtsamkeit in der frühen Neuzeit*. 2 vols. Wiesbaden: Harrasowitz, 1987.

Williams, Alan. *The Police of Paris, 1718–1789*. Baton Rouge: Louisiana State University Press, 1979.

Wilson, Arthur. *Diderot*. New York: Oxford University Press, 1972.

Index